INSIGHT GUIDE

Nepal

APA PUBLICATIONS
Part of the Langenscheidt Publishing Group

ABOUT THIS BOOK

Editorial

Project Editor
Zoë Ross
Managing Editor
Tom Le Bas
Editorial Director
Brian Bell

Distribution

UK & Ireland
GeoCenter International Ltd
The Viables Centre, Harrow Way
Basingstoke, Hants RG22 4BJ
Fax: (44) 1256-817988

United States
Langenscheidt Publishers, Inc.
46–35 54th Road, Maspeth, NY 11378
Fax: (718) 784-0640

Canada
Prologue Inc.
1650 Lionel Bertrand Blvd., Boisbriand
Québec, Canada J7H 1N7
Tel: (450) 434-0306. Fax: (450) 434-2627

Worldwide
Apa Publications GmbH & Co.
Verlag KG (Singapore branch)
38 Joo Koon Road, Singapore 628990
Tel: (65) 865-1600. Fax: (65) 861-6438

Printing

Insight Print Services (Pte) Ltd
38 Joo Koon Road, Singapore 628990
Tel: (65) 865-1600. Fax: (65) 861-6438

CONTACTING THE EDITORS
Although every effort is made to
provide accurate information, we
live in a fast-changing world and
would appreciate it if readers
would call our attention to any
errors or outdated information
that may occur by writing to:
**Insight Guides, P.O. Box 7910,
London SE1 1WE, England.
Fax: (44 20) 7403-0290.**
e-mail:
insight@apaguide.demon.co.uk

www.insightguides.com

This guidebook combines the
interests and enthusiasms of
two of the world's best known information providers: Insight Guides,
whose titles have set the standard
for visual travel guides since 1970,
and Discovery Channel, the world's
premier source of non-fiction television programming.

The editors of Insight Guides provide both practical advice and general
understanding about a destination's
history, culture, institutions
and people. Discovery
Channel and its Web site,
www.discovery.com,
help millions of viewers
explore their world from
the comfort of their
own home and also
encourage them to
explore it first hand.
This fully updated
edition of *Insight Guide: Nepal* is
carefully structured to convey an
understanding of Nepal and its culture as well as to guide readers
through its sights and activities:
♦ The **Features** section, indicated
by a yellow bar at the top of each
page, covers history and culture in a
series of informative essays.
♦ The main **Places** section, indicated by a blue bar, is a complete
guide to all the sights and areas
worth visiting. Places of special
interest are coordinated by
number with the maps.
♦ The **Travel Tips**
listings section, with
an orange bar, pro-
vides a handy point
of reference for
information on travel,
hotels, shops, restau-
rants and more.

EXPLORE YOUR WORLD

Discovery
CHANNEL

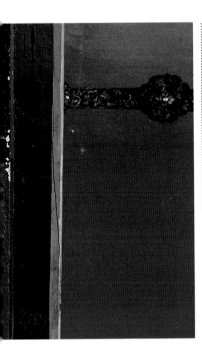

and the Pacific. She updated much of the Places text, as well as fully revising the Travel Tips. Conservation architect **John Sanday** has lived in Nepal since 1972 and worked throughout Asia advising international foundations on repairing and conserving historic sites, including the Imperial Palace, Beijing, with the China Heritage Fund. **Robert Peirce**, who wrote on the Sherpas, has been leading treks to Nepal for 20 years and has many Sherpa friends. He is the freelance editor of *News from Nepal*, a publication for readers in the USA and Canada. **David Allardice** put together the River Rafting chapter. He owns and operates "Ultimate Descents", specialising in river expeditions in the Himalaya. **Kunda Dixit** is co-publisher of *Himal* magazine and author of several books on media and the environment. For this edition he wrote on the Annapurna Conservation Project, and updated Environmental Issues and National Reserves. **Linda Kentro** is a Kathmandu-based architect who updated Hikes in the Kathmandu Valley, Mountain Biking, Mountain Flight and The Remote West. **Robin Marston** updated the Trekking chapter. **Elizabeth Hawley** updated her own original chapter on Mountaineering.

The current edition also builds on the foundations of editors and writers of previous editions, including **Dr Harkah Bahadur Gurung** on geology and the Gurkhas, **Dor Bahadur Bista** on the people of Nepal, **Father John K. Locke** on religion and **Bill O'Connor** on the 8,000-Metre Peaks.

Thanks also to **Alison Copland** for proofreading the book and to **Penny Phenix** for indexing it.

The contributors

This edition of *Insight Guide: Nepal* was revised by **Zoë Ross**, a London-based editor, and managing editor **Tom Le Bas** at Insight Guides. The book has been completely updated with the invaluable help of the following writers:

Kerry Moran lived in Kathmandu for 13 years and has written several books on Nepal and Tibet. She updated a large proportion of the Places and History chapters, as well as writing on Nepal's wool industry and arts and crafts. **Lisa Choegyal** has been resident in Kathmandu since 1974. She is a director of the Tiger Mountain Group, pioneers of responsible wildlife and adventure travel in Nepal and, as an independent ecotourism consultant, she advises governments, agencies and the private sector throughout Asia

Map Legend

— ·· —	International Boundary
– – – –	State Boundary
⊖	Border Crossing
— · —	National Park/Reserve
✈ ✈	Airport: International/Regional
🚌	Bus Station
❶	Tourist Information
✉	Post Office
✝ ✝	Church/Ruins
✝	Monastery
☾	Mosque
✡	Synagogue
🏰	Castle/Ruins
∴	Archaeological Site
∩	Cave
🗿	Statue/Monument
★	Place of Interest

The main places of interest in the Places section are coordinated by number with a full-colour map (e.g. ❶), and a symbol at the top of every right-hand page tells you where to find the map.

CONTENTS

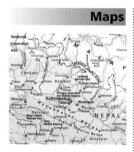

Introduction

History

Features

Houses at Manakamana

Information panels

Insight on ...

Places

Travel Tips

◆ Full Travel Tips index
   is on page 321

HIMALAYAN HARMONY

Nepal may be tiny in comparison with its giant neighbours, but within its borders lies a remarkable range of landscapes

N epal is one of the world's most extraordinary countries: a geographical wonder and an ethnological crossroads. Contrast is the common denominator, the unifying thread linking a profusion of customs, cultures, peoples, languages and landscapes.

The terrain stretches from the Terai, a flat, fertile strip of land along the country's southern border, to the summit of Mount Everest, the highest point on earth. Subtropical jungles, rhododendron forests, high-altitude deserts and frozen peaks are all to be found within the kingdom. Breathtakingly high mountains march along the northern border, including eight of the world's ten highest. Ancient traditions honour the Himalaya as the embodiment of the gods, and it is easy to see why: the mountains are on a superhuman scale, both beautiful and dangerous.

Tucked between peaks and plains are the Middle Hills, a rugged landscape on which farmers have eked out a living for centuries, equipped only with hand tools and determination. Rural realities dictate the terms of life for more than 80 percent of the population: Nepal is still largely a country of villages and agriculture.

Nothing manifests in a single variety in Nepal, neither religions (Hinduism and Buddhism combine with each other, with Shamanism and with various local religious traditions) nor holidays (four separate New Year's Days are celebrated), and especially not people, who are as diverse as the terrain. More than 60 linguistic groups have been recognised, each with their own cultural identity. Today there are 22 million Nepalese of various ethnic groups, castes and tribes.

Located between the two regional superpowers of India and China, Nepal is well placed to weave a rich cross-cultural tapestry. The pattern of Hinduism to the south and Buddhism to the north is intertwined with Tantrism, animist rites and shamanistic practices. These strands come together in the Kathmandu Valley to create the sophisticated civilisation of the Newars, the indigenous inhabitants of the valley.

The new millennium offers both promises and challenges. Age-old patterns are altering as the nation develops. The fabric of Kathmandu's society is being re-woven to incorporate modern influences: motorised transport, popular culture, mass tourism. It is a time of transition. Yet, regardless of the changes in Kathmandu, Nepal's reputation as a land where gods and mortals mingle and the inaccessibility of its rugged terrain make it likely that the hills and valleys, sheltered beneath the protecting peaks of the Himalaya, will long nurture the country's magnificent diversity and heritage. ❑

PRECEDING PAGES: Sherpa guide with Everest in his eyes; trekkers gaze at Ama Dablam; Buddhist monk at the temple of Boudhanath; enjoying a *hookah* in a hill village. **LEFT:** Thyangboche monastery, the Khumbu region.

THE BEGINNING

*Nepal's mountainous landscape is a legacy of a cataclysmic collision
between the Indian subcontinent and the Eurasian landmass*

The traditional concept of the Himalaya is one of utter immanence, the eternal home of the gods, an object of awe and devotion and not for men to enquire and fathom. However, a reflection on the genesis of the shaligram ammonite, the black fossil revered by the Hindus as an embodiment of Vishnu, leads to a geological past far beyond the age of mankind. The making of the ammonite fossil is related to the initial emergence of the Himalayan heights from the depths of an ancient sea millions of years ago.

The collision of continents

It was only as recently as the 1920s that Alfred Wegener first postulated the theory of Continental Drift. The continents as we know them today were said to have broken off from a single landmass some hundreds of millions of years ago and "drifted" apart, riding on underlying plastic materials. Though discussions persist as to the actual cause and extent of the drift, modern geologists have reaffirmed the movement of continents, or plates, within the theory of Plate Tectonics.

It is now largely accepted that the Himalaya were formed as a result of the collision of two large continental plates, the Indian subcontinent and Eurasia, in a process that began as early as 130 million years ago. This was at the time when reptiles and dinosaurs still roamed the earth. Having split off from a much larger southern continent called Gondwanaland – from which also emerged modern-day Australasia, Antarctica, Africa and parts of South America – the Indian subcontinent travelled 4,400 km (2,700 miles) northwards at an estimated rate of 20–25 cm (8–10 inches) per year. It eventually collided with part of the northern landmass, Eurasia, approximately 50 or 60 million years ago.

PRECEDING PAGES: the turquoise waters of Gokyo Lake, Everest region.
LEFT: a misty morning on Nuptse.
RIGHT: ammonite fossil from the ancient Tethys Sea.

The Tethys Sea

Studies of rock layers have been used to reconstruct the origins of the Himalaya, suggesting early periods of alternating subsidence and uplift of the earth's surface. An extensive sea once existed in the region where the Himalaya now rise, stretching right across the southern

margin of Eurasia wedged between Laurasia and Gondwana. The sea, known as the Tethys, came into being some 250 million years ago during the Late Palaeozoic era, when the first reptiles appeared, and dried up gradually about 40 or 50 million years ago, when mammals came into being. Some scientists now think that the Tethys was actually a series of seas that repeatedly subsided, were uplifted and drained away with the passing of a number of land fragments set adrift from Gondwana.

During this time, almost all of the now highly elevated areas between India and Central Asia were invaded by the Tethys Sea. The sinking and widening of the earth's surface commenced around 200 million years ago. By 40 to 65 million years ago, the bottom had risen so much as to cause the water to spill over and flood much of the surrounding land. This deluge was followed by the ultimate dissolution of the Himalayan sea, as evidenced by the fact that all later rock types found within the Himalaya (except those in localised basins) were laid down above water.

Thus, the rising of the Tethys Sea was primarily due to the build-up of marine sediments, accumulating to thicknesses of more than 4,500 metres (15,000 ft) over a period of some 200 million years. Earlier, however, during the Jurassic and late Cretaceous era (between 70 and 195 million years ago), upheavals created some minor sub-marine ridges and valleys, accompanied by the appearance of volcanoes and subterranean bodies of molten rock.

The Himalaya are born

These upheavals were the first spasms of the birth of the Himalaya, which actually took place in a series of stupendous periods of uplift punctuated by intervals of comparative quiescence. A second upheaval occurred during the Upper Eocene era (38 to 45 million years ago),

THE EARLIEST SETTLERS

Very little is known of the earliest human activities in the Himalaya; the facts tend to be shrouded in myths and legends. Take the "yeti", for instance *(see page 64)*. If it does exist, as many seem to think, it could be an ape-like primate trapped in the high mountains and forced to adapt to the conditions as the Himalaya rose.

There is also the legend of Manjushri, the Tibetan saint who came across the mountains and saw a large lake, then cleft a mountain in half to let the water out, creating the Kathmandu Valley. There is a deep limestone canyon where Manjushri is said to have used his sword.

raising the primary ridges and basins of the Tethys Sea into vast mountain ranges, with intervening shallow marshes and large river valleys. It was, however, the intense mountain-building epoch of the mid-Miocene (7 to 26 million years ago) that created the major structure of the present-day Himalaya.

This third uplift was followed by a relatively dormant period, coinciding with the Ice Age, when these first Himalayan chains were steadily eroded down to form the Siwalik Hills to the south of the country *(see page 24)*. Siwalik deposits consist of coarse boulder conglomerates, from 1,000 to 1,500 metres (3,000 to 5,000 ft) thick.

The fourth sequence in the uplift occurred about two million years ago when older layers of rock were overthrust onto the deposits of the Siwalik Range, demarcated by the fault plane called the "main boundary thrust".

The fifth and final upheaval ensued during the Pleistocene period, between one and two million years ago – a time of much glacial activity when the progenitors of human beings were also stirring. The impact of this period was felt most in the lower reaches of the Himalaya, where layers of rock were gradually being pushed up as much as 2,000 metres (6,000 ft).

shed their outer layers. Glaciers also play their part: each year, snow accumulates and is compressed into ice to depths of several hundred metres. The weight pushes the glacier's lowest edge down the mountain, scraping away debris and carving out the valleys. Higher up, glaciers scoop out rounded valleys (cirques), which define the mountain ridges. From its terminus, the glacial "snout", a milky stream, runs thick with sediments which will eventually wash all the way down to the Ganges river. Ice-scooped basins found at lower elevations indicate a wider glacial provenance in the past.

Mountain relief is asymmetrical, with rock

Mountain geography

Away from the narrow strip of plain along its southern border and the temperate valleys spread across its middle, these giant mountains dominate the Nepalese landscape. The highest ranges are crowned by jagged peaks. The Himalaya, however, are constantly wearing down, as all "young" (i.e. relatively recently formed) mountains do. The monsoon rains pound at their sides, and constant freezing and thawing cracks the rocks which cause them to

LEFT: wildly folded sedimentary rock high on Nuptse, photographed from 7,000 metres (24,000 ft).
ABOVE: Buri Gandaki river in central Nepal.

TENSIONS AND EARTHQUAKES

Ever since the first collision of continents, the Himalayan region has been subjected to compression, contortion, elevation and denudation. The area is still adjusting: the Indian subcontinent continues to push into Asia at a rate of about 5 cm (2 inches) per year, seen by the frequency of slips along major faultlines beneath the Himalaya causing periodic earthquakes and more localised geologic events. Most geologists agree that the Himalaya are still rising, noting Pliocene "overthrusting" in the foothills and a 50-degree tilt of rock layers in the west. The rate of uplift is hard to tell as measurements have only been made over the last 100 years.

strata inclined to the north, leaving steep south faces. The south-tending spurs of the main range are covered with temperate forests at lower altitudes, their steep valleys marked with occasional waterfalls. Thunderstorms are frequent and winter frosts limit agriculture. Nevertheless, mountain pastoralists, in an effort to survive this harsh landscape, have succeeded in growing potatoes to 4,000 metres (13,000 ft) and barley even higher.

North of the main range, the prospect is much more desolate with bare mountain slopes and undulating valleys filled with rock debris and sparse vegetation. This is a marginal area for human settlement and man's influence on the landscape is minimal. Summers are short, winters severe and dry with high snowfall, low temperatures and strong winds.

In the northwest of the country a fourth, trans-Himalayan range defines the boundary between Nepal and Tibet. Peaks of between 6,000 and 7,000 metres (19,700–23,000 ft) lie about 35 km (22 miles) north of the main range; their relief is less rugged and wind-eroded land-forms predominate. Here elevated *bhot* valleys – broad with open profiles and a dry climate – are reminiscent of Tibet, particularly where the Himalayan rainshadow blocks the monsoon.

MONSOON RAINS

The monsoon begins in June and lasts for almost four months, but its distribution of rain varies. East Nepal is affected first by the wet winds from the Bay of Bengal and has a longer monsoon and more rain. West Nepal lies in the hinterland of the monsoon's progress and is under the influence of the *lhu*, the dry wind that blows across western India. The high Himalaya block the north-ward passage of the rains and much of the northwest lies in the rainshadow. Pokhara, exposed by a dip in the middle ranges, receives over 300 cm (120 inches) of rain while Jomsom, just 65 km (40 miles) further north, gets less than 30 cm (12 inches).

Survival is difficult here. The Thakalis of the Kali Gandaki Valley and the people of Manang originally came from Tibet, but the harsh terrain of the Himalayan rainshadow made farming difficult. So both groups turned to trading as their livelihood, traversing the mountains on foot, bartering and selling. Today, they remain known for their business acumen.

The central part of the Himalayan chain stretches for approximately 900 km (550 miles) from the Mahakali River on Nepal's western border to the Tista River in India in the east. It can be divided into three regions, principally on the basis of the types of vegetation found. These subdivisions generally correspond to the three major river systems of Nepal: the Karnali, the Gandaki and the Koshi.

The main spine of the Great Himalayan Range is not the watershed between the Ganges and Tsangpo rivers. This lies further north in Tibet. Geologists say this is proof that the rivers are older than the mountains – as the mountains rose, the rivers cut their gorges and rose with them. Consequently even those trans-Himalayan regions which fall within Nepal are drained by tributaries of the Ganges.

CITY LATITUDE

People are often surprised to learn that Kathmandu's latitude – about 27°41 North – is the same as that of southern Florida and Kuwait, and slightly south of New Delhi.

river valleys. While the smaller valleys make narrow, steep defiles, the larger ones have an easy gradient and a wide open character. The main north-south trending valleys and their upper tributary extensions make deep indentations in the middle hill topography, and these low valleys have numerous old river terraces indicating changing geologic or climatic conditions at the time of alluvial deposits. Landslides and landslips are very common in these areas and tributary streams, overloaded

Middle hills

Below the Himalaya, running in a similar west-northwest to east-southeast direction 90 km (56 miles) south of the great rise is the Mahabharat Range, reaching elevations between 1,500 and 2,700 metres (4,900–8,900 ft). These are referred to as the sub-Himalaya. The middle hill region, also called the *pahar*, extends between the Mahabharat and the high Himalaya. Its characteristic landforms are low hills and sinuous ridges, dissected by numerous

LEFT: a remote monastery is protected by trees in a valley sculpted with terraces in east Nepal.
ABOVE: the Himalaya seen from the Terai plains.

with washed-down materials, unload alluvial cones at their termini.

The mild subtropical climate and adequate rainfall have made the central area a favourable zone for agricultural settlement. The Tamangs of central Nepal, also originally from Tibet, have assimilated into the local culture through farming – the typical scenery of the middle hill country is flights of terraced fields carved out of steep slopes. However, over time they have inevitably cleared most of the forest cover to make way for cultivation, thereby hastening the process of soil erosion. This depletion of a critical natural resource is reflected in the increasing migration of farmers to the Terai.

The Kathmandu Valley also falls within this belt. The moderate climate in this region permits three harvests a year and small plantings in between. Summer maximum temperatures are about 30°C (86°F) and mean winter temperatures about 10°C (50°F). Winters can be frosty but they are dry and snowless, while summer monsoons bring substantial rain. The Newars of the Kathmandu Valley have developed a talent for growing food on the fertile alluvium of the valley floor.

> **WORSHIPPING THE LAND**
>
> The geography of Nepal has always meant a struggle for survival. Little wonder that the Nepalese deify the mountains that divide them and sanctify the rivers that unite them.

The lowland landscape

The area of the country to the south of the Mahabharat Range is most commonly known as the Terai. Despite the intervening Siwalik Range, this southern region is predominantly flat, a finely graded alluvial plain overlain with silt and sand. About 25 to 40 km (15 to 25 miles) in width, the Terai is a northern extension of India's vast Ganges plain *(see page 293)*. The Siwalik (sometimes called the Churia) Range stands out conspicuously from the swampy, jungle-like lowlands. These low hills generally rise to heights of 750 to 1,500 metres (2,450 to 4,900 ft), but they are higher in the west.

At a slightly higher elevation than the Terai plain, but with similar vegetation, lie the *dun* or Inner Terai valleys between the Siwalik and Mahabharat hills. These longitudinal valleys have been formed mainly by the depositions worn away from the slopes of the enclosing Mahabharat and Siwalik ranges. Summers are very hot in the Terai and the *dun*, with temperatures often rising well beyond 38°C (100°F). Winters are much cooler, with temperatures falling to 10°C (50°F). Rainfall is predominantly concentrated in the June-to-September monsoon period and is heaviest in the east.

The Terai's natural environment has changed considerably over the past two decades, partly due to the eradication of malaria; the southern strip has been transformed into an extensive belt of farms and new settlers, such as those from the Middle Hills, have made deep inroads into the area by clearing forest and draining marshes. The Tharus of the southern plains have an agriculture-based culture and an elaborate system of irrigation, homestead construction and rotational grazing. The primary crop of the region is wheat.

Surviving the landscape

The attempt of human beings to adapt to the natural environment of this mountainous and climatically diverse nation has left an imprint on the landscape in the process.

The livelihood of the Nepalese has always been dictated by the altitude at which they live. From mountain pastoralists and migrant traders to the successful farmers of the Kathmandu Valley and the Terai, it is the land that has shaped these cultures rather than culture shaping the land.

However, change is afoot. The Nepalese have traditionally lived in harmony with their environment, honouring their surroundings and taking only what they need to survive. But many traditions are gradually being eroded by environmental destruction, new technology and the ongoing march of modernity. ❏

LEFT: carrying wood in the Godavari region, above Kathmandu.
RIGHT: the beauty of the Kathmandu Valley.

Decisive Dates

EARLY HISTORY: 8000 BC–AD 1200

8000–600 BC Nepal's first known residents are the eastern Kirati kings; warrior hill people, their history is inextricably woven with legend.

543 BC Lord Buddha is born at Lumbini as Prince Siddhartha Gautama.

350–100 BC Ashoka, ruler of the Mauryan empire, spreads Buddhism throughout the Indian subcontinent. Hinduism returns to the north after the Mauryan dynasty falls.

AD 300–600 The first golden age of Nepalese arts

flourishes during the Licchavi dynasty. The Kathmandu Valley's earliest stone inscription describes Nepal's first great historical figure, King Manadeva I. As well as leaving a legacy of superb stone sculptures, the Licchavis also instigate the tradition of a hierarchical Hindu caste system.

637 Chinese pilgrim Hsuan Chuang encounters the Newars of Kathmandu Valley.

600–879 Licchavi ruler Amsuvarman (605–21) composes the first Sanskrit text. His daughter, Princess Bhrikuti of Nepal, marries King Songtsen Gampo of Tibet and is deified as the Green Tara for converting him and Tibet to Buddhism, along with her Chinese co-wife, Princess Wencheng, who is later deified as the White Tara.

880–1200 The "Dark Ages" of turmoil begin under the Thakuris, a people from northern India. The Khasas from Tibet establish a dynasty around the Himalaya and Pokhara.

MALLA AND SHAH DYNASTIES: 1200–1846

1200 King Arideva assumes the title Malla and sets up a new, highly accomplished dynasty. The Mallas bring riches and recognition to Nepal, and reinforce the caste system.

1350–1482 Jayasthiti Malla (1354–95) establishes the 64 Hindu working castes, which remain operational in society until 1964. Yaksha Malla (1428–82) extends his rule from Biratnagar on the Indo-Nepal border to Gorkha, just outside the Kathmandu Valley.

1482 Following the death of King Yaksha Malla, the Kathmandu Valley is divided and ruled as three city-states: Kathmandu, Patan (Lalitpur) and Bhaktapur (Bhadgaon). Agriculture and cottage industries thrive but political rivalries fragment the empire.

1559 Druvya Shah captures the fort of Gorkha.

1768 After more than 20 years of attrition, Prithvi Narayan Shah (1722–75), ruler of Gorkha, conquers Kathmandu and Patan, and takes Bhaktapur a year later, thus founding a united Nepal and the present Shah dynasty. Expansionist policies and conflicts of trading interests lead to clashes with Nepal's neighbours. Nepal is off-limits to foreigners, a rule that remains in force until the 1950s.

1792 Invasion by Chinese troops follows several years of war with Tibet. Nepal is forced to pledge that it will not attack Tibet and to pay tribute regularly to the Chinese emperor in Peking.

1811 The first Himalayan peak to be measured, Dhaulagiri, is estimated to be 26,795 feet (8,167 metres) in height.

1814 Nepalese expansion to the south results in war with British India.

1816 The "Treaty of Friendship" is signed which ends two years of war. Nepal's territory is divided in half; the Terai plains are now part of British India. A British representative is established in Kathmandu, the first and only western envoy resident in Nepal. The first Gurkha regiments join the British armed forces.

THE RANA DYNASTY: 1846–1951

1846 Jung Bahadur Rana takes advantage of palace intrigue to stage the "Kot Massacre" in Kathmandu's Durbar Square, in which more than 50 men are killed. He then establishes the Rana regime of hereditary ruling prime ministers. The Ranas rule Nepal, with the the royal family kept as virtual prisoners, restricted to public exhibition for ceremonial and religious purposes only.

1852 "Peak XV", later named Mount Everest, is discovered to be the highest point on earth.

1857 Britain returns the Terai plains to Nepal in gratitude for their support during the Indian Mutiny.

1865 Nain and Mani Singh, known as the Pundits, secretly enter Nepal, bringing back a wealth of information about the country to British India.

1897 Englishman Henry Savage Landor claims to have reached the summit of Mount Api in his book *In the Forbidden Land*. His claims are later disputed by mountaineer Tom Longstaff.

1901 Chandra Shamsher Rana deposes his brother and becomes prime minister. He builds the Singha Durbar in Kathmandu and the country's first railway and paved roads, as well as colleges and the first hydroelectric plant. He also abolishes slavery.

1940 Juddha Shamsher Rana organises the execution of four men who had been plotting the downfall of the Rana dynasty; the men are later proclaimed as martyrs.

1950 India signs the "Peace and Friendship" treaty with Nepal. The Nepali Congress Party (NCP) is formed in Calcutta and launches a campaign against the Ranas. The "Delhi Compromise" leads to shared power between the the Ranas and the NCP, under the direct rulership of the king, and the Nepalese win the right to vote. However, members of the Rana dynasty still retain most positions of power.

MONARCHY RESTORED: 1951–1990

1951 King Tribhuvan (1951–55) regains royal power, aided by India, and dismisses the Rana prime minister. Foreigners are now allowed into Nepal.

1953 Mount Everest is climbed for the first time, by Sir Edmund Hillary and Sherpa Tenzing.

1962–1970 After an experiment with parliamentary rule, King Mahendra (1955–72) institutes the party-less *panchayat* ("village council") system of government, imprisoning all leaders of Nepal's political parties. Major roads are built, linking Nepal with both India and Tibet.

1972 King Birendra succeeds the throne on the death of his father, King Mahendra.

1975 The king declares Nepal as a "Zone of Peace", making it a neutral country in times of war.

1980 A national referendum is called by King Birendra following unrest, and reaffirms the people's confidence in the *panchayat* system.

PRECEDING PAGES: Jung Bahadur Rana and family.
LEFT: Bhimsen Tapa, an early prime minister.
RIGHT: celebrating the lifting of the ban on political parties, 1990.

1988 Corruption charges force the king's brother, Dhirendra, to abandon his title as prince.

1989 India enforces a trade embargo on Nepal, under its prime minister Rajiv Ghandi, increasingly dissatisfied with Nepal's absolutist monarchy.

DEMOCRACY AND REVOLT: 1990–2000

1990 Following riots, King Birendra lifts the ban on political parties. The constitution of 9 November invests sovereignty in the people, guarantees human rights and introduces a parliamentary system. The king is now a constitutional monarch.

1991 The general election on 12 May is won by the Nepali Congress, with a small majority, and Girija

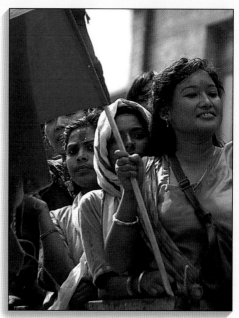

Prasad Koirala becomes Prime Minister.

1994 Koirala steps down and Manmohan Adhikari, leader of the Communist Party of Nepal, is voted in as prime minister.

1995 The Supreme Court announces the previous year's election results void, and the former parliament is returned to power. Over the next five years, six governments of opposing leanings, from centre left to centre right, attempt coalitions, leading to political chaos in the country.

1996 The Nepal Communist Party (Maoist) begins the "People's War" with bomb attacks and political kidnappings and assassinations

1999 Nepal is governed by a coalition of the Congress Party and the Rastriya Prajatantra Party. ❑

NEPAL CHRONICLE

Like many of its neighbours, Nepal has a long history steeped in legend,

but its recent past is more troubled, blighted by political wrangles

This awesome mountainous land was named by the ancients *Himarant* or *Himalaya*, the "Abode of Snow". Set deep in the mountains, between the Great Himalayan Range and the lower Mahabharat, was a holy lake. Nepalese legends speak of an island on this lake upon which grew a blue lotus containing the eternal flame of the Primordial Buddha. Manjushri, a manifestation of the Buddha, came to worship here and, to make access easier for pilgrims, he cut a passage through the Mahabharat hills and so drained the lake. A fertile valley was revealed, men settled here to farm and build cities and this became Nepal. Swayambhunath's stupa *(see page 193)* marks the site of the original island. Chobhar Gorge, through which the Bagmati River drains the Kathmandu Valley, is where the *bodhisattva* made his cut through the mountains *(see page 213)*.

Early kingdoms

The first kingdoms of Nepal were confined to the Kathmandu Valley. Other centres of civilisation developed in what is now the Terai, Nepal's southern plains. One of these was at Lumbini, where in 543 BC was born the "Light of Asia", Prince Siddhartha Gautama, son of a local ruler, who achieved enlightenment to become the Buddha *(see page 311)*.

Of the Kathmandu Valley, the Nepalese chronicles detail the rise and fall of successive dynasties of rulers: the Gopalas, the Kiratis, the Licchavis. In AD 637 the Chinese pilgrim, Hsuan Chuang, found its inhabitants to be of a "hard nature" but with many talents. These were the Newars, still the majority population in the valley. Even 1,400 years ago their artistic and mercantile skills were evident: "The houses are of wood, painted and sculpted. The people are fond of bathing, of dramatic performances, of astrology and of blood sacrifices. Irrigation, carefully and skilfully applied, makes the soil

LEFT: King Prithvi Narayan Shah, the founder of modern Nepal.
RIGHT: Licchavi stone statue of Vishnu.

rich. Both Buddhism and Brahmanism (Hinduism) flourish in the main temples, which are wealthy and well supported. Commerce prospers and trade is well organised."

Already Nepal had built up profitable trading links with its powerful neighbours to the north and south, acting as middleman between two

strong cultures, and in the process building up a distinctive culture of its own. This Nepalese culture came into full flower during the extended dynasty of the Malla kings. The first Malla came to power in AD 1200, and the last was deposed in 1769.

Greatest of the Malla kings was Jayasthiti Malla, who transformed late-14th-century Nepal into a prosperous, well-ordered nation. However, three generations later, in 1482, the country was divided among three Malla brothers and a sister. Each became ruler of one of the four valley towns – Kathmandu, Bhaktapur, Banepa and Lalitpur (now Patan) – and each established an independent ruling dynasty.

Rivalry between these city-states led to nearly three centuries of artistic competition as the Malla kings vied to outdo each other in splendour. Newari artistry soon transformed Kathmandu Valley into one of the world's richest repositories of art and architecture.

Feuding among themselves weakened the political supremacy of the Mallas in the region, and in the surrounding hills other local rulers began to bid for power. The Muslim conquest of northern India had driven a number of Rajput princes and their fol-

WARRIOR NATION

Following defeat by the British in 1816, volunteers from Nepal's army formed the first of the famous Gurkha regiments. They serve the British Crown to this day.

lowers into the mountains. In 1559 one of these chieftains, Druvya Shah, seized the hill-fort of Gorkha, three days' march west of Kathmandu *(see page 223)*. From this stronghold his descendants gradually extended their authority over the *paharis* or hill-people of the Chaubasi Raj, the "24 Kingdoms" of central Nepal.

The pattern culminated with a particularly brilliant and ambitious ruler named Prithvi Narayan Shah, who when little more than a boy set his heart on the conquest of the valley. It took 26 years of planning, sieges and battles, but by 1769 his conquest was complete. The Malla kings were dethroned and the Shahs became the new rulers of Nepal. His successors

continued his policy of expansion after his death at the age of 52 in 1775. In effect, King Prithvi Narayan Shah laid the foundations of the present-day Kingdom of Nepal.

War and peace

Nepal then entered a period of conquest that pushed its boundaries west along the Himalaya as far as Kashmir and eastwards to Sikkim. The Nepalese next laid claim to the fertile plains to the south, where the authority of the Moghul emperors had long been in decline. But here they came up against a rival power, the British East India Company, that was also expanding to fill the political vacuum. Diplomacy failed and in 1814 Nepal and Britain went to war. The East India Company sent four armies into the hills. Two failed to make any headway, one was repulsed, but the fourth eventually proved too strong, and the Nepalese were defeated.

A peace treaty was signed in 1816 at Segauli, resulting in an arrangement that benefited both parties. Nepal secured her frontiers and diverted Britain's empire-building ambitions elsewhere, while the British gained a staunch ally. Only one feature of the "Treaty of Friendship" really irked the Nepalese: a clause requiring the Government of Nepal to accept a British Resident in Kathmandu. The Nepalese had always been fiercely protective of their independence and had never made strangers welcome, unless they came as pilgrims. Two European Jesuits had passed safely through Kathmandu in 1661 while travelling from China to India, but a party of Capuchin missionaries who followed met with disaster when it was discovered that they had come to win converts. Following the 1816 treaty, successive British Residents scarcely fared any better. The British Residency was deliberately sited on waste land said to be haunted by evil spirits, and its human occupants found themselves virtual prisoners with their movements severely restricted.

Nepal's self-imposed isolation from the outside world was greatly intensified when, in 1846, an army officer named Jung Bahadur Rana took advantage of a crisis meeting being held in the government armoury, known as the Kot, to massacre virtually everybody present *(see page 171)*. The king was spared, but Jung Bahadur took over the reins of power as prime minister and Commander-in-Chief, also ensuring that after his death both posts would be inherited by a member of his family. The Shahs remained as monarchs, but real power was in the hands of the Ranas.

For a century the Rana dynasty stuck to a policy of despotic self-quarantine. Writing in 1928, the journalist Percival Landon estimated that no more than 120 English and 10 other Europeans had entered the Kathmandu Valley before him. Of those who had, none had been permitted to set foot in the surrounding hills except when entering or leaving Nepal, although a privileged few had joined their Rana

north of the Great Himalayan Range and is the home of tribal groups of Tibetan-influenced peoples collectively known as Bhotia. They include the famous mountain guides of Solu Khumbu, the Sherpas, yak farmers and traders settled in the upper reaches of the Dudh Kosi in eastern Nepal, who in the summer months traded into Tibet by way of the 5,716-metre (18,753-ft) Nangpa La pass. Another notable northern community is the Buddhist people of Mustang at the headwaters of the Kali Gandaki in western Nepal, who traded grain for salt across the Mustang Pass *(see page 243)*. Two other crossing points into Tibet served as con-

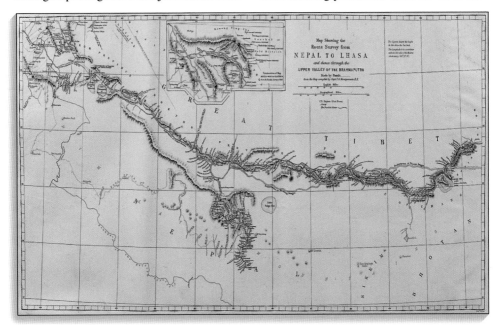

hosts in tiger and rhinoceros shoots in the Terai. Trade with British India was strictly controlled and what few goods were imported, chiefly to grace the palaces of the Ranas, had to be carried in on the backs of porters, since no roads were allowed to be developed.

Trade and exploration

Only along Nepal's borders with Tibet were local communities permitted to maintain links with their neighbours. This border area lies

duits for trade, both river passes: the Khirong La on the Trisuli River north of Kathmandu, and the Kuti La on the upper Sun Kosi, the main trade route to Lhasa and therefore the most closely guarded.

The first European to grasp the extraordinary nature of Nepal's mountains was the map-maker James Rennell, who in 1788 observed that the highest snow peaks could be seen from the Indian plains at a distance of 240 km (150 miles). When it was declared that some of the peaks might be as high as 8,000 metres (26,250 ft) there was disbelief, but in 1811 a peak in west Nepal, observed from four survey stations in the Indian plains, was calculated to be

LEFT: a Malla king honours Indra in a 15th-century fresco at the Palace of Bhaktapur.

ABOVE: the ancient route from Nepal to Tibet.

8,167 metres (26,795 ft). This was the Dhaula-giri massif, the world's seventh-highest mountain. For the next 30 years the map-makers of the Survey of India concentrated their efforts on mapping India, using a system of triangulation devised by the Surveyor-General of India, Sir George Everest. After his retirement in 1843 interest once more returned to the Nepalese Himalaya. This was partly a result of increasing British concern at what was perceived as the vulnerability of India to attack from the north. Russian agents and spies were believed to be at large in Tibet and the northwestern approaches to the subcontinent. By mapping the

Himalaya the British hoped to identify any likely invasion routes through the mountain passes, and to secure them as necessary.

By 1852 the two great cornerstones at the far reaches of Nepal, the 8,586-metre (28,169-ft) Kanchenjunga massif in the east and Gurla Mandhata (7,728 metres/25,355 ft) in the Nalakankar Himal in the west, had been accurately plotted, but the 800 km (500 miles) of mountains and valleys between these two points lay unmapped and out of reach. All the Survey of India could do was to take theodolite bearings from the plains and compute them to produce a rough map. In 1849 bearings were

EVEREST DISCOVERED

Once the first figure of 8,840 metres (29,002 ft) for the height of Everest, then known as "Peak XV", had been verified in 1852, strenuous efforts were made to find the mountain's local name. This proved fruitless, with the result that in 1865 Peak XV was named Mount Everest, after the Surveyor-General of India, Sir George Everest. Years later it was found that the peak did indeed have a Tibetan name, *Chomolungma*, which has been translated variously as "Mother Goddess", "Lady Cow" or "The Mountain So High That No Bird Can Fly Over It". The Nepalese name was discovered to be *Sagarmatha*, which honours the demon-slaying King Sagar of Hindu legend.

The true altitude of Mount Everest, at 8,848 metres (29,028 ft) (this has recently been revised to 8,850 metres/29,035 ft), was established by improved measuring techniques. What is remarkable is that from the time of its "discovery" Everest was to remain inviolate for another full century. In 1903 an officer of the Survey of India was permitted by the government to come to Kathmandu so that Everest could be identified from the surrounding hills. Attempts to scale the mountain from the Tibetan side to the north were unsuccessful and it was not until 1949 that the first climbing party was permitted to enter any great distance into the country.

taken from six different stations on a peak in east Nepal, identified only as Peak XV. Three years passed before a clerk rushed into the office of the Surveyor-General claiming he had "discovered the highest mountain in the world".

The Pundits

If official visitors were forbidden to explore Nepal, what was to stop unofficial visitors from venturing in disguise? In 1863 the Survey of India hit upon the idea of using Himalayan traders to act as their surveyors. Two such men, Nain Singh and Mani Singh from Kumaon Himalaya, were the first of these explorer-spies,

Kathmandu. The two then split up, Mani Singh heading west to attempt a crossing via Mustang while Nain Singh tried the Khirong La. Mani Singh failed, but brought back detailed information on west Nepal. Nain Singh had better luck, returning to his base in India in July 1866 after an epic journey of 2,000 km (1,200 miles).

These were the first of many journeys of exploration through forbidden territory made by these two men and their successors. The exploits of these brave men remained a closely guarded secret for some years and, when accounts of their journeys were first revealed, their identities were concealed and details with-

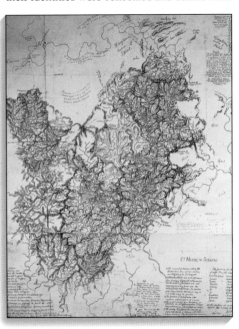

later known as the Pundits. They were trained for two years, given a disguise and then sent into the Himalaya with their survey instruments hidden in secret compartments in their luggage. Lhasa was their main target but Nepal was their means of entry into Tibet. In March 1865 they crossed into Nepal and after a brief stay in Kathmandu attempted to enter Tibet by way of the Khirong La. Suspicious Nepalese customs officials detained them, then sent them back to

---

LEFT: Mallory and Irving on their fated 1924 expedition to Everest.
ABOVE LEFT: the Pundit Nain Singh.
ABOVE RIGHT: nineteenth-century map of Nepal.

held. The British were also anxious to preserve good relations with the Ranas, so very little was ever written about the "opening up" of Nepal by the Pundits, who would certainly have faced years of imprisonment or death had their spying been discovered.

As a result, the name of Hari Ram, code-name "M.H." or "Number 9", is hardly known today. Yet this forgotten Pundit, also a Kumaoni, did more to put Nepal on the map than any other single individual. In 1871 he made the first circuit of eastern Nepal and the Everest region in a 1,300-km (800-mile) route survey. Two years later he entered western Nepal from Kumaon and traversed the northern belt as far as the Kali Gandaki gorge, with a brief foray into Tibet, then returned to follow the river down into India. Fourteen years later, Hari Ram set out to survey central Nepal: he first made his way eastward across the high country that drains into the Sun Kosi river and up into Solu Khumbu to cross into Tibet over the Nangpa La. He then marched east for 160 km (100 miles) before crossing back into Nepal by way of the Khirong La. The last section of this seven-month survey – all of it paced out on foot by counted, measured steps and compass-bearings – took him through the Gorkha region between Kathmandu and Pokhara.

that in 1864 Smyth led a totally unauthorised expedition through the northwestern corner of Nepal and over a 6,000-metre (20,000-ft) pass for a spot of yak hunting in Tibet.

If Smyth was the most reticent of explorers, Henry Savage Landor was the most boastful. This English gentleman-cad bullied his way through the same corner of west Nepal in 1897 and, after being beaten up by the Tibetan authorities, was thrown out. To round off his trip, later enlarged upon in a book *In the Forbidden Land*, Savage Landor made a record-breaking ascent of the 7,000-metre (23,400-ft) Nepalese peak Mt Api. Another trespasser into Nepal, the

Mountaineers and pilgrims

Forbidden Nepal drew other trespassers besides the Pundits. The most secretive was an Englishman named Edmund Smyth who, as Kumaon's first Education Officer, chose Nain Singh and Mani Singh for their new profession. Smyth's chief interests lay in mountaineering, exploring and hunting rather than his work. He made two illicit journeys over the Himalayan ranges and was probably the first westerner to "climb" in the Himalaya, following his introduction to this new sport in the Alps in 1854. He left no record of his activities, but a book of reminiscences published by a Forest Officer in 1902 gives away at least one of his secrets –

mountaineer Tom Longstaff, came that same way six years later and was not surprised to find that Landor's climb had lost some 2,000 metres (6,500 ft) over the intervening years, Landor having never reached the summit.

Others trespassed with higher motives, most notably the Japanese Zen Buddhist monk Ekai Kawaguchi, who first entered Nepal in 1899 dressed as a Tibetan monk. This highly eccentric traveller came in search of the original scriptures of Buddhism, which he believed he would find hidden in the monasteries of Nepal and Tibet. Lhasa was his goal, but, beguiled by the austere charms of the upper Kali Gandaki valley, he lingered in Nepal for 15 months before moving on into Tibet. He then gathered funds for a second journey, returning to Nepal in 1903. This time he came quite openly as a Japanese seeking Sanskrit texts. The Rana prime minister of the day, Chandra Shamsher, happened to be on a hunting trip in the Terai. Kawaguchi secured an audience with him and was given permission to proceed to Kathmandu Valley – only to find himself as restricted in his movements as any British Resident. A month later he was given his scriptures and escorted back across

DISBELIEF

Kawaguchi's accounts of his adventures, later published as *Three Years in Tibet*, were dismissed as fiction when he returned to Japan.

stages of World War II that the Ranas began to relax their grip on the country. In 1944 King Tribhuvan, who had ascended to the throne as a minor in 1911, was able to visit India and Europe. He initiated contacts with progressive forces outside Nepal, including the fledgling National Congress Party, which supported him as a symbol of promised freedom. In November 1950 he put his demands for a return to constitutional monarchy to the Rana government. The king received a hero's welcome on 16 February 1951; two

the border. In 1905 he returned for a third time to Kathmandu, living for 10 months at the Buddhist centre of pilgrimage at Boudhanath. He was now a well-known and much-respected figure – but remained as much a prisoner of the Ranas as before.

The doors open

Despite the assistance in terms of soldiers and funds given to Britain and India by Nepal during the two world wars, it was not until the latter

days later, he proclaimed a multiparty democracy that overthrew the Ranas and re-established the Shahs as the rulers of Nepal.

A cabinet drawn from the Nepalese Congress Party was formed to govern the country, and for almost a decade a succession of cabinets and prime ministers came and went without providing the effective government that Nepal needed. Yet this return to democratic rule allowed Nepal to open its doors to the outside world. Roads, schools and hospitals were built and foreigners were gradually welcomed into the country.

In 1950 a French mountaineering expedition had been granted access to western Nepal, where it made the first ascent of Annapurna I, at

FAR LEFT: Henry Savage Landor.
LEFT: the imposing face of Mount Everest.
ABOVE: King Tribhuvan with Nehru in India, 1951.

8,091 metres (26,545 ft) the highest mountain yet climbed and the first 8,000-metre (26,250-ft) peak to be successfully scaled. This set the pattern for future mountaineering expeditions. In 1951 a British expedition made the first reconnaissance of Mount Everest from the Nepal side. A Swiss party followed in 1952 and, the next year, Edmund Hillary from New Zealand and the heroic Tenzing Norgay, then on his seventh expedition to Everest, finally conquer the world's highest mountain.

FOREIGN VISITORS

The first tourists to Nepal – a total of 600 – were admitted in 1951. The number has since grown to more than 400,000 per year.

(panch) man village council. It offered locally elected, non-party representation and government at ward, village, district and zone levels, as well as a National Panchayat Assembly to ratify decisions taken by a Council of Ministers appointed by the king.

Following King Mahendra's death in 1972, his son, King Birendra Bir Bikram Shah Dev, inherited the throne. The youthful new king amended the constitution in 1980, following public discontent and a national referendum. Although it maintained the single-party system,

Transition and revolution

King Tribhuvan died in March 1955 and was succeeded by his son, Mahendra. The political merry-go-round continued: between 1951 and 1960 Nepal had no fewer than 10 different governments. Political tensions grew and in December 1960 King Mahendra declared a state of emergency, dissolving Parliament and assuming direct rule. In 1962 a new constitution was implemented, investing all powers in the king.

The new political scheme was based on the king's conviction that Western-style parliamentary democracy could not work in Nepal. In its place he instituted the *panchayat* system, based on the traditional Hindu model of the five

the new constitution granted more powers to the assembly, who appointed the cabinet and prime minister if the king endorsed the choice.

On 18 February 1990, the 40th anniversary of the declaration of a multi-party democracy, Nepal's outlawed political parties announced a campaign to restore the multi-party system. The Nepalese Congress and a coalition of Nepal Communist Party factions joined in a movement headed by Congress Party leader Ganesh Man Singh. Demonstrations swept the country and tensions grew as police shootings of demonstrators spurred further dissent. On 6 April a crowd rallied at Kathmandu's Tundikhel and began a march down Durbar Marg to the

Royal Palace. Police tried to turn the crowd back with tear gas; when that failed, they turned to bullets. Reports vary, but between several dozen and several hundred people were killed.

The violence shocked the country and provoked major reforms. King Birendra lifted the ban on political parties. The *panchayat* system was dissolved. An interim government led by the Congress Party was formed until the 1991 elections and an independent commission wrote a new constitution.

> ### POLITICS AND RELIGION
> At one point Nepal had the distinction of being the world's first, and only, Communist Hindu monarchical democracy.

Council. The Congress Party (NCP), which won the 1991 election, has since traded power regularly with the Communist Party of Nepal (CPN-UML). The Rastriya Prajatantra Party (RPP) and the Sadbhawana Party provide the deciding vote in shifts of power. Prime Minister G.P. Koirala heads a coalition-government with the RPP.

Democracy has not cured Nepal's problems. Corruption, inefficiency and power struggles continue. While wealth has grown, most of it is focused in Kathmandu. But Nepal's new democracy has brought positives

A new start
The new constitution defines the country as "a multi-ethnic, multi-lingual, democratic, independent, indivisible, sovereign, Hindu and constitutional monarchical kingdom". While the king's power is now limited, he retains political influence. The executive branch of government is made up of the king and a Council of Ministers; the legislative branch is composed of a directly elected 205-member House of Representatives (Parliament) and a National

LEFT: demonstrators clashing with police, April 1990.
ABOVE LEFT: King Birendra and Queen Aishwarya.
ABOVE RIGHT: prime minister G.P. Koirala.

as well. People feel freer to criticise the system and voter turnout is high. More than 70 political parties were registered for the 1994 mid-term elections, each assigned a symbol that identifies it to illiterate voters. "Tree" (NCP) and "Sun" (CPN-UML) are the most popular parties, evidenced by graffiti seen at election time.

Since 1996 the Maoist Nepal Communist Party has been carrying out bomb attacks, political kidnappings and assassinations. In the summer of 2000, the group was controlling a large area of central-west Nepal. There have been allegations of massacres of suspected sympathisers by police, but the brutality appears to be on both sides. ❏

PEOPLE AND SOCIETY

For such a small country, Nepal is astonishingly diverse in its ethnic
make-up, from ancient tribal societies to refugees from neighbouring lands

Nepal is a veritable mosaic of different ethnic groups whose languages, cultures and religions have over the centuries penetrated and settled the hills and valleys from the north, south, east and west. Despite this diversity, Nepal has a tradition of harmony rather than conflict. In this land of ethnic elements as varied as its landscape, the principles of integration and synthesis have been accepted since ancient times, accommodating new ideas, new values and new peoples from afar.

Watch the faces of the Nepalese people at any busy intersection in Kathmandu and you will soon discover what a fascinating melting pot of Himalayan cultures the city is. And when you leave the valley to visit outlying regions, you will surely find dozens of isolated pockets of distinct peoples and cultures.

The genius of the Newars

Typical of this synthesis of peoples and cultures are the Newars of Kathmandu Valley, who descend from both Tibeto-Burman- and Indo-European-speaking peoples. The genius of Newari artisans, long patronised by the ruling nobility, can be seen in the temples, palaces, bahals (monasteries) and chowks (courtyards) that constitute the man-made environment of the valley today.

The original Newar settlements of the valley and beyond reflect concern for the prudent use of valuable agricultural land. Often located along ridge spines, Newari houses clustered around sites of religious significance, expanding on the basis of each family's structure. Villages extended laterally along these plateaux, leaving the fertile low-lying areas for farming. In this way, organic wastes found their way to the farms, adding nutrients to the soil.

The Gorkha invasion of 1768 brought a concept of nationhood into this ancient milieu.

PRECEDING PAGES: an ethnic mosaic of women and children watching the Indrajatra Festival.
LEFT: spinning a prayer wheel.
RIGHT: a Nepalese Hindu boy.

With the establishment of the capital of a united Nepal in Kathmandu, the homogeneity of the valley was interjected with new values. The Gorkhas' more independent family structure spilled over into the traditional urban precincts.

What one sees today in Kathmandu is precisely this mixture: a medieval township that

finds itself at the beginning of the 21st century, a blending of the essence of old Kathmandu with the effects of latter-day migration from outside the valley.

In a valley where there are said to be more religious monuments than houses, it is sometimes difficult to tell the difference between the divine and the worldly. A Newari house can only be built with sacred permission, which must come prior to the foundation-laying ceremony and then again after the roofing of the house. The fire-baked bricks are prepared in the valley, though not in the wedge-shapes which give the palaces such a distinctive air. The intricately worked wood window frames and doorways are carved as lovingly as on any temple *(see page 69)*.

The extended family is the cornerstone of Newari society and acts as both a support and a refuge. From an early age, a Newar learns how to fit within the social nucleus and how to relate to clan and caste, through respect for relatives and patron deities. Joint families can include three generations with 30 or more members.

The Newari *guthi* is on a higher plane than the family but symbolises a deep aspiration to community living. These brotherhoods maintain local temple and communal services, organise feasts, festivals and processions, arrange burials, maintain family sanctuaries, care for the ailing and elderly, and even assist in the collective preparation of fields. The *guthi* provides substantial advantages to its members and is indicative of the social rank and economic potential of each family. This institution, present since Malla times, has been both a factor of social integration and a means of perpetuating cultural values and achievements.

Elsewhere in Kathmandu, life goes on – in the streets, courtyards, temples and on the rooftops – blending the tight bonds of Newari tradition and customs of past with the concrete reality of the present.

RITES OF PASSAGE

From birth to death, special rites and celebrations mark the important events of a Newar's existence.

One of the more colourful initiations is when the young girls are "married" to the god Narayan before they reach puberty, with all the symbolic rituals of a typical wedding. Although the human marriage will come later, it will technically be her second, thus ensuring that the girl will never become a widow and also making any future divorce a mere formality.

In a country where death comes early, age is also respected and celebrated. The old are venerated, and when a relative reaches the auspicious age of 77 years, seven months and seven days there is a reenactment of the *pasni*, or rice-feeding ceremony, that all children go through when they are seven months old.

When death finally comes, the deceased must be taken, often in the pre-dawn hours, to the cremation ghats by the riverside. The sons must walk three times around their parent's corpse, carrying the butter lamp that will be placed on the face of the deceased. As the priest sets the pyre ablaze, the dead person's relatives have their heads shaved and ritually purify themselves with a bath in the sacred river. The ashes are scattered in the river which flows into the sacred Ganges.

Brahmans and Chhetris

Brahmans and Chhetris, along with the occupational castes of Nepal, have also played an important role in Nepalese society. Originally from west Nepal, the majority have a preference for the temperate middle hills, although they have dispersed all over the Terai.

Orthodox Hindus, they believe in a hierarchical structure known as caste. "Caste", a word first brought to Nepal and the Indian subcontinent by the Portuguese, is often misunderstood. It was first instigated by the early Malla rulers to protect their regime. Most societies in the world have hierarchical systems in the Hindu world for the degree to which economic, political and romantic deviations from the caste norms are accepted and incorporated into society.

Brahmans and Chhetris are predominantly subsistence farmers. However, the literary and priestly tradition of the Brahmans has facilitated their taking important roles in modern Nepalese government, education and business. Similarly, most of the ruling families, including the famous Ranas, have been drawn from the Chhetri caste. The distinguished Thakuris are also Chhetris, but they claim to have come from Rajasthan, in contrast to the rest of the clan who

based on birth and pedigree as well as wealth and position, groups with whom they prefer to socialise and intermarry, and groups whom they consider different. Hinduism merely institutionalises this concept.

In Nepal, the Hindu caste system socially, occupationally and ritually defines all people by the group into which they are born. It is elaborated into a number of rules for eating, marrying, working and touching. But, as strong and pervasive as this system is, Nepal is unique

originally migratedinto Nepal from the east.

Together, the Brahmans and Chhetris have provided the lingua franca, Nepali, and the main cultural and legal framework for Nepal's national identity.

The Tamang "horse soldiers"

Outside the valley rim, and well beyond it, live the Tamangs. "Tamang" is derived from the Tibetan term for "horse soldiers", and it is supposed that they descended from Tibetan cavalry. Today, they are mostly small farmers, although some work as porters and craftsmen. Their elaborate two-storey stone-and-wood houses are clustered along cobbled streets.

LEFT: three Newar girls from the Kathmandu Valley.
ABOVE LEFT: a Buddhist child with its sacred strings.
ABOVE RIGHT: Brahman with *tika* and *topi* hat.

Tamangs are often seen in the streets of Kathmandu carrying large *doko* (baskets) by headstraps supported on their foreheads. The men and boys dress in loincloths and long black tunics; in winter, they wear short-sleeved sheep-wool jackets, frequently with a *khukri* knife thrust in the waistband. They are a familiar sight carrying their handmade, grey, beige and white *rhadis* (flat-weave carpets) for sale from house to house. Women wear above-the-ankle saris of homemade cotton, and blouses adorned with ornaments and jewellery.

Tamangs practise Tibetan Buddhism, as do most upper Himalayan peoples *(see page 58).*

They have *gompas* (monasteries) in every sizeable village. The gods, religious paintings and texts, festivals and rituals are all of Tibetan style. Some follow the pre-Buddhist Bön religion, although variations between this and other forms of Buddhism are now minimal: whereas a Buddhist walks to the left of a shrine and spins his prayer wheel clockwise, a Bön believer walks to the right and spins his wheel counter-clockwise. The Tamangs also retain shamans in addition to priests *(see page 62).*

Polygamy is not uncommon, even though the government has attempted to restrict it. There is an ambivalent attitude to sexual activities, with

REFUGEES IN NEPAL

After China's invasion of Tibet in 1950, almost two decades of violence ensued, including torture and famine, as the strictly atheist Communists took control over this Buddhist country. It is estimated that more than 100,000 Tibetans fled the invaders, including the Dalai Lama. Some 15,000 exiles crossed the Himalaya into Nepal.

The Tibetans have been successful in forging new lives. They have built up a thriving wool industry *(see page 80)* and created a centre of Tibetan Buddhism at Boudhanath *(see page 195).* However, the Nepalese government's dependence on Chinese aid means the "Free Tibet" movement in Nepal is largely conducted underground.

Nepal is also home to a large number of Bhutanese refugees. Originally hailing from Nepal, the Lhotshampas migrated during the 1880s in search of farmland, and settled in southern Bhutan. They retained their culture and religion (Hindu), in contrast to the Buddhist Bhutanese (Drukpas), and enjoyed a conflict-free existence for 100 years. However, the Bhutanese government, threatened by the rising number of Lhotshampas and their infiltration into politics, issued legislation in 1985 that all citizens adopt the Drukpa culture. Many Lhotshampas demonstrated and violence erupted. More than 100,000 fled to Nepal, where they continue to live in refugee camps.

money as a soothing influence. If a Tamang man abducts the wife of another, for example, the new husband compensates the former spouse with money.

Mountain people

The high Himalayan settlements of Tibetan-speaking peoples perch precariously on mountain ledges and precipitous slopes. Life here is a delicate balance of hard work and social frivolity, tempered by a culture deeply rooted in religious tradition. The best

MOUNTAIN FESTIVALS

Mountain celebrations occur on the full-moon days of May, June, July, August and November, including the Yartung festival of Muktinath; and the Dyokyabsi fest of Mustang.

requires long journeys and much of the year is spent in temporary shelters, moving with the seasons to provide grazing for their animals. Among the inhabitants of these harsh climes are the people of Mustang, numbering around 8,000. They live in oasis villages on a reddish-brown rock desert, battling against freezing winds to cultivate grains and potatoes in sheltered plots. The hard grind of survival is interrupted by seasons of feasts and festivals, marked by drinking and dancing. Most festivals

known of the high-mountain peoples are the Sherpas *(see page 50)*.

The southern limits of these Himalayan regions – places such as Phaplu, Junbesi, Tarkeghyang and Jomsom – are sometimes thought of as attractive, even romantic, examples of high-altitude settlements. Indeed, many are. But the far north and other communities on higher slopes are neither comfortable nor prosperous. These border settlements are few and far between; interaction with other villages

LEFT: ornate silver jewellery is characteristic of Tamang women.
ABOVE: a sherpa girl.

are of a religious nature and centre around the temples and monasteries, with rites conducted by priests and shamans.

The Thakalis

Among the most interesting northern peoples of Nepal are the Thakalis, residing in the upper Kali Gandaki river region. Over several centuries, the Thakalis have integrated Tibetan Buddhism and Hinduism into their own colourful faith, and have mastered the art of trade and commerce to emerge as the most successful entrepreneurs in Nepal. Their careers began with the salt trade between Tibet and India, but today they have spread into all spheres of contemporary life – including construction, politics, business, academia and the arts.

The secret of this expansion is the *dighur* system. A group of friends or relatives pool a given amount of money, sometimes thousands of rupees each, and give the whole sum every year to one among them. The recipient uses the sum as he sees fit; whether he loses or gains money is his own affair, and his only obligation is to feed the *dighur* (group). When everyone has taken a turn, the

dighur is dissolved. A self-financing device based on mutual trust, the system does away with interest rates and presupposes stability of currency.

Most Thakalis are small farmers, growing barley and potatoes. Savings are often invested in herds of yaks to gain from their milk, cheese, wool and hide *(see page 102)*.

People of the middle hills

The people living in Nepal's middle hills are often referred to *en masse* as Gurkhas, but there is no such single ethnic group. Most Gurkhas, in fact, come from the Gurung, Magar, Rai, Limbu, Yakha and Sunuwar peoples.

MODERN ATTITUDES

An example of Thakali life can be seen in the village of Marpha in the Annapurnas. Clean and organised, there is running water and a drainage system, a relative rarity in Nepal.

The Gurungs are self-sufficient hill people characterised by high cheekbones, and generally live in central and western Nepal along the Kali Gandaki watershed. Farmers and herders, they cultivate maize, millet, mustard seeds and potatoes. Cattle are kept and buffaloes provide meat, but sheep are of paramount importance for their wool and suitability to the middle hill grazing. Families own perhaps a dozen sheep, grouped in village flocks of 200 to 300. Four or five shepherds take them to the upper pastures from April to September, when the shearing is done. The flocks return to the village in October, for the Dasain festival when all the family gathers; then they head south for the winter, sometimes as far as the inner Terai hills. Wool is soaked and washed, then woven in traditional patterns by Gurung women *(see page 89)*.

Magars are also predominant. They have earned a reputation for martial qualities, though they are basically self-sufficient hill farmers. They grow rice, maize, millet, wheat and potatoes, depending upon the suitability of the terrain they occupy. Spread out from the Himalayan valleys to the Terai plains, the Magars, of Tibeto-Burman origin, have adopted whatever language, culture, religion, dress and architecture is dictated by their settlement area.

The Rai, Limbu, Yakha and Sunuwar people of the eastern hills, like Magars and Gurungs, favour military service to all other professions, mainly because soldiers return home with prestige and income. But the majority of them practise subsistence agriculture. They are nominally Hindu, although some have adopted Buddhism or shamanistic practices.

Peoples of the Terai

The Terai Hindus tend to be more orthodox and conservative than the hill people. Although the caste system has lost its legal support, the higher castes still control most of the region's wealth and carry political clout. Movement across the India-Nepal border is unrestricted, and there are close ties with India here. Villages are typically clusters of 30 to 100 dwellings, with bamboo walls plastered with cow dung and mud. Concrete walls and cement roofs are signs of wealth.

Lowland groups such as the Tharu, Danuwar, Majhi and Darai live in the southern, north-eastern and western Terai. Rajbansi, Satar, Dhimal and Bodo peoples live in the far eastern districts of Jhapa and Morang. Muslims are found along the central and western Terai.

Numbering about half a million people, the Tharu are the most ancient people inhabiting the Terai. The name Tharu is one of the few common factors uniting these "tribal" people whose cultures vary greatly. The main Tharu groups are the Kochila in the eastern Terai, Mahaton and Nawalpuria in the Chitwan Valley, Dangaura in Dang and Deokhuri valleys, Katharya or Rajathya in Karnali and Rana in the far west. Their agrarian lifestyle remained isolated until the eradication of malaria in the 1950s and the land reforms of the 1960s, which enabled the hill people to compete for the rich land of the Terai.

In most areas, the Tharu grow rice, maize, wheat, barley, lentils and mustard seed. They keep chickens and ducks, breed pigs, goats and buffaloes, and practise fishing – casting nets, damming streams or catching fish with their bare hands. Fish, shrimps and snails are the daily diet, eaten with rice. They collect medic-inal herbs, grasses and wood from the jungle and occasionally hunt small animals. Creepers are made into rope and marsh reeds are used to weave mats and baskets, decorated with shells, seeds and tassels. The women use these to carry goods on their heads.

Tharu women marry early, although their life does not change much until they give birth. Their husbands-to-be often work for their future parents-in-law for two or three years before they "earn" the right to marry. Age defines authority; the old man is the overlord and the mother or elder sister rules over the female household. Tharu worship their own local spirits and some Hindu deities. A goddess is worshipped by each community at a shrine tended by priests *(gurwas)*.

The Dangaura Tharu have managed to preserve their traditions to the greatest extent.

LEFT: Tharu lady in distinctive hat.
RIGHT: wicker baskets are used to transport goods in the hill regions.

NATURAL IMMUNITY

The Tharu were able to remain in the lowland Terai because of a mysterious immunity to malaria among their people.

They live in villages of mud longhouses, with as many as 150 family members clustered together under one roof. The small entrances to the houses lead into a large central room, which is often decorated with wall paintings, nets and hanging baskets. Animals live on the right; on the left the family rooms are divided by tall grain jars providing both privacy and storage. Dangaura wear mostly white, and the women are tattooed with peacock designs. They often marry by sister exchange: two families exchange their

sons and daughters. During the wedding cere-mony, the newlyweds knock their heads together as a sign of union. The Nawalpuria Tharu of Chitwan speak a similar dialect to the Dangaura and also wear white.

In the far west, the Katharya Tharu claim to be descendants of the Rajputs. The women wear distinctive short, embroidered skirts, and their blouses are covered with coins. They adorn their necks and ankles with silver jewellery. Also concentrated in the western plains, the Rana Tharu are similar, but tend to live in smaller villages and decorate their houses with orange and white designs set with small mirrors. ❑

The Sherpas

There are still many people who think that to be a Sherpa means simply to be a high-altitude porter, rather than a member of a distinct ethnic group. "How long have you *been* a Sherpa?" is a question that is frequently asked of Sherpas who venture outside of their own country. It is true that Sherpas first came to be known to the Western world through their remarkable help in getting mountaineering expeditions to the high summits of the Himalaya. Yet Sherpas do other things besides carry loads and climb mountains.

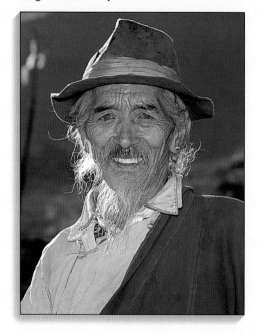

Sherpas are members of an ethnic group that has been living in the mountainous regions of northern Nepal for several centuries. Their name in Tibetan means "people from the east", and it is generally assumed that they came here from east-ern Tibet during the 16th century. They were able to make a living in this inhospitable environment by balancing a commercial and agrarian way of life, combining the growing of meagre crops with the raising of yaks (and the yak-cow crossbreed, *zopkio* or *dzum*), as well as trading with their former home-land. After they became officially incorporated inside the borders of the political state of Nepal, the northernmost Khumbu Sherpas were granted the exclusive privilege of carrying trade goods over

the Nangpa La, one of the few accessible routes to Tibet. This, and the introduction of the potato, gave them and their Sherpa neighbours in Solu to the south a degree of wealth that allowed them to establish monasteries and, for many families, to develop a relatively prosperous lifestyle.

However, the Chinese invasion of Tibet in the 1950s ended this long-standing way of life. The border closed down and hundreds if not thousands of Tibetan refugees streamed over the Nangpa La into the Sherpa homeland. Some Tibetans stayed behind to become leading citizens in the Sherpa community but most moved farther south. Yet luck and an innate adaptability and resilience of char-acter have favoured the Sherpas. At almost the same time that the Tibetan trade was cut off, Nepal's borders were opened to foreigners and Westerners were beginning to discover the joys of trekking. Sherpas played an important part in the first ascent of Mount Everest in 1953 (Tenzing Nor-gay, originally from Thame, a village in the Khumbu, was one of the first two climbers to set foot on the summit), and continued to excel in this role in the many climbing expeditions that have followed. Starting with a handful of adventurers in the 1950s and 1960s, trekking has mushroomed into an activity that brings some 20,000 visitors from all over the world to the Sherpa homeland each year *(see page 123)*. Sherpas remain in demand not just for their climbing prowess but also for their renowned loyalty and friendly demeanour.

The influx of trekkers and climbers has had its benefits and its disadvantages. It has undoubtedly brought a new prosperity to the Sherpas: many homes have been converted into lodges or tea houses, most able-bodied Sherpas can find work in trekking crews, and almost every Sherpa family has come to depend in one way or another on the trekking industry. While some rich foreigners have helped their Sherpa friends build large hotels or start trekking companies, others have funded schools, medical stations, and projects designed to conserve the Sherpa environment.

However, probably the most important change is the conversion of the Sherpa world from what was largely a barter economy to a money economy, and with it a concomitant disruption of their tradi-tional social patterns. With the increase in tourism, many Sherpas have become dollar

LEFT: Konjo Chumbi, a Sherpa elder statesman from Khumjung village.
RIGHT: Sherpani sisters tend the family hearth.

millionaires, and have moved into more high-profile careers, including politics. At the same time, the centre of authority has in many ways moved outside the area. Sagarmatha National Park, established with the help of New Zealanders in the 1960s, has taken control of the forests out of local hands. Kathmandu, where most trekking companies have their headquarters and hire their crews, has become a dominant focus for Sherpa life, with many moving there for part or all of the year. The construction, with Austrian help, of a hydro-electric plant in the Khumbu has given a new look to many of its villages. One of them, Namche Bazar, now boasts a laundrette, disco and cin-

Trekkers who visit the homeland of the Sherpas often worry about the possible negative impact they and their fellow trekkers may be having on the Sherpas and their way of life. Even way back in 1950, Charles Houston, who, with Bill Tilman, could claim to be one of the first trekkers to set foot in the Khumbu, was concerned about the "damage we might have set in train for this innocent, backward country. We were all sad, knowing that this was the end of something unique and wild, and the beginning of a period of great danger and immense change for this wonderful land."

Yet, as noted above, the Sherpas are wonderfully adaptable and at the same time resilient. They

ema, as well as the world's highest internet café *(see page 264)*. Many young Sherpas are now being drawn by the attractions of a larger world beyond even the big city: the United States, Japan, India or the Middle East.

There is, also, the inherent risk involved with the sport of mountaineering, and the Sherpas are at the front of the queue if disaster strikes. As Sir Edmund Hillary commented: "While foreign expedition members waited in their tents for the next thrust forward up the mountain, Sherpas were relaying loads backward and forward up the slopes. They were constantly in peril. Many died in crevasses, in avalanches and in tumbles down the mountainsides."

may, many of them, now be wearing Western dress, dancing to Western music, or browsing the Internet on Western computers, but, as anyone who deals with them knows, they are made of the same stuff as the ancestors who first made such an impression on early Western mountaineers. Sir Edmund Hillary, who has worked with the Sherpas for half a century and devoted much of his life to helping them, still finds them "cheerful, hardworking, agreeable and lacking in any sense of inferiority... The warmth and hospitality remain... They introduce you so readily into their culture and religion; they ask so little from you except politeness and friendship; they laugh so easily at your jokes and their own." ❑

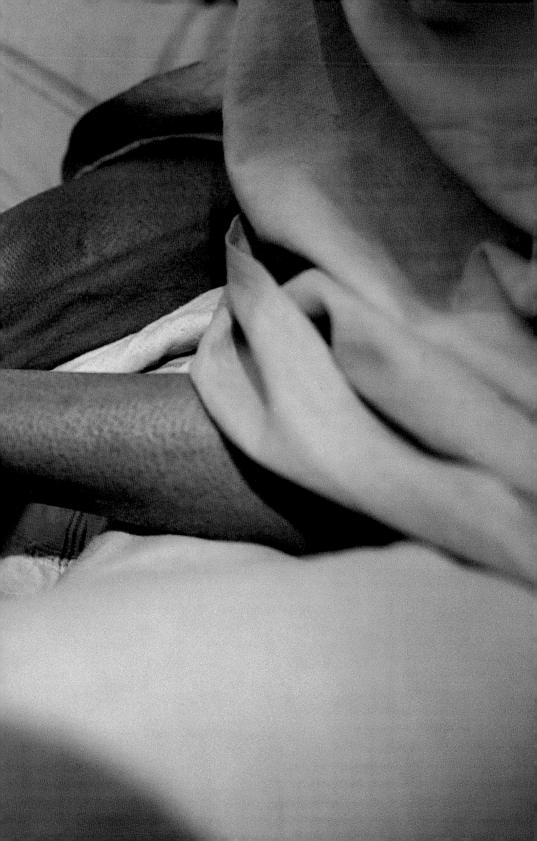

CENTRE OF THE UNIVERSE

The two main religions of Nepal, Hinduism and Buddhism, are often
worshipped side by side, but there are also more unusual rites such as Shamanism

The sacred Mount Kailas (6,714 metres, 22,028 ft), situated beyond the main Himalayan range in Tibet, is regarded by millions as the spiritual centre of the universe. Worshipped by sages and celebrated by poets, this is the divine home where the gods descended to earth from heaven. Kailas and nearby Lake Manasarovar have for centuries captured the imagination with the classic images of creation, such as the Garden of Eden, the mountain of the Ark and the primordial ocean where creation of cosmos began. This oddly shaped mountain is only visible on the clearest of days from an aircraft flying in the far west of the Nepalese Himalaya. It is the object of pilgrimages by only a privileged few, due to the difficulties of travel to such a remote region.

Both Hinduism and Buddhism relate to the Himalaya as a sacred source and those that live in its shadow are ever-mindful of its spiritual power – "An embodiment of the godly, fit to be worshipped" (Kalidasa, 5th century).

Religious mainstreams

The majority of Nepal's population calls itself Hindu, followed by a strong Buddhist faction, with a small percentage of Muslims and a few Christians. The two main spiritual currents are, however, often hard to distinguish, since they are interwoven with the exotica of Tantrism and the influences of various local religions. The result is a cornucopia of sects, deities and celebrations unknown elsewhere on earth. With such diverse beliefs, religious tolerance is of the essence. In fact, proselytism is forbidden by law – with a lengthy jail sentence awaiting offending parties, both converter and convert.

The bulk of Kathmandu's Newars *(see page 43)* can be called Buddhist, in the sense that their family priests are Tantric Buddhist priests rather than Hindu Brahmans. Such classifica-

tion, however, has never prevented a villager from worshipping Tantric Hindu gods who are the village's patron deities. By becoming a follower of the Buddha, one does not cease to be a Hindu. Buddhists, in fact, regard the Hindu trinity of Brahma, Shiva and Vishnu as avatars (incarnations) of the Buddha and give the triad

an importance in the Buddhist cosmology. Hindus likewise revere the Buddha as an incarnation of Vishnu. It has been said that, if one asks a Newar whether he is Hindu or Buddhist, the answer will be "Yes"; the question implies an exclusive choice which is alien to the religious experience of Nepal's people.

The political leaders of Kathmandu Valley have always been Hindus, but most of them have also supported development of their peoples' other faiths. The 7th-century King Narendradev, for instance, received Chinese Buddhist travellers with utmost respect. Chinese journals describe the king as a devout Buddhist who wore an emblem of the Buddha

---

PRECEDING PAGES: a sadhu's praying hands play the sacred cymbals.
LEFT: marigolds are devout offerings for Hindus.
RIGHT: Shiva devotees gather at Pashupatinath.

on his belt. But inscriptions left behind from Narendradev's reign insist that he regarded Shiva as his principal god.

From the time of King Jayasthiti Malla in the 14th century, growing pressure was put on Nepal's population to conform to the social structure of Hindu society. Even the Malla family deity, the goddess Taleju, was an import from South India. This trend was strengthened when the present Shah dynasty acceded to the throne, adopting as its patron

> ### SACRIFICIAL GIFT
>
> The sacrifice of a male chicken, goat or buffalo is not only a way of slaying a beast before the divine but gives an "unfortunate brother" a release from his imprisonment as an animal.

deity a deified Shaivite yogi, Gorakhnath.

The Rana prime ministers increased the caste differences during their century of power, enhancing the wealth of the ruling class. Innovation in religious arts was discouraged and architects turned to building palaces rather than temples. In recent years, however, Nepalese governments have realised the importance of religious diversity and have promoted this cultural legacy.

Daily devotion

Every day before dawn, when sacred cows and stray dogs roam aimlessly in empty streets and farmers hurry to market with their loads of vegetables or chickens, devotees of Nepal's religious cults wake up their gods in sacred temples. As the misty rays of dawn begin to stream through the doorways, men, women and children set out for Hindu and Buddhist temples, carrying ritual offerings *(puja)* for the multiple gods of their pantheons.

They carry small copper plates piled high with grains of rice, red powder and tiny yellow flower petals to scatter on the deities' images. Afterwards, they mix the offerings into a paste and apply a small amount of the mixture to their own foreheads, between the eyes: this is *tika*, a symbol of the presence of the divine.

Puja such as this are made at any and all times in Nepal, for any occasion or celebration. This is a cornerstone of Nepalese religion, inherited from the most ancient of ancestors. Offerings renew communion with the deities most important to each individual's particular problem, caste or inclination.

Some of the devout have a special sequence of offerings, carefully arranged in a partitioned copper tray; they go from god to god for the best part of the morning. Others arrive with a couple of cups of yoghurt or *ghee*, and perhaps a few coins for the priests. Still other people may stay near their homes, contenting their deities by throwing rice, powder and petals on a particular rock or tree.

Ritual sacrifice is another foundation of Nepal's Hindu faith. Whether it is for a wedding or initiation rite or a seasonal festival for a deity, sacrifices are carried out with utter simplicity or with utmost pomp and ceremony.

At the time of Nepal's biggest feast, the Dasain festival of early autumn *(see page 89)*, some 10,000 animals, mainly goats, are sacrificed in the space of a few days. More commonly, there are regular animal sacrifices at the Dakshinkali Temple in the southwest of the Kathmandu Valley – to the fascination of tourists crowding outside the sacrificial pits.

The Hindu heritage

Nepal's religions actually had their origins with the first Aryan invaders, who settled in the north of India about 1700 BC. They recorded the Vedas, a collection of more than 1,000 hymns defining a polytheistic religion. Out of this grew the caste-conscious Brahmanism, linking all men to the god-creator Brahma. The brahmans, or priest class, were said to have come from Brahma's mouth; the Chhetris, or warrior caste, from his arms; the Vaisyas, artisans and traders, from his thighs; and the Sudras, or serfs, from his feet.

As Brahmanism evolved into modern Hinduism, followers began to feel increasingly that existence and reality were subjects too vast to be encompassed within a single set of beliefs. The Hindu religion of today, therefore, comprises many different metaphysical systems and viewpoints, some of which are mutually

with Brahma "the creator", Vishnu "the preserver" and Shiva "the destroyer".

Most Nepalese Hindus regard Brahma's role as being essentially completed. Having created the world, he can now sit back astride his swan and keep out of everyday affairs. Both Vishnu and Shiva, however, remain very important.

Vishnu, whose duty it is to assure the preservation of life and of the world, is traditionally considered to have visited earth as 10 different avatars. Nepalese art pictures him as a fish, a tortoise, a boar, a lion, a dwarf, and as various men – among them Narayan, the embodiment of universal love and knowledge; Rama, a

contradictory. The individual opts for whichever belief or practice suits him and his inclinations the best.

Hinduism has no formal creed or universal governing organisation. Brahman priests serve as spiritual advisers to upper-caste families, but the only real authority is the ancient Vedic texts. Most important is that the individual complies with his family and social group.

Different sects have developed a particular affinity with one or another deity – especially

LEFT: ritual sacrifice is a cornerstone of Hindu worship in Nepal.
ABOVE: *baba* at Pashupatinath.

prince; Krishna, a cowherd and charioteer; and Gautama Buddha, who corrupted the demons. The King of Nepal is also regarded as an incarnation of Vishnu.

Despite all the devotion paid to Vishnu, it is Shiva who gets the most attention in Nepal. Those who worship Shiva do so not out of love of destruction, but because man must respect the fact that all things eventually will come to an end, and from that end will come a new beginning. Like Vishnu, Shiva takes different forms. He is Pashupati, the lord of the beasts who guides all species in their development and serves benevolently as the tutelary god of Nepal. He is also Mahadev, lord of knowledge and procreation, symbolised by the *lingam*. And he is the terrifying Tantric Bhairav, depicted with huge teeth and a necklace of skulls, intent on destroying everything he sees, including ignorance.

One of Shiva's sons, by his consort Parvati (also known as Annapurna, goddess of abundance), is the elephant-headed god, Ganesh. It is said he was born as a normal child, but had his head accidentally severed and the elephant's head was grafted onto his neck. It is Ganesh's responsibility to decide between success and failure, to remove obstacles or create them as necessary.

The idea of "new beginnings", made manifest in the doctrine of reincarnation, is what keeps the Hindu caste system strong. Hindus believe that they must accept and act according to their station in life, no matter what it may be. Their birthright is a reward or punishment for actions – *karma* – accrued in a previous life. Their behaviour in this life will help determine their next one.

Teachings of the Buddha

Brahmanism was the dominant faith in the Indian subcontinent at the time of the emergence of Buddhism in the 6th century BC. The new religion's founder, a Sakya prince named Siddhartha Gautama, was born about 543 BC (the actual date is disputed) near present-day Lumbini in Nepal's western Terai *(see page 311)*. At the age of 29, he convinced his charioteer to take him outside the palace grounds where he lived a life of protected luxury. There, the sight of an old man, a crippled man and a corpse persuaded him to abandon his family and his lavish lifestyle for that of a wandering ascetic.

For more than five years, Gautama roamed from place to place, nearly dying of self-deprivation as he sought a solution to the suffering he saw. He finally abandoned his asceticism, and while meditating under a pipal tree near Benares (now Varanasi) in India, oblivious to all distractions and temptations, he became enlightened.

Now known as the Buddha, the "Enlightened One", Gautama preached a doctrine based on the "Four Noble Truths" and the "Eightfold Path". We suffer, he said, because of our

---

RELIGION AND LITERATURE

The stories of Rama and Krishna are particularly important to Hindus, not just in Nepal but all over the Asian continent. Rama is the hero of the *Ramayana*, perhaps Asia's greatest epic tale which has been translated and adapted into numerous versions from India to Indonesia.

The ideal man, Rama is brave, noble and virtuous. His beautiful wife Sita, whose legendary home is Janakpur *(see page 297)*, is the perfect wife, loyal and devoted. On a forest foray, Sita is captured by the demon Rawana, who carries her off to his lair on the isle of Lanka. Rama enlists the help of the monkey people and their general, Hanuman, as well as the mythical eagle, Garuda. Together, they rescue

Sita and slay Rawana. Despite Rawana's advances, Sita proves her purity after the abduction by entering a fire and emerging unscathed. In Nepal, Hanuman and Garuda, Vishnu's vehicle, are revered.

Krishna is the central figure of the other great Indian epic, the *Mahabharata*, particularly in the part of the tale known as the Bhagavad-Gita. Nepalis love the many tales of Krishna's pranks and antics as a cowherd. It is said he once appeared to the *gopis*, the cowherd girls, in as many embodiments as there were women, and made love to each of them in the way she liked best. However, Krishna is also revered as the embodiment of moral conduct.

attachment to people and material objects in a world where nothing is permanent. We can rid ourselves of desire, and do away with suffering, by living our lives with attention to right views, right intent, right speech, right conduct, right livelihood, right effort, right mindfulness and right meditation.

The "self", said the Buddha, is only an illusion trapped in the endless cycle of *samsara*, or rebirth, and created by *karma*, the chain of cause and effect. By following the Buddhist doctrine, the *dharma*, he said, one can

was the break between the Theravada or Hinayana school, which adhered more closely to the original teachings and today predominates in Southeast Asia and Sri Lanka, and the Mahayana school, which spread north and east from India.

It was Mahayana Buddhism which took hold in Nepal. One of the central beliefs of all Mahayanists is that one can achieve *nirvana* by following the example of bodhisattvas, or "Buddhas-to-be". These enlightened beings have, in the course of many lifetimes, acquired

put an end to the effects of *karma*, thereby escaping *samsara* and achieving *nirvana*, which is essentially extinction of "self".

Gautama preached his doctrine for 45 years after his enlightenment, finally dying at the age of 80 and transcending to *nirvana*. Nepalis claim he visited the Kathmandu Valley with his disciple, Ananda, during his ministry.

In the centuries following the Buddha's life, many doctrinal disputes arose, leading to various schisms in the philosophy. Most important

LEFT: Ganesh is one of the most popular and helpful gods in the Kathmandu Valley.
ABOVE: the wheel of life at Boudhanath.

the knowledge and virtues necessary to attain *nirvana*, but have indefinitely delayed their transcendence to help other mortals reach a similar state of perfection.

The Buddhist emperor Ashoka, of India's Mauryan dynasty, is believed to have made a pilgrimage to the Buddha's birthplace near Lumbini in the 3rd century BC. He or his missionaries may have introduced some basic teachings while building stupas in the Kathmandu Valley. Nearly 1,000 years later, in the 7th century AD, a Tibetan king, Songtsen Gampo, invaded the valley and carried back a Nepalese princess, Bhrikuti, as his wife. Both the Nepalese lady (later incarnated and revered as the Green Tara) and the king's Chinese consort, Princess Wencheng (who became the White Tara), were Buddhists, and they persuaded Songtsen Gampo to convert to Buddhism.

Tibetan Buddhism

Since that time, the form of Buddhism which evolved in Tibet has exerted a significant influence on Buddhist belief in Nepal. Altered in part by the indigenous Tibetan Bön religion, it has taken on a unique form in the world of Buddhism.

his predecessor. Upon the death of a Dalai Lama, a party of elder monks goes on a pilgrimage among Tibetan people to discover where their leader was reborn immediately following his physical death. The correct child is determined by his recognition of possessions from his previous life.

Tibetans believe that there are, at any one time, several hundred more *tulkus*, people identified in similar fashion as reincarnations of other important religious figures. These people generally go on to become

The shamanistic Bön faith, elements of which still exist in Tibet and some remote corners of Nepal, has certain affinities with Buddhism. Bönpos (followers of Bön) claim their religion was carried from the west, possibly Kashmir, by their founder, Shen-rab, who, in common with the Buddha, endured hardship and meditated to achieve his spiritual knowledge. In medieval times, interchange between Bön and Buddhism led to a mutual adoption of sections of each other's pantheon under different names and guises.

The leading figure of Tibetan Buddhism – its pope, as it were – is the Dalai Lama. Every Dalai Lama is regarded as the reincarnation of

leading monks themselves *(see page 279)*.

There are four main sects of Tibetan Buddhism, the most important of which is the Gelugpa (Yellow Hats). Although himself a Gelugpa, the Dalai Lama preaches free access to all teachings, including the Kagyupa (Red Hats), Nyingmapa (Ancients) and Sakyapa (People of the Earth). Each group has made important contributions to the Tibetan Buddhist doctrine.

Tibetan Buddhism stresses the interrelatedness of all things. Universal cosmic forces and the energies of the individual human being are one and the same, and through meditation one can learn to apply one's knowledge of these energies. This can even involve an altered state of consciousness: skilled Tibetan monks are said to be able to levitate, to travel across land at the speed of the wind, and to perform other actions which Westerners tend to relegate to the realms of fantasy or the occult.

Learning proper meditation, under the guidance of a personal teacher, is the first step toward understanding the doctrine of interdependence. The most important tools of meditation are *mantra* (sacred sound) and *mandala* (sacred diagram). In *mantra* meditation, chanting of and concentration on certain syllables is believed to intensify the spiritual power of those indoctrinated to the meaning. *Mandala* meditation requires one to visualise certain circular images to assist in orienting the self to the universe.

Another important aspect of Tibetan Buddhism is the perception of death. Accounts of pre-death and post-death experiences are an integral part of Tibet's religious archives. Because mental and emotional states are believed to affect one's afterlife and rebirth, the dying person – accompanied by family, friends and lamas – meditates through the period of transition from life to death, making it easier for his spirit, or consciousness, to give up its residence in the body.

The Tantric cults

Nepal's religions, whether Hindu, Buddhist or otherwise, are strongly influenced by the practices of Tantrism, a legacy of the Indian subcontinent's medieval culture. While the Islamic conquest, the British Raj and modern secularism have largely eliminated Tantrism elsewhere, it has lived on in Nepal.

Tantra is a Sanskrit word, referring to the basic warp of threads in weaving. Literally, Tantrism reiterates the Buddhist philosophy of the interwovenness of all things and actions.

But Tantrism, with its roots in the Vedas and the Upanishads, pre-Buddhist Brahmanistic verses, is more than that. In its medieval growth, it expanded the realm of Hindu gods and rites, and added a new element to the speculative philosophy and yogic practices of

---

LEFT: prayer flags above Thyangboche waft prayers to the gods.
RIGHT: a Buddhist lama celebrates Tibetan New Year.

WHEELS AND FLAGS

The mantra *Om mani padre hum* ("Hail to the jewel in the lotus") is written on prayer wheels to aid meditation. Prayer flags offer thoughts to the wind.

---

the time. Within Buddhism, it created a major trend called Vajrayana, the "Path of the Thunderbolt", which reached its greatest importance in Nepal.

The *vajra*, known as the *dorje* in Tibetan Buddhism, is the ritual object for Tantric Buddhist monks, a sceptre, at each end of which are five digits curved in a global shape, said to represent the infinite in three dimensions. It is the symbol of the Absolute, a male instrument. Its female counterpart is a bell *(ghanta)*.

The prolific Tantric gods are represented in

numerous human and animal forms, often with multiple arms, legs and heads as symbols of the omnipresence and omnipotence of the divine. Many of these deities have a terrifying appearance, such as forbidding Bhairav, bloodthirsty Kali or Shiva, who in Tantrism is both the creator and destroyer. Their appearance is said to reflect man's when confronted with unknown forces.

Opposed to contemplative meditation, Tantrism substituted concrete action and direct experience, but it soon evolved into more esoteric practices, often of a sexual nature, purportedly to go beyond one's own limitations and to reach a divine bliss. Shaktism is one such cult, praising the *shakti*, the female counterpart of a god. Some ritual Tantric texts proclaim: "Wine, flesh, fish, women and sexual congress: these are the five-fold boons that remove all sin."

At a higher level, Tantrism is an attempt to synthesise spiritualism and materialism. Practitioners seek to expand their mental faculties by mastering the forces of nature and achieving peace of mind. In the sexual act is seen wisdom, tranquillity and bliss, along with the mystery inherent in human union.

The image depicting sexual union is called *yab-yum*, not unlike the Chinese *yin-yang*, a

symbol of oneness in polarity. Around Kathmandu Valley *yab-yum* and other erotica are carved in wooden relief on the struts of temples. Their significance depends less on what they show than on who looks at them.

Shamanism

There are few cultures in the world that lack an indigenous tradition of faith healers. While the broad outlines of Nepalese shamanism are influenced by Tibetan and Indian traditions, a great variety of local Himalayan forms has evolved parallelling the diverse ethnic groups in the country. Most of Nepal's tribal languages have their own terms for those specialists more commonly known as *jhankri* and *dhami*. The term shaman, a Siberian expression, encompasses the tremendous variety of forms.

A shaman is a man (or, less commonly, a woman) who mediates between this world and the supernatural realm of ghosts, demons, witches, ancestors and the like. His task is to restore the proper relationship between the two worlds when it has been upset. Since the commonest manifestation of imbalance is illness, the shaman is, above all, a healer.

The methods which the healers use to tackle spirits and diseases are legion. The shaman invokes one or more divinities, his familiar spirits, who enter his body and speak through him. Once possessed, the shaman falls into a trance which may involve violent shaking and wild dancing. Possession may be accompanied by dramatic demonstrations of the power temporarily bestowed by the gods: licking red-hot iron, for example, or tying swords in knots. In this case it is the gods who answer questions,

SHAMAN PERFORMANCES

Dressed in a long robe and a headdress of peacock feathers, protected by straps or bells, ironmongery and cowries, and armed with his flat, double-sided drum, the shaman usually accompanies his spiritual performance with the recitation of a myth that may continue for many hours, revealing both his prodigious memory and his gift for storytelling.

The story, which is usually sung to the accompaniment of the drum, begins with the origin of the world, and continues with the appearance and ultimate resolution of crises between the forces of good and evil. The therapeutic power of these stories should not be underestimated: the

bards of ancient Tibet, for example, were regarded as the protectors of the kingdom.

Part of the shaman's technique involves forging an identity between the myth he recites and the circumstances of the pathology with which he is faced. Through ritual performance and sheer thespian virtuosity the shaman relates the myth to the everyday world; the mundane and the supernatural merge, and healing is achieved in sympathy with the narrative's resolution.

Today, the theatricality of shamanism has entered the commercial world; many shaman performances are now given in hotels for the entertainment of tourists.

make oracular statements and banish evil influences, speaking through their human medium in strange voices or unfamiliar languages.

Another approach involves the healer achieving ecstasy – literally "standing outside". The patient has fallen ill because his soul or life force has been stolen by a malign entity, perhaps a witch, a demon or the ghost of a restless dead person. The shaman must leave his body and fly through the other world in search of the lost soul and bribe, cajole or force the captor into relinquishing it. The shaman negotiates the terms of his patient's recovery and will do battle with the assailants if all else fails.

medicinal plants and the shaman's repertoire normally includes a mastery of herbal lore. The plants are not cultivated but must be gathered from the wilderness. Pharmaceutical knowledge is only one branch of an overall familiarity with the wild and the undomesticated.

Images of the hunt also characterise many of the rituals that are performed over the course of the long shamanic nights: malign ghosts must be tracked down and brought to bay, and lost souls recaptured like wild animals.

Among the skills a shaman must learn is divination, which is essentially a magical diagnosis to establish the cause of a problem.

Animal sacrifice is usually a prerequisite of shamanic sessions, even in some nominally Buddhist communities who technically do not condone ritual killing. The sacrifice is an important component of the commerce between the two worlds in which the shaman is the broker. The client wants something from the spirits and in exchange for this concession he must send across something from the domestic sphere, such as a chicken, a goat or a pig.

The Himalayan region is a rich store of

LEFT: village shaman in the Helambu region.
ABOVE: Rai shaman performing rites at the Gosainkund Festival.

Methods include the scrutiny of egg yolks or the entrails of animals; the way grain moves on a lightly tapped drumskin; the number of beads in a section of a rosary (used primarily by Buddhist shamans); or, among the Rai people of east Nepal, the way in which pieces of sliced ginger fall on a sample of the patient's clothing.

Shamanism appears in Hindu and Buddhist communities of Nepal and parallels the activity of priests of these religions. The exponents of the literate religions cater to demand by including healing and exorcism among more spiritual services; but the continuing popularity of spirit-mediums leaves little doubt that these revered shamans are still masters in Nepal. ❏

The Yeti

Of all the myths and legends of the high Himalaya, perhaps the best known is that of the yeti or "abominable snowman". But is it a myth? Or is there, in fact, a creature roaming the frozen wastes, preying on yaks and frightening human intruders?

Such a beast was first described to the West as a shaggy wild man by a European mercenary in Mongolia in the early 15th century. Himalayan peoples who lived in remote areas below the snow line spoke of him as anything from ape to supernatural

being. To the Sikkimese, for instance, he was the spirit of the hunt, only visible to the devout: votive offerings of any kill had to be made to him.

The British tended to dismiss, as colourful legend, native sightings of strange snow creatures. In 1899, however, Major L.A. Waddell, an authority on Tibetan Buddhism, described finding footprints that "were alleged to be the trail of the hairy wild men who are believed to live among the eternal snows". In 1921, Colonel C.K. Howard-Bury, who led the reconnaissance on the north side of Everest through Tibet, saw dark figures moving across the snow and came upon enormous footprints.

Stories continued to flow from Tibet and Sikkim, and the great snowman debate was on. It was given credence by a British columnist who mistranslated the beast's Tibetan name, *migyu*, as "the abominable snowman". The name stuck.

Years later, when Nepal allowed foreigners to climb Mount Everest, the "snowman" became fixed in the world's imagination. The Sherpas who assisted on those early expeditions told climbers stories about the *yeh-tch*, or yeti. Giant footprints were seen by such well-known mountaineers as Frank Smythe, Bill Tilman and John Hunt.

On a November afternoon in 1951, climber Eric Shipton found a clear trail of naked human-looking footprints high up in the snow of the Menlungtse Glacier. He and his companion, Sherpa Sen Tenzing, followed the trail for about 1.5 km (1 mile) until it disappeared in moraine. Shipton took clear and well-defined photographs of the yeti footprints; they were oval in shape, more than a foot long and very wide, with a distinctive protruding big toe. Suddenly, all those mysterious sightings, the unknown yells and whistles, the stones and branches hurled at startled travellers, seemed to make sense. There was something out there.

According to the Sherpas, the *yeh-tch* – literally "man of the rocky places" – is of three types. There is the huge, cattle-eating *dzu-tch* (or juti), about 2.5 metres (8 ft) tall when standing on its hind legs but usually on all fours, which is almost certainly the blue bear of Tibet. There is the *thelma*, a small ape-like creature which walks on its hind legs, has long dangling arms and is covered in red or blond hair; this is probably the Assam gibbon strayed far from home. And there is the *mih-tch* (or miti), a man-sized ape, which but for its face and stomach is covered in shaggy red hair. By all accounts, it is an abominable creature, attacking on sight. Some say it is a man-eater.

The *mih-tch* is the true yeti for which there is no definite explanation. It is this anthropoid that is painted on monastery murals and religious scrolls. Sherpas single out the orang-utan when shown photographs of known animals; fossils of extinct giant orang-utans have been found in the Himalayan foothills. Could some have survived by sheltering in the once remote reaches below the snow line? Some theorise this *mih-tch* could be a direct descendant of *Gigantopithecus*, Peking Man of one million years BC. This ape man, they say, could have evolved in obscurity, in inhospitable habitats.

Several expeditions have set out in search of the yeti. In 1954, London's *Daily Mail* fielded an impressive team of experts which, though it failed to find the yeti, returned with a bank of knowledge on the creature. Mountaineer Norman Dyhrenfurth in 1958 found footprints similar to those photographed by Shipton.

In 1960, Sir Edmund Hillary led an expedition to Shipton's yeti country, below the great peaks of Gauri Shankar and Menlungtse. The expedition was equipped with the latest scientific equipment and a signed-and-sealed order from the Nepalese government that the yeti, if found, was on no account to be killed or kept in captivity. Hillary's expedition procured furs alleged to be those of yetis and found endless suspicious tracks in the snow. It also borrowed the legendary "yeti scalp", a sacred relic, from the Sherpa monastery of Khumjung. This iron-

But the yeti refuses to be killed so easily. There are two other scalps in Sherpa country, in the monasteries of Pangboche and Namche Bazar, and a skeletal yeti hand at Pangboche. One of these scalps was examined in Europe in the early 1970s; some declared it a blatant fake while others said it was genuine. A Sherpa girl was said to have been savaged in 1974. Yaks' necks were broken by something that grabbed them by the horns and twisted their heads. The high whistles have been heard again. Expedition camps have been visited at night by a creature that left footprints in the snow. When members began following and photographing, something screamed at them.

hard dome of leather and red bristles had baffled climbers and other observers for years but, when taken for examination to Chicago, Paris and London, the "scalp" was declared to be a 200-year-old artifact made from the hide of a wild Himalayan goat, the serow. Hillary's furs, meanwhile, were discovered to be those of the Tibetan blue bear. Many of the footprints were those of foxes and ravens, whose tracks had melted and taken on grotesque sizes and shapes. Western "experts" were quick to debunk the yeti legend.

LEFT: a priest displaying what is thought to be a yeti scalp – many believe it is genuine.
ABOVE: yeti footprint photographed in 1980.

Author Bruce Chatwin wrote of his discovery of tracks in the Gokyo Valley in 1983 and Reinhold Messner found traces in Tibet in 1986. Chris Bonington led a 1988 expedition to Menlungtse, although journalists' reports of sightings and samples continued to be treated with disdain by the scientific community. Proof remains inconclusive, to say the least. There is even an irreverent though forever-to-be-unconfirmed theory that Shipton's 1951 yeti footprints were an elaborate hoax.

Ape, sub-human, wild man of the snows, or demon – the myth lives on and perhaps someday the yeti will be found. It was not very long ago, after all, that China's giant panda and Africa's mountain gorilla were mere legends. ❏

ARCHITECTURE

Nepal's architecture has developed according to local climate, religious needs and dynastic rulers, who commandeered great craftsmanship as a sign of wealth

rchitecture, for the most part, in Nepal is dictated by climate. The country has the greatest transect of climate, height and ethnography of anywhere in the world, which consequently leads to a diversity of architecture. Styles range from those of the arid zones of the Tibetan Plateau, where the buildings are of rammed earth or large mud-brick blocks with a flat-roof construction designed to resist the harsh climate of the Himalaya, to the wattle-and-daub buildings of the Tharus, which render a cool environment against the oppressive heat of the Terai. However, the greatest concentration of architectural styles in Nepal is to be found in the Newar communities of the Kathmandu Valley. Little changed over the centuries in the differing types of domestic structures until the arrival of modern materials such as cement and steel, together with all the trimmings of Western culture.

Only a few buildings survive from the early years of Nepal's history. This period is mostly represented by stupas or *chorten* – memorials to holy men consisting of solid domes, ranging from the great stupa of Swayambhunath, thought to be the oldest structure in Nepal *(see page 193)*, to the thousands of smaller *chorten* dating from the Licchavi period which are associated with the earlier settlements in Nepal.

The culture still extant in the Kathmandu Valley, however, dates from the great Malla period of the 17th century and consists of a combination of temples and palaces centred around the former capitals of the valley's petty kingdoms.

Newari temples and shrines

The most interesting and most prolific form of Newari architecture is the brick-built temple with diminishing tiered roofs. The survival of this style in certain remote areas of India, and the descriptions by Chinese pilgrims of Indian

---

PRECEDING PAGES: Tamang girls enjoying a laugh at Boudhanath stupa.
LEFT: Hanuman Dhoka Palace, Kathmandu.
RIGHT: wood carving in the Royal Palace in Patan.

temples more than 1,000 years ago, confirms that the style was derived from an ancient Indian format.

All Newari-style temples are based on this concept, but differ in shape and size. The main structures are built of brick, often faced with special glazed bricks. The heavy multi-tiered

sloping roofs are supported by carved timber struts *(tunasi)* and are mostly covered with small clay tiles *(jingathi)* – the more enriched temples have gilded copper or brass roof coverings. The top roof is capped with a decorative gilded copper or brass pinnacle *(gajur)*. The diminishing stepped plinths achieve a sense of height and majesty.

A temple may be free-standing or attached to a terrace of domestic structures. It can be square, rectangular or even octagonal in plan and it can measure anything from a 2 sq. metre (21 sq. ft) structure to something the size of the Taleju Mandir in Kathmandu's Durbar Square *(see page 168)*, which is more than 30 metres

(100 ft) high. Most temples have three roof tiers whereas the smaller attendant shrines generally have only two. Temples dedicated to Pashupati always have two large projecting roofs and there are only two free-standing temples with five roofs: the Nyatapola Temple in Bhaktapur and the Kumbeshwar Temple in Patan.

Another striking architectural style that has become common over the last two centuries is the *shikhara* – a tower-like structure built of brick, stone or terracotta. The central tower is geometric and rises to the heavens, suggesting the Himalayan peaks. Like most other religious buildings the *shikhara* is set on a stepped plinth and encloses a small sanctuary containing the principal divinity. The main structure is generally symmetrical in form around a central spire or tower, which is capped with a *gajur*. The *shikhara* style is typical of most Hindu shrines in India and it was first introduced into Nepal in the 17th century.

Newari houses

The development of urban settlements and their street patterns has caused dwellings to be formed either around groups of interlocking courtyards *(chowks)* or terraces facing onto a street. Passages may run beneath the dwellings

STUPAS AND *CHAITYAS*

Nepal's major stupas are dedicated exclusively to the Buddha and are solid hemispherical structures enshrining relics, whether it be his mortal remains, as in the case of the Swayambhunath, or some of his belongings. Smaller stupas, or *chaityas*, usually contain holy scripts, mantras or, in the hills, the mortal remains of a holy *lama*.

The stupas vary greatly in size, from the massive structure at Boudhanath *(see page 195)* to smaller versions found in towns where Buddhists predominate. Their style of construction is basically uniform: the hemispherical mound is either made-up ground or a small hillock or rocky outcrop from which, as is the case at Swayambhunath, the dome is formed. According to tradition, this mound of earth often covers a series of small *chaityas* grouped around a central one. Centrally placed on the mound is a small square structure *(chaku)* which supports the elaborate, usually gilded, pinnacle of 13 stages, on the base of which are the eyes of the Buddha surveying the cardinal points. The 3rd-century Ashoka stupas of Patan are much simpler in form and have only a plain brick *chaku*. The mounds of the later stupas are generally covered with brick or lime-concrete and are whitewashed. During Buddhist festivals the dome is decorated with yellow clay poured over the whitewashed dome to resemble the lotus flower.

linking the courtyards. The facades are symmetrical and contain finely carved windows and doors. The houses usually comprise two or three storeys, and where the ground floor is not used as a shop or a workshop it remains unadorned with a low door flanked by two small windows. The living area is marked by a special window consisting of either three or five bays known as *tikejayal*.

In the common three-storeyed house, the second floor is the main living and family area.

CASTE RESTRICTIONS

Because of their religious significance, strangers and members of lower castes are banned from entering the kitchens or shrines of high-caste dwellings.

general term for Newari Buddhist religious buildings. *Vihara* is used to describe two styles, the *bahil* and the *bahal*. The *bahil*, set on a raised platform above street level, is a two-storeyed structure surrounding a courtyard. Except for the main entrance, consisting of a small, central doorway flanked by two blind windows in the main elevation, the ground floor is sealed off from the outside. Arcaded porticos on all four elevations overlook the internal yard. Directly opposite the main entrance is the free-standing

The spine wall is replaced by a row of twin columns forming a large, ventilated, hall-like room suitable for family gatherings. On the exterior, large, finely carved windows emphasise the position of this living area. The kitchen and the family shrine are usually located in the attic.

Vihara: the Buddhist monastery

The Buddhist monasteries in the Kathmandu Valley – as opposed to monastic buildings of the north *(see page 278)* – are called *viharas*, a

LEFT: Ashok stupa in Patan.
ABOVE: old Newar architecture in Kathmandu.

shrine with a passageway around it. The shrine itself is a small, dark and simple rectangular room containing the image. To the left of the entrance is a stone staircase leading to the upper floor. Over the main entrance, a projecting window forms the central axis to the main facade.

The *bahal* is also a two-storeyed building enclosing a courtyard, but, unlike the *bahil*, both its ground and upper floors are subdivided into several rooms. The building is generally of a more robust construction, set on a low plinth and overlooking a sunken courtyard. The main entrance, flanked on either side by windows, leads into an ante room with benches. As before, the main shrine is situated opposite this entrance and consists of a large, enclosed room containing the main divinity. In the four corners of the building are stairways to the upper floor, each with a separate doorway leading from the courtyard, which lead to a separate group of three-room units with no intercommunicating doors or passages.

Perfect symmetry is achieved in *bahals* by projecting the central and corner sections of the brickwork on all facades and by the placement of windows and doors on a central axis. Although unglazed, the quality of the brickwork is excellent and is usually left exposed on the external facades. The interior facades are rendered with a mud plaster and whitewashed. A carved tympanum or *torana* indicates the entrance to the *bahal* and to the main shrine.

Math: the Hindu priest house

The Hindu *math* or priest house is clearly distinct from the Buddhist monastic complex. Firstly, it is governed by specific regulations and secondly its location, orientation and internal planning correspond closely to that of a typical lay dwelling. The larger *math* generally comprises several small house-units around a courtyard. It is usually a three-storeyed building, which is fully integrated into a terrace.

PALATIAL ARCHITECTURE

All the palaces in the Kathmandu Valley built by the Malla kings are recognisable for their extravagant style and, in the major cities, for their scale and complexity. These buildings are much larger than the general domestic scale; as prestige buildings they were often constructed in competition with the rival petty kingdoms elsewhere in the valley. The palaces exhibit the best examples of their period of architecture, since the local craftsmen were encouraged to produce the finest quality of workmanship. They are solidly built, not as fortresses but rather as examples of artistic beauty, and incorporate qualities of religious, monastic and domestic architecture.

A dramatic change in style can be seen in the vast white stucco palaces introduced by the Rana regime from the mid-19th century. Most of these palaces boast several hundred rooms and scores of courtyards. Large workforces were employed to build them in only a few years. All materials were available locally – bricks, mud, mortar, timber and floor tiles. The external decorative stucco was executed in local clays, copying the intricate designs at that time popular in Europe. The interiors were furnished with reproduction period furniture and decorated with crystal chandeliers and mirrors, all conforming to the neoclassical revival of Europe.

Utilisation of space on the different levels is similar to that of a domestic dwelling. The ground floor serves as stables, stores, servants' quarters and guardrooms and there are usually shrines dedicated to Shiva and a *puja* room. The first and second floors contain the living and sleeping quarters, while the third floor contains the private shrine and kitchen. The exterior and courtyard facades are faced with glazed bricks and the windows are heavily carved, as are the cornices and the brick lintels. Occasionally the rooms occupied by the chief priest are more ornately decorated, with painted panels adorning the walls. The internal walls are otherwise plastered with mud and whitewashed.

DOMESTIC HABITS

In general Brahmans live in separate buildings in isolation whereas most other settlements are communal terraces or dwellings grouped together.

Dharmasala: public resthouse

A building common to all towns and villages is the *dharmasala* or public resthouse, a place where travellers or pilgrims may rest free of charge. In Nepal these resthouses can range from the simple *pathi*, a small shelter usually at the intersection of important routes to the *mandapa* which formerly served as the town assembly hall. These resthouses were donated by wealthy individuals or religious groups, who were also responsible for their upkeep. The *pathi* is a small, raised and covered brick platform, which is either free-standing or incorporated into a dwelling. As it is sited to overlook access routes, the front is always open and of simple post-and-lintel construction.

Sattal is a general term for the larger public building enclosing a courtyard. The *sattal* was intended for longer sojourns by members of religious communities. Idols erected in the *sattals* were most likely features of later origin. The *sattal* is commonly found in the Durbar Squares and might originally have quartered a part of the palace guard or other military unit. The two-storeyed unit consists of a simple rectangular platform with a small door at the rear leading into the shrine. The upper floor is reached by an external stairway at the back. On the upper floor there is another shrine housing a private divinity directly above the one below.

The *mandapa* is a square, single or multi-storeyed building mainly designed as a community hall. It is generally a free-standing open pavilion, facilitating large gatherings of people in or around it and is open on all sides. The roof is supported by pillars. In some cases, a further upper floor is constructed with a separate roof, following the typical temple structure. *Mandapas* vary considerably according to the area they are serving, hence the Kasthamandap in Kathmandu is the largest *(see page 161)*.

High-altitude architecture

Architecture has also developed to cope with the harsh conditions prevalent at altitudes above 3,000 metres (10,000 ft). Timber is scarce and buildings are set out on modules, dividing up space by columns and partitions. The walls are built of thick rammed earth (adobe) or large mud bricks. Windows, if any, face south and west. Roofs are flat and built of clay laid on brushwood or stones. More sophisticated roofs are laid with a mix of clay and oil which is rammed in great ceremony by singing workers. In some of these structures, such as the temples of Lo-Manthang *(see page 243)*, are wall paintings depicting the Buddha. ❑

LEFT: Pujari Math, Bhaktapur.
RIGHT: a typical rural dwelling.

ARTS AND CRAFTS

Like many of its Asian neighbours, Nepal has a long history of art, from

religious inspired paintings to traditional dance rituals

The art of Nepal is dedicated to the glory of the gods. Art, religion and daily life are inextricably intertwined in the Kathmandu Valley, where images of deities preside over local water taps and laundry is laid out to dry on the tiered steps of magnificent multi-roofed temples. The valley's tremendous artistic wealth was created by its original inhabitants, the Newars *(see page 43)*, who drew on the rich cross-cultural influences brought in by successive waves of traders, pilgrims, religious scholars and refugees. Motifs were adopted from Hinduism and Buddhism, while stylistic influences came from India, China and Tibet.

Most works of art were commissioned by wealthy patrons for donation to a temple or monastery. Portraits of people are rare, but the gods are all-pervasive, rendered in a highly formalised context according to iconographic canons that dictate a deity's pose and appearance, down to the smallest details. Creativity was expressed in the general composition and the skilful rendering of fine details.

Metal and stone

Some of the most glorious art to emerge from valley ateliers are cast images of gilt, copper and bronze deities, produced by the ancient *cire perdue* or "lost wax" technique for more than 1,000 years.

A wax model is formed and coated with clay to create a cast. The wax is then melted and drained out and molten metal is poured into the mould and left to cool. The mould is broken to release the image, which is then filed, polished and engraved to a satiny finish. Larger images require several moulds which are then joined together. Statues may be coated with gold and inlaid with semi-precious stones such as coral, turquoise or agate. These statues generally follow the Tibetan Buddhist tradition, with numerous images of the Lord Buddha in his

traditional poses. Patan is one of the main casting centres *(see page 177)*.

Another ancient art is *repoussé*, which involves hammering metal sheets into intricate embossed designs, generally used to create the lavish temple ornamentation so abundant in the Kathmandu Valley. Metalworkers also excel in

creating finely detailed accessories such as temple bells and implements, and fine jewellery in gold and silver.

Stone sculpture also abounds throughout the valley. Stone was the first medium Nepalese artists fully mastered and Licchavi-era pieces from as early as the 5th century are still breathtakingly powerful. Sculptures generally depict Hindu deities, Vishnu being a particular favourite. A slightly less solemn form are *makara*, stone water spouts carved in the form of serpents with water gushing from their open mouths. Set in *dhunge dhara* (sunken stone taps), they serve as a combination public bath, laundry place, water source and social centre.

LEFT: this distinctive Sherpa painting shows Thyangboche *gompa* and a yeti climbing the mountains.
RIGHT: a metalworker in Janakpur.

Paintings

The classical paintings of the Kathmandu Valley blend cultural influences from India and China with an exquisite sense of form and colour. Gracefully posed figures are depicted in highly stylised and symbolic settings.

The favoured medium was the scroll painting, which was easy to transport for use in teaching, worship or decoration. Called *thangka* in Tibetan, *paubha* in Newari, they constitute two very distinct schools of painting.

> **NATURAL COLOURS**
>
> Paints made out of mineral and vegetable dyes are still used on traditional *thangkas*, as well as an abundance of gold-based paint on the more valuable works.

devices, somewhat akin to comic strips. Modern *paubha*-derived paintings produced for the tourist trade use naive folk-art style to depict animals, and an assortment of minor deities and valley landmarks.

Along the streets of Patan and Kathmandu there is also now a trend for ethnic images of Nepalese village life, painted in oil or acrylic. Charming as these may be, they have only come to light in the past couple of decades, and are mainly catering to the tourist trade.

Thangkas depict deities, either peaceful or wrathful; the painstaking level of detail in these traditional paintings can be astonishing, and the artists have followed a complex set of rules for each individual image. Modern renditions of *thangkas* crowd Thamel tourist shops today *(see page 174)*, though in terms of detail these are distinctly inferior to any of the traditional works.

Paubha are purely Newari paintings involving more vibrant and flowing renditions of deities. Traditional *paubha* may appear as horizontal scrolls up to 12 metres (39 ft) long, which were intended to be slowly unrolled; in this way they functioned as story-telling

Outside the valley, a vigorous folk-art tradition continues in paintings rendered in vivid colours on handmade paper by the Maithili women of Janakpur in the Terai *(see page 298)*. These striking primitive paintings utilise folk designs originally painted on the walls of houses. Centuries of tradition and legend are condensed into a highly stylised symbolic art, in which every motif carries a wealth of meaning. Pictures may depict a range of subjects, the most common being deities or fertility symbols such as bamboo, fish or whimsical pregnant elephants. The main images are surrounded by intricate borders and detailed designs fill all empty spaces.

An abundance of vessels

Simple, useful crafts are an equally vibrant tradition in Nepal. Metalware includes brass water pots or *ghada*, and graceful vessels such as the *anti*, used to pour *raksi* at festival feasts. Finely wrought ritual items are more formal in use, such as oil lamps, incense burners and the classic metal baskets favoured by Newari women to carry temple offerings. The patina of age makes it easy to distinguish old pieces from shiny new products.

Unglazed red clay pottery formed from the valley's earth is a common and highly practical product produced by the local *kumal* (potters).

Textiles and clothing

From the red-bordered black *patasi* worn by Newari peasant women to the intricately patterned colourful *dhaka* that are quintessential Nepal, hand-woven cloth embodies the country in its very weave.

Kathmandu is also an outlet for other Asian fabrics: brilliant Chinese brocades and delicate silks and sturdy Bhutanese cloth. Old Bhutanese textiles of cotton, intricately embroidered with silken thread, are particularly interesting. Nepal's major export is hand-woven Tibetan carpets, which make a unique and useful souvenir. So do shawls and scarves of

Pottery is used for a variety of purposes, from transporting yoghurt to, again, serving *raksi* at ritual feasts. Flowerpots, small and large, in the form of rhinos, elephants and griffins are among the more amusing variations.

Potter's Square in Bhaktapur is the best place to observe the pottery-making process from start to finish. Heavy clay is shaped on spinning wheels into vessels, formed into a final shape, then baked in temporary kilns of straw *(see page 188)*.

LEFT: a *thangka* portraying Padmasambhava, creator of the hidden valleys of Shangrila.
ABOVE: colourful fabrics on sale in Kathmandu.

A WEALTH OF JEWELLERY

Nepal is famous for its silver jewellery, often set with semi-precious stones. Silver and gold are sold by the *tola*, a measurement equalling 11 grams (0.3 oz); the fine craftsmanship is included in the price. Traditional jewellery designs tend towards the dramatic, ranging from necklaces of old silver coins favoured by hill women to Tibetan ornaments composed of enormous chunks of antique turquoise, coral and amber. The most popular semi-precious stones include tourmaline, citrine, aquamarine, ruby and garnet which are found in the Ganesh Himal region, and amethyst and sapphire, imported from Tibet.

pashmina, now an up-market fashion accessory in the West *(see page 81)*.

The local clothing industry centres around rayon dresses produced for export. More distinctive garments include the striking designs of local boutiques, utilising local hand-weaves of linen, *allo* (nettle), hemp and silk.

Overflowing handicrafts

Nepal offers a cornucopia of miscellaneous handicrafts. Hand-woven baskets range from the ubiquitous *dokko*, Nepal's own "backpack", to the elegant coiled baskets of the Terai, decorated with cowrie shells and coloured grasses.

Kathmandu as well, and include silk carpets, chain-stitch tapestries and brightly painted *papier mâché* wares.

Performance art

Like the visual arts, Nepal's traditional music and dance are deeply influenced by religion. They range from exuberant expressions of folk-songs to the highly sophisticated dance-dramas of the Kathmandu Valley. Ethnic diversity has spawned a huge variety of performance art, but this traditional wealth is sadly being eroded by the popularity of mainstream Hindu culture, spearheaded by Radio Nepal and Hindi films.

Another distinctive symbol is the wickedly curved *khukri* knife, the preferred weapon of Gurkha soldiers *(see page 224)* and a handy tool for hillsmen across the country. A *khukri* can be used to sharpen a stick or lop off a goat's head with equal ease.

Soft, textured handmade *lokta* paper, produced from the soaked and pounded bark of the daphne shrub, is produced in a range of colours and products. Colourful wooden toys, block-printed fabrics, cushion covers and hand-knitted sweaters are also abundant in local handicraft shops.

Indian handicrafts, many of them from Kashmir, can be easily found on the streets of

Nasa Dyo, the god of music and dance, presides over Newari music and dance, and a special *puja* or worship to him precedes all performances. In the old sections of Kathmandu, Newari men still gather to sing *bhajan*, devotional hymns accompanied by harmonium and tabla. Evening walks in the old bazaar may uncover songs wafting out from a resthouse or upstairs window, and during major festivals such as Indrajatra, the singing goes on all night *(see page 88)*. Bhaktapur has its own variation in the *dhimey guthi*, bands built around the *dhimey* or drum, an ancient Newari instrument traditionally made from a hollowed-out tree trunk (now usually a kerosene can).

Wandering minstrels or *gaine* are major carriers of Nepalese folk music. Claiming to be descended from the *gandharva*, celestial musicians of Hindu mythology, they roam from village to village, accompanying themselves with a small wooden fiddle or *sarangi*. In pre-radio days, the *gaine*'s long, topical ballads served as an important means of spreading news. A few can be found on the back streets of Kathmandu during the Dasain season, and the Pokhara Valley is one of their strongholds.

FARMERS' DANCE

The vigorous motions of the Tharu stick dance, popular with tourists in the Terai, are said to be based on the rhythmic movements of the annual harvest.

Spontaneous village dances range from the long, shuffling line dances of Tibetan-influenced peoples to circles of hand-clapping viewers clustered around a solo performer.

Costumed, masked Newari dancers perform in the great cities of the Kathmandu Valley during festivals such as Dasain, enacting trance-like dance-drama pageants depicting various religious themes such as the 10 *avatars* of Vishnu or the eight Mother Goddesses or Ashta Matrika.

Dance

While folk dance shows are held year-round at tourist hotels, festivals and weddings are the prime time for authentic dance performances. Often these are marked by humorous or satirical dance, as in the wild masquerade of Gai Jatra. Nepalese women do not generally dance in public, apart from the wonderful festival of Teej *(see page 89)*. Female roles are thus left to men dressed in drag, with often hilarious results.

LEFT: a woman at Chame weaves on a traditional weaving loom.
ABOVE: Makakala dance in Kathmandu.

The Newari Buddhist ritual dance tradition of *charya nritya* dates back to 7th-century India. A combination of worship, meditation and performance, it was originally only performed inside temple precincts to audiences of initiated male members. The Tibetan Buddhist equivalent is *cham* dancing, in which richly costumed monks impersonate deities in performances that can last for days. These ceremonies combine religious symbolism with equally important social get-togethers – an occasion for locals to mingle, chat and celebrate. Best-known are the dance-dramas of Mani Rimdu, performed yearly at Buddhist monasteries in Solu Khumbu *(see page 90)*. ❏

NEPAL'S WOOL INDUSTRY

Nepal's Tibetan carpet industry has thrived at an unprecedented rate; it is now undoubtedly the country's largest industrial employer

Over the past four decades the Tibetan carpet industry has transformed from a self-help scheme for newly arrived Tibetan refugees to a booming industry. It provides Nepal with its principal source of foreign exchange and produces its major export – hand-knotted carpets based on traditional Tibetan designs are a strikingly modern and useful product developed out of ancient traditions.

PRODUCING OLD FROM NEW

Most modern Tibetan carpets are now woven of a blend of New Zealand and Tibetan wool; the latter is preferred for its greater durability and lustre. The knot ratio of the carpets is relatively low compared to other Asian rugs, averaging 40-60 knots per square inch, and even up to 100 knots per square inch in the best new carpets.

The carpets are woven in specially arranged rooms in private homes or in cavernous factories. Generally the weavers sit shoulder-to-shoulder as they deftly knot the yarn according to patterns drawn on graph paper. Weavers work long hours, from dawn to dusk, to meet the demands of the tourist market.

The finished product is trimmed to accent the contours of the design, then immersed in a chemical bath to soften the wool and make it more lustrous. A new trend is to add a "tea wash" to the finished rug that produces an antiqued golden sheen.

▷ **RAW MATERIAL**
Raw wool is sorted, carded and handspun into yarn, then dyed with natural or chemical colours, often in copper pots over wood fires.

△ **CARPET TRADING**
In many of Nepal's market areas, particularly in Kathmandu, rows of carpet sellers can be seen plying the Tibetan handicraft.

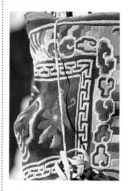

△ **CARPET RIDE**
The durability of Tibetan wool makes it suitable for hard-wearing objects, such as this blanket saddle from the Mustang region.

▽ **COMMUNITY SPIRIT**
Tibetan carpet factories are not only a place of work but a source of social activity, with weavers chatting and singing throughout the day.

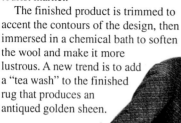

△ WEAVING STYLE
Tibetan carpets use the senna loop, an ancient technique in which the yarn is knotted around a gauge rod slipped out with each row.

△ RETURN TO NATURE
Tibetans loved the intense aniline dyes introduced in the 19th century, but recently they have begun to return to natural vegetable dyes.

▷ TIBETAN MINIMALISM
Old Tibetan carpets are a riot of colour, while modern designs are rendered in muted pastels that harmonise better with western interiors.

PASHMINA SHAWLS

As well as carpets, Himalayan wool is also transformed into a more elegant fashion product, the pashmina shawl. Often called the "cashmere of cashmeres", it is considered the *crème de la crème* of textiles.

The popularity of pashminas is their combination of cloud-light weight and great warmth, ideal for wearing on balmy summer evenings. The pashmina is woven of fine wool spun from the silky long fleece that constitutes the undercoat of Himalayan goats. Workers spin the thread and weave the fabric on special wooden looms, often combining it with silk to add sheen, lustre and durability.

Dyed in brilliant jewel tones or subtle pastels, this luxury fabric is now transformed not only into shawls but also scarves, pillow slipcovers and hats. Natural, undyed hues of cream, white and light brown are also available.

Pashminas can be bought all over Nepal, particularly in the many shops around the Thamel district of Kathmandu (*see page 174*) and their recent high fashion status in the West makes them an ideal souvenir, at considerably lower prices.

FESTIVALS

With an annual calendar packed with festivals, visitors are likely to witness at least one colourful event regardless of when they arrive

I t has been observed that in Nepal every other building is a temple and every other day is a festival. With more than 50 festivals spread over 120 days each year, celebrations are so frequent that they often overlap.

Thousands of gods and goddesses, demons and ogres, restless spirits and the family dead must be appeased and remembered. The various seasons must be honoured and there are appropriate rites for the blessing of seeds to be planted and crops harvested. Some of Nepal's festivals are ancient indeed, having their origins in animism and legend. Others are more recent, the direct result of a monarch's command and government decree.

The majority are tied to one or both of the two great religions of the land, Hinduism and Buddhism. The devotees of one religion often take part in the other's festivals, adapting some of the rites of the other faith to their own festivals. Hindu festivals generally combine mass pilgrimages and *puja* offerings at temples followed by large *melas* (fairs), feasts and animal sacrifices. Buddhist festivals tend to be quieter, but equally colourful.

The major festivals of Nepal are listed here according to the months in which they are normally held. Always check locally with tourist offices, however, as dates vary due to the lunar calendar and complicated astrological calculations, making precise date predictions virtually impossible.

Maha (January and February)

The festival year begins with **Maha Sankranti** (usually on 14 or 15 January), an important day for ritual bathing in sacred rivers celebrating the passing of the previous unholy month of Pousch and the promise of warmth to come. This is a particularly important day at Devghat, north of Narayanghat.

PRECEDING PAGES: Holi Festival in Kathmandu. **LEFT:** the great stupa of Boudhanath is blessed at Losar, Tibetan New Year. **RIGHT:** autumn festival in Manang.

Basant Panchami is the festival of spring on the fifth day after the full moon, and also of Saraswati, goddess of learning. The season is inaugurated before the king in Hanuman Dhoka in central Kathmandu and Saraswati's birthday is celebrated colourfully at the temple of Swayambhunath *(see page 193)* by hundreds

of students, artists, weavers and schoolchildren. Schools are also decorated.

The Hindu shrine of Pashupatinath *(see page 196)* or the nearby village of Sankhu are the places to be for the ceremony of **Maha Snan**, which is the holy bath given to Lord Shiva in which he is washed with milk, yoghurt, honey and *ghee*, then dressed anew.

Falgun (February and March)

One of the most beautiful celebrations of the year is **Losar** or Tibetan New Year when Tibetans and Sherpas feast, enjoy *lama* dances and parade on the freshly decorated stupa of Boudhanath *(see page 195)*.

Shivaratri, the birthday of Shiva, the Hindu god of destruction and rebirth, is one of the great festivals of the year. Thousands of townspeople, holy men and pilgrims flock to the *mela* at Pashupatinath for the happy celebration and all-night vigil. *Sadhus*, or *yogis*, some dressed in nothing but a loin cloth and carrying a metal trident, gather from all over India and Nepal to perform rites.

> **LUNAR CALENDAR**
>
> The lunar cycle is divided into two halves, "bright" and "dark", and within each half are 14 specific lunar "days" on which festivals are held.

The rowdy week-long festival of colour, **Holi**, is a chaotic springtime carnival during

Chaitra Dasain, exactly six months to the day before the spectacular Dasain festival of October. **Seto Machhendranath** is a four-day procession through Kathmandu, eight days after full moon, in which the deity of compassion is paraded from his temple in Asan in a towering chariot and visited by the *Kumari* (Living Goddess).

Solu's Junbesi monastery performs exorcist rites at one of the Sherpas' greatest annual festivals, **Dumje**, which takes place in April *(see page 262)*.

which children roam the streets pelting each other (and anyone who gets in the way) with water balloons and coloured powder. A day to wear your oldest clothes and have fun.

Chaitra (March and April)

The horse festival of **Ghorajatra** takes place on the Tundhikhel in Kathmandu with a display of horsemanship and gymnastics. The same evening, the festival of **Pasa Chare** assures protection against an underground demon in a midnight procession.

Two separate festivals occur simultaneously towards the end of March. Ritual offerings are made to the goddess Durga at midday on

During the full moon is **Chaitra Purnima**, when Buddha's mother Mayadevi is worshipped by thousands of pilgrims in Lumbini *(see page 311)*.

One of the great Janakpur festivals, **Ram Nawami**, Ram's birthday, is celebrated in April *(see page 299)*.

Baisakh (April and May)

Baisakh (usually on 13 or 14 April) is the beginning of the Nepalese New Year which marks the week-long Bisket Jatra celebration in Bhaktapur *(see page 187)*. The wrathful god Bhairav and his consort Bhadrakali are pulled on great chariots through the city streets, culminating in the raising of a long pole. The citizens of Bhaktapur play a lively game of tug-of-war to topple the pole, assuring a year of good fortune.

West of Bhaktapur in Thimi, **Bal Kumari Jatra** is celebrated at night with torchlight processions and devotees covered with vermilion powder (the colour of joy).

Matatirtha Snan, the Nepalese version of Mothers' Day, takes place near Thankot and is for persons whose mothers have died during the year. Living mothers are also honoured.

The birthday and enlightenment of the Lord Buddha, **Buddha Jayanti**, is celebrated with

Jesth (May and June)

Sithinakha is the birthday of Kumar, the handsome warrior son of Shiva, and is celebrated at Jaisedewal, south of the Kathmandu Durbar Square.

The **Ganga Deshara** festival attracts thousands of Hindu devotees to the holy river confluence at Khaptad National Park in west Nepal *(see page 106)*.

Asadh (June and July)

Tulsi Bijropan is one of the most important *Ekadasis*, the eleventh day of each lunar fortnight, when no animal can be slaughtered and

pilgrimages and celebrations at Buddhist shrines during the full moon. Swayambhunath and Boudhanath temples are particularly colourful at this time.

Thame monastery, high in the Khumbu region of east Nepal *(see page 272)*, holds its **Mani Rimdu** dance-drama festival in May during which Sherpa monks enact age-old legends and evoke protector deities. A similar festival is held at Thyangboche during November and December.

LEFT: a torchlight procession at Thimi.
ABOVE: Gaijatra, festival of the cow; chariot for Rato Machhendranath in Patan.

a day of fasting is mandatory for the religious. Primarily a woman's ritual, the *tulsi* (basil) plant is planted in a specially chosen place within the home and then reverently worshipped.

The Khumbu Sherpas' **Dumje** celebration brings the entire community together in much gaiety and merry-making, but, more importantly, to drive out evil forces with an elaborate liturgy and much chanting.

Srawan (July and August)

Patan sees one of its biggest and most spectacular annual festivals in the summer, though the exact date varies according to astrologers.

During **Bhoto Jatra** a sacred jewelled waistcoat *(bhoto)* is ritually displayed in front of the royal family. This is the culmination of **Rato Machhendranath**, the protector deity of the valley, who is paraded through Patan for months in his huge 2-metre (6-ft) high chariot and is designed to ensure good monsoon rainfall *(see page 177)*.

Traditionally the last day for rice planting, **Ghanta Karna** is the night of the devil, sworn enemy of Vishnu, who was outwitted by a frog. Small boys make

---

WEDDING CELEBRATIONS

Nepalese also marry according to the lunar calendar, choosing auspicious days on which to wed. The wedding party is preceded by a brass band, followed by the bride, dressed in red.

---

the sacred lakes and make offerings, celebrating with dancing and feasting. Shamans, dressed in long white-belted robes and crowns of peacock feathers *(see page 62)*, gather at both Patan and Gosainkund to chant and perform rites of purification.

Snake gods *(nags)* are widely worshipped as controllers of rainfall, earthquakes and guardians of treasure in Kathmandu Valley. During **Naga Panchami** prayers are said at Pashupatinath and pictures of the *nags* are displayed on every

leafy arches and collect money in the street to pay for the demon's funeral.

The birth of the popular Hindu god, Krishna, is celebrated at **Krishna Jayanti** in all Krishna temples. Women carrying oil lights make offerings, chant and sing as they keep vigil all night on the Krishna Mandir in Patan.

Raksha Bandhan or **Janai Purnima** is the full-moon day *(Saaun)* on which every Brahman male must renew the sacred thread worn over his shoulder and all Brahmans and Chhetris receive a new thread around their wrists. Go to the Kumbeshwar temple in Patan. At Gosainkund, high in the Helambu *(see page 255)*, thousands of devotees throng to bathe in

house. Milk, the snake's favoured drink, is offered to the pictures.

Late summer is the time for the important **Yartung** festival celebrated annually by mountain people with wild horse-racing displays, drinking and celebrating, at holy Muktinath, high in the Kali Gandaki valley of the Annapurna region *(see page 242)*.

Bhadra (August and September)

Musical processions of little boys dressed as holy men and stylised cows, followed by their family and friends, take place throughout Kathmandu, Patan and Bhaktapur during the festival of **Gaijatra**. A carnival evening follows of satire and fantastic costumes. Originally devised as a comic-relief parade to cheer the inconsolable Queen of Nepal who had lost a son to smallpox, these rituals also ease the spiritual transition of those who have died during the previous year.

The most spectacular of all the Kathmandu Valley festivals is the eight-day **Indrajatra** around the full moon. Best seen from the Hanuman Dhoka, the Hindu god Indra is feted with dancing and processions. Homage is paid to the *Kumari* (Living Goddess) *(see page 167)* and

SACRED COW

The cow *(gaai)*, the sacred Hindu animal, is thought to assist the path of the deceased to heaven, leading them by its tail.

Teej, three days after full moon, is the most colourful women's festival in Nepal, celebrated over three days. After fasting and ritual bathing, a period of dancing and singing takes place. Pashupatinath is the best place to watch these women in their finest red saris and jewels. Offerings are made to their husbands and their sins are washed away.

Ashwin (September and October)

The great 10-day festival of **Dasain** is the most important Hindu festival of the whole year and

she is escorted, beautifully adorned, in a special chariot to give the king a *tika* (auspicious mark on the forehead). Bhairav is also honoured during this festival, the only time his great mask is exposed to the public with *chhang* (beer) pouring from his mouth to refresh revellers.

Gokarna Aunshi or Fathers' Day is celebrated with ritual bathing at the Mahadev temple by the river at Gokarna *(see page 199)* for those whose fathers have died during the previous year.

normal life throughout the country comes to a standstill for up to a week. Families gather to worship the mother goddess Durga who is assuaged with offerings and animal sacrifices performed in community courtyards and in mammoth proportions in Kathmandu's Hanuman Dhoka. Priests swirl and gyrate through the streets of Patan for eight nights prior to the main day, Vijaya Dasain, when each family's elder male adorns all with a red *tika* before a feast on the sacrificial meat.

Although Hindu in origin, the majority of non-Hindus in Nepal join in the festivities – the streets are overcrowded with revellers and funfairs are set up in open spaces.

LEFT: incense is burned in oil lamps during Krishna Jayanti in Patan.
ABOVE: crowds enjoying the Indrajatra festival.

Kartik (October and November)

Diwali or **Tihar**, the "festival of lights", is a more joyous five-day holiday of family gatherings, feasts, gifts and offerings. Cows, dogs and crows are blessed with treats, and brothers travel for days to receive a *tika* from their sisters on Bhai Tika. On the fifth day Lakshmi Puja, the goddess of prosperity, is attracted to homes by lamps and lights on all windows and doors throughout the city. This is also an auspicious day for gambling.

> ### BIG BANGS
>
> It is hard to miss the sounds, let alone the sights, of the Diwali festival. Nepalese children rejoice in setting off firecrackers throughout the event in streets all over the country.

Chhath takes place during the Diwali festival and is an important event for the Maithili people of Janakpur *(see page 299)*. Women pray and bathe in sacred rivers and make offerings to the sun god, Surya. They also paint their distinctive murals on exterior walls, which remain in place until the spring.

The Newars also celebrate **Mha Puja** at this time to honour the self and to mark their calendar New Year.

The yearly **Mani Rimdu** dance-drama festival is held at Thyangboche monastery in the Khumbu, high on the trekking route to Everest *(see page 265)*. Monks enact Sherpa legends and evoke the protector gods with colourful masked dances, celebrating their victory over the Bön religion. Mani Rimdu is also held during the full moon of this month at Solu's Chiwong monastery.

Reminiscent of Mani Rimdu are the dance festivals of **Dyokyabsi**, celebrated at various monasteries in the Thak Khola (upper Kali Gandaki River valley) and Mustang during October and November *(see page 243)*.

Haribodhini Ekadasi welcomes Vishnu back from his annual four-month sleep in the underworld. Budhanilkantha is the culmination of celebrations after fasting devotees have concluded the long pilgrimage, singing and chanting, to the four peripheral Kathmandu Valley temples of Changu Narayan, Bishankhu Narayan, Sekh Narayan and Ichangu Narayan *(see page 203)*.

Marga (November and December)

Yomari Purnima is celebrated by Newars with a *mela* at Panauti in December *(see page 209)*. A special cake *(yomari)* is made out of rice flour and ritually offered to the family rice store for protection.

Indrayani Jatra takes place in Kirtipur at new moon, when deities are paraded through the streets *(see page 205)*.

Bala Chaturdashi is a night-time vigil held at Pashupatinath during new moon, when Hindu families pray and make offerings to their dead relatives.

Pousch (December and January)

His Majesty the **King's Birthday**, celebrated on 28 or 29 December (depending on the calendar), is one of several public holidays. Well-wishers flock to the Royal Palace to make offerings to their monarch.

In Janakpur in December the festival of **Biha Panchami** reenacts Ram and Sita's marriage from the great Hindu epic the *Ramayana*, complete with a colourful five-day procession of elephants, horses and chariots. Thousands of pilgrims flock to this small town in the Terai to witness the event. ❏

LEFT: Mani Rimdu festival in Thyangboche.
RIGHT: Seto Machhendra is paraded annually in a huge chariot through the streets of Kathmandu.

FLORA AND FAUNA

Nepal has an unusually high number of national parks and reserves, designed to protect its rich variety of indigenous wildlife and vegetation

Nowhere else in the world does the landscape change so greatly over so short a distance as in Nepal, from the mountain areas of the Himalaya, down through lush valleys and into the tropical plains of the south. Consequently, the flora and fauna, much of it indigenous, is remarkably diverse for such a small area.

Vegetation zones

Nepal's natural vegetation zones are determined by the distribution of the annual monsoon rains, as well as by altitude and, to some extent, by aspect. Eastern Nepal experiences a longer wet season than the west, while those areas to the north of the main Himalaya are arid due to a strong rainshadow effect. This is more pronounced in northwestern parts of the country.

In terms of altitude, the tropical Terai and lower Siwalik (Churia) hills extend up to about 1,000 metres (3,300 ft) and are followed by the subtropical zone from 1,000 to 2,000 metres (3,300–6,500 ft). The warm temperate belt runs from 2,000 to 3,000 metres (6,500–10,000 ft) and is succeeded by the cool temperate or subalpine zone, which ends with the treeline at about 4,000 metres (13,000 ft).

Most of the remaining vegetation falls within the Alpine belt between 4,000 and 5,000 metres (13,000–16,500 ft). The region above 5,500 metres (18,000 ft) is referred to as the *nival* or aeolian zone, euphemisms for what is effectively a windswept desolation of snow and ice.

The tropical belt

The vegetation of the tropical Terai plains remains remarkably uniform throughout the length of Nepal. The prevailing type of forest is sal, named after its dominant tree, *Shorea robusta*. This hardwood tree, valued for its

PRECEDING PAGES: the one-horned rhino, grazing on elephant grass in Royal Chitwan National Park.
LEFT: an elephant ride is a great way to see wildlife.
RIGHT: strangler fig on a sal tree.

timber, grows in association with a number of other species, including *Lagerstroemia parviflora* which has a pinkish-brown bark that falls away in flakes, *Dillenia pentagyna*, the fruits of which are favoured for making pickles, and *Semecarpus anacardium*, the marking-nut tree, so called for the dark juice of the fruit which is used as ink (and also as an abortifacient).

Spatholobus roxburgii is an enormous vine which winds clockwise around its hosts – local lore has it that, if you find one growing anti-clockwise, a nail hammered into it will turn to gold. There are a number of *Terminalia* species including *Terminalia belerica*, the delicious kernel of whose fruit contains a mild narcotic. *Holarrhena antidysenterica* is used for the purpose indicated in its name in ayurvedic medicine. Its milky sap is the source of its Nepali name, *dudhkare* (*dudh* means milk). Some ethnic groups bury their dead babies near the roots of this tree so they will have milk to drink in the afterworld.

Evergreens and deciduous trees

The eastern and central regions of the Terai are dominated by two evergreens: *Schima wallichii* and three species of *Castanopsis*. The little chestnuts of the latter are roasted in their shells and eaten by villagers; the foliage is prized for livestock fodder. The lower forests include *Bombax ceiba*, the silk cotton tree, valued for the kapok yielded by the pods. *Mallotus philippinensis* produces a red powder from its fruit that was traditionally used as the ceremonial

> **FLOWER POWER**
>
> Rhododendron flowers are often pickled by villagers but honey made from the nectar contains a natural hallucinogen, producing bizarre visual distortions.

dust in Hindu rituals, before the advent of chemical dyes. The drier conditions of western Nepal favour the growth of chir pine *(Pinus roxburghii)*, where it proliferates on north-facing hillsides. Interestingly, elsewhere in its distribution it is only found on south-facing slopes. Chir pine is an important source of resin and turpentine. Other trees become more abundant in the upper ranges: the deciduous *Engelhardtia spicata*, *Michelia champaca*, a beautiful magnolia whose yellowish wood is valued for furniture, and the indigenous Nepalese alder *(Alnus nepalensis)*.

The temperate zone in eastern and central Nepal is characterised by mixed broad-leaved forest, usually on north and west slopes. It is sometimes referred to as "laurel forest" because of the abundance of *Lauraceae*. *Michelia champaca* and *Castanopsis* find their way into this belt from the lower regions, together with a few tree-ferns and screw pines. Evergreen oaks (*Quercus* spp.) begin to appear at 1,200 metres (4,000 ft) and share the upper temperate forests with various species of maple as well as *Prunus, Magnolia* and *Osmanthus*.

The national flower

Rhododendrons (*laligurans* in Nepali) are found from around 1,100 metres (3,600 ft). The red bloom of *Rhododendron arboreum* was declared the national flower of Nepal in 1962. The colour of the flower fades with altitude, progressing through paler shades of pink until it turns white at about 2,500 metres (8,200 ft). Colours of other rhododendron species range from white, cream and yellow to lilac and purple. While rhododendrons usually constitute the understorey, there are regions where they grow 15 metres (50 ft) high, almost to the exclusion of other trees.

Rhododendrons decrease in stature with altitude and dwarf species form a low carpet in certain Alpine areas. Two of these, *Rhododendron cowanlum* which has purplish flowers and the pale yellow *Rhododendron lowndesii*, are the only two rhododendrons endemic to Nepal. People of the Alpine zone value dwarf rhododendrons for incense and as a substitute for snuff. The diminutive *Rhododendron nivale*, which attains a height of just 5 centimetres (2 inches), holds the altitude record for woody plants at 5,500 metres (18,000 ft).

Except for the sun-loving dwarf species, rhododendrons prefer moist habitats. They therefore thrive in eastern Nepal which boasts 30 species, whereas only five have been recorded from the Karnali Basin.

Oak, conifer and birch

The vegetation of the temperate hill zone in western Nepal is generally quite different from the eastern region. The dominant species of oak in the west is *Quercus incana*. Frequently occurring with *Rhododendron arboreum*, it gives way at higher altitudes to mixed deciduous forests of other species of oak, the chestnut *Aesculus indica*, the maple *Acer caesium* and the walnut *Juglans regia*.

Conifers are much more in evidence in west Nepal. The low-altitude fir, *Abies pindrow*, soars up to a height of 45 metres (150 ft). In the lower parts of its range, extending from about 2,100 to 3,500 metres (7,000–11,500 ft), it is found with the majestic Himalayan cedar *(Cedrus deodara)* which forms magnificent forests along the Karnali. Further up is the West Himalayan spruce *(Picea smithiana)*, the silver fir *(Abies spectabilis)* and the blue pine *(Pinus excelsa)*. Like the blue pine, the Himalayan

Alpine plants and fibres

Vegetation above the treeline is divisible into moist and dry Alpine scrub. In addition to dwarf rhododendrons, there are several species of juniper, two of which reach 10–15 metres (33–50 ft) in the moister highlands. Those in the dry, higher elevations of central and western Nepal grow as a prostrate shrub no more than 2 metres (6 ft) high. Other scrubland plants include shrubs such as *Hippophae*, *Spiraca*, *Berberis* and *Cotoneaster*. The arid western regions of Mustang, Dolpo and Manang are dominated by thorny *Caragana* and *Lonicera* bushes.

hemlock *(Tsuga dumosa)* is distributed throughout the subalpine region of Nepal, but the cypress *(Cupressus torulosa)*, which grows between 1,800 and 3,500 metres (5,900–11,500 ft), occurs nowhere east of the Kali Gandaki.

Much of the treeline in Nepal is defined by birch *(Betula utilis)*. Its papery bark is used by highland villagers for a number of purposes including as a ceiling material in flat-roofed Muktinath and as a natural greaseproof paper for wrapping yak butter.

LEFT: a beautiful rhododendron forest near Machhapuchare.
ABOVE: orchids abound in the jungles of the Terai.

Above all, the Alpine flora makes the mountains worth visiting in the summer for those willing to brave the heat, rain and leeches. Primulas (70 species are found in the Himalaya) grow in abundance; larkspurs, fumitories, edelweiss, anemones and potentillas and gentians flower into October. The ice-blue Himalayan poppy is found on lower hillsides.

While impossible to do justice to the whole spectrum of Himalayan flora, some mention must be made of Nepal's orchids which number a staggering 319 species, in 89 genera. Orchids fall into two main groups, terrestrial and epiphytic. The majority of the former, which grow in soil, are found in the temperate and subalpine zones and include the spectacular lady's slipper (*Cypripedium* spp.). There are also a few saprophytic varieties, such as the tall, yellow-flowering *Galeola*, whose leaves grow beneath the humus layer of the soil. Most epiphytes (which have aerial roots) favour the subtropical and warm temperate zones. All orchids are protected by law and their export is banned.

Another important plant is the bamboo. Twenty species occur in Nepal and are fundamental to the lifestyles of many ethnic groups. The Rai creation myth gives pride of place to bamboo as one of the first living things to emerge from the womb of the goddess-creator. One survey counted 57 bamboo artefacts used in a single Rai house. Common items include baskets, mats, cradles and water vessels, but there are also more exotic objects such as bows and arrows, rat-traps and a brush used in shaman seances. People who have lived for generations on the margins of the forest have come to learn how best to use its resources.

A great number of species at different altitudes are valued for their fibres but none is more versatile than *Girardinia*, the Himalayan nettle. This plant, which may reach 3 metres (10 ft) in height, grows best in clearings in

MEDICINAL PLANTS

In a country where modern medical facilities are few, it is natural that a vast lore of medicinal herbs should have developed. Nepal has 600 indigenous plants with recognised therapeutic properties, more than half of which occur in the subtropical zone. Some are in high demand on the international market and large quantities are exported in bulk to India, Europe and the Far East.

A number of lichens are valued as medicinal plants; some 352 species, grouped in 67 genera, have been identified in Nepal. Two species of *Parmelia* are especially in demand in India for use in spice and incense. Lichen extracts are used in perfume and some are valued for their antibiotic properties. Lichens cover a vast altitudinal range and the wealth of species found above the treeline remains practially unstudied.

Ferns, too, include a number of species (30 are listed by the Nepal Pharmaceutical Association) with medicinal properties, valued for use in respiratory ailments, for intestinal worms and for the treatment of cuts and bruises. In total there are 375 species of ferns, grouped into 84 genera, although the diversity decreases as one moves westwards to the drier regions. Young shoots of several varieties are eaten as a green vegetable and may even be found on sale in the markets of Kathmandu.

mixed deciduous forests between 1,500 and 3,000 metres (5,000–10,000 ft). Its jagged leaves, which can deliver an impressive sting, are enjoyed as a vegetable when young and tender. But it is the stems, containing among the longest-known plant fibres, in which the villagers are chiefly interested. Processing takes over four weeks and is carried out by women (bamboo by contrast is worked by men). The bark is stripped from the stems with their teeth and the fibres soaked, pounded, boiled and spun into a rough yarn. It is then woven on looms into a durable cloth.

Of the many other plants that are valued for their fibres, three species of the Thymeliaceae family are important because of their use in paper-making. These shrubs, especially daphne, grow abundantly in oak-laurel and oak-rhododendron forests. Workers pound the plant stems with mallets to extract the pulp, then spread it over taut muslin screens to dry into sheets of coarse paper.

Butterflies and moths

One of the great pleasures of Nepal for the visitor is the profusion of butterfly and moth species, many of which have diminished in developed countries as a consequence of modern agricultural practices. For example, the swallowtail *Papilio machaon* is still common in Nepal (while in England it is now confined to Norfolk). The rare Queen of Spain fritillary *(Issoria issaea)* is frequently encountered and there are some half-dozen species of clouded yellows (*Colias* spp.), a Palaearctic genus which has extended its range down to the Terai. Not unusual in Nepal are some of the very rare British hawk moths, such as the Death's Head *(Acherontia)*.

Eleven of the world's 15 families of butterflies are represented in Nepal and 614 species have been identified. This high number is due largely to the presence of both Palaearctic and Oriental species, the dividing line for which corresponds roughly to the upper limit of the temperate zone at 3,000 metres (10,000 ft). The line, of course, is somewhat blurred as there are strong fliers from both regions which transgress the frontier by a large margin.

LEFT: ferns and leaves flourish during the summer monsoon rains.
RIGHT: peacock pansy butterfly *(Precis almana).*

The butterfly season varies with altitude. Lowland species proliferate between March and November, and a few may be seen throughout the winter months. During the wet season, greater size and brighter colours are the rule.

The most spectacular butterflies of the Terai and midlands are undoubtedly the swallowtails (Papilionidae), although the name is a misnomer as many are tailless. Other highly visible species include tawny tigers (*Danaus* spp.), close relatives of the American milkweed or monarch. They can afford to fly unhurriedly as their orange-and-black wings warn predatory birds that their bodies contain

poisons. This colour scheme has proved so successful that it is mimicked by perfectly edible species. The swallowtail family is also represented in the opposite altitudinal extreme. The rare banded apollo *(Papilio acdestis)* has been found only at 5,000–5,500 metres (16,500– 18,000 ft), protected from brisk temperatures by its hairy body. The highland season is considerably shorter than the lowland, lasting only from May to August.

Over 5,000 species of moths are found in Nepal, some of which are still to be scientifically described. The spectacular Saturniidae family of the atlas, moon and silk moths are represented by 20 species. These include the giant atlas moth *(Attacus atlas)*, the world's largest moth with a wingspan of nearly 30 centimetres (1 ft). More than 90 species have been recorded of the handsome Sphingidae family in Nepal (8 percent of the world population) and include many of the world's rarest hawk moths.

Bird paradise

Nepal is a paradise for bird-lovers, with more than 800 species recorded, representing 10 percent of the world's population in a fraction of the landmass.

NATIONAL BIRD

Nepal's national bird is the brightly coloured *danphe* (impeyan pheasant), a common sight in the Everest region.

represents the westward limit of such birds as the blood pheasant, the brown parrotbill, the golden-breasted tit babbler and the rufous-bellied shrike babbler.

The highlands are home to impressive birds of prey, such as the lammergeier, the golden eagle and the Himalayan griffon vulture. The last of these is common around the Annapurnas but is declining in the Everest region. There is also a large range of high-altitude passerines, including a number of mountain finches, rose finches, accentors and redstarts.

The avian wealth of the Terai is discussed in detail later in the book *(see page 296)* but the midlands and highlands also have a great deal to offer. While altitude is the principal criterion that separates the northern Palaearctic species from the predominantly Oriental varieties of the south, the longitudinal factor is also important.

In the case of birds, however, the central division of the Nepal Himalaya seems to be a largely meaningless category. Instead, the distribution of birds points to the Kali Gandaki as a clear divide between east and west. For example, three species of titmouse *(Parus spp.)* and two nuthatches *(Sitta spp.)* do not occur east of the Kali Gandaki Valley, which also

Mountain mammals

Most large mammals of Nepal, such as the elephant, rhinoceros, gaur and tiger, are restricted to the lowland Terai but the higher-altitude parks afford protection for a number of species.

Sagarmatha National Park, for example, contains the largest concentration of Himalayan tahr *(Hemitragus jemlahicus)* anywhere in the animal's wide range from Kashmir to Sikkim. The preferred altitude of this wild goat coincides with the upper haunts of the ghoral or Himalayan chamois *(Nemorhaedus goral)*. This goat-antelope may be found at altitudes of more than 4,000 metres (13,000 ft) to as low as 900 metres (3,000 ft) where it descends to raid village crops. The ghoral and its near relative, the odd-looking serow *(Capricornis sumatrensis)*, which prefers forest habitats, are widely hunted for their meat outside protected areas.

Another crop raider is the bear. There are two species in the mountains of Nepal. The Himalayan black bear *(Selanarctos thibetanus)*, like the sloth bear of the Terai, has a white V-shaped bib, but ranges through the middle hills up to the limit of the forest. The brown bear *(Ursus arctos)*, a Palaearctic species, is more confined to higher altitudes. Both are hunted for their gall bladders, which are in demand as ingredients for Chinese

strictly protected, musk is worth several times its weight in gold and a single pod may yield over 50 grams (2 ounces), providing the incentive to risk the penalties.

Above the treeline, between 4,000 and 5,000 metres (13,000–16,500 ft), it is often possible to see the blue sheep *(Pseudois nayaur)*, locally known as a *bharal*.

With exceptional luck one also might glimpse the blue sheep's chief predator, the elusive snow leopard *(Uncia uncia)*. This elegant cat has long been persecuted for its beautiful coat, paler and thicker than that of its cousin, the common leopard, and because of its

medicine. The capacity of these animals to defend themselves against, and occasionally to attack, villagers is evident by the injuries that sometimes occur in mountain villages.

No animal has been the object of hunters' attention as much as the musk deer *(Moschus moschiferus)*, which ranges from around 2,000 to 4,500 metres (6,500–14,800 ft). The musk, secreted by the male in a pod under its tail, is valued in Chinese medicine, Tibetan incense and the western perfume industry. Although

FAR LEFT: Iora on its nest in Chitwan National Park.
LEFT: impeyan pheasant.
ABOVE: Himalayan brown bear.

penchant for domestic sheep, goats and occasionally even yaks. Its numbers are increasing in response to protection, although it has not yet reappeared in the Everest region where the last was killed in 1966. When it does return, however, it will no longer lack natural prey.

Chitwan's ecology: fire and flood

Nearly a quarter of Royal Chitwan National Park consists of alluvial floodplain at only 150 metres (500 ft) above sea level. The remainder is low hills rising to 760 metres (2,565 ft), covered with tropical deciduous forest, dominated by the towering sal tree. On the highest ridges there are chir pine.

Yaks

Ask anybody which animal they associate with the Himalaya and most people will mention yaks. Yaks occupy a significant place in Tibetan life, providing food, clothing, shelter and transport. The Tibetan term for the animals is itself revealing: the collective expression is *nor*, meaning "material wealth", recalling the old English synonymity between cattle and chattel.

Yet the Tibetans' appreciation of their indigenous bovine has never toppled over into worship. Yaks are eaten without qualms and with relish.

Killing the animals is more problematic because of the Buddhist reluctance to take life, but there are many cliffs off which animals can be encouraged to fall. Some indigent is also often willing to take on the slaughter in exchange for a portion of *digsha*, literally "sin-meat". Nothing is wasted. The head is often dried and eaten as a festive dish during New Year celebrations, while the horns may be used to adorn doorways and rooftops as a deterrent against demons.

Yaks are perfectly adapted to high altitudes, and function best between 3,000 and 6,000 metres (10,000–18,000 ft). They were originally domesticated from the wild drong, now rare due to unchecked hunting. Drongs are huge – a bull may stand up to 2 metres (6 ft) and weigh almost a ton. They also have a nervous temperament and very large horns. Bred down to more manageable proportions, yaks rarely exceed half a ton in weight and most are considerably smaller.

Pastoral patterns accord with the yak's natural inclination to follow the receding snow up to the high grasslands in warmer weather and to retreat to lower settlements at the onset of winter. Yaks can obtain water by eating frozen snow and can dig down to eat the grass beneath. They have also been the main form of transport in trans-Himalayan trade, especially in the long-distance commerce in salt.

Dairy products head the list of the yak's bounties. Yak-milk contains about twice as much fat as that of lowland cattle and has a rich, golden appearance. Fresh milk is rarely drunk but is subjected to processing: yogurt is a favourite. Butter is also extracted by churning the milk. It is consumed mainly in tea or as a lubricant for *tsampa* (barley flour), but is also smeared on faces and heads as protection against the atmosphere. Butter is one of the principal offerings by the faithful to monasteries, where it is used to fuel votive lamps and to make religious sculptures. The residual buttermilk is boiled and the solids skimmed off and made into cheese *(churpi)* by the Sherpas. *Churpi* is delicious if eaten within a few days, but beyond that consuming the hard, dried cheese is daunting. *Churpi* should not be confused with the eminently edible yak-cheese, made by Tibetan refugees to a Swiss recipe.

The most obvious adaptation of yaks to their environment is their fur. The longer, coarser hair is used for making ropes, slings, sacks and blankets. It also provides the raw material for the black tents of the Tibetan nomads. The weave allows smoke to escape and light to enter, while the oil on the hair keeps the structure waterproof. Yak-hair tents are also warmer and more durable than canvas, which can be shredded by winter winds. The soft wool beneath the hair is spun into yarn for clothing or felted to make boots. Usually the fur is pulled out by hand.

The yak's tail is valued in central Nepal for royal flywhisks and healing aids for shamans. The shaman may brandish it while dancing or plunge it into boiling water before whipping the illness out of the patient *(see page 62)*. ❑

LEFT: yaks carry double the load of a person and work with treks and expeditions.

The beautiful grasslands are dominated by different species of saccharum, often reaching more than 6 metres (20 ft) in height. The grasslands are interspersed with riverine-forests, featuring shisham *(Dalbergia sisso)*, khair *(Acacia catechu)*, simal or kapok *(Bombax ceiba)* and bilar trees *(Trewia nudiflora)*.

The grasslands periodically flood during the monsoon, when 90 percent of Chitwan's annual 2,150 millimetres (85 inches) of rain falls between June and September. This introduces a dynamic element into the ecology, changing river courses so as to create ox-bow lakes or tals where wildlife concentrates.

Another factor of great importance is fire. The dying grasses have been burnt annually for centuries so that fresh shoots can appear. Now controlled by the park authorities, thousands of local villagers are first permitted to collect grass for thatching in January. The black, burnt areas become a mosaic of grasses in different stages of regeneration, providing grazing for ungulates during the dry months. Fire tends to preserve the grassland at the expense of the forest saplings. The "cool burn" in the sal forest does not affect the fire-resistant trees.

Chitwan's animal life

More than 50 species of mammals are found in Royal Chitwan National Park. Sadly, some species have disappeared over the past few decades. Wild elephant *(Elephas maximus)* are now confined to a single herd of about 20, resident in the adjacent 500 sq. km (193 sq. mile) Parsa Wildlife Reserve.

The greater one-horned rhinoceros *(Rhinoceros unicornis)* has made a dramatic comeback and now numbers are more than 450, a quarter of the world population. The preferred habitat of these primeval beasts, with their great folds of skin, is the marshy grassland where they like to wallow in the tals.

There are a few hundred gaur *(Bos gaurus)*, the largest of the world's wild cattle, chiefly confined to the densely forested hillslopes of the Siwaliks. The best time to glimpse their sleek, dark coats is in the spring when they descend to feed on the fresh new grasses.

Four species of deer are found in the park; most numerous and gregarious is the elegant

chital or spotted deer *(Axis axis)* which gather in large herds in the spring. There are also the stately sambar *(Cervus unicolor)*, the stocky hog deer *(Axis porcinus)* and the barking deer *(Muntiacus muntjak)* named for its dog-like alarm call.

Wild pigs *(Sus scrofa)* are found throughout the park. There are two primates, the langur monkey *(Presbytis entellus)*, with its grey coat and black face, and the reddish-coloured rhesus *(Macaca mulatta)*. Much of the park provides a habitat for the sloth bear *(Melursus ursinus)*.

The Narayani River supports dwindling numbers of the freshwater Gangetic dolphin

(Platanista gangetica). A few wild dog *(Cuon alpinus)* course through the Chitwan in search of prey. More common are their scavenging relatives, the golden jackal *(Canis aureus)*.

There is a great variety of smaller mammals including mongooses, civets, martens, honey badgers and two species of hare. There are three small cats, the jungle cat *(Felis chaus)*, the fishing cat *(Felis viverrina)* and the leopard cat *(Felis bengalensis)*. A number of rodents includes squirrels, flying squirrels, porcupines, bats and rats.

Other than the rhino, Chitwan is most famous for its population of the Royal Bengal tiger *(Panthera tigris)*. Containing an estimated 40

RIGHT: rhesus monkeys at Pashupatinath Temple outside Kathmandu.

breeding adults, the total number of tigers fluctuates around 120. The park's tigers are part of a larger regional population of about 200. This includes individuals protected in the eastern Parsa Wildlife Reserve and the Valmiki Tiger Reserve in India, adjoining the southern boundary of the park, a total area of 1,875 sq. km (724 sq. miles).

Chitwan's tigers prefer the floodplain where the abundance of prey species allows them to exist at comparatively high density. The most secretive and retiring of all the cats, the tiger is nocturnal and it is only a few lucky visitors who catch a glimpse of these splendid creatures.

There are not many leopards *(Panthera pardus)* in Chitwan, probably because of the intolerance of the tigers. What few there are live on the periphery of the park.

The gharial *(Gavialus gangeticus)* is one of two species of crocodile. It is a specialised fish-eater with an elongated snout and lives in the rivers running through the park. It is harmless to man. The marsh mugger *(Crocodylus palustris)* eats anything it can catch and lives mainly in the ox-bow lakes. Pythons *(Python molurus)* frequent the edges of ponds and streams. The world's largest venomous snake, the king cobra *(Ophiophagus hannah)* also lives in the park

TIGER CONSERVATION: NEPAL'S SUCCESS STORY

One of the most dramatic conservation success stories in Nepal is the comeback of the Royal Bengal tiger. After royal hunts of the past, the tiger population of Chitwan's jungles dwindled to a few dozen. But when Chitwan was declared Nepal's first national park in 1973, tigers began to rebound. By 1980, there were nearly 80; now there are as many as 130 adults. There are some 30 more in Bardia and Parsa.

Unfortunately, the number of tigers outside national parks is now negligible because of habitat loss. The disappearance of jungle corridors between parks also means that natural breeding no longer takes place. Experts are also concerned about overcrowding. Adult males mark

out territory of as much as 60 sq. km (23 sq. miles), females more than 15 sq. km (6 sq. miles). When territories overlap there are fights. Wounded tigers cannot hunt traditional prey and turn into man-eaters, picking on cattle and humans on the park's fringes.

Tiger poaching is not the problem it is in India, since national parks are guarded by the army, but Nepal is still a conduit for smuggling of tiger parts into China. India and Nepal plan anti-poaching activities along their border.

The tiger is at the top of the food chain: protecting tigers protects the habitat on which it depends, and it has become symbolic of Nepal's entire conservation effort.

with a number of smaller, though no less poisonous cousins, kraits and vipers.

More than 450 species of birds have been counted in Chitwan – 38 percent of all those found in the subcontinent. Just under half of these are residents. Two of the spectacular and endangered species found in the park are the rare Bengal florican *(Eupodotis bengalensis)* and the giant hornbill *(Buceros bicornis)*.

Royal Bardia National Park

The alluvial floodplain of the Geruwa River and its many islands are covered with tall grasses and a rich assemblage of riverine forest,

management. The largest are the Baghaura and Lamkhole Phantas.

Once endemic, the greater one-horned rhinoceros had become extinct in Bardia. In 1985, 13 rhinos were captured in Chitwan, then the western limit of their range, and moved here where they are now established and breeding.

Bardia has the same four species of deer as Chitwan but in addition has the endangered swamp deer or *barasingha (Cervus duvauceli)*. Two species of antelope live in the park: the *nilgai* or blue bull *(Boselaphus tragocamelus)* frequents the riverine forest; smaller and more graceful is the blackbuck *(Antilope cervicapra)*

though most of Royal Bardia National Park *(see page 308)* is covered with sal forest. In 1984 1,500 inhabitants of the Babai Valley were relocated onto better land outside the park. Still in the process of regeneration, the Babai valley promises to develop into one of the finest wildlife regions of the park.

Characteristic of Bardia are the *phantas*, the short grassland meadows on the forest edge. These so facilitate wildlife viewing that they are now artificially maintained by the park

which once thrived on the Baghaura Phanta. Predation has all but wiped them out, though there are plans to relocate some of the remaining population to the Babai Valley. No gaur exist in Bardia but a few wild elephants roam the park. There are estimated to be less than ten and some of the solitary bulls make their presence felt by raiding the village fields.

Despite disturbance caused by development in the Karnali Gorge, some crocodiles have managed to survive – there are populations of both gharial and marsh mugger species. Some 350 species of birds have been recorded in the park including such endangered species as the sarus crane *(Grus antigone)*. ❏

LEFT: a Royal Bengal tiger shrouded in thick grass.
ABOVE: green pit viper.
RIGHT: gharial crocodile.

National Parks and Reserves

Nepal has a staggering amount of nationally protected landscapes for such a small country. In total there are eight national parks, four wildlife reserves and one hunting reserve, all administered by the National Parks and Wildlife Conservation Department of His Majesty's Government, as well as the Annapurna Conservation Area Project, the first ecotourism area in Nepal. These 14 protected areas total 17,000 sq.

km (6,560 sq. miles) and represent 12 percent of Nepal's land area. Details of the country's wealth of natural wonders are as follows:

The **Annapurna Conservation Area Project** (ACAP), northwest of Pokhara *(see page 119)*, covers an area of 2,660 sq. km (1,027 sq. miles) and is successfully managed by the non-governmental King Mahendra Trust for Nature Conservation (KMTNC).

Dhorpatan Hunting Reserve contains a large number of blue sheep *(bharal)* in the western mountains and covers an area of 1,325 sq. km (512 sq. miles).

Khaptad National Park contains one of the last examples of Nepal's middle hill forests, situated in the far west of the country. It was gazetted in 1984 with an area of 225 sq. km (87 sq. miles). In the middle of the park is a centre of pilgrimage filled with Hindu shrines.

Kosi Tappu Wildlife Reserve is located on the Kosi River in the east Terai and contains the only population of wild buffaloes in Nepal. It is also a sanctuary for a wide range of migratory waterfowl. It was gazetted in 1976 with an area of 175 sq. km (68 sq. miles).

Langtang National Park, in the mountain region of central Nepal just south of the Tibet border *(see page 253)*, was gazetted in 1976 with an area of 1,710 sq. km (660 sq. miles). The red panda (also known as the lesser panda) lives mainly on bamboo on the forest canopies of this park, as well as in a few other areas in Nepal, although sightings of this rust-coloured, fox-like mammal are very rare.

Makalu-Barun National Park and Conservation Area was set up in 1992 and is contiguous with the Sagarmatha National Park. It covers an area of 2,330 sq. km (900 sq. miles). This sanctuary is being managed using the same ecotourism strategy as the Annapurna Conservation Area, employing locals in conservation projects and attempting to stem the tide of tourism.

Parsa Wildlife Reserve, adjacent to Royal Chitwan National Park, contains Nepal's largest resident herd of wild elephants. It covers a land mass of 499 sq. km (193 sq. miles) and was gazetted in 1984.

Rara National Park, which includes the beautiful Rara Lake and its surroundings in far west Nepal, was established in 1976 with an area of 106 sq. km (41 sq. miles). Mountain wildlife is particularly abundant here, including musk deer and the Himalayan black bear.

Royal Bardia National Park, situated in the remote and largely untouched far western Terai was formerly a wildlife reserve established in 1976 and extended in 1984 to its present size of 968 sq. km (374 sq. miles). It finally achieved national park status in 1988 and is comparable to Chitwan for its richness of wildlife, including tigers and wild elephant herds *(see page 308)*.

Royal Chitwan National Park, located in the central inner Terai region, was the kingdom's first national park and is today the best known and most popular *(see page 301)*. It was gazetted in 1973, with an area of 544 sq. km (210 sq. miles) and was extended in 1976 to its present size of 1,040 sq. km (402 sq. miles). This former royal hunting reserve and rhinoceros sanctuary contains abundant wildlife and is most famous for its tigers and wild elephant herds. The greater one-horned rhinoceros has been rescued from the brink of extinction in Chitwan and sightings are now common. Due to overcrowding some have been translocated to Bardia, and the numbers have now risen to almost 600. The Royal Bengal tiger is another conservation success story *(see page 104)*. After being hunted into near oblivion, the numbers have now risen to about 150 in Nepal's national parks, including Chitwan. Gharial crocodiles are also bred here.

Royal Sukla Phanta Wildlife Reserve in the far

Everest) but also many villages of the Sherpa mountain guides *(see page 262)*. It was established in 1976 to preserve the local forest, with an area of 1,243 sq. km (480 sq. miles).

Shey Phoksundo National Park, the country's largest park and the only national park in the trans-Himalayan zone, was gazetted in 1984 with an area of 3,555 sq. km (1,373 sq. miles). The snow leopard's range stretches right across the Nepal Himalaya and population concentrations are found in the park, as well as in the Annapurna Conservation Area and on the slopes of Mount Kangchenjunga in the east. However, it is extremely rare to catch sight of this elusive cat.

western Terai, not far from Royal Bardia National Park, contains a large population of swamp deer *(barasingha)*, as well as a few tigers and elephants and a range of other wildlife, including more than 450 species of birds. As its name suggests, it is also known for its tall, savannah-like *phanta* grass. It was gazetted in 1976 with an area of 155 sq. km (60 sq. miles).

Sagarmatha National Park includes not only the peaks and valleys of the southern half of Mount Everest (Sagarmatha is the Nepali name for

LEFT: rhododendrons in the Himalaya.
ABOVE: *tal* (lake) at Royal Chitwan
National Park.

Shivapuri Watershed and Wildlife Reserve is at the northern rim of Kathmandu Valley. Although this is not managed by the Department of Wildlife, like most of the country's national parks, it is a walled sanctuary designed to protect the watershed of the Bagmati River that flows through the valley. Shivapuri is the nature sanctuary closest to the capital and is therefore an easy day trip from Kathmandu. It has abundant bird species, leopards and brown bears.

Another endangered and protected species that finds its habitat in the higher reaches of many of Nepal's national parks and sanctuaries, particularly Sagarmatha, is the multicoloured impeyan pheasant, Nepal's national bird. ❏

ENVIRONMENTAL ISSUES

Threatened by the pressures of population growth and tourism,

Nepal's fragile environment needs to be carefully managed

It is hardly surprising that Nepal has begun to take its environment and its conservation very seriously: it is, after all, home to the most spectacular mountains in the world. The icy chaos of the Himalaya is really a gigantic pile-up resulting from the head-on collision millions of years ago of two continental plates. The force of that impact squeezed out layer upon overlapping layer of rock like toothpaste all along the impact zone. The antecedent of what is now the Annapurna massif used to be a stupendous hulk soaring as high as 9,500 metres (31,000 ft) above sea level. Mount Everest's granite pyramid was the product of later upheavals. Interestingly, although the black massif of the world's highest mountain is made of granite, the top 300 metres (1,000 ft) is yellow limestone which millions of years ago was lying at the bottom of the sea.

Rainstorms, prototypes of present-day monsoons, soon started breaking down the southern slopes and eroding the adolescent Himalaya as they grew. Enormous volumes of silt were washed down to the Ganges which became clogged with detritus and alluvium.

One of the best ways of putting the mountains in their geological perspective and seeing the true wonder of this environment is to take a mountain flight *(see page 280)*. On the ground, the vertical tends to be exaggerated. From 10 km (6 miles) up, the mountains become no more than folds on a bedsheet. The brown expanse of the Tibetan plateau is visible below, just as the twin spires of Machhapuchhre glide by. The majestic south face of Annapurna looks like a living-room sofa draped in white, while Dhaulagiri stands aloof. The foothills are humps veiled in blue haze, stacked in progressively lighter shades right up to the western horizon. To the left, the Gangetic basin stretches in an ocean-like flatness underneath a pall of dust.

It is incredible, seeing all this from one spot. This is the vantage point of the gods, who are reputed to hover over the mountains that they created. In the cockpit, where there is no other sound besides the roaring rush of wind, the flight becomes a religious experience. A brief pilgrimage to the heavens.

First humans

It was only after the Himalaya were moulded out of the thin crust of a molten planet that the first human beings settled along the Siwalik (Churia) foothills. Echoes from the clash of continents were still reverberating as frequent earthquakes shook the land. The power and mystery of nature, the purity and inaccessibility of distant snow peaks struck resonance with the spiritual mind.

As the population of the foothills expanded, the principalities and princedoms took the great natural barriers as their boundaries. The towering peaks of the north became not only a frontier but also a deterrent for invaders from

---

LEFT: a porter in the Solu Khumbu region of Nepal.
RIGHT: landslides are a result of continued deforestation in Nepal.

Central Asia and Tibet. Further hemmed in by dense malarial jungles to the south, the Himalayan kingdoms became isolated, and fiercely independent, centres of culture.

Lying on the trade route between India and Tibet, Kathmandu thrived commercially and evolved a culture that was a blend of Hindu and Buddhist ways of life. Belligerent Gorkha kings sent troops across the mountains to raid Lhasa and at one point controlled the entire Himalayan arc from Kashmir to Bhutan.

Topographical reality soon imposed a limit on how far the Gorkha conquest could stretch. Generals paid the price as campaigns failed because of long supply routes across rugged inhospitable terrain. Despite two wars, the British in India could not penetrate Nepal's mountain fastness. The Nepali troops, skilled at guerilla warfare, used hilltop forts to guard strategic passes with great effect, until the British brought in cannons and started using siege tactics.

Roads and wheels

Although the British built railways and highways across the south Asian subcontinent, the Himalayan foothills remained as inaccessible as ever. Only a few Indian hill-resorts such as

SACRED MOUNTAINS

The pre-Vedic tribes of the Indo-Gangetic plains must have been the originators of Hindu reverence for mountains. Rivers that flowed out of the hills became fountainheads of life. Geologists maintain that Himalayan rivers are actually older than the mountains, the relics of prehistoric river systems that carved gorges and valleys even as the mountains were rising. Sources of these rivers lie along the watershed of the pre-Himalayan mountains of Tibet.

The mountains were named with reverence – for instance "Giver of Grain" (Annapurna) – and were considered symbols of deities. Their topography was vital: because of their height the mountains became monsoon traps that brought life-giving moisture to farms and water to rivers. The snow and glaciers were huge storage systems for ice which melted in spring, supplying water to downstream areas during the dry season. The snows rested on the border between temporal and spiritual, between earth and heaven.

Most mountains became sacred. Kailas, the perfect cone reflected in the holy waters of Mansarovar, became the symbol of Shiva, the god of creation and destruction. Gauri Shankar, revered by Hindus as a manifestation of Shiva (Shankar) and his consort Parvati (Gauri), was also regarded by the Buddhist inhabitants of Rolwaling as Tseringma, one of the holy Five Long Life Sisters.

Simla and Darjeeling were connected to the plains, usually by narrow-gauge railways that were more fun than functional. Nepal remained for the most part roadless. The people of Pokhara, for example, saw the wheel for the first time when a DC-3 landed on a grass field in the middle of town in 1952 *(see page 229)*.

WATER-LOGGED

In the rainy season, landslides can wipe entire sections of Nepal's highway network off the map

Roads were enormously expensive to build and the serpentine eternity of the Tribhuvan Raj Path from the Indian border to Kathmandu became the classic horror story of a Himalayan bus ride. Nevertheless, willing foreign govern-

summit of Himalchuli is visible far on the northern horizon. Twenty years ago, it would have taken up to three weeks to walk from Chitwan to the base of that mountain. The trail traversed a perilous malarial jungle, ran along the swift-flowing Nara-yani River where crocodiles sunned on sandy banks, up tracks carved out of the sheer cliffs at the Narayani's confluence with the Marsyangdi and Trisuli rivers, up and down the awesome vertical distances of the midhills, finally to the hilltop fortress of Gorkha, the birthplace of

ments were ready to build Nepal all the roads it wanted. Twisted coils of asphalt began to spread up the steep mountainsides, down the foothill slopes, along river gorges and across the valleys.

For anyone who knew Nepal before the roads were built, the difference is as dramatic as between the days of the covered wagons and jet-age America. From the banks of the Rapti in the lush jungles of Royal Chitwan National Park, the distinctive *khukri*-shaped

LEFT: the magnificent Manang Valley.
ABOVE: road trouble, as seen here in the Annapurna region, is a frequent sight all over Nepal.

modern Nepal, standing boldly at the base of Himal Chuli.

Today that same journey takes less than three hours. A Chinese-built highway has sliced through the mountains and through time. Sleek Japanese cars chartered by tourists and smoke-belching Tata trucks zoom past heavily laden porters walking by the roadside. The road is pitifully thin, a fragile thread of asphalt stretched across a precipitous mountainside.

Social upheaval

Distances, not only in Nepal but all across the Himalaya, have shrunk over the years, bringing social, economic and political changes to the hinterlands. Speedier access and communications have introduced new concepts and a growing materialism from the outside world, and have also facilitated major political changes and greater interaction within.

Before the road arrived, Gorkha was a peaceful, self-contained village perched on a barren hillside west of Kathmandu. The brick buildings existed in harmony with the surrounding countryside. Indeed, all the materials used to build them were locally available. The market place was stocked with items people needed for their traditional lifestyles, sold by local businessmen and women.

Today Gorkha is full of the trappings of the modern age. Corrugated roofs reflect sunlight off new buildings; the bazaar is festooned with brightly coloured plastic buckets, replacements for the traditional hand-tapped brass pots. Coca Cola advertisements adorn the town square. In addition to the obvious material advancement, the roads have brought profound demographic changes. Once-isolated villages are now populated by people from all over Nepal and beyond; the roadside vendors may be migrants from the plains, the barber shaving a local official is from the Indian district of Darbhanga. Indeed not all change has come from the west.

ETHNIC BLENDING

The construction of roads is rapidly bringing about ethnic unification in Nepal. It is not uncommon today to see traders from Dolpo and hill tribesmen from the Ganesh Himal step off a bus at the terminal in Kathmandu. Dressed in their yak-wool jackets and robes, they mingle in Kathmandu's urban mêlée with Tharu people from the plains. Nepal's ethnic diversity endured for so long largely because of the ridges and valleys which isolate communities. These barriers still exist to some extent in the hills, but are fading in the cities where it has become hard to tell a Rai man from a Gurung for their adapted Western dress.

Until very recently, there were six directions in Nepal's remote hills: north, south, east, west, up and down. The terrain kept the inhabitants of these lands isolated, but also self-sufficient, hard-working and clear-headed. The construction of roads has eased the vertical and introduced unaffordable "luxury" goods into a predominantly cashless society. Villagers now often prefer the appearance of imported polyester cloth, however impractical, over locally made durable weaves. Young people, swayed by magazines, television and now videos' flashy hype, are choosing short-term gratifications over longer-term investments in a better lifestyle such as medical care, sanitation or education.

Many say these changes are inevitable and unstoppable. Perhaps, given time, the villagers of the Himalaya could have adjusted, differentiating the good from the bad. But part of the problem is that it all happened virtually overnight.

Nepal's hills are no longer carved into isolated districts that can be governed from far-off Kathmandu through the writ of centrally appointed powerful officials. After centuries of autocratic and near-feudal rule, democracy has brought greater demands for decentralisation and a freely elected choice in leadership.

school, a road or electricity – the answer was: "None of the above." They wanted bridges. For them the raging torrents of Himalayan rivers are the most glaring obstacles to progress. The waters cut them off from markets and imposed long detours on their way to the towns to find work; children die because they cannot be taken to a health post on the other side of the river.

Population pressure

Many of the problems of health, nutrition and education are compounded by Nepal's burgeoning population. In 25 years, Nepal's 22 million population will double. Settlers of the

Rural development

"Let's split the mountains to usher in an era of progress", used to be a popular patriotic song over Radio Nepal. Today, "economic development" translates as "overcoming the physical and psychological barriers of the mountains". Dynamite charges rend the air as new roads are blasted, another hydroelectric project is launched or bridges are built. When rural Nepalese were asked in a survey some years ago what they wanted most – a hospital, a

LEFT: a community forestry poster encourages reforestation.
ABOVE: Tharu shepherds on the Terai landscape.

HEALTH HAZARDS

The child mortality rate in the far western Humla district is several times the national average. Of 1,000 children born in Humla, barely 400 live to be five years old. Most of them die of respiratory infections caused by breathing the smoke of pine-wood cooking fires. In other areas of the country, contaminated water kills thousands of babies and hundreds of adults every year. Ironically, Western multinational soft drinks are available in villages where there is not even safe potable water. Some experts say a tap with clean drinking water would do more for the general health of most of Nepal's districts than a fully equipped hospital.

Himalaya's southern slopes have now far surpassed the land's capacity to sustain them.

Projecting these problems into the future, it is not difficult to see human misery on a massive scale. The swelling population is putting a strain on nature's capacity to regenerate. The steep flanks of Himalayan mountains are constantly crumbling simply because of gravity. Avalanches cut across high snow slopes, sharpening the ridges and making peaks more jagged. Monsoon rains pound the lower foothills triggering landslides and washing off the topsoil. The process is called "mass-wasting" and began the moment the mountains started rising.

Denudation of the Himalayan foothills by deforestation and overgrazing is adding to the problem. More than half of Nepal's forest disappeared between 1961 and 1981 after village woods were nationalised. Not only is wood needed for cooking, heating and construction, but vast tracts of land must be cleared to grow crops for the burgeoning population. Trees stripped of their greenery for livestock fodder eventually fall to the axe, and in the meantime provide no protection to the soil from the rains which lash the country from June to September. Without trees or grass to hold the hillsides, the soil is easily washed away. The effect of this erosion is especially marked in

the Siwalik hills, where the sandy soils are particularly vulnerable. Once the trees disappear, entire hillsides can be washed off during one rainy season. However, experts now discount the theory that deforestation-induced erosion of the Himalaya is the main cause of worsening floods downstream in Bangladesh and India. "Natural" erosion of the Himalaya has probably contributed most of the silt to the Ganges and the Bay of Bengal long before people settled in the hills.

The not-so-fragile mountain

There is, however, some cause for optimism. Many ecologists refute the claims of those Doomsday theorists who believe that the extent of forest loss in the mountains is catastrophic, arguing that deforestation is now largely confined to the jungles of the Terai. Indeed, recent studies of satellite data show that forest cover has increased by as much as 15 percent in the middle hills since 1981. The reason for this is the silent success of Nepal's community forestry programme, which allows villagers to grow and protect their own forests.

The intrepid inhabitants of the Himalaya have long known how to live with nature. Mountainsides sculptured with meticulously carved terraces are proof of the hill farmers' ingenuity. Hydrologically engineered terraces save the soil from washing away and help grow food on non-irrigated steep slopes with only a thin skin of topsoil. Long before development specialists were talking about ecological sustainability, high mountain dwellers practised rotational grazing on the summer pastures and learned how to tap the forests' resources for food, fodder and fuel without doing permanent damage. From east to west, many communities had laws governing the use of their forests, some with forest guards and public deliberations over what penalty the culprit should pay. In hindsight, the most disastrous single blow to Nepal's forests was the nationalisation of all forest lands in 1957, a centralist decision which dissolved people's interest in nurturing the resources and land, and instigated uncontrolled overuse to the detriment of all.

But these traditional conservation ethics are being severely tested by Nepal's burgeoning population. The hill farmer is driven to cultivate ever-steeper, unsuitable slopes, slashing forests and shrubs to make way for the plough.

Sons inherit ever-smaller plots of land, making agriculture as a sole occupation less and less viable. In some communities, a traditional land distribution system has prevented the division of land among successive generations. The Sherpas, for example, passed all land to the eldest son, leaving younger brothers the choice of sharing his household (and wife), making it on their own, or joining a monastery. This practice also served to keep the population down. The contemporary preference for monogamous marriages fortunately coincided with a general rise in the living conditions of Sherpas, the group which has benefited most from mountain tourism *(see page 50)*.

JOB CREATION

One job is created for every 7.5 tourists who visit, a ratio that rises to 1 to 3 in the trekking industry.

The impact of tourism

Many of Nepal's environmental and social concerns preceded the arrival of tourists, but the indulgent habits and cultural contrasts of an alien influx undoubtedly leave a mark on a country which was long isolated – inherently by physical barriers and later with political blinds – from the world. Some of the effects of tourism are positive, others are not.

Tourism currently pumps more than US$60 million worth of hard currency into Nepal every year. Trekkers and mountaineers contribute more than their share, spending longer periods in the country than do other tourists. This labour-intensive industry provides a wider and more equitable distribution of cash in the hills, where it is most needed. Crucially, that income is more likely to stay within the country than be spent outside on costly imports to furnish Western-style hotels and restaurants.

There is great potential to develop tourism-related cottage industries and food production to further stimulate the rural economies; for example setting up small-scale handicraft centres in the hills and organising vegetable and meat production units to supply trekkers with fresh produce. Tourism has revived the dying arts and crafts of Bhaktapur *(see page 183)* and has fuelled a carpet and pashmina industry which rivals tourism as the country's top generator of foreign revenue *(see page 80)*.

LEFT: deforestation is all too evident on this mountain slope.

RIGHT: cooking *dhal bhaat* on a low-watt cooker.

While tourism, directly and indirectly, brings precious foreign exchange to the national coffers, it also contributes to inflation and disrupts local markets. New-found income is making its way into mountain homes accustomed to centuries of subsistence living, driving prices for basic commodities way beyond what farming families can afford. Foreigners' intended generosity, or ignorance over a fair price, has the same effect; at Khumbu's Namche Saturday market, the only people who buy eggs, which until recently were carried in

on porters' backs out of respect for the mountain god who dislikes chickens, are lodge-owners who can pass the hefty price onto trekkers.

More serious is the fear that mountaineering and tourism will further strain the Himalaya's fragile environment. The Barun Valley in eastern Nepal and the trekkers' "highways" through Solu Khumbu and the Annapurnas are vivid examples of what uncontrolled visitor traffic can do. In the Barun, the moraines are crumbling because mountaineering expeditions on Mount Makalu have uprooted the dwarf junipers to burn at the base-camp kitchen. The Annapurna Sanctuary's frail ecosystem is slow to recover from the tramping boots of the 10,000 trekkers who visit it every year.

The receding forests all along the Annapurna and Solu Khumbu trails are tragic reminders of the effects of indiscriminate tourism. National Park and Annapurna Conservation Area Project *(see page 119)* rules now require trekkers to be self-sufficient in cooking fuel, but Khumbu lodge-owners still rely on wood supplemented by yak dung to cook for hungry guests. Trekking agencies supply kerosene for their clients' cooking needs but porters must fend for themselves and no-one fends for the trees. Solu, where there are no tree-felling restrictions, is losing its rhododendron forests to the construction of more and more tea houses to serve the ever-increasing independent trekkers.

Responsible travel

The tourism debate has changed the way both tourists and locals look at the industry. Tourists know that they can't keep going to the next exotic place and fouling it up. Countries like Nepal have realised that they have to be careful that the benefits of tourism always outweigh its harm. Nepal declared 1998 "Visit Nepal Year", and the slogan was: "Sustainable Tourism for Sustainable Development".

KEEPING NEPAL TIDY

Like the proverbial goose that lays the golden egg, the tourism goose also fouls its nest. Conservation-minded planners in Nepal, conscientious trekking agencies and trekkers are worried that more hikers will mean more litter along the mountain trails. Toilet paper, biscuit wrappers and non-biodegradable rubbish marks the over-trodden trails and campsites, although growing ecological awareness has cleaned up the trails in many areas. Toilet facilities, if they exist at all, are often poorly maintained or dangerously close to water sources.

Slowly, awareness is growing. Initiatives such as the Annapurna Conservation Area Project are teaching the lodge owners how to build decomposing toilets and to keep rubbish pits. Some trekking agencies have vowed to carry out trash, but the problem then remains of how to dispose of it at roadheads or airfields.

Even the high mountains have not escaped the problems. At almost 8,000 metres (26,250 ft), the South Col of Mount Everest is known as the "world's highest garbage dump". Discarded oxygen cylinders, stoves and climbing gear are strewn about. In recent years, several clean-up crews have made a difference, but ultimately responsibility lies with each expedition and with the government to enforce environmental regulations.

Dense concentrations of tourists can erode the exotica factor. Thamel in Kathmandu has become a tourist ghetto. Ironically, although many visitors complain about it they don't seem to mind being there since that's where the good restaurants, shops and travel agents have also congregated. Like Bangkok's Banglamphu area, this is where young travellers can be seen in their thousands during the season.

Most tourists to Nepal today are adventure-minded (rafting, trekking, mountaineering) and

SOUND ADVICE

In Nepal's national parks, the dos and don'ts for travellers are summarised very simply: "Take nothing but pictures, and leave nothing but footprints."

from local materials (slate roof, stone masonry, no cement, no excessive wood). Does everyone eat together and therefore save firewood? It is also interesting to look at where the money you pay a trekking agent ultimately ends up: with a businessman in Kathmandu or a wholesaler in Hamburg, or does it benefit the porters who carry your bags? Does the porter spend most of his earnings gambling and drinking, or does he take it home to his family? Is the chief porter paying his men proper wages?

tend to be ecologically aware and responsible. However, tourism – being a major employer – also becomes a magnet for people from surrounding districts. This swells the population of local towns and villages beyond their capacity. Examples can be seen all across Nepal.

Tourists can have their own ecological checklist of where to stay and what kind of restaurants to eat in. For example, is the hot water in your lodge heated by solar power or does the owner burn firewood? Is the inn constructed

LEFT: Machhapuchhre Base Camp on the Annapurna Circuit trek.
ABOVE: tourists shopping near Namche Bazar.

Across Nepal, it has become common to see schoolchildren asking for sweets or money. Three decades of tourism and well-intentioned donations have turned many proud Nepalese villagers needlessly into beggars. If you really want to give, introduce local children to books. One of Nepal's most pressing problems is the low status of women and the low enrolment of girls in schools. Helping girls by talking to them in English will bolster their confidence.

Locals observe tourists wherever they go, looking at what they wear, carry and eat. Tourism often raises expectations of local people, which by itself may not be bad, but these expectations are way beyond their reach and can enforce a sense of inferiority. All guide-books advise you to avoid ostentatious displays of wealth, but whatever you wear or carry is already ostentatious, such is the income disparity between the visitor and the local. Blend as much as possible with the surroundings.

Hikers can help save the forests by bringing adequate clothing and thus not relying for warmth on the lodge fireplace. Group trekkers can choose a trekking company which is environmentally conscientious, one which uses kerosene on all treks whether required by park regulations or not, and which provides warm clothing for porters on high-elevation treks.

Innovative planning

The Annapurna Conservation Area Project (ACAP) is innovative in more than one way. An entry fee collected from all visitors is used specifically on environmental protection and development activities which benefit the local inhabitants and help them accommodate trekkers in a sound manner – entrance fees from all the other national parks are absorbed into central government coffers. ACAP is also helping to instill a pride in indigenous ways by training young people to lead tourists on cultural tours and by instigating cooperation in villages where traditional ways still exist.

The debate continues over whether the gov-ernment should open more new trekking areas. It recently lifted the requirement for trekking permits to the Everest area, Annapurna and Langtang, but permits are still required for Dolpo, Kanchenjunga and other areas. The Mustang region is a special protection zone for which a fee of US$70 for 10 days is charged, but the winds of change are blowing here too, with a road soon to link it with Tibet.

Some say that remote regions thus far spared from the negative effects of tourism should be protected in an unspoilt state, while others argue that all mountain peoples should be entitled to share in the wealth which tourism undoubtedly brings. Would opening more areas lessen the litter and deterioration of overburdened areas, or should these heavily burdened regions such as Khumbu and Anna-purna be closed for several years to allow them to rejuvenate? Whatever the answers, all agree that the government and tourism indus-try must plan for the future so as not to spoil the object which attracts tourists here in the first place.

Hydroelectric potential

Another hugely important environmental factor is the potential for foreign governments to facilitate change in Nepal through large-scale projects such as hydroelectric generating plants. Nepal's total feasible hydropower potential is estimated at 83,000 megawatts, one of the highest per capita in the world. To date only 350 megawatts have been harnessed, with the help of foreign governments. The main obstacle to more dams is the initial capital needed for construction. The proposed 3,600 megawatt Chisapani plant (on the Karnali River) in far west Nepal, for instance, could cost up to US$4 billion and be a major boost to Nepal's economy. But unless Nepal can agree with neighbouring countries about sharing the project costs in return for power and flood-control benefits, and on a worthwhile price for the power, there is little likelihood of it taking on projects of that scale on its own. In the meantime, there are six new medium-scale hydroelectric projects under way, which should go some way towards meet the increasing demand for power in the years ahead. ❏

LEFT: a solar panel set up on a post in a Himalayan village.

Annapurna Conservation Area

Ecotourism has become a buzzword, and in some places a false label for old-fashioned mass tourism. But Nepal now has a model of how ecotourism should work, and it has given it back its true meaning: investing tourism receipts into the village economy for environmental protection, education, health and higher living standards.

This is exactly what the Annapurna Area Conservation Project (ACAP) has been doing. About 80,000 (nearly 60 percent) of all trekkers who come to Nepal hike in the Annapurna region – an area of spectacular scenery, mountain hamlets and a diversity of plants and animals. ACAP covers an area of 7,600 sq. km (2,934 sq. miles) to the north of the town of Pokhara *(see page 229)*. Only 25 km (15½ miles) away rises the hulk of the 8,000-metre (26,246-ft) Annapurna range.

Heavy monsoon rains and the altitude variation gives the Annapurna region one of the richest biodiversity in the Himalaya. On the slopes of Annapurna lives the snow leopard, the endangered blue sheep, pheasants and some 1,300 species of plants and 100 species of mammals. But there is also a human population of 120,000 living here. It is to ensure their development, so that they will protect the biodiversity, that the ACAP project was set up in 1986 by the King Mahendra Trust for Nature Conservation and the government of Nepal.

ACAP was prompted by the destruction of forests and the denudation along the trails that was observed during the late 1970s as more and more visitors started coming here. ACAP works with local communities on forest management, community woods, solar power, health clinics, schools, water supply and sanitation. Local communities clean up the trails so that they are relatively litter-free. There is also tourism training in tasks such as cooking Western foods, a committee to standardise prices and accommodation for trekkers. ACAP charges a fee of 1,000 rupees for every trekker entering the area; most visitors happily pay this.

The Ghorapani Pass, which in the early 1980s was virtually denuded, is now showing signs of regeneration. The oak and rhododendron forests are growing back. Young forests drape the

RIGHT: Namaste Lodge on the Annapurna Sanctuary trekking route.

mountains on either side of the trails leading up to the Annapurna Sanctuary, and villagers have formed groups to sustainably use deadwood and fodder for their daily needs. In 15 years, ACAP's achievements are already impressive. Satellite mapping shows that there has been a dramatic increase in both crown cover and undergrowth. Wildlife has returned and in some cases even caused problems because leopards are carrying away livestock and wild monkeys raid crops. Efforts to augment poultry and vegetable farming has also ensured that almost half of what trekkers spend is retained in the local economy – the figure was 20 percent in 1987.

Although ACAP has demonstrated that there is a way to benefit local communities and protect the environment through sustainable tourism, challenges remain. ACAP is a non-governmental project but there are government and district authorities with competing interests. Pokhara, the area's main town, draws about 115,000 tourists each year and thus brings in people from all over Nepal in search of jobs, putting a strain on resources.

Despite the problems, ACAP planners say the model can be replicated. The Makalu-Barun Conservation Area near Everest is trying to use the formula for conservation. The Worldwide Fund for Nature is keen to do the same in the Kanchenjunga National Park. ❏

TREKKING

For those who seek breathtaking mountain scenery,
nothing can beat the exhilarating treks of the Himalaya

The call of the wild has roused a spirit of adventure from the earliest times, inspiring people to explore every corner of the earth. Contemporary Marco Polos have now turned their attention to the endless horizons of outer space; yet as recently as the 1940s one of earth's greatest natural wonders, Mount Everest, remained sequestered from all but the Nepalese who revered its pre-eminence but were loath to tread its sacred slopes.

Until 1949, Nepal was closed to foreign visitors; even the few who were invited by the Rana rulers were not allowed out of the Kathmandu Valley *(see page 36)*, although Henry Savage Landor and Tom Longstaff had managed to make tentative forays elsewhere. In the middle of the twentieth century, Nepal was the largest inhabited country yet to be explored by Europeans. The restrictions were especially frustrating for Alpinists who had climbed the most challenging European peaks and were eager to test their skills on the summits of the Himalaya.

With the easing of the restrictions on foreigners in 1949, exploration of the Himalaya by Western mountaineers began. In that year a small British expedition led by Bill Tilman was allowed by the king to visit Langtang, a short distance to the north of Kathmandu. Tilman, in particular, was interested in the cols at the eastern end of the Langtang Valley which gave access to the lofty bulk of Xixapangma in Tibet (8,046 metres/26,398 ft), eventually the last of the giants to be climbed.

Late in the season, with the monsoon approaching, Bill Tilman, Peter Lloyd and an aspiring and as yet unknown Sherpa, Tenzing Norgay *(see page 141)*, crossed the Bhote Kosi and explored the extreme southeast corner of the Ganesh Himal. During that sortie an interesting, if small, mountain called Paldor

(5,928 metres/19,450 ft) was climbed. It was the first peak in Nepal to be scaled.

These first foreign explorers in Nepal all shared a willingness to endure the rigours of a rugged landscape cut off from all communication and modern amenities. There were no roads and, other than supplies carried with

them, for months only local food and basic camping accommodation were available.

Birth of the trekking industry

Lieutenant Colonel Jimmy Roberts was the first to ply a trade from the booming interest in mountain tourism. An officer in the British Gurkha army, Roberts was a pioneer of numerous first ascents of peaks in Nepal and Pakistan, and had organised logistical support for major Himalayan expeditions. Roberts borrowed the new sport's name from the South African Boer "trekkers" and refined the camping concept from walking and climbing trips he did as a boy in Garhwal in the Indian Himalaya. He

---

PRECEDING PAGES: backpacking through the Himalaya is an unbeatable experience.
LEFT: a trekker pauses above Namche Bazar.
RIGHT: a porter and his load on the Annapurna Circuit.

advertised his first trek in *Holiday* magazine. Three sporting middle-aged American women responded and in 1964 Nepal's trekking industry was born. Roberts opened Nepal's first trekking agency, Mountain Travel Nepal, which still exists today, although Roberts died at his home in Pokhara in November 1997.

International news coverage of the conquering of Mount Everest and other great Himalayan peaks, together with tales from returning mountaineers and journalists, sparked a huge growth in mountain tourism. Between 1966 and 1970, the number of annual visitors quadrupled to 46,000, and by 1976 it had passed 100,000.

Today roughly 450,000 tourists visit Nepal each year; of these about a third are Indians who mostly come for religious pilgrimages, shopping and sightseeing. Of the others, more than a quarter come for trekking and mountaineering, contributing a lion's share of the country's annual foreign-exchange earnings. From a single trek outfitter in the mid-1960s, 100-plus registered trekking agencies now vie in a competitive market.

A boon to hill traders

Mountain tourism has been a boon to many of Nepal's hill economies, providing seasonal

TREKKING CHARGES AND ROUTES

In 1999 the trek permit system was abandoned for all non-restricted areas. The only payments that now have to be made are an initial one-month tourist visa (US$30) and fees for the following areas: Everest National Park (around US$10); Annapurna Conservation Area (around US$15); Makalu/Barun and Kanchenjunga (around US$15); parts of Mustang and Dolpo (around US$70 per day). Improved roads have made access via Dumre to the Besishahar-Khudi area for the Annapurna or Manang trek easier and more comfortable. The new road from Pokhara to the Kali Gandaki Valley can also cut days off a trek by starting or ending at Beni or Baglung.

jobs to hundreds of skilled guides (mostly from Kathmandu) and to thousands of subsistence farmers as porters, and a much-needed source of cash to villagers with the ingenuity to set up tourist shops and lodges.

In the 1950s, mountaineering injected the Khumbu Sherpas with an employment boost just at the time that trans-Himalayan trade with China was brought to its knees. Hill farmers, who for centuries had depended on trade as a source of supplemental income, suddenly faced very tough times.

The Sherpas, living year-round at elevations upward of 3,000 metres (10,000 ft), were naturally adept at scaling precipitous heights and proved a pleasure to work with. Many early foreigner-Sherpa partnerships have turned into life-long relationships. Some children of Sherpa climbers receive educational scholarships abroad. Many of those who so diligently served the first foreign expeditions nowadays have their own trekking agencies *(see page 50)*.

With the closure of the Tibet border in 1959, the Thakali people of the upper Kali Gandaki Valley in the Annapurna region faced a similar dilemma. The choice was to eke out a living in this high mountain desert, devoid of trade's supplemental income, or to move to lower, more productive farmlands far from their her-

railway to a few eastern foothill bazaar towns. Not even Kathmandu was linked to the outside world. In 1950 Herzog described in the last chapter of his classic saga *Annapurna: First Conquest of an 8,000-Metre Peak* their final walk (those with frost-bitten toes were carried) to Kathmandu to receive the king's congratulations. The early Everest explorations set out from Darjeeling through Tibet, but even after Nepal was opened to foreigners, the trek from Kathmandu to Everest Base Camp still took more than a month.

Nowadays Nepal's east-west road network plus its 27 STOL (short take-off and landing)

itage and homeland. Although some sought jobs in the mountains, many Thakalis turned their well-reputed traders' inns called *bhattis* into trekkers' lodges. Today they offer the cleanest, most popular restaurants on the circuit, serving some of the best food.

Tourism's inroads

There were no roads to speak of in Nepal when the first foreigners arrived in 1949: only a short roadway extended from the Indian border

---

LEFT: trekking among the villages of the Annapurnas.
ABOVE: resting at Annapurna Base Camp.
RIGHT: rescue doctors advise future trekkers.

GRADING SYSTEM

The grading system has no relationship to accessibility or technical difficulty. For instance the normal route on Mera, 6,654 metres (21,830 ft), the highest of all the Trekking Peaks, is probably the easiest climb of all via the northern approach from the Mera La. However, anyone wishing to attempt the south face, only ever climbed once, is faced with a sheer 2,000-metre (6,500-ft) rock face!

Gradings are not changed during the winter, but the onset of a winter storm could easily leave climbers exposed in extreme temperatures and conditions, so caution in attempting some of the more remote peaks is advised during the December–February period.

mountain airstrips make the mountains much more accessible to visitors. In just a matter of two or three weeks, trekkers can reach Everest Base Camp and see much of Khumbu, or go hiking around the Annapurna massif.

Trekking accommodation

The mushrooming of small lodges along popular trekking routes, many converted from homes that once served the trans-Himalayan traders, has sped tourism's inroads into certain mountain areas. During the 1970s, the peak of Kathmandu's ignominy as a drug haven, low-budget travellers began wandering into the hills

of Nepalese home life, along with the charm can come problems. Not all lodge kitchens are hygienic and sickness out on trek can delay travellers by days or even for the whole trip. The monotony of *dal bhaat* (rice and lentils) can also be tedious, as can the lack of privacy or security of dormitory living.

Jimmy Roberts's vision of high-quality service was reminiscent of that provided by affluent early Himalayan mountaineering expeditions on their trek to Base Camp, of which he had much experience. The Sherpas proved not only to be good climbers but capable also of giving friendly and professional support for

unaccompanied by Nepalese guides and staying in village tea houses, coining the phrase "tea-house trekking".

The villagers caught on and built more lodges. Most are simple shelters offering wooden cots and a hot meal. Others, particularly in the Annapurna and Solu Khumbu areas, are more elaborate, patterned after Alpine huts with wood-panelled dining areas separate from the kitchen, private rooms and flower-garden terraces. Conveniently spaced several hours to a day's hike apart, tea houses have enabled the independent trekker to travel light, with sleeping bag but without tent, food or cooking gear.

While lodge-to-lodge trekking gives a taste

tented trekking in Nepal. Nowadays improved equipment, food and toilet facilities add to the level of comfort.

Indeed, Nepal has set the standards for quality adventure travel worldwide. It is not uncommon for a group of six trekkers to be accompanied by an entourage of 12 to 15, comprising porters, a cook and several kitchen staff, two or three Sherpas and a chief guide called a *sirdar*. The porters carry all food needed for the trip, camp equipment including sleeping and dining tents, stools and the members' personal belongings. Each night, camp is made by a stream or water source, often in an idyllic setting beneath the snow-crested Himalaya or overlooking a jigsaw pattern of brilliant green rice paddies. The cook and his assistants create a variety of savoury Western and Asian meals over a kerosene stove. It is indeed a moveable feast. Sherpas accompany individual members on the trail, and the *sirdar* (usually fluent in English) oversees the entire operation from the hiring and firing (and placating) of local porters, to seeing to the clients' comfort and safety.

Many first-time trekkers, especially those used to backpacking, feel their conscience twinge upon seeing the porters, some just adolescent males and females, bend under two or three duffel bags. But to the Nepalese, who

Planning a trek

First-time and many return trekkers find it easier to let the experts do all the preparatory work, and contact a trekking company either at home or in Nepal *(see page 330)*. Their assistance in arranging for any relevant permits, equipment, food and transportation, hiring reliable staff and arranging porter insurance (a government requirement) can certainly help make the most out of limited time. In planning and discussing a possible trek itinerary, make it clear how many days you wish to spend on the trail as this, along with the season and your personal interests, are the

have transported all kinds of loads on foot for centuries, such work is a chance to earn hard cash to buy household necessities or a new pair of high-tops.

The camaraderie that grows between clients and staff, despite there often being a language barrier, is heartfelt and is one of the bonuses of trekking with an agency. At the end of the trek all members of the party generally join in communal dances and songs, ignoring their sore muscles and the cold.

LEFT: Namaste Lodge at Ghorapani, part of the Annapurna Circuit.
ABOVE: a lunchtime break with a game of cards.

primary determinants in deciding where to go.

Treks need not be long and rigorous; they vary from two to three days' walking on relatively easy, low-level terrain to rugged and often demanding expeditions of three weeks or more. Do not make the mistake of thinking a short trek is necessarily easier – there are still hills and less time to get fit and into the trek rhythm. You can go virtually anywhere, except restricted zones.

Trekking with an agency, self-sufficient in all aspects, often allows you the chance to penetrate deep into the Himalayan wilderness, leaving behind overcrowded trails. Entry into the recently opened Dolpo and Mustang areas requires special permits and is limited to those with a registered agency who must be self-sufficient in food and fuel. Dolpo and other remote, food-poor regions simply do not have any surplus to support tea-house trekkers *(see page 319)*.

The appeal of Shangri La

What do so many trekkers find in Nepal that they cannot find hiking in their own or other foreign countries?

The early Tibetan scripts and Hindu epics tell of the wondrous Himalaya, where gods dwelt on high and mortals could find heaven-on-earth in hidden valleys. An air of mysticism indeed permeates musty monasteries *(see page 278)* and resides thick amid a circle of gyrating, possessed shamans.

But what many travellers to Nepal find most appealing is the Nepalese people, who still retain a charm and friendliness that is unique. In the Nepalese's simple yet arduous life, the visitor sees a clarity of values: family strength, self-respect, purity of heart, kindness to others and a wonderful sense of humour.

The vigilant mountains and mesmerising patterns of hard-wrought "staircases" of terraces can also massage the mind into

SPECIALITY TREKS

A more structured approach and an educational forum appeals to some travellers, and companies now combine scientific, religious, photographic, art and cultural study with a trekking holiday. Tour leaders double as instructors in yoga, herbal medicine, photography, birdwatching, sketching, language study and cultural interaction.

Family treks can be planned with a less ambitious schedule, finding time for children's' activities and extra staff to tend to youngsters. Pony treks are conducted out of Pokhara for those who do not wish to or cannot walk. A group of blind trekkers recently set a world record climbing 6,654-metre (21,830-ft) Mera Peak.

contemplation; a moment's rest on a mountain top, an interlude by a rushing stream, the flash of a passing smile, can reveal long-cloistered moments of truth to those who are prepared to listen. The physical effort required of carrying one's body up and down this immense landscape, of paring one's daily essentials, of relishing in mundane accomplishments, all invite reflection on a cluttered or distracted life back home. This is aided by the wonderful natural beauty of the mountains, and the silence from being so far from busy roads and urban environments. The rewards of trekking are unquantifiable yet uniquely addictive. Once is rarely enough.

Trekking Peaks

Nepal, as Tilman said, is a "singularly mountainous country". Despite this, mountaineers are only permitted onto a small proportion of the hundreds of peaks; 128 summits are officially climbable, and of these 110 are classified as Expedition Peaks. This means they can only be climbed by expeditions endorsed by Alpine Clubs who have bought a permit and are accompanied by a liaison officer.

In 1978, the Nepal Mountaineering Association (NMA) announced that 18 Trekking Peaks were climbable without the "red tape" of a full-scale expedition. They ranged in height from

further skills than the ability to walk. This is most definitely *not* the case. To attempt a trekking peak it is necessary to have some previous climbing experience and a knowledge of how to use equipment such as ropes, ice axes and crampons.

It is true that some peaks have a high success rate with large commercial groups – these include, amongst others, Island Peak, Mera, Tent Peak and Chulu Far East. However, most of these achievements can be attributed to good leadership and the use of strong Sherpas to carry loads, fix ropes and blaze the trail.

5,587 metres (18,330 ft) to 6,654 metres (21,830 ft). Apart from a proviso that attempts must be accompanied as far as Base Camp by Sherpa guides, these mountains can be attempted with little formality and within a time-scale that suits an annual holiday period.

Not so easy

Inherent in the name "Trekking Peaks" is a serious misnomer which might indicate to the uninformed that their ascent requires no

LEFT: dome tents camped in the Everest Region, near Cho Oyu.
ABOVE: descending from an Annapurna trek.

Among the 18 peaks are several coveted summits, such as Kusum Kanguru, Hiunchuli, Fluted Peak and Kwangde, which over the years have acquired a reputation of inaccessibility that has attracted some of the world's most respected climbers. They offer technical routes of the highest standard and are not suitable for the ambitious amateur.

As might be expected, Trekking Peaks are concentrated in the Khumbu and Annapurna Himal, the most popular trekking destinations. As yet there are no Trekking Peaks in recently opened areas such as Dolpo, Dhaulagiri, Manaslu or Kanchenjunga, although the situation may change in the near future. ❏

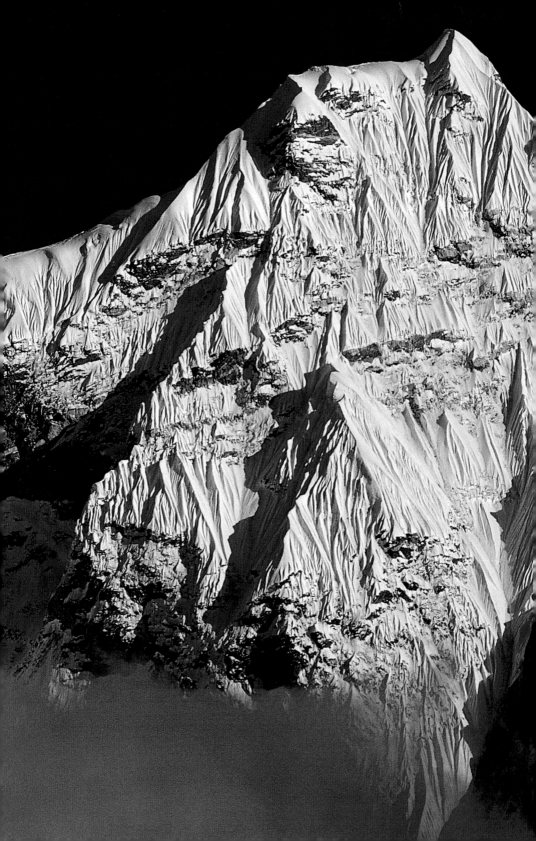

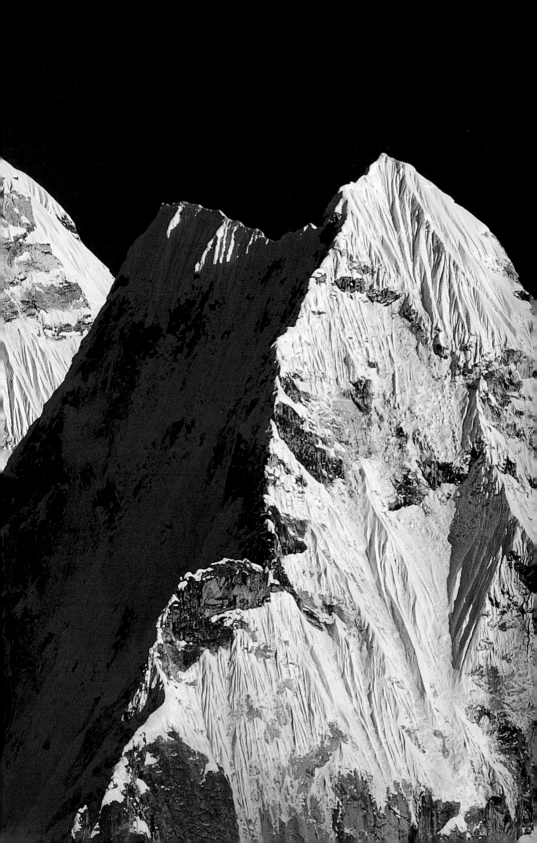

MOUNTAINEERING

*Home to eight of the world's ten highest mountains, Nepal has long been
a Mecca for mountaineers, both professionals and ambitious amateurs*

The shattering force of the tectonic collision which formed the Nepal Himalaya gave birth to eight of the world's fourteen 8,000-metre (26,250-ft) mountains and eight of the ten highest mountains in the world. These huge mountain masses range eastwards from Dhaulagiri to form a natural frontier with Nepal's neighbours. Everest and Cho Oyu border with Tibet, while Kanchenjunga shares its multi-summited crest with the Indian state of Sikkim. The history of the ascents of these awesome 8,000-metre mountains by teams from an increasing number of developed and emerging nations reflects the importance today of "sporting" success. As yardsticks of national and personal achievement, Nepal's peaks have become the ultimate playground for the mountaineering elite.

Scaling the heights

The true age of mountaineering began at the end of the 1940s, when Nepal, and therefore its mountains, was opened up to the outside world. Climbers were quick to take up the challenge. From this point, the development of mountaineering mirrored the evolution of Alpine exploration in Europe: early expeditions sought to reach summits by the easiest or most obvious routes. The major difference between Nepal and Europe was that the effort, cost and size were escalated for Himalayan expeditions. Vast armies of climbers, porters and Sherpas marched towards base camps to lay siege to the mountain in question. The expeditions often lasted for months.

Once the virgin summits had been scaled, those at the cutting-edge of mountaineering looked towards more difficult routes on steeper ridges and faces. In recent years, Himalayan endeavour has taken individuals to the very limits of endurance in solo, turbo-charged,

PRECEDING PAGES: an avalanche-fluted range.
LEFT: during the 1982 ascent of Cholatse, US climber John Roskelley negotiates the final ice wall.
RIGHT: Everest Base Camp.

record-breaking climbs. The mountains have seen an increasing number of wild performances – flying in hot air balloons or hang-gliding and ski descents.

Yet, despite predictions for a future of multi-ascents and even faster descents, in reality this approach to Himalayan climbing will remain

the preserve of the extreme few because of the high level of expertise required. In the meantime, the majority of mountaineers are confined to the traditional approach utilising fixed camps, fixed ropes, "tinned" air, and the help of Sherpas.

Everest – highest point on earth

The "Mother of the Universe" is known as Sagarmatha in Nepal and Chomolungma (Mother Goddess or Goddess Langma) in Tibet. In 1999 the height of the summit was recalculated, using the Global Positioning System (GPS) satellite, to be 8,850 metres (29,035 ft); previously it had been measured at 8,848 metres (29,028 ft). The increase is due to the movements of the earth's plates; as the Indian plate continues to push into the Eurasian, the Himalaya continue to be thrust upwards.

Everest had challenged the skills of British mountaineers over several decades prior to the opening up of Nepal, although always from the north and without success. The closing of Tibet coincided fortuitously with Nepal's opening, and efforts were renewed to find a way to the top from the south side of the mountain.

The leading lights of British mountaineering were soon probing the corrugated foothills east of Kathmandu to find an approach to the

top. Two days later, on 29 May 1953, New Zealander Edmund Hillary and Sherpa Tenzing Norgay were the first people to stand on the summit of the highest mountain in the world.

They proudly brought to a close what has been called "an Edwardian quest for the poles of the earth" and made an auspicious start to the new Elizabethan age as the news reached London for the coronation of Queen Elizabeth II.

Kanchenjunga – third highest

Visible in the distant mists from Darjeeling and with access from Sikkim, the history of Kanchenjunga (8,586 metres/28,169 ft), like

Khumbu. Bill Tilman and American Charles Houston traced a way to the foot of the Khumbu icefall in 1950 and a year later Eric Shipton's team went through the icefall to reach the Western Cwm. The British, however, were not alone in their endeavour and all but lost the great prize in 1952 when a Swiss expedition came close to success.

The following spring an expedition led by Colonel John Hunt renewed the British assault on Everest. This was a strong expedition gathered from the finest mountaineers of Britain and New Zealand. On the first summit bid Charles Evans and Tom Bourdillon reached the South Summit, laying the way open to the

that of Everest, goes back far beyond the opening of Nepal to foreigners. This mountain is the best documented of all, having been attempted as early as 1905.

Kanchenjunga is vast: some 13 km (8 miles) in length by 8 km (5 miles) wide. After an optimistic British reconnaissance in 1954, the Alpine Club and the Royal Geographical Society of London dispatched an expedition the following spring, led by Charles Evans. This particularly strong team included George Band, Joe Brown, John Jackson and Tony Streather.

After a hard struggle, plagued by avalanches and not without mishap – a young Sherpa died after falling into a crevasse – Band and Brown left for the summit, using artificial oxygen, on 25 May 1955. They had chosen a route on the southwest face and, having gained the main ridge, the top lay beyond a tower of grey-green rock. Joe Brown, acclaimed as the finest rock climber of his generation, managed to overcome this obstacle to reach the easy slope leading to the summit. Next day, two teammates followed in their footsteps.

> ### DAUNTING FACE
>
> The south face of Lhotse is ranked as "amongst the most difficult in the world". As Reinhold Messner wrote in 1977: "…this vertical face may well be impossible."

The four climbers kept a promise made to the Sikkimese not to stand on the sacred summit of the highest point so, although credited with the first ascent, Kanchenjunga remained the "Untrodden Peak".

Lhotse – fourth highest

For a long time the fourth peak, Lhotse (8,516 metres/27,940 ft), had no separate identity from its dominating neighbour to the north, Mount Everest. Even its name, which translates as "South Peak", implies it is not a mountain in its own right. Once Nepal opened its borders the error became all too clear – from the south Lhotse forms an enormous mountain wall.

Although unattempted until 1953, Norman Dyhrenfurth had identified a route to the summit from the South Col of Everest. European and US assaults did not make much impact until spring 1956 when a Swiss expedition established a Base Camp beneath the Khumbu icefall. Poor weather hampered progress, but on 18 May Swiss climbers Ernest Reiss and Fritz Luchsinger reached the summit of the world's fourth highest peak.

The most recent star in the firmament of Himalayan climbing was thought to be Tomo Cesen from Yugoslavia, who at first confounded his peers by climbing the massive south face of Lhotse in April 1990. The 30-year-old sports journalist claimed he had climbed not only without fixed camps or bottled oxygen but also entirely alone, with very little fixed rope and in the amazing total elapsed time of 45 hours and 20 minutes from the

bottom of the face to the summit. This is now widely disbelieved, however, following an investigation by Yugoslavian mountaineering experts. This has in turn led to many of Cesen's earlier claims being discredited.

Lhotse's south face was successfully climbed in the autumn of 1990, however, by a large Russian expedition consisting of 17 mountaineers and 13 Sherpas; two Soviet members, Sergei Bershov and Vladimir Karataev reached the summit on 16 October.

Makalu – fifth highest

Makalu (8,463 metres/27,766 ft), in eastern Nepal, is the highest peak between Everest and Kanchenjunga and is a mountain of exceptional beauty. As with Annapurna I *(see page 137)*, the French have laid claim to Makalu, although US and New Zealand teams had explored the region earlier the same year. The French reconnaissance party headed by Jean Franco visited the mountain in 1954, returning a year later with an expedition consisting of the very best guides Alpinist France could muster, among them Jean Couzy, Lionel Terray, Guido Magnone and Serge Coupe. They were also ably supported by an expedition doctor,

---

LEFT: the British Everest expedition of 1933.

RIGHT: mighty Makalu is the fifth tallest mountain in the world.

geologists, some 23 Sherpas and an army of no less than 315 porters.

Their route to Camp 5 on the Makalu La proved technically very difficult and required a large amount of fixed rope. From there, they were able to traverse easy slopes on the north side. A steep couloir led to the knife-edged ridge leading to the summit, first reached on 15 May 1955 by Couzy and Terray. In total eight Frenchmen and one Sherpa reached the summit that year.

> ### PEAK OF JOY
>
> On reaching Cho Oyu's summit, Tichy felt "...a sense of complete harmony such as we had never known before, an almost unearthly sense of joy – worth far more than a few frozen fingers."

was an experienced team including many who were to take part in the first ascent of Everest. From the Nangpa La, the traditional yak trade route to Tibet, a route was found that looked feasible, though the north flank was out of bounds in closed Tibet.

In 1954 a Viennese author, Dr Herbert Tichy, put together an expedition which proved the exception to the rule that 8,000-metre mountains needed large-scale expeditions. With only two European companions he organised a lightweight party

This outstandingly successful expedition was a combination of a strong, well-organised and highly motivated team aided by the finest equipment and blessed with good weather providing ideal climbing conditions. The latter is critical to success on 8,000-metre mountains.

Cho Oyu – sixth highest

Cho Oyu (8,201 metres/26,906 ft) rises 32 km (20 miles) west of Everest. Known as the "Goddess of Turquoise", it was the third of Nepal's 8,000-metre peaks to be climbed.

The first reconnaissance took place in 1951, followed a year later by the British Cho Oyu expedition led by Eric Shipton. Once again this

very much in keeping with the "small is beautiful" philosophy expounded by Tilman and Shipton. Accompanied by half a dozen Sherpas they left Namche Bazar for the Nangpa La in late September. Finding a way through the icefall they established a high camp but a storm drove them down and left Tichy with frostbitten hands.

In the meantime two members of a Swiss/ French expedition to Gauri Shankar arrived at Base Camp, hoping to "poach" Cho Oyu. Though not yet fully recuperated, the Austrians were driven back onto the mountain and an epic ascent followed. Unable to use his damaged hands, Tichy had to be helped over the rock band, but at 3pm on 19 October 1954 the summit was reached by Tichy, Sepp Joechler and Pasang Dawa Lama. It was the first ascent of an 8,000-metre peak in Nepal without the use of artificial oxygen.

Dhaulagiri I – seventh highest

This spectacular peak's name means, benignly enough, the "White Mountain", but Dhaulagiri (8,167 metres/26,795 ft) has come to be known as the mountain of storms and sorrows.

Although the first of the 8,000-metre peaks to be attempted by the French in 1950, who abandoned their bid in favour of Annapurna I,

Manaslu – eighth highest

If Europeans can lay claim to many of the Himalayan giants, Manaslu (8,163 metres/26,781 ft) is determinedly an Asian mountain. Not only was it first climbed by a Japanese expedition, but a high number of Nepalese, Japanese and South Korean lives have been lost on this daunting mountain whose name means "Soul" in Sanskrit. During two days of avalanches during the spring of 1972, in the largest death toll yet on any Nepalese peak, 15 men lost their lives.

The mountain itself is stunning; the highest of a cluster of glorious summits including

ironically it was the very last 8,000-metre peak in Nepal to be climbed.

Seven expeditions attempted Dhaulagiri, including one sponsored by President Perón of Argentina, but it was not until 1960 that a massive Swiss attempt was successful via the northeast spur. Supplied by a small glacier plane piloted by Ernst Saxer, the expedition finally ended the "Golden Decade" of Nepal's giants by putting two Europeans and two Sherpas on the summit on 23 May 1960.

LEFT: Cho Oyu, the world's sixth highest mountain, first scaled in 1954.

ABOVE: ice seracs on the Khumbu glacier.

Peak 29 (Ngadi Himal) and Himal Chuli *(see page 239)*, Manaslu stands in splendid isolation, between the Annapurna range and Ganesh Himal.

Between 1953 and 1956 the Japanese mountaineering elite served their Himalayan apprenticeship by making several attempts on Manaslu. In 1956 the venerable 62-year-old expedition leader, Yuka Maki, approached via the Buri Gandaki. The Japanese set about climbing the northeast face, despite some disputes with the local villagers. Toshio Imanishi and Sirdar Gyalzen Norbu Sherpa reached the rocky pinnacle of the summit by midday on 9 May.

Annapurna I – tenth highest

Annapurna I (8,091 metres/26,545 ft) was the first 8,000-metre mountain to be climbed when, in 1950, a strong French expedition, led by Maurice Herzog, reached the summit by the north face. Having failed to find a way up Dhaulagiri, they had turned their attention to the tenth highest peak.

The team included such notable Chamonix guides as Gaston Rebuffat, Lionel Terray and Louis Lachenal. Lachenal and Herzog reached the summit, but deteriorating weather and a series of mishaps almost turned success into disaster. Herzog suffered severe frostbite during an epic descent, resulting in amputations. Despite this, their success is generally credited with heralding the beginning of the "Golden Decade" of Nepal's 8,000-metre mountains.

Problems at high altitude

Heroic feats by some of the world's finest mountaineers has led the way for more amateur climbers eager to test their skills on Nepal's highest peaks, but scaling such heights has its own, very specific problems. Will I make it up Kala Pattar (5,545 metres/18,192 ft) or over Thorong La (5,416 metres/17,769 ft)? These are the questions that begin months

THE EVEREST 1996 DISASTER AND IMAX FILM

Despite its size and and perilous conditions, Everest is now big business. Tibet and China have opened the peak to tourism, charging climbers up to $65,000 to be walked to the top, often regardless of their expertise. On 11 May 1996, however, the mountain's worst disaster took place, which may go some way to halt this dangerous onslaught.

In spring 1996, 14 groups from 11 countries swarmed Base Camp, including a 26-member New Zealand team, headed by Rob Hall, a US group led by Scott Fischer and teams from Japan, South Africa and Taiwan. Though the south ridge is barely wide enough to accommodate one climber at a time, 33 people planned to climb to the top the same day. This human "traffic jam", combined with an unpredicted blizzard, led to tragedy. Hall and Fischer were among the eight who perished, along with two Sherpas, two clients and two other leaders.

The disaster, one of the worst in climbing history, became the subject of TV specials and books, notably the bestseller *Into Thin Air* by survivor Jon Krakauer. Also on the mountain that week were film-makers David Breashears and Ed Viesturs, there to capture the ascent on the realistic IMAX format film. Unwittingly, their film, completed on the summit on 23 May, tells not only the story of Everest, but the tragedy that unfolded on it 12 days earlier.

before the trip. Some people have never hiked in a true mountain atmosphere, and have no experience with feeling breathless walking uphill. Others have been to 4,000 metres (13,000 ft) or more, and wonder what an additional 1,500 metres (4,900 ft) in altitude will add to the exertion. Although these questions are valid (some people will find it too difficult to get to these heights at all), it is important to remember that these apparently enormous heights are just at the base of the peaks in the Himalaya.

RATES OF ASCENT

The recommended rate of ascent is 500 metres (1,650 ft) per day at altitudes above 3,000 metres (10,000 ft). Beyond 5,000 metres (16,500 ft) more caution is required.

At Mount Everest Base Camp (5,357 metres/17,575 ft) the amount of oxygen in each breath is half that of sea level. At the top of Everest this has shrunk to one third of that at sea level. The tiny amount of oxygen in each breath at that altitude was at one time thought to be inadequate to support human exertion, and that therefore the summit could not be reached without carrying and breathing supplemental oxygen. This was the feeling of many scientists prior to 1978, when Reinhold Messner and Peter Habeler set off from the Base Camp of Everest with no artificial oxygen and went all the way to the summit. Some people even doubted their claims when they came down, so convinced were they that it was impossible! Messner put the issue to rest two years later when he left Base Camp on the Tibet side of Everest all alone without oxygen, and went to the summit and back in four days *(see page 141)*.

Messner himself, the first man to climb all of the earth's 14 8,000-metre peaks, speaks of the environment above 8,000 metres (26,250 ft) as the "death zone". At these heights the body cannot adjust, it can only slowly deteriorate. Thinking is slowed and neurologic function is impaired (and remains impaired for months after descent). You inevitably lose weight, both fat and muscle, and along with that you lose strength. Panting rapidly in the high dry air causes you to lose litres of fluid that must be painstakingly replaced by chop-

ping ice, melting it on a stove, forcing the lukewarm result past parched lips, spending up to four or five hours a day replacing what has been lost. Four or five days above 8,000 metres (26,250 ft) is the most time that a human has spent at that height and survived; people have perished who have tried to stay longer, trapped by storms or delayed by injuries. In a sense, they "vanished" into thin air.

Human beings evolved genetically at sea level. Yet the potential to adapt to even these

great heights is built into our bodies. Breathing automatically accelerates and red cell production is increased to carry more oxygen. Other, as yet undefined, changes also facilitate carrying oxygen from the lungs to the tissues that need it. If you were deposited by helicopter at the summit of Everest, without prior acclimatisation and without artificial oxygen, you would lose consciousness within minutes and die within hours. The fact that an acclimatised person can live and function at that height is a genetic miracle. Further mystery is added by the discovery that the summit of Everest is probably exactly the limit that a human being could go on earth without supplemental

LEFT: a sick trekker is treated in the Hongu with Baruntse behind.

RIGHT: altimeter from Mallory and Irvine's ill-fated Everest expedition.

oxygen. In other words, the highest point on the planet is the highest point at which a human being could survive.

The weather at high altitude can also change abruptly. Winds can exceed 200 kph (125 mph) and temperatures drop far below freezing. Frostbite is a constant risk but stopping to warm frozen toes or fingers can be impossible in precarious, exposed situations. The throat and lungs become parched and coughing becomes severe and uncontrollable. Climbers have been known to break their ribs during severe coughing spells and have had to climb down unassisted with this additional pain.

Coping with altitude

The speed at which the human body can adapt to altitude is limited by a condition known as acute mountain sickness (AMS). This results when you ascend to altitude faster than your body can adjust. Initially you have headaches, nausea and tiredness, but the symptoms can progress to coma or fluid on the lungs. Usually this process takes several days. Dr Charles Clarke, the British climber and physician, feels that this process may be even more accelerated at high altitude. Case reports suggest that a milder, preventable form of AMS may prevail at altitudes up to 5,500 metres (18,000 ft), what Dr Clarke refers to as the

"mountain sickness of acclimatisation". Above that height, the syndrome can sometimes strike with devastating speed and often gets worse even as the victim struggles to descend. He calls this the "mountain sickness of extreme altitude".

Climbers are always trying to strike a balance between spending sufficient time adapting to altitude and safeguarding the route, whilst trying to restrict the time spent at high altitude to a minimum. However, as climbers attempt to ascend more quickly, minimising exposure to altitude and weather, they are liable to succumb to the sudden onset of severe altitude sickness.

Physical fitness also plays a large role in helping climbers at extreme altitude. Most mountaineers who have ambitions to climb high already have some success and experience in scaling lesser peaks and have a high degree of fitness. World-class mountaineers moreover have a different concept of fitness compared to ordinary people. At what many would think was the end of a hard day's climbing, these strong men and women say, "It's not dark for half an hour yet, let's climb…". However, even these great athletes are levelled by exposure to altitudes above 8,000 metres (26,250 ft). Messner has stated that fitness no longer matters at these heights; it is willpower and experience alone, from there to the summit and back.

What does this mean for the Himalayan trekker? Suddenly 5,500 metres (18,000 ft) does not seem so high. If you have an interest in hiking, do it regularly and are willing to take time to adjust as you gain altitude, you have every chance of being able to comfortably gain your trekking goal. Not allowing enough time is the road to defeat in the Himalaya. Although the air is thin, you can be quite comfortable at rest at 5,500 metres (18,000 ft), only noticing the altitude when you start to walk uphill. The air is clean and dry, the sky is a deep blue and the surrounding walls are white and massive. These moderate heights (by Himalayan standards) are an environment to be enjoyed rather than a goal to be accomplished. For a few days, your worldly problems can be left behind as your mind soars free. ❏

LEFT: frostbitten fingers are one of the commonest hazards of the ill-prepared mountaineer.

A Tale of Two Mountaineers

The two best-known mountaineers in the world are New Zealander Sir Edmund Hillary and South Tyrolean Reinhold Messner. In 1953 Hillary, a former beekeeper, became the first man to scale Mount Everest. Messner belongs to the next generation of climbers and was the first person to scale all of the world's 14 giant 8,000-metre (26,250-ft) peaks.

Hillary came late to mountaineering: he was 16 years old before he even saw a real mountain, and 20 when he ventured into New Zealand's rugged Southern Alps in 1939. But, once his interest had been sparked, there was no stopping him. He began with climbs in New Zealand before embarking on the Himalaya in 1951. In Nepal, Hillary met Eric Shipton, the British climber-explorer. Together they charted the most feasible route up Everest on the Nepalese side of the border. Hillary returned in 1953 with a British expedition and, as every schoolchild knows, he and his Sherpa companion Tenzing Norgay became the first men to reach the top of the world. "We knocked the bastard off" was Hillary's summary of the achievement.

Hillary's adventures have not been restricted to the Himalaya. In 1957 and 1958 he led a small party in a tractor race across the Antarctic to the South Pole. In 1977, he led a group of friends by jet-boat from the mouth of the Ganges to one of its mountain sources. But Nepal has always been close to his heart. As late as 1981, he was back on Everest, accompanying a US mountaineering team on an east-face attempt, by way of Tibet. Hillary also became increasingly involved in the problems of the Sherpas, particularly their illiteracy and health problems *(see page 50)*. The organisation which Hillary founded, the Himalayan Trust, now supports 27 schools and two hospitals that he himself has taken a hand in building. He was New Zealand's ambassador to Nepal from 1985 to 1989 and now lives back in New Zealand.

Reinhold Messner, born in 1944, grew up in a village surrounded by the Dolomite mountains in South Tyrol. Until he first ventured to the Himalaya in 1970, Messner worked as a teacher. Messner's first attempt to conquer a Himalayan peak was

successful. He and his brother Guenther, members of a German expedition to Pakistan's Nanga Parbat (8,126 metres/26,660 ft), made history's third ascent of the mountain and the first by its Rupal face, although his brother tragically died in an avalanche on the descent.

There are 14 of these 8,000-metre mountains on earth and Messner soon set about scaling them all. In 1972, he alone, among members of an Austrian team, gained the summit of Manaslu (8,163 metres/26,781 ft) on a new route. In May 1978, Messner and Austrian Peter Habeler made the first ascent of Everest without artificial oxygen. In August 1978, Messner made the first solo ascent

of any 8,000-metre peak on Nanga Parbat again. Messner returned to Everest in 1980 for what many consider his greatest achievement: a solo ascent of the highest mountain on earth. In four days, he climbed from Base Camp to the summit and back, without the support of fixed camps, companions or bottled oxygen.

On 16 October 1986 Messner became the first person to have scaled all 8,000-metre mountains when he made it to the summit of the world's fourth highest, Lhotse, 8,516 metres (27,940 ft) above sea level, just 20 days after having been to the top of the fifth highest, Makalu, 8,463 metres (27,766 ft). He achieved this formidable goal the hard way, without taking bottled oxygen. ❏

RIGHT: Sir Edmund Hillary (left) and Reinhold Messner in the Himalaya.

RIVER RAFTING

Flowing down from the Himalaya through the country's varied landscapes, rivers provide one of the most popular and exhilarating ways of seeing Nepal

Fed by the glaciers of the world's highest mountains and the snows of the Tibetan plateau, Nepal's feverish rivers provide exciting opportunities for whitewater rafting or kayaking and an unbeatable profile of an ever-changing landscape. On their way to India's sacred Ganges, the waters surge through Himalayan gorges, traverse rugged foothills, course between tropical forests and meander across the Terai plains.

River running is one of the best and most thrilling ways to abandon the cities and experience the rural life of Nepal without investing the time and energy required for a long trek.

Sacred waters

The Himalayan rivers are considered sacred to the Nepalese. Ashes of the cremated dead are scattered into rivers to be eventually carried to the Ganges. The confluence of two rivers is usually revered as a holy site for ritual bathing. Water brings life, but the rivers are also feared, which explains why on the hottest days few Nepalese will be seen swimming.

The first people to run Nepal's rivers were therefore foreigners. Exalting at the opportunity to test virgin waters, early pioneers set about exploring the rivers soon after Nepal opened its borders in the late 1940s. Sir Edmund Hillary attempted a journey to the source of the Sun Kosi in 1968. Various rivers were kayaked and rafted by visiting adventurers, including Michael Peissel who tried to drive a hovercraft up the Kali Gandaki in 1973.

But it was not until 1976 when American Al Read started running and charting the rapids of the Trisuli and upper Sun Kosi rivers that river running began in earnest, with foreign experts brought in to train Nepalese river guides. Today local guides handle the rafts, supervise the camp staff and interpret the flora and fauna of the Himalaya for guests' added appreciation.

LEFT: nothing can compare with the adrenaline rush of running the rivers of Nepal.
RIGHT: Bembo Bridge over the Marsyangdi River.

Selecting a river

Nepal's rivers link the mountains and plains like blue veins. Tumbling out of the highlands they are sometimes violent, sometimes calm but always beautiful. Trips are available from one to 13 days on different rivers, all offering dramatically different experiences.

The Karnali, descending from Tibet's Mount Kailas, is Nepal's mightiest river. Ten days of wilderness, excitement and exploration make this the classic Himalayan expedition. Finish with a visit to Royal Bardia National Park *(see page 105)* for an unbeatable combination.

The Sun Kosi, Nepal's "River of Gold", traverses 270 km (165 miles) through the beautiful Mahabharat Range. At the right flow it's an incredible combination of white water, scenery, villages and quiet, introspective evenings along what many people consider to be one of the world's definitive river journeys. An eight- or nine-day trip finishes in far eastern Nepal.

In east Nepal the snows of Kanchenjunga feed a challenging cousin of the Sun Kosi. The Tamur combines one of the best short Himalayan treks over a 3,000-metre (10,000-ft) pass, offering mountain views with an exhilarating river expedition.

The Trisuli, named after Shiva's trident, parallels the road from Kathmandu to Mugling before joining the Gandaki river system and becoming the Narayani River. One- to three-day trips conclude at Royal Chitwan National Park (see page 301).

> ### WATER LEVELS
>
> Himalayan rivers can fluctuate dramatically and as a general rule the higher the flows the more challenging the rafting will be.

The Annapurna and Dhaulagiri mountains feed the Kali Gandaki west of Pokhara. Being Kali's river, the Kali Gandaki is considered particularly sacred, and at the confluence of tributaries there are temples and cremation sights in abundance. A three-day trip gives a good wilderness alternative to the Trisuli.

The Marsyangdi is one of the most challenging whitewater runs in the world. A five-day trip combines a short trek with demanding whitewater rafting and stunning scenery.

The Bhote Kosi, three hours from Kathmandu on the road to Tibet, is a turbulent mountain stream offering the steepest rafting in Nepal. An overnight stay at one of the luxurious new resorts can include bungee-jumping, canyoning or trekking.

The Seti is an excellent two- to three-day trip in an isolated area with easy rapids and can be combined with trekking and jungle safaris, while the Bheri, in west Nepal, is a trip with great jungle scenery and lots of wildlife. This is one of the best fishing rivers and can be combined with a visit to Royal Bardia National Park.

The Arun River from Tumlingtar makes an excellent three-day wilderness trip, although getting to the starting point is rather complicated and time-consuming.

Seasons and expeditions

Late September to mid-December and March through to early May are the best times to run rivers in Nepal, avoiding the coldest time and the monsoon. The water temperature is only 6–10°C (43–50°F) but the air clear and warm.

Most trips let passengers partake in the paddling, with the professional guide steering with a series of commands. Others allow you to relax and enjoy the fun while the guide controls the boat using centre-mounted oars. Either way, rafting combines tranquillity and thrills.

Many of Nepal's rivers are remote and unpredictable and a responsible rafting company is vital to ensure your safety. Reputable companies employ guides trained to international standards with years of experience on Nepal's rivers. Their training includes first aid, rescue, sanitation and environmental awareness. The best outfitters provide all the essentials for a safe and fun trip: fully trained staff, self bailing rafts and safety kayakers on more difficult rivers, river rescue equipment, high-buoyancy lifejackets and helmets, first-aid and raft-repair kits, tents, camping gear and transport.

On longer trips time is set aside for hiking into side canyons, visiting nearby villages and swimming in the river or lazing on beaches. River rafting is an exceptional experience anywhere, but with Nepal's unique topography, cheerful people and traditional culture it is all the more rewarding. ❑

LEFT: rafting the Trisuli River is one of Nepal's most popular river trips.

Mountain Biking

Mountain biking is one of the most recent adventure sports and already its suitability to the cobweb of dirt roads that crisscross Nepal is evident. From the trading trails of the mountains to the lowland plains of the Terai, the mountain bike has proven itself the ultimate way to explore the rural countryside.

Mountain bikes were developed in the 1970s by a group of enthusiasts in California to handle rough, rocky trails and steep hill climbs. Old bicycles were modified with five- to ten-speed gears, front and rear drum brakes, motorcycle brake levers and big, knobby tyres. These were tested in California hills that dropped 400 metres (1,300 ft) in 2.4 km (1.8 miles) averaging a 14 percent gradient – an ideal testing ground for the Himalaya. In the mid-1980s mountain bikes were introduced to Nepal by some of the more enterprising expatriates of Kathmandu. Intrigued children in distant villages would run up shouting "*Gearwallas Aayo*! – the people of the geared bikes have come!" And they keep coming.

Mountain biking is an incomparable way to explore the temples, medieval cities and rural settlements of the Kathmandu Valley *(see page 203)*. Daily village life can be observed from a dirt road without the intrusion of vehicles or the constraints of travelling on foot. If you choose to leave town under your own steam, a pollution mask is a valuable precaution and available from many department stores. Once beyond the Ring Road the air freshens up quickly. Without much time to roam you may want to stick to the roads shown on the various valley maps. The fields in all four directions offer endless scope for single-track adventure. Beyond the valley a mountain bike is a wonderful way to reach a trek start point, the beginning of a river trip or just to tour the country.

A more pleasant route to Pokhara on a mountain bike follows the longer, more scenic old Raj Path down to the Terai (stop off for a few nights in Royal Chitwan National Park), then takes the Siddhartha Highway up to Pokhara. Other great routes around the country include biking from Kathmandu to the Tibetan border at Kodari *(see page 288)*, Kathmandu to Jiri and Kathmandu to Dhunche, with a side trip to the ancient palace of Nuwakot *(see*

RIGHT: mountain biking through the beautiful and peaceful Kathmandu Valley.

page 221). More ambitious trips go from Pokhara to Royal Bardia National Park in the far west *(see page 308)*, from Kathmandu to the Arun Valley in the east *(see page 283)* or even the Annapurna circuit through Jomsom *(see page 239)*.

Mountain bikes do have shortcomings – they are suitable only for selected trekking trails, for safety and ecological reasons. At the other end of the spectrum, some of the main roads of Nepal, such as from Kathmandu to Pokhara, are too trafficked with lorries and buses for enjoyable biking.

Day-rental bike stands have now been overshadowed by bicycle touring companies that offer higher-quality bikes and dependable maintenance

and guides. Of these, the leader is still Himalayan Mountain Bikes, located in Adventure Centre Nepal, at the gate of Northfield Café in Thamel *(see page 174)*. They have 40 new, well-maintained bikes, all with front shocks, jel seats and good touring equipment. They set up classic routes and and offer trip advice, as well as pioneering combination adventures that team up biking with canyoning, hot springs, bungee-jumping, monastery tours or jungle treks. The Dawn till Dusk company also knows their routes and offers some cheaper rates, but with older equipment. But any good bike company should be able to help you to assess the best routes for you, given your ability, schedule and what you want to see. ❏

ADVENTURE SPORTS: FROM PEAK TO JUNGLE

From the jungle to the mountain crests, few countries in the world offer the range of sporting opportunities available in Nepal.

Anyone with a taste of adventure and a certain level of fitness will find something to thrill them within Nepal's varied landscape.

Commercial river rafting got underway in 1976 when the company Himalayan River Exploration started plying the Seti and Trisuli rivers, floating visitors down to Royal Chitwan National Park. Today it is one of the country's most popular sports. Enterprising kayakers occasionally shoot the rapids as well; some rafting companies can arrange kayak rentals by the day. Boating on Pokhara's Phewa Lake is more restful than sporting. Row boats are readily available; when the afternoon winds pick up, search out a sailboat for hire.

Spring and autumn are the best seasons for sport fishing in lowland lakes and rivers. Trout-like species make the best eating and the large *mahseer* are the most fun.

In the mid-19th century, Nepal was a favoured ground for big game hunters, a privilege granted only to invitees of the ruling Rana regime. However, the rhinos and tigers of Chitwan are now strictly protected and hunting is only permitted with a licensed guide in designated areas.

Just as mountain climbing has become a contest of ingenuity using high-tech gadgetry, the latest lightweight, tough sports equipment is finding a niche in the Himalaya, particularly mountain bikes. The Himalaya's up-drafts and incomparable views send the imagination soaring with airborne sport opportunities.

▷ **HANG-GLIDING**
Some mountaineers avoid the walking descent by carrying light-weight wings to the tops of peaks and sailing down.

△ **ON THE PISTE**
Nepal's slopes are generally too rocky, remote and high for ski runs, though there are some gentle runs in Langtang and Jomsom.

△ **AERIAL VIEWS**
In recent years hot-air ballooning has become popular: it is possible to arrange balloon flights over the Kathmandu Valley.

◁ **GAME HUNTING**
Highland hunters come in search of the blue sheep, bearing a world-class prize rack, and the shaggy Himalayan *tahr*.

WILDLIFE VIEWING ON SAFARI

Wildlife viewing, tracking and photographing in the Terai jungles is a thrill which takes many mountain-engrossed tourists by surprise. Tiger Tops' world famous Jungle Lodge in the trees was the first private safari outfitter in Nepal. It flourished from one house on stilts in 1965 to a multi-dimensional enterprise and continues to set standards in comfort and wildlife operations. Tiger Tops' annual World Elephant Polo tournament pits maharajahs and film stars against national park officials and corporate heads in a folly staged near the Meghauly airfield.

In total seven lodges are now licensed to lead wildlife safaris within Royal Chitwan National Park, searching for rhino, tiger and deer from atop a trained elephant; crocodiles and water fowl from canoes; wild boar and sloth bear and all of the above on foot or in vehicles. Dozens of smaller lodges operate from outside the park. Increasingly popular is the triad of outdoor excursions featuring a well planned itinerary of trekking, rafting and jungle safaris.

△ **CYCLE TERRAIN**
Mountain bikes are ideal on Nepal's labyrinth of dirt roads, pedalling around the Kathmandu Valley or venturing into the mountains.

▽ **RIVER-RAFTING**
Nepal's whitewater thrills are divided among five commercially operable rivers and attract thousands of tourists every year.

△ **FREE AS A BIRD**
Sports such as para-gliding combine high-tech equipment with nature's most spectacular views.

◁ **MOUNTAIN FLIGHT**
Microlight flights over the peaks of the Himalaya are an exhilarating way to feel close to the mountains.

PLACES

*A detailed guide to the country, with principal sites
clearly cross-referenced by number to the maps*

The unexpected oasis of the Kathmandu Valley is a green oval nestled beneath the highest mountains on earth. The valley covers an area of some 570 sq. km (220 sq. miles) and is small enough to walk across in a single day. It abounds with monuments, palaces and temples, including seven UNESCO World Heritage Sites, and a vibrant traditional culture that has managed to survive into the 21st century. The great shrines of Pashupatinath, Swayambhunath and Boudhanath exhibit the enormous wealth and devotion that has been poured into them over the centuries.

A visit to Nepal generally begins with a day in Kathmandu's Durbar Square, the old palace complex. This ensemble of art and architecture is complemented by the Durbar Squares of Patan and Bhaktapur. Each of the three former kingdoms has its own unique atmosphere. Kathmandu blends antiquity with an edgy modernity, Patan's Buddhist-influenced culture is more elegiac, while Bhaktapur has a rural feel. Like other Asian cities, Kathmandu is deluged with urban stress: roaring motorcycles and *tempos* jam the streets, and concrete "boxes" are replacing the traditional red-brick dwellings. Yet most of the valley remains peaceful countryside. Here the old ways linger, in festivals and customs. The best way to explore this realm is on foot or bicycle. At every turn natural wonders are evident: the towering white Himalaya to the north, the emerald green of paddy fields or the shimmering gold of a mustard field.

But Kathmandu Valley is not the only destination in Nepal. There is also the laid-back resort of Pokhara, where mountain peaks appear to float above the serene lake. The sal-forested hills and riverine grasslands of Royal Chitwan National Park shelter tigers and the Asian one-horned rhinoceros. Other destinations in Central Nepal include Gorkha, ancestral home of the Shah kings; Lumbini, the birthplace of Lord Buddha; the mountain views of Daman; the road to Tibet; or a rafting trip down the Trisuli River.

Because of its rugged terrain, much of Nepal is inaccessible by road and it is necessary to do as the locals do: walk. A trek can range from a half-hour to a month or more, from low-altitude farmland to high mountain landscapes. The Annapurna region is rich in easy, short rambles as well as longer treks. Solu-Khumbu, the home of Mount Everest, and the Langtang, Gosainkund and Helambu regions all offer a number of short or long treks. Beyond these three trekking regions lies a wealth of opportunities: the Manaslu Circuit; the Kanchenjunga region; mysterious Mustang. After the scenery, many trekkers find their most vivid memories focus on the friendliness of the people met along the way and the exposure to traditional life.❏

PRECEDING PAGES: Kalinchowk, a holy Shiva site; terracing in the Himalayan foothills; prayer flags at Pharping; King Bhupathindra surveys Bhaktapur Durbar Square.
LEFT: Buddhist monk in the high Sherpa country of east Nepal.

Nepal

0   50 km
0   50 miles

CHINA

Zhari Namco
Tangra
Numco
Ngangze
Co

Ruldoy Zangbo
Amzhong
Cogen Zangbo
Monco
Bunnyi

Budarongding
Daggyai
Co

Xuru
Co

N y a i n q e n t a n g l h a   S h a n

Quinglag

Linkakuoka

Yagmo

Liasi
Nyugu
Patsakuh

Lhasa

Linkuo

Lage
Gyatro
Sangsang
Rutog

Tibet

Gyagya

Pabai
Dzong
Kaika
Nigapring
Kyim

Raka Zangbo

Silong

Chhatan Bhanjyang
5666
Zhonka
Zhong
Tatzu
Zangbo Jiang

T s i e r i   R a n g e

Quxar

Lugula Bhanjyang
5870
Baruduksun

Paikü
Co

Mainpu

B u r t r a   R a n g e

L a d a k h   R a n g e

Xegar
Sa'gya

Annapurna
Conservation
Area

Nylma
Zongga
Siling

Chamuta

Dinggye
Dobzha
Como
Chamling

Manaslu
8163
Himal Chuli
7893

Lukuwa

Lapsang Karbo
7150

H I M A L

Xixabangma
Feng
8013

Phurbichachu Himal

Yala

Niehen

Tashikhang
Changmu

MarSyangdi

Buri Gandaki

Dhunche

Cho Oyu
8201

A Y A

Besisahar
Gandaki
Gorkha
Dhabe

Langtang
Himal

Langtang
National Park

Melamchigaun

Sermathang

Khumbu Himal

Sagarmatha
National
Park

8501
Lhotse

Dashingha

Janak Himal

Tharpu
Dumre
Manakamana
Trisuli
Bazaar

Mahakal

Barabise

Chhule
8850
Mount
Everest

Makalu
8463

Chamlan Himal

Umbak Himal

Kangchenjunga
8586

Muglin
Bhatapur
Shivapuri Watershed
and Wildlife Reserve

Bhote Kosi

Namche
Bazar

Lukla

Bharatpur
Jagatpur

Kathmandu
Patan
Bhaktapur

Charikot
Jiri

Najin

Makalu-Barun
National
Park

Uwa

Thudam

Helok

Narayani
Royal Chitwan
National Park
Parsa
Wildlife Reserve

Pharping

Dhulikhel
Panauti

Lele
Hetauda

Ringmo

Kerun

Kosi

Dobhan

Mechi

Gobarthana

Amlekhganj

S i w a l i k (C h u r i a) R a n g e

N E P A L

Okhaldhunga
Sun Kosi

Lamidanda

Bhojpur

Terhathum

Phidim

INDIA

Phatalaia

Sindhulimadi

Tamur

Narkatiaganj
Chanpatia

Simra

Janakpur

Katari

Dhankuta

Ilam

Darjiling
Cart
Road

Bettiah
Raxaul
Birganj

Patharkot

Dhalkebar

Sagarmatha

Dharan

Kannem
Uttar Bagdogra

Sonbarsa

Balragnia

Sitamarhi

Madhwapur

Janakpur

Mahendranagar

Kosi Tappu
Wildlife Reserve

Madhumalla

Birtamod

Motihari

Belsand

Jaynagar

Rajbiraj

Bhantaban
Birpur

Bhadrapur

Gopalganj
Mirganj

Deoria

Madhubani
Ihanjharpur

Nirmali

Forbesganj

Biratnagar

Gopalpur

Siwan
Maharaganj

Muzaffarpur

Darbhanga

Supaul

Raiganj

Basantpur

BANGLADESH

Laiganj

Samastipur

Saharsa

Dalkola

Chhapra

Rusera

Kishanganj

Purnia

Arrah
Dinapur
Patna
Teghra

Katihar

KATHMANDU

*Nepal's capital is slowly turning into a modern metropolis, but
within its bustling streets and squares remain numerous temples
and monuments of great beauty and historical significance*

Map
on page
162–3

Kathmandu

The founding of Kathmandu, the capital of Nepal and its only large city, is estimated to have taken place during the Licchavi period, beginning in about AD 300, although recent archaeological excavations at Hadigaon indicate even earlier settlements. However, it was not until the time of the Mallas, from the 14th century onwards, that the city began to develop in earnest, together with neighbouring Patan and Bhaktapur. During the golden age of these Malla city-states, their splendid Durbar Squares vied for artistic ascendancy. Today, Kathmandu forms the hub of the surrounding valley, its atmospheric temples and shrines holding their own amid the growing urban sprawl, clamouring traffic and increasing pollution that is the modern legacy.

The centre of Kathmandu's old city and the structure from which it derives its name, is the Kasthamandap or "House of Wood". This impressively large pavilion was built in the 12th century at the crossroads of two important trade routes and was originally used as a community centre for trade and barter. The city developed in radial fashion from this hub, the old Royal Palace and Durbar Square being constructed soon afterwards.

With the unification of the valley in the 14th century, King Jayasthiti Malla selected Kathmandu as his capital. Considerable expansion took place from this time, with the main activity focusing on the palace complex itself, which also served as the administrative headquarters. Nevertheless, the diagonal trade route running from the Kasthamandap through Asan Tol maintained its commercial importance, as indeed it still does today as a thriving and busy bazaar.

LEFT: Asan Tol.
BELOW: the former
Royal Palace.

Architectural legacy

The forest of temples that comprises Kathmandu's Durbar Square represents a style of architecture that generally changed very little throughout the centuries. Only a trained eye can differentiate between earlier and later artistry in traditional Nepalese buildings. When damaged by age or earthquakes, temples would customarily be replaced in the same form as the old building. While King Prithvi Narayan Shah, the founder of the Shah dynasty who conquered the valley in 1769, enhanced the magnificent Malla buildings, richly decorated with woodcarving, metalwork and gilding, it was not until the mid-19th century that dramatic changes in architecture occurred, with the introduction of European neoclassical styles by the Rana rulers. The contrast with Nepalese architecture was striking. Jung Bahadur, the founder of the Rana regime, returned in 1850 from a visit to France and England with visions of grandeur. Ladies were encouraged to adapt their styles to Victorian fashions, and anything European was admired.

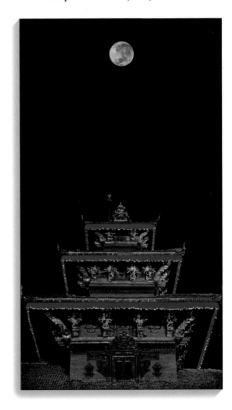

Kathmandu

200 m
200 yds

Pashupatinath, Boudhanath

Budhanilkantha

NAXAL

GAHIRIDHARA

Tukucha Khola

Siwa Mandir

Nag Pokhari

HATTISAAR

Kamal Pokhari

Jai Nepal Chitra Ghar

LAZIMPAT

Lazimpat

Narayan Mandir

Naxal
Narayan Hiti

Nepal International Clinic

Casino Royale

Royal Nepal Academy

Lal Durbar

BAGH BAZAR

DILLI BAZAR

Narayanhiti Royal Palace

Seto Durbar

Everest Cultural Society

KAMALADI

Kamaladi

French Cultural Centre

Durbar Marg

Kanti Path

LAINCHAUR

British Council

Bishojyoti Cinema Hall

Clock Tower

Rani Pokhari
(Queen's Pond)

Lekhnath Marg

Keshar Mahal

Library

Tridevi Marg

Bahadur Bhawan

Jyatha

National Theatre

ASAN TOL

Bhagwan Bahal

THAMEL

KWABAHAL

Chusya Bahal

KAMALACHI

Annapurna Mandir

MAHABUDDHA

PAKNAJOL

Chhetrapati

Kwa Bahal

Swachagu Ganesh

Musya Bahal

Thahiti Stupa

Dhoka Bahal

Uma-Maheshvara

Ikha Narayan

Ugratara

Haku Bahal

Vaisha Dev

Krishna Temple

Lunchen
Lun Bun Ajima

Seto Machhendranath

KHEL TOL

Chhetrapati Bandstand

Kathe Simbhu

THAHITI

NAGHAL

Jana Bahal

Hum Bahal

BANGEMUDHA

Bangemudha

Dhobichaur

DHALKO

CHHETRAPATI

Nyata Ganesh

Nara Devi

Narsingh Mandir

Yatkha Bahal

Kanga

KALDHARA

Kaldhara

DHOBICHAUR

Raktakali

TENGAL

NARDEVI

Kankeswari

Luti Ajima Mandir

Vishnumati

Swayambhunath
Natural History Museum

Balaju

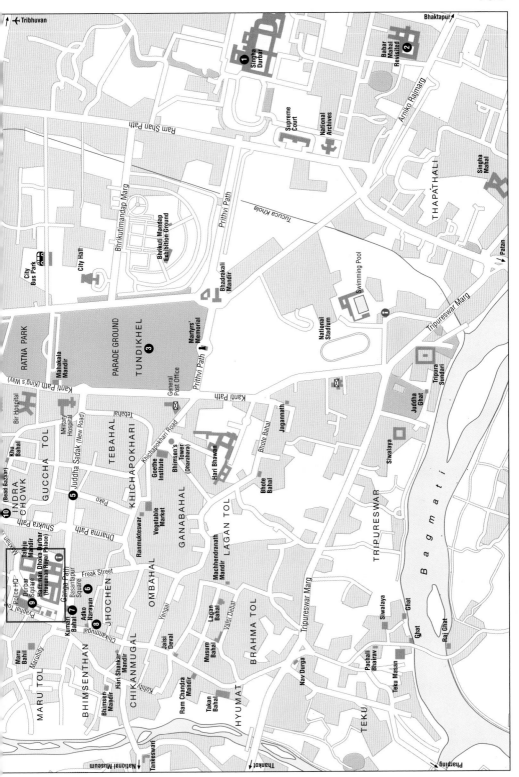

← Tribhuvan

Bhaktapur ➚

1 Singha Durbar

2 Bahar Mahal Revisited

Supreme Court

National Archives

Ram Shah Path

Prithvi Path

Tucuca Khola

THAPATHALI

Singha Mahal

↘ Patan

Bhrikutimandap Marg

Bhrikuti Mandap Exhibition Ground

City Hall

City Bus Park

Bhadrakali Mandir

Swimming Pool

Tripureswar Marg

RATNA PARK

Mahakala Mandir

PARADE GROUND

TUNDIKHEL

3

Martyrs' Memorial

National Stadium

i

Tripura Sundari

Juddha Ghat

Kanti Path (King's Way)

General Post Office

Prithvi Path

Kanti Path

Bir Hospital

Khu Bahal

Military Hospital

Tebahal

Goethe Institute

Bhimsen's Tower (Dharahara)

Jaganath

Bhote Bahal

Siwalaya

GUCCHA TOL

Khichapokhari Road

Hari Bhawan

Bhote Bahal

INDRA CHOWK

(Bead Bazaar)

10

Juddha Sadak (New Road)

5

Pako

TEBAHAL

KHICHAPOKHARI

Ranmukteswar

Vegetable Market

GANABAHAL

LAGAN TOL

TRIPURESWAR

B a g m a t i

Shukra Path

Dharma Path

Machhendranath Mandir

OMBAHAL

Freak Street

Basantapur Square

6

Yengal

Tripureswar Marg

Siwalaya

Ghat

Talèju Mandir

Hanuman Dhoka Durbar (Hanuman Royal Palace)

Ganga Path

Durbar Square

i

Police HQ

9

Paphal Tol

Kumari Bahal

7

Adko Narayan

8

JHOCHEN

Lagan Bahal

Tatsi Debal

BRAHMA TOL

Pachali Bharav

Teku Masan

Ghat

Raj Ghat

Maru Bahil

Marulity

Bhimsen Mandir

BHIMSENTHAN

Hari Shankar Mandir

Kohiti

CHIKANMUGAL

Chikanmugal

Jaisi Deval

Musum Bahal

Nav Durga

Siwalaya

MARU TOL

Ram Chandra Mandir

Takan Bahal

HYUMAT

TEKU

Tankeswari

National Museum

↙ Thankot

↙ Pharping

The sumptuous Rana palaces of Jung Bahadur and his family numbered several hundred throughout the valley. They boasted elaborate plasterwork and imposing columns and were entirely furnished from Europe, with crystal chandeliers and gilt and velvet furniture. Many still survive, though in a rather tarnished condition. Taken over by the government or private organisations for offices or schools, today they are mere shadows of their former selves.

Rows of flagpoles at the Royal Palace bear the world's only non-rectangular flag: Nepal's flag is two superimposed red triangles with white sun and moon emblems.

The culmination of this architectural vogue was the grand palace of **Singha Durbar ❶**, which now houses Nepal's Parliament, the prime minister's office and several ministries. A building of gigantic proportion and size, it consisted of 17 courtyards and as many as 1,700 rooms and was reputed to be the largest palace in Asia. It was built over a period of only 11 months in 1901. In 1973 much of it was damaged by a mysterious fire but several courtyards were rebuilt and the imposing white facade restored.

Another example of fine architecture can be seen in the city's most elegant shopping venue, **Babar Mahal Revisited ❷**. An old Rana palace has been restored and converted into a number of smart boutiques, bars and restaurants. Treasures range from colourful Indian handicrafts to hand-woven silks, exquisite *thangkas*, sturdy old brass and fine Tibetan carpets. Babar Mahal lies just south of Singha Durbar, in the neighbourhood of Maitighar.

Modern Kathmandu

BELOW: Singha Durbar, home of parliament and government ministries.

Under the Ranas, the suburbs of Kathmandu began to expand and the traditional Newari concept of a tightly knit city preserving every square metre of precious arable land was lost. By the 1960s Western-style dwellings of concrete and glass began appearing on the outskirts of the city. In the past two decades Kath-

mandu's growing pains have multiplied considerably with explosive urbanisation. Increased industry and a population that numbers over 800,000 has led to widespread and indiscriminate "infilling" that is changing the face of the city. Precious rice-growing land is being lost to brick factories and private houses are built on every available terrace. Very little land within the Ring Road is left undeveloped – a marked contrast to even the recent past, when vegetable plots could still be found within city limits.

As a result of the different styles of planning, Kathmandu is divided into two quite distinct parts. The **Tundikhel ❸**, the long open expanse of grassland used as the central parade ground and meeting place, separates the old medieval city to the west from the expanding eastern part with its mushrooming modern buildings. Traffic flows clockwise around the Tundikhel – or, more and more frequently nowadays, becomes snarled in enormous honking traffic jams (the number of vehicles in the city has tripled in the past 10 years). The southern end is marked by the Martyrs' Memorial and the slim white landmark form of the **Bhimsen Tower**. At the northern end is Rani Pokhari, a tank with a small white shrine in the centre, built by Pratap Malla's queen in memory of their dead son.

Two main thoroughfares extend north from Tundikhel. Kanti Path leads up to Thamel, with its backpacker hostels and restaurants, eventually becoming Lazimpat and running through the embassy district. Parallel to Kanti Path to the east is the premier office street of **Durbar Marg**, at the north end of which is the modern **Narayanhiti Royal Palace ❹** (open daily 10am–5pm; entrance fee) the residence of the royal family. Durbar Marg is the main artery of the modern, commercial part of town with its banks, travel agencies, airline offices and restaurants, and is the city's most desirable address.

Map on page 162–3

The Bhimsen Tower, built in 1832 by Prime Minister Bhimsen Thapa.

BELOW: curd shop

Despite all the development, Kathmandu still manages to retain its rural atmosphere, even in downtown areas with their veneer of sophistication. A herd of goats or ducks may crowd the pavement and cows, seemingly aware of their sacred status, ruminate contentedly in the middle of the road. The crime of cow-slaughter in Hindu Nepal is punishable by imprisonment and a hefty fine.

New Road

The old city of Kathmandu has remained intact through the centuries, except for **Juddha Sadak (New Road)** ❺, so called as it was rebuilt after the major earthquake of 1934. This wide street runs west from the Tundikhel, where an arch spans the road adjacent to the Royal Nepal Airlines Building, notable for the bronze sculpture of a yeti bearing a tray. Further west the road becomes known as Ganga Path.

This major commercial axis is the hub of the new consumer society that has flourished since Nepal opened up to the West. Electronic goods, imported clothes, cameras, rental videos, watches and jewellery are all available here. Halfway up on the left, shoeshine boys congregate beneath a spreading pipal tree where men gather to peruse the morning newspapers.

At the statue of Juddha Shamsher Rana, under whose direction the street was built, is the cavernous supermarket of Bishal Bazaar. But the area's modern image is only skin-deep. Branching off from here, narrow side-lanes thrust between rows of traditional houses. These alleys end in squares with corner *patis*, central *chaityas* and shrines.

The first lane off to the left after the statue is **Freak Street**, the famous 1960s haunt of long-haired hippies. Today's young world travellers favour the laid-

BELOW:
sacred cows mingle with traffic and children in the Kathmandu bazaar.

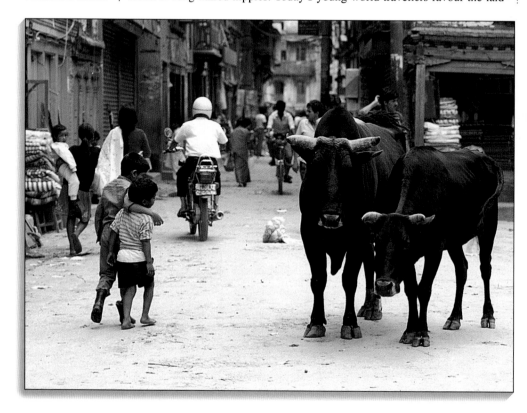

back atmosphere of the lake at Pokhara as their hangout *(see page 229)*, or the lodges and restaurants of Thamel and Chetrapati, in the northern part of Kathmandu. The hippies have long since gone – King Birendra's coronation in 1975 initially encouraged their departure and today's visa laws discourage dalliance.

The open brick platform at the top of New Road on the left is **Basantapur Square ❻**, formerly a vegetable market and before that, the home of the royal elephants. Souvenir and trinket vendors display their wares on long tables lined with red cloth. The Hanuman Dhoka *(see page 170)* looms on the right and the graceful temple silhouettes beckon visitors into the Kathmandu Durbar Square.

The living goddess

Kumari Bahal (House of the Living Goddess) ❼, is the 18th-century stucco temple with intricately carved windows on the far (west) side of the square. The elaborate woodcarving in the inner courtyard, where the *Kumari* or "living goddess" herself may be glimpsed, is even more remarkable than that on the exterior. The *Kumari* is considered to be the incarnation of the "virgin goddess". Stories of her origins vary, but this particular *Kumari* is known as the "Royal *Kumari*", to distinguish her from others in the valley and because she is worshipped by the king. Except for the religious festival of Indrajatra *(see page 89)* she never leaves her *bahal*, and then she is escorted in a suitably splendid procession in a flower-bedecked chariot pulled by devotees. Custom dictates her feet must never touch the ground.

The living goddess is chosen from a selection of girls of four or five years of age, all belonging to the Sakya clan of Newari goldsmiths and silversmiths. The *Kumari*'s body must be flawless and must satisfy 32 specified, distinctive

Maps: City 162–3 Square 168

Khukris *on sale at Basantapur Square.*

LEFT: the *Kumari,* the living goddess.
BELOW: *torana* on the Kumari Bahal.

Torana over the door at the Kumari Bahal.

signs. After enduring a number of tests, she confirms her selection to the attendant priests by choosing the clothing and ornaments of the previous *Kumari* from among a large collection of similar items. Astrologers must be assured that her horoscope is in harmony with that of the king and then she is settled into the *bahal*, which becomes her home until she reaches puberty or otherwise loses blood, as from a small wound.

When the term of the *Kumari* comes to an end, the girl leaves the temple richly endowed and free to marry. Recent *Kumaris* have returned to normal lives, though there is an unhappy tradition that the ex-goddess brings bad luck to a household and early death to her husband.

As you leave the *bahal* of the *Kumari*, the **Adko Narayan (Temple of Narayan)** ❽ is on your immediate left. The triple-roofed structure on a five-tiered plinth was built in 1670 and provides an excellent vantage point during festivals. On ordinary days the plinths are thronged with traders hawking their wares, farmers resting with their burdens and people chatting or simply watching and enjoying the atmosphere.

Durbar Square

BELOW:
Ganesh figurine at Ashok Binayak.

Kathmandu's **Durbar Square** ❾, with more than 50 temples and monuments packed into its compact area, is at the heart of the old city and top of the list on most people's sightseeing itineraries. Start at the western end to enjoy the most complete view of the square, and then walk into the beginning of the small street called Maru Tol to find the famed **Kasthamandap (House of Wood)** Ⓐ which represents the very centre of the city. One of the oldest buildings in the valley, it dates from the 12th century and supposedly gave Kathmandu its name.

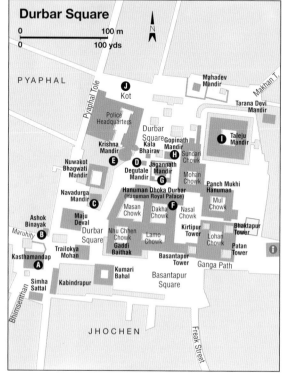

The Kasthamandap was originally a community centre, and was later turned into a temple dedicated to Gorakhnath. The god sits in the centre of the platform in a wooden enclosure. A pair of bronze lions guard the entrance and carvings along the first-storey cornice depict Hindu epic literature.

Hidden behind the Kasthamandap is the small but very important golden shrine of **Ashok Binayak Ⓑ**, also known as Maru Ganesh. A constant flow of worshippers here offers devotions to the obliging elephant-headed god; in particular those departing on a journey pay a visit beforehand to ensure a safe trip. The number of visitors increases noticeably on Tuesdays and Saturdays, unlucky days dedicated to Ganesh. Across the way is a large and amusing gilt image of Ganesh's mount, the rat.

Returning to the square, the large Maju Deval Shiva Temple dominates the left side, its three roofs towering over a steep nine-step plinth. Note the **Navadurga Temple Ⓒ** on the left. A folksy image of Shiva and Parvati, carved in wood and painted crudely but with great charm, gazes benignly down from the central window of the upper balcony.

A statue of King Pratap Malla is set on a stone column at the entrance of the second part of the square. He faces the inner sanctum of his private prayer room on the third floor of the **Degutale Temple Ⓓ** dedicated to the royal deity. Opposite the entrance to Hanuman Dhoka Durbar stands the small octagonal **Krishna Mandir Ⓔ**. On the right a large wooden lattice screen hides the huge gilded face of the Seto Bhairav, a fierce figure who is revealed only during the Indrajatra festival between August and September. At that time he is showered with rice and flowers and *chhang* (rice beer) flows out of his mouth, poured from a tank above to refresh the crowd.

Maps: City 162–3 Square 168

BELOW: the White Bhairav in Durbar Square.

The Hanuman statue's evil eye is said to deter the entrance of malign spirits, while the thick sindhur paste protects innocent devotees from coming to harm.

BELOW:
setting up shop in Durbar Square.

Hanuman Dhoka Durbar

The Durbar Square is dominated by **Hanuman Dhoka Durbar (Hanuman Royal Palace)** , the former seat of power (open Wed–Mon 10.30am–4pm; closes 2pm on Friday; entrance fee). It is flanked by a 1672 statue of the monkey-god Hanuman, smeared with red paste and shaded by an umbrella. The palace gate is colourfully painted and guarded by soldiers in the black-and-white Malla uniform.

On the immediate left as you enter is a sculpture of Narsingh, an incarnation of Vishnu as a man-lion tearing apart the demon Hiranya-Kashipu. The first courtyard is Nassal Chowk where important royal ceremonies and festivals take place, including coronations – *nassal* means "the dancing one". The north end of the courtyard is an arched gallery with portraits of the modern Shah dynasty. In the corner are the five round roofs of a temple dedicated to the five-faced deity Pancha Mukhi Hanuman.

The palace complex is a series of 14 courtyards whose main structure was built by the Mallas, though its origins are Licchavi. The superb woodcarvings for which it is renowned testify to the Mallas' artistry *(see page 75)*. The construction began in the north with the two courtyards, Mohan Chowk and Sundari Chowk, built for King Pratap Malla in the 16th century, and progressed south. King Prithvi Narayan Shah renovated and added to the palace complex after his conquest of the valley in 1769. He is responsible for the nine-storey Basantapur Tower and the smaller towers of Kirtipur, Patan and Bhaktapur. All four are set around the Lohan Chowk and are said to have been contributed by citizens of the towns after which they are named.

Climb up the steep staircase of Basantapur Tower for superb views of the

STOLEN RELICS

The Kathmandu Valley is often called an "open-air museum" and part of its charm comes from the great quantity of ancient art found in temple courtyards and riverside fields. Sadly, organised art trafficking has moved in to despoil this heritage, fuelled in recent years by the desire of private collectors for "chic" Asian images. Even holy relics are not exempt: several years ago a sacred artefact said to be a piece of the Buddha's bone, donated to Nepal by Sri Lanka, was dug up from its site in Swayambhunath. Artist and historian Lain Singh Bangdel documents this cultural plunder in his book *The Stolen Images of Nepal.* Page after page of ancient stone sculptures are depicted, alongside photos of their now-vacant settings. The overall effect is heartbreaking. Images may be wrenched out of their settings or sawn off at the feet. If the head alone is considered valuable enough, the figure may be decapitated. Local people have sought to protect remaining images by caging them behind elaborate metalwork, as with the grilles enclosing Kathmandu's Seto Machhendranath Temple or encasing two gilt Tara images at Swayambhunath, although clumsy efforts to cement stone images to their setting have predictably diminished the beauty of the sculpture.

city spread out below, ringed by snowy mountains, and admire the erotic carvings on the base of the struts of the tower.

After the Ranas came to power in 1846, further changes were made and the white stucco western wing with the neoclassical facade was added. Hanuman Dhoka Durbar was extensively restored by a UNESCO programme prior to King Birendra's coronation in 1975. The palace complex houses three small museums dedicated to kings Birendra, Mahendra and Tribhuvan. Admission to the exhibits is included in the ticket to the palace complex. Displays include personal memorabilia, old photographs and news clippings documenting the dynasty's recent history.

The royal deity

Returning to the square, there are more erotic carvings on the struts of the two-tiered 17th-century **Jagannath Mandir G**, the oldest structure in this area. Next to this temple is **Gopinath Mandir H** with three roofs and a three-stepped plinth. Nearby, the terrifying **Black (Kala) Bhairav** relief is a masterpiece, highly admired and revered as a form of Shiva. This fierce god wears a garland of skulls and has eight arms, carrying six swords, an axe and a shield. He tramples a corpse, the symbol of human ignorance. He is never without offerings of the faithful, placed in his skull bowl. The Black Bhairav is believed to punish anyone who tells lies in front of him by causing them to bleed to death. In the past, criminals were dragged before the image and forced to swear their innocence while touching its feet. Conveniently, the image is located directly across from the city's main police station.

This northeastern end of Durbar Square is dominated by the magnificent

Maps:
City 162–3
Square
168

The Black (Kala) Bhairav peers down over dishonest citizens.

BELOW:
Jagannath Mandir
in Durbar Square.

Beads for sale at the Potey Pasaal market-place, Indra Chowk.

three-tiered gilded **Taleju Mandir** , Kathmandu's largest temple, built on a huge stepped platform and dedicated to the royal deity, the goddess Taleju Bhawani. The walled precinct is considered so sacred that it is off-limits to all but the king and certain priests; ordinary Hindus are allowed access once a year during the Durga Puja of the Dasain festival *(see page 89)*. The Taleju Bhawani is a South Indian goddess who was brought to Nepal in the 14th century and enshrined as the ruling family's special deity – shrines to her were also erected in Bhaktapur and Patan. The temple was built in 1562 by King Mahendra Malla and, according to legend, human sacrifices used to be performed here until the goddess became displeased with such practices. Human sacrifices were outlawed in 1780.

At the northwestern end of Durbar Square is an open courtyard called the **Kot** ❾ or "armoury". Now part of police quarters and army barracks, this is the site of the terrible "Kot Massacre" in which the young army officer Jung Bahadur Rana murdered almost all the Nepal aristocracy and his political rivals, enabling him to establish the Rana regime in 1846 *(see page 32)*.

Bazaars and temples

Leaving Durbar Square, a *garuda* statue lies half-buried in the street. Cast a glance at the little Tarana Devi Mandir hidden behind the Taleju Mandir before getting swallowed up in the activity and distractions of the Makhan Tol bazaar. There are many temples and courtyards of interest and it is worth detouring as you explore the old bazaar areas on foot.

BELOW: rickshaw for hire in Thamel.

Indra Chowk ❿ is an animated and picturesque junction of six streets. The gilded griffins rearing their bodies up in front of the rambling shrine to Akash Bhairav are particularly distinctive. This temple houses a deity said to have fallen magically from the sky. The image of the deity is displayed in public only once a year, during the lively eight-day Indrajatra festival – one of Kathmandu's most important celebrations *(see page 89)*.

This area traditionally sells blankets and textiles, including the soft wool pashmina shawls which have recently become popular as fashion items in the West *(see page 81)*. Shop carefully, however, as cheaper acrylic substitutes abound.

Tucked behind an old building through a narrow entrance is the glittering magic of the **Potey Pasaal**, or "Bead Bazaar", where every day is like Christmas. Cross-legged merchants sit in tiny stalls, presiding over colourful displays of glass beads imported from as far afield as Europe and Japan. Combinations can be pieced together while you wait into any item you wish – earrings, necklaces, bracelets or belts. Nepalese women prefer red or green beads, often adorned with a single faceted gold bead or *tilhari* that symbolises marriage.

Khel Tol ⓫, which is beyond Indra Chowk, is the oldest trading segment of the bazaar and there is a constant coming and going of farmers, pedestrians, rickshaws, motorcycles and cars forcing their way through the narrow lane. All manner of goods can be bought in the shops, ranging from bangles, saris and the red yarn tassels that women braid into their hair, to the large copper pots for festival feasts.

Turn left into a courtyard marked by a tall carved pillar and enter one of the most venerated shrines in the whole kingdom. The **Seto Machhendranath** ⓬ is a beautiful structure standing in the middle of a monastic courtyard. Within the shrine is a form of Avalokiteshvara, known as Machhendra, the guardian deity of the valley and the most compassionate of all the gods. This white *(seto)* god is pulled in a huge chariot through the streets of Kathmandu during the lively four-day Seto Machhendra festival held annually between March and April *(see page 86)*. The entrance to this temple is guarded by magnificent brass lions. Within the courtyard there is rich ornamentation and decoration, most of it dating from the 17th century, though the complex almost certainly has earlier origins.

It could be said that **Asan Tol** is the real heart of the old city. Traditionally a grain market and a place to hire porters, this crossroads is constantly thronged with people. It also features several temples. Most notable among these is the elaborately decorated little Annapurna Temple, dedicated to the goddess of plenty, here represented by an overflowing pot or *purna kalash* which symbolises abundance. Devotees often toss in offerings of a few coins to bring good fortune. Produce sellers line the streets feeding into Asan, providing fresh vegetables daily for Kathmandu's downtown residents.

Two roads lead east from Asan Tol, both emerging on Kanti Path, opposite Rani Pokhari. Beyond this fenced-in lake the solid white clocktower of the **Trichandra College** is visible, built by the Ranas. To the right is the open expanse of the Tundikhel *(see page 165)*.

Maps: City
162–3
Square
168

BELOW: Asan Tol is always teeming with people.

Map on page 162–3

Showing the way to the gentlemen's public bathrooms.

To see more of the old city take the road leading directly north from Indra Chowk, which passes several shrines, stupas and courtyards worth exploring. In the Bangemudha neighbourhood look for the "Toothache Shrine", a nail-studded chunk of wood. Toothache sufferers transfer their pain by hammering in a nail around the tiny gilded image of Vaisha Dev, the "god of toothache". Nearby dentists, with their window displays of dentures, take a more worldly approach.

A few steps further is the striking white Buddhist stupa of **Kathe Simbhu** ⑬, built as a replica of Swayambhunath as a convenience for those who are physically unable to climb up the steep steps to that hilltop shrine *(see page 193)*. Across the road, look for a beautiful 9th-century sculpture of Shiva and Parvati, also known as Uma-Mahesvara. Shops in this area specialise in cloth from neighbouring countries, from brilliant Chinese brocades to Bhutanese striped cottons and bolts of Tibetan prayer flags. The white stupa of Thahiti, ringed with prayer wheels, marks the transition from old town into new.

World travellers

BELOW:
Thamel caters to all backpackers' needs.
RIGHT:
masked dancers in the courtyard of Hanuman Dhoka Durbar.

The narrow streets north of here take on a distinctly Western air as you reach the tourist areas of **Chhetrapati** ⑭ and eventually **Thamel** ⑮. Favoured by world travellers and cost-conscious trekkers, Thamel is a jumble of budget hotels, lodges and restaurants, a neighbourhood where trekking equipment and *thangka* shops jostle for space with carpet and clothes stalls. This is the place to buy embroidered T-shirts, turquoise-encrusted silver jewellery, cotton dresses, English-language paperbacks, excellent chocolate cake and any number of souvenirs and fake antiques proffered by vendors. More illicit items such as hashish are also plentiful, as hissing street salesman ("hashhhhhhh, madame...") will soon inform you. Thamel is a world in itself, a budget paradise or hell, depending on your perspective. Its international flavour and bargains are intriguing, but it bears little resemblance to anything Nepalese.

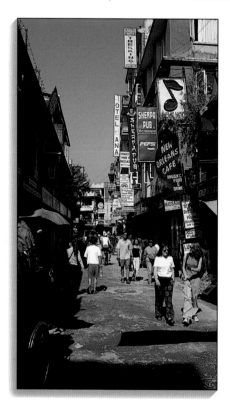

The name "Thamel" encompasses a number of smaller neighbourhoods, but the heart of the action is focused in the area around the Kathmandu Guesthouse. Several blocks east, Tridevi Marg runs into Kanti Path and Narayanhiti Royal Palace. At the intersection is **Keshar Mahal**, an old Rana palace now housing the Ministry of Education and Culture. The extensive book collection of its owner, historian Kaiser J.B. Rana, is open to the public. The setting alone is worth a visit: suits of armour and a stuffed tiger mingle with marble nymphs, old oil paintings and a fine collection of Rana hunting photographs.

To the west of Thamel, more traditional old Newari neighbourhoods such as Dhalko and Dhobichaur stretch down to the Vishnumati River. Both the Luti Ajima Temple on the river's near bank and the Shobha Bhagwati Temple on the far bank are well-patronised local shrines, interspersed with cremation sites. Further on is the Hotel Vajra, with its art gallery, library and cultural events. The nearby **Natural History Museum** (open Wed–Mon; entrance fee) displays local flora and fauna . ❑

PATAN

Maps:
Area 194
City 178

*One of the Kathmandu Valley's three ancient capitals, Patan is rich
in temples and traditional architecture, as well as being
the centre of Nepal's thriving carpet industry*

L ocated on a plateau above the Bagmati River a short distance south of
Kathmandu, **Patan ❶** is known as a centre of fine arts, partly due to the
superb craftsmanship of its artisans. Essentially a Buddhist city, Patan is
said to have been founded by Emperor Ashoka in the 3rd century BC although no
historical proof of this exists. Patan is also called Lalitpur, "The Beautiful City".

Four main roads radiate from the **Durbar Square** to the four Ashoka stupas, brick and grass mounds marking the boundaries of the city, more evocative
for their historical relevance than their architectural interest. Historic inscriptions
establish Patan as an important town from early times. **Mangal Bazaar**, an
area adjoining the Durbar Square, may have been the site of King Manadeva's
palace in the 5th century. The city's greatest building period took place under the
Mallas from the 16th to 18th centuries. Most of the monuments seen today
were built or rebuilt at that time. With no fewer that 136 *bahals* or courtyards
and 55 major temples, Patan is really the cradle of arts and architecture of the
valley, a great centre both of the Newari Buddhist religion and of traditional arts
and crafts *(see page 75)*. Patan's Durbar Square has been acclaimed as one of
the finest urban streetscapes in the world.

LEFT: Vishnu,
preserver of life.
BELOW: Patan's
Durbar Square.

The Royal Palace

The ancient north-south and east-west access roads
divide Patan neatly into four geographic sections,
which meet at the Durbar Square and Royal Palace
complex. A spectacular example of Newari architecture, the **Royal Palace ❹**, with its walled gardens on
the eastern side of the square, is faced by a dozen temples of various sizes and styles. Residential houses
occupy the other three sides of the square.

The palace consists of three main *chowks* or courtyards which open onto the square. The southernmost
and smallest is the Sundari Chowk which has in its
centre a masterpiece of stone architecture and carving,
the sunken royal bath called Tusha Hiti. Created
around 1670, the walls of the bath are decorated with
a double row of statuettes representing the eight Ashta
Matrikas, the eight Bhairavs and the eight Nagas.
Many of these are now missing. Two stone snakes
(*nagas*) girdle the top of the basin into which water
flows through a stone spout gilded with metal. The
three-storey buildings around the chowk contain a
corner temple and have wonderfully carved windows
and grilles in metal and ivory. Stone images of
Ganesh, Hanuman and Narsingh guard the outside of
this courtyard.

The oldest courtyard is the central Mul Chowk,
built in 1666 for Srinivasa Malla. The low two-storey
residence of the Patan royal family encloses a

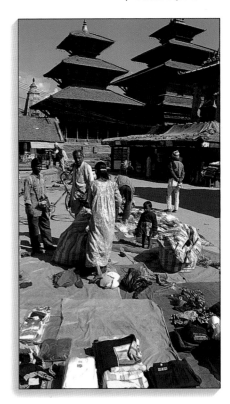

A sadhu with his snake at Patan's Durbar Square.

courtyard with a small gilded central shrine, the Bidya Mandir. The Shrine of Taleju is guarded by two fine *repoussé* brass images of Ganga on a tortoise and Jamuna on a mythical crocodile-like figure.

Towering over this part of the palace, in the northeast corner of the Mul Chowk is the triple-roofed octagonal tower of the **Taleju Bhawani Temple**, built in about 1666 and housing the royal deity. Images of Shiva and Parvati crown the much-admired "Golden Gate" leading to the third northern courtyard, the Mani Keshab Narayan Chowk. Recently restored, it now houses the **Patan Museum ③** (open Wed–Mon 10am–5pm, Fri closes at 3pm; entrance fee). Beautifully designed galleries are dedicated to Hindu and Buddhist art, and the display concludes with an exhibit of rare photographs. The small open-air restaurant is a pleasant place for lunch. Between this and the central chowk is the temple of Degutale, the personal deity of the Malla kings. Surmounted with a four-roof tower and originally built in 1640, the kings once performed their sacred Tantric rites here.

Krishna Mandir

Facing the Sundari Chowk at the southern end of the square is the Chyasin Deval, an octagonal stone *shikhara*-style building raised by the daughter of an 18th-century king in memory of the eight wives who followed her father onto his funeral pyre. To the west is the Bhai Dega with a Shiva *lingam* within.

To the north a huge bell hangs between two pillars; nearby is the triple-roofed 17th-century **Hari Shankar Mandir ③**, with its carved roof struts and guardian stone elephants. Just north, a gilded statue of King Yoganarendra Malla prays atop a pillar, shaded by the hood of a royal cobra. The stone *shikhara* behind

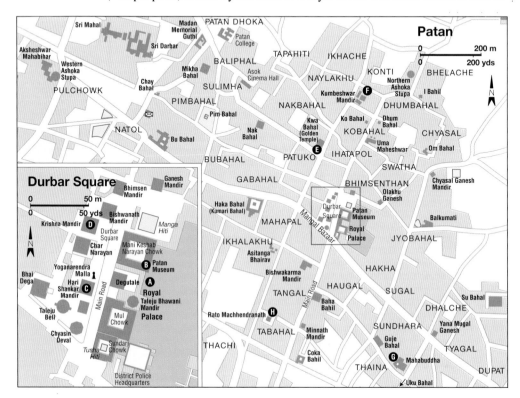

Map on page 178

dates from 1590. Beyond is a small Narayan temple that is probably the oldest surviving temple in the square, built for the god Char Narayan in 1565.

Opposite the northern courtyard of the palace is the **Krishna Mandir D**, one of the most exquisite buildings in Kathmandu Valley. Its airy colonnades show the influence of Moghul architecture from India. The first two storeys comprise a series of pavilions in smooth black stone. Encircling these are carved friezes depicting scenes from two Hindu epics, the *Mahabharata* and the *Ramayana*, with explanations etched in Newari. A slender *shikhara* emerges from the top. The temple was built in 1637 at the command of King Siddhi Narsingh Malla, following a dream he had of Krishna and Radha. A gilt statue of Garuda mounted on a high pillar faces this elegant shrine.

The next temple is the **Bishwanath Mandir**, a profusely carved and decorated double-roofed pagoda. The building collapsed in the 1990 monsoon but has been reconstructed, though the stone elephants guarding the steps are the worse for wear. The last temple is the highly venerated **Bhimsen Mandir** dedicated to Bhimsen, the god of traders, and decorated in silver and gold. This brick structure was erected in the late 17th century but the marble facade dates from Rana times. At the corner of the northern chowk is the lotus-shaped, recessed **Manga Hiti** with three carved water spouts in the shape of crocodile heads.

Northern Patan

On leaving Durbar Square there is a maze of small streets, rich in monuments of great interest. Patan is known for its *bahals*, two-storey Newari Buddhist monasteries built around courtyards, and the less elaborate *bahils*. The most renowned of these is the **Kwa Bahal E**, known as the "Golden Temple", a few minutes' walk north of Durbar Square.

This is an ancient sanctuary and legend connects its origins with a 12th-century queen. This actively patronised monastery is a large, rectangular building with three roofs and a facade richly embossed with gilded copper. The entrance is guarded by a pair of lions. Within the shrine are many images and some early bronzes. A small gilded frieze banding the temple facade depicts the life of the Buddha. The metalwork and gilding shows great craftsmanship and the central shrine is lavishly embellished. Up a wooden staircase is a Tibetan Buddhist shrine, decorated with frescoes and rafters painted with sacred *mantra*.

A little further north, the towering **Kumbeshwar Temple F** dominates an area of rural streets. The Kumbeshwar, the Nyatapola in Bhaktapur and Panch Mukhi Hanuman in Hanuman Dhoka Palace are the only temples in the valley with five roofs. Founded in 1392, the Kumbeshwar is the oldest existing temple in Patan. Its precincts are scattered with rare early sculptures and its struts, cornices and door frame are intricately carved. Two ponds in the courtyard are believed to be fed from the holy Gosainkund Lakes (*see page 254*). Dedicated to Shiva in his form of "Lord of the Water Pot", the Kumbeshwar is the focus of several colourful festivals. During the Janai Purnima pilgrims pay homage to a silver and gold *lingam* in the middle of the tank (*see page 88*).

BELOW:
Moghul-inspired
Krishna Mandir.

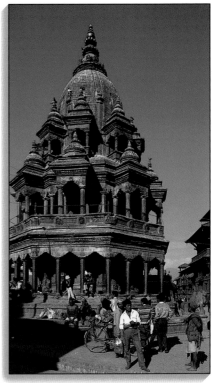

Terracotta plaque at Mahabuddha, the Temple of the Thousand Buddhas.

Patan's northern Ashoka Stupa lies a few minutes beyond Kumbeshwar in a secluded courtyard. The hemispheric mound, topped with mysterious painted eyes, is the most impressive of the city's four stupas. The road continues through fertile fields to the banks of the Bagmati River. The shrine of Sankhamul Ghat is a fascinating collection of crumbling courtyards and temples. Most notable is the brick *shikhara* of Jagat Narayan, encircled by terracotta snakes or *nagas*.

Southern Patan

Down a narrow street southeast of Durbar Square is the architectural masterpiece of **Mahabuddha** , "Temple of the Thousand Buddhas". The entrance is well marked down a lane to the right and curio shops line the route. Many specialise in the metalwork that Patan is famous for: images of Buddhist and Hindu deities and mythical animals.

Mahabuddha stands in a cramped courtyard and is a tall *shikhara* structure entirely covered by terracotta plaques depicting the Buddha. The best view is from the roof terrace of an adjacent house. Built at the end of the 16th century, the monument was damaged and rebuilt after the 1934 earthquake. The spare parts "left over" from the restoration were used to construct a smaller *shikhara* dedicated to Maya Devi, the mother of the Buddha. Further south is another monastery, the Uku Bahal, with gilded roofs and animal sculptures. The carved wooden struts on the courtyard's rear wall date from the 13th century. Written records of this shrine go back to AD 1117, making it the oldest in Patan.

Double back west through the metalworking neighbourhood of Thaina, where craftsmen make the air ring with their hammers on metal, then turn south at the Mangal Bazaar road to visit the brightly painted shrine of Minnath, a minor

BELOW: mother and child at Patan.

Map on page 178

local deity known as the "son" or "daughter" of the famous **Rato Machhendranath** Ⓗ nearby. Rato ("Red") Machhendranath dwells across the street, in a three-storey temple set in a grassy compound. A local form of the Buddhist deity Avalokiteshvara, he is venerated as Shiva by Hindus and is worshipped by all as the guardian of the valley and the god of rain and plenty. The present temple was built in 1673 and is a fine example of Newari architecture. A row of prayer wheels lines the base, while carved roof struts show the tortures of condemned souls in hell. Statues of various animals on pillars face the shrine.

The painted idol of Rato Machhendra is taken out of his shrine every year and paraded through Patan in a chariot for several weeks during the summer. This is Patan's biggest festival, designed to ensure plentiful monsoon rain *(see page 87)*. It culminates in the Bhoto Jatra festival when the king presides and the sacred bejewelled waistcoat *(bhoto)* of the serpent king is displayed. Following this ritual, the chariot is dismantled. However, every 12 years the chariot is dragged all the way to Bungamati *(see page 213)*, a village 6 km (4 miles) south of Patan where the deity spends the winter. Progress over the uneven road is slow, punctuated with prayers and offerings. Other years the deity is carried in a palanquin to his winter quarters, a 16th-century tradition.

The southern neighbourhood of **Jawalakhel** is home to Nepal's only zoo (open Tues–Sun 10am–5pm; entrance fee), a collection of rhinos, monkeys, tigers and leopards. It is also a major centre of the carpet industry *(see page 80)*. The **Tibetan Refugee Camp** established in the 1960s promoted a craft that has now become Nepal's biggest export and the largest employer in the valley. Watch the manufacturing process at the Tibetan Handicraft Centre. Weavers knot wool into traditional patterns in the main hall, chatting and singing all the while. ❑

TIP

Patan provides excellent shopping opportunities for souvenir hunters. Handicraft shops lining the Kopundol Road offer block-printed fabrics, quilted cushion covers, pottery, paintings and wooden toys.

BELOW:
Tibetan carpet weaver at work.

BHAKTAPUR

Now preserved as a UNESCO World Heritage Site, this former capital of the Kathmandu Valley is today the best-preserved medieval town in Nepal, rich in temples and traditional architecture

Maps:
City 184
Area 194

With its skyline of ancient temple roofs set against the white peaks of the Himalaya, the city of **Bhaktapur ❷**, also known as Bhadgaon, is one of the highlights of any visit to Nepal. It is said to have been founded in the shape of Vishnu's conch shell by King Ananda Malla in the 9th century (in fact, the ancient city is a double S-shape). A former capital of the valley, and a flourishing city on the trade route to Tibet, Bhaktapur has preserved its traditional character better than Kathmandu and Patan, in part due to its more isolated location. The old city was comprehensively restored with German assistance between 1974 and 1986 and is regarded as a classic showcase of "medieval" Nepalese town life *(see page 190)*.

The town, with 150,000 inhabitants, is also the most self-contained and self-sufficient of the valley's major urban settlements. Its farmers supply food from the surrounding fields, the craftsmen are still able to restore and decorate the ancient houses and temples, and its people have maintained their religious and cultural traditions. An entrance fee (NRS 300) is collected from tourists by the municipality and used to maintain a clean urban environment and for the conservation of historic and religious monuments.

Bhaktapur is situated 16 km (10 miles) east of Kathmandu along an increasingly congested road which leads to Banepa, Dhulikhel and eventually to the Chinese border. Industrial development lines the road. A more interesting rural route takes you through the pottery village of **Sano Thimi**, famous for its terracotta work, including delightful peacock and elephant flowerpots and imaginative moulded candlesticks and ashtrays. The significant settlement of Thimi, a name that derives from *chhemi* meaning "capable people", is north of the road. Thimi is also known for its colourful painted masks and dolls.

LEFT: drying chillis at Dattatraya Temple.
BELOW: view from Nyatapola Temple.

Durbar Square

The traditional approach road from Kathmandu passes a grove of pine trees on a hillock and the recently restored **Siddhi Pokhari**, the largest of the city's network of historic water tanks.

Follow the tarmac road through narrow medieval streets to the **Durbar Square**. This part of town was originally outside the city boundaries which was centred further east around Dattatraya Square. Between the 14th and 16th centuries, when Bhaktapur was capital of Kathmandu Valley, the centre moved west to Taumadhi Tol. Durbar Square became integrated during the reign of King Bupathindra Malla around the beginning of the 18th century.

Entering Durbar Square through a 19th-century gate, the sparseness of the temples is immediately

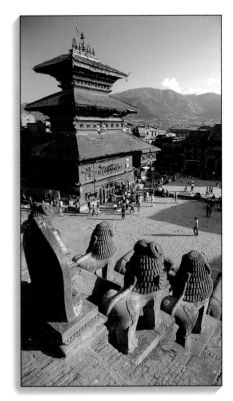

The gilded copper Sun Dhoka (Golden Gate), entrance to the Royal Palace.

apparent, compared to the profusion in the Durbar Squares of Kathmandu and Patan. The devastating 1934 earthquake destroyed many of the highly decorated buildings of all shapes and sizes that once crowded the square. Legend claims there were 99 courtyards here, though this is hard to believe. Today, by contrast, the brick paved square has a pleasant, open feeling.

On the left a pair of very fine stone statues represent Durga with her 18 arms and Bhairav with 12, both guarding the entrance to a lost part of the palace. The houses on the south side of the square are used for offices. Nearby is the Rameshwar Temple dedicated to Shiva and a brick *shikhara*-style temple dedicated to Durga with images of Hanuman and Narsingh. The most striking feature ahead of you as you enter the square is the exquisite gilded statue of King Bupathindra Malla, seated on a tall stone pillar.

The Royal Palace

The Bupathindra Malla statue faces the superb **Sun Dhoka** or "Golden Gate", generally considered the greatest single masterpiece of art in the valley, which leads into the Royal Palace. Created in 1753 by Jaya Ranjit Malla, it is a monument to the skill and artistry of the craftsmen who produced it. In gilded copper the door frame illustrates many divinities and the gate itself, set in brickwork, is capped with a gilded roof with finials of elephants and lions.

Standing back from the Sun Dhoka, what remains of the former **Royal Palace Ⓐ** can be seen, though it was much damaged in the 1934 earthquake. The 18th-century Palace of 55 Windows is on the right, built of brick with an upper floor of carved wooden windows. To the left is a plastered and whitewashed section of the palace built in the early 19th century. It now houses the

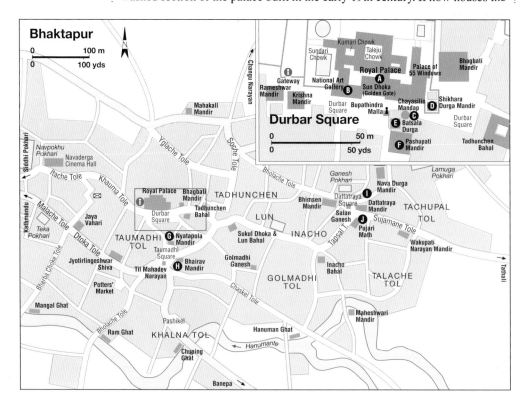

National Art Gallery 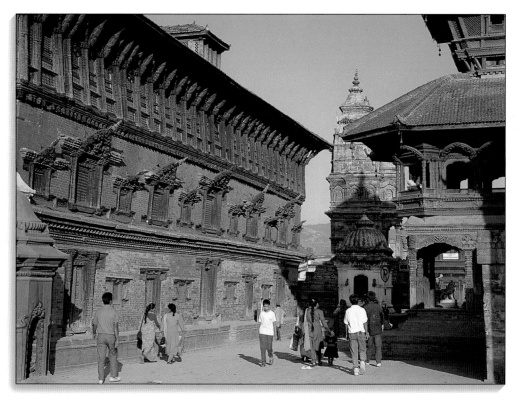 (open Wed–Mon 10.30am–3.30pm; entrance fee), with its collection of fine artworks, though sadly over-restored *thangkas*. The entrance is flanked by Hanuman, the monkey god, and Narsingh, the man-lion.

Walk through the Sun Dhoka into the religious and ritual courtyards of the royal palace. Pass under a couple of low doorways across small courtyards and wind your way around to the back where the elaborately carved entrance to the Taleju Chowk is on the left. This is as far as non-Hindu visitors may go as the two *chowks* of the Taleju and Kumari are sacrosanct. Try to persuade the guards (who are usually very amenable) to allow a glimpse into the courtyard and in particular note the Taleju God-house on the southern side with its rich carving and decoration.

Nearby is the Sundari Chowk, the ritual bathing courtyard of the Bhaktapur kings. Unlike others, this one is no longer surrounded with buildings but the tank itself has some stone divinities and is unusually large. From the centre of the tank rises a magnificent *naga* or sacred serpent.

Although no longer complete, the Bhaktapur palace is a place to linger a while and contemplate the beauties contained in what must have once been the most impressive of all the Durbar Squares in the valley.

Pavilions and pillars

Return to the Durbar Square. Ahead is the **Chayasilin Mandap** , an octagonal pavilion destroyed by the 1934 earthquake but entirely reconstructed between 1987 and 1990 as a gift of the German government. Note the fine woodcarving with hardly a difference between the new and original pieces, and the interior steel girders, ensuring a longer life than that of the previous

Map on page 184

BELOW: the Palace of 55 Windows.

building. Great effort has gone into detecting and integrating original timber components from the period.

Turn to the eastern plaza and pass on the left the fine stone **Shikhara Durga Mandir**  with interesting animal guardians and a beautiful royal couple at the bottom. A two-storey arcaded building frames this corner of the main square. Up a lane to the east is an intimate and unusual Buddhist monastery called Tadhunchen Bahal, restored with great care by the municipality in 1999.

Reorient yourself by the pillar of Bupathindra and note the big bell that was erected in the 18th century. Next to the bell, the stone *shikhara* of **Batsala Durga** ❺ is a symphony of pillars and arches with many divinities represented by stone carvings. The *shikhara* is surmounted by copper pinnacles and wind bells. A sunken stone *hiti* or water fountain is behind.

Further on is the large, two-roofed **Pashupati Mandir** ❻, one of the oldest temples in the valley, dating from the 15th century. Beyond, a narrow lane, Taumadhi Tol, which is lined with inviting shops and small restaurants, leads down to the lower square.

Two great shrines

Taumadhi Tol contains two great mystical temples, both of which have been restored in the late 1990s with revenue from tourist entrance fees.

The **Nyatapola Mandir** ❼ is Nepal's tallest, standing more than 30 metres (98 ft) with a total of five storeys (*nyata* in Nepali means "five-stepped"). Carved wooden columns support five lofty roofs and form a balcony around the sanctum. The temple is balanced superbly upon five receding square plinths. The steep central stairway is flanked by huge stone guardians on each plinth. Each

Langur monkeys are a common sight in the urban areas of the Kathmandu Valley.

BELOW: Nyatapola Temple towers above the skyline.

Map on page 184

pair is believed to have ten times the strength of the pair on the plinth immediately below them. The two famous Malla wrestlers at the bottom of the stairway are ten times as strong as ordinary people, and the elephants above them ten times as strong as the wrestlers, and so on. The list extends with lions, griffins, and the goddesses Baghini and Singhini.

Thus, metaphysical power culminates on the top in the Nyatapola's secret deity, Siddhi Lakshmi, a Tantric goddess to whom her patron-king Bupathindra Malla dedicated the temple in 1702. Exactly 108 painted wooden struts supporting the roofs show the goddess in her different forms. Despite this exhortion of Tantric power, people gather on the brick platforms of the temple for a chat in the sun and to trade goods, though no ordinary Bhaktapurian has ever seen the goddess, nor cared to do so. The huge steps are periodically daubed with political slogans and are a perfect platform for political meetings.

By contrast the **Bhairav Mandir** ⓞ is set at right angles to the Nyatapola and is a perfect architectural foil to its spire-like lines. The rectangular base rests directly onto the square and its three-tiered roof gives a massive, solid appearance. Dedicated to the city's patron god Bhairav, his awesome powers also counterbalance those of the Tantric goddess, portraying a peculiar Newari perception of the balance of spiritual terror.

The image of Bhairav is taken out for chariot processions across the town during the week-long, annual Bisket Jatra festival. It is barely 30 centimetres (1 ft) in height, and usually rests in a niche close to the ground, protected by a brass door through which offerings are thrust into the mysterious inner space of the temple. The real entrance to the temple is from behind, through the small neighbouring Betal Temple.

BELOW: the steps of Nyatapola Temple are guarded by mythical beasts.

Potters and ghats

The Nyatapola Café pavilion opposite the Bhairav Temple is a pleasant place to overlook the square and watch the constant activity. A street behind winds its way southwest to the pottery market, where hundreds of pots dry in the open square. The huge potters' wheels are spinning all day long and women pound grain as the men mould the wet clay. Ganesh, the elephant-headed patron of potters, presides from his Jeth Ganesh Temple, donated by a potter in 1646.

Follow the narrow lanes heading west out of the pottery market to several interesting temples, courtyards and *bahals*. A lane to the south leads downhill to the Hanumante River and the Ram Ghat, one of the bathing and cremation places serving the western part of the city.

Southeast from Taumadhi Tol, the steep flagstoned lane marks the processional route taken by the chariots of Bhairav and his goddess Bhadrakali during the annual Bisket festival on their way down to a square near the river *(see page 86)*. Thousands of people gather for this most boisterous of valley festivals, which marks the New Year in April with the raising of a 25-metre (82-ft) *lingam* pole.

To the south at **Chuping Ghat** a serene riverside temple compound houses the Music Department of Kathmandu University. Here both foreign and local musicians can study the traditional music of Nepal and learn its various instruments and dance forms.

Across the Hanumante Bridge, a stretch of Nepal's traditional main route to Tibet and the east still exists as a pleasant country walk upstream to the confluence at Hanuman Ghat. This is Bhaktapur's major cremation site with a profusion of shrines and ancient statuary under huge pipal trees.

BELOW: Potters' Square in Bhaktapur.

Uphill to the north is the oldest part of Bhaktapur and the narrow lanes are a maze of passages, courtyards and old houses. This was the area most damaged in the August 1988 earthquake, when many Bhaktapurians lost their lives.

Map on page 184

Dattatraya Square

This part of the city is called Tachupal Tol and **Dattatraya Square** ❶, with its commanding Dattatraya Temple, was the former centre of ancient Bhaktapur. The Dattatraya Temple was originally a community centre and dates from 1427. This is the only temple in the valley dedicated to Dattatraya, who is worshipped by followers of both Shiva and Vishnu as well as Buddhists who consider the god to be a cousin of the Lord Buddha.

Wooden eye wall decoration on a Bhaktapur street.

At the opposite lower end of the square is the two-storey Bhimsen Temple, which was erected in 1605 in front of a deeply recessed water fountain. The **Pujari Math** ❶ next to Dattatraya is the oldest and most important of 13 such *maths* or pilgrim hostels in Bhaktapur, this one also serving as the residence for the Dattatraya priests. It now houses a sadly neglected woodcarving museum, but don't miss the exquisite wood adornments in the courtyard and the windows. Round the corner down a narrow lane is the much-acclaimed Peacock Window. On the north side of the Tachupal Tol is the little Salan Ganesh, erected in 1654 in a lavishly decorated temple.

The road east out of the square passes the temple courtyard of Wakupati Narayan on the right, and leaves the city northeast to join the main road past an army encampment to the hilltop village of Nagarkot *(see page 208)*.

Southwest from Dattatraya Square the main bazaar road leads directly back to the Taumadhi and Durbar squares. ❏

BELOW: quiet moment during a Bhaktapur festival.

NEPAL'S WORLD HERITAGE SITES

There are a total of ten World Heritage Sites in Nepal nominated by UNESCO, eight of which are outstanding cultural sites, two natural treasures.

Kathmandu Durbar Square is the most extensive of the three royal squares in the valley. It consists of two smaller squares incorporating the palace compound, Hanuman Dhoka. There is an extraordinary mix of *shikaras*, divine images and palace complexes of immense grandeur. Patan Durbar Square is the most spectacular example of Malla architecture. The palace was constructed from 1668 to 1734. In Bhaktapur the two main temples are the Nyatapola and the Kasi Biswanath. The palace was constructed from the 13th to 18th centuries.

Boudhanath, the largest stupa in Nepal, dates back to the 5th century. Numerous renovations are recorded, in particular those of the 6th, 17th and 20th centuries. Pashupatinath is the largest Hindu shrine in the valley, dating back to the Licchavi period. It has undergone repeated renovations, mainly in the 17th and 19th centuries. The sacred Bagmati River is the major religious feature of the site. Changu Narayan is believed to be one of the valley's earliest settlements. The two-roofed temple was built in 1702 and a courtyard contains 13 Hindu shrines dating from the 5th century.

Other cultural sites are the stupa of Swayambhunath and Lumbini, birthplace of the Buddha. The two natural sites are Sagarmatha National Park and Royal Chitwan National Park.

◁ **BUDDHA'S HOME TOWN**
Lumbini, birthplace of the Lord Buddha, is the most recent site to be nominated for World Heritage status by the government of Nepal.

◁ **RELIGIOUS CENTRE**
Pashupatinath is a pilgrimage centre and includes many temples, votive *shikharas*, shrines and ghats for ritual bathing and cremation. Yogis come here to meditate.

◁ **CAPITAL SQUARE**
Kathmandu Durbar Square contains 60 important individual structures, the great majority of which date from the17th and 18th centuries.

△ **TOP OF THE WORLD**
Sagarmatha National Park includes the highest point on the earth's surface, Mount Everest, also known as Sagarmatha by the Nepalese.

▽ **JUNGLE RIDES**
Safaris in Royal Chitwan National Park offer the chance to see one-horned rhinoceros, barking deer, leopards and crocodiles.

△ **BOUDHANATH STUPA**
This stupa rises in stepped terraces to a giant white-washed hemisphere, topped by the "all-seeing" eyes of the Buddha.

▷ **MONKEY TEMPLE**
Swayambhunath temple is another ancient sacred site for Buddhists, and worshipping place for *rinpoches*.

RESTORING THE MONUMENTS

In the early 1970s a group of German architects from Dharmstad University began the first restoration programme at the Pujahari-math in Bhaktapur. After this success the German government began the Bhaktapur Redevelopment Project which as well as providing water and sewage disposal to the northeast of the town also rehabilitated the temples around Dattatraya Square. UNESCO began the Hanuman Dhoka Conservation Project in 1973 in collaboration with the Department of Archaeology, which both repaired and conserved an architectural masterpiece and trained craftsmen in monument repair.

Private foundations such as the World Monuments Fund New York, The Kathmandu Valley Preservation Trust and the American Himalayan Foundation continue an assortment of conservation projects such as Gorkana Temple, the Panauti temples and the Patan Museum. The American Himalayan Foundation has funded conservation of the *gompas* of Mustang while training locals to conserve and maintain some of the finest monuments on the Tibetan Plateau.

AROUND KATHMANDU

In the course of one day, visitors to Kathmandu can journey around the outskirts of the city and take in three of the most impressive temples in Nepal, revered by both Buddhists and Hindus

Map on page 194–5

Kathmandu

The area around **Kathmandu** ❸ is extraordinarily rich in places to visit. Three of Nepal's finest temples, Swayambhunath, Boudhanath and Pashupatinath, exist in the near vicinity of the capital and are places of pilgrimage for the country's Hindus and Buddhists. There are also countless smaller shrines of both faiths in the region.

Ancient Swayambhunath

Atop a green hillock on the western edge of Kathmandu stands the great stupa of **Swayambhunath** ❹, a site more than 2,500 years old marking the point where the legendary patriarch Manjushri discovered the lotus of the ancient valley lake. For centuries an important centre of Buddhist learning, the painted eyes of the Buddha gaze out from all four sides of this monument.

Constructed to specific rules, each with a symbolic meaning, the stupa of Swayambhunath is a model of its kind. Its dazzling white hemispherical mound represents creation, inset by statues of meditating Buddhas representing the four elements of earth, fire, air and water. The 13 gilded rings of the spire are the 13 degrees of knowledge required to ascend the path to enlightenment and nirvana, itself symbolised by the umbrella on top. The whole is hung with multicoloured prayer flags whose every flutter releases holy prayers. The faithful circumambulate the stupa clockwise, turning the banks of prayer wheels and even prostrating full-length in reverence.

The pilgrim's approach to the shrine is through a wooded park up a steep flight of 300 stone steps, lined with stone sculptures of animals and birds – vehicles of the gods. Cars can drive part-way up the rear side of the hill and park near one of the Tibetan monasteries. Legend relates how Manjushri had his hair cut at Swayambhunath, each hair becoming a tree, and the lice becoming monkeys – the monkeys that line the route up to the temple are appropriately persistent. Banks of new prayer wheels and stupas have recently been constructed around the base of the hill by the faithful.

Statues of the Buddha repose in richly decorated niches at the four cardinal points of the stupa. Statues of the goddesses Ganga and Jamuna, masterpieces of Newari bronze art, guard the eternal flame in a gilded cage behind the stupa. On the surrounding terrace are many *chaityas*, small stupas, two *shikhara*-style temples and a huge *vajra* (symbolic thunderbolt). An adjacent *gompa* (Buddhist monastery) conducts daily services in the light of flickering butter lamps, overlooked by its vast Buddha statue. The local communities have organised cleaners and guardians to regularly maintain the heavily visited shrine areas.

LEFT:
all-seeing eyes.
BELOW:
Buddhist monk at Swayambhunath Temple.

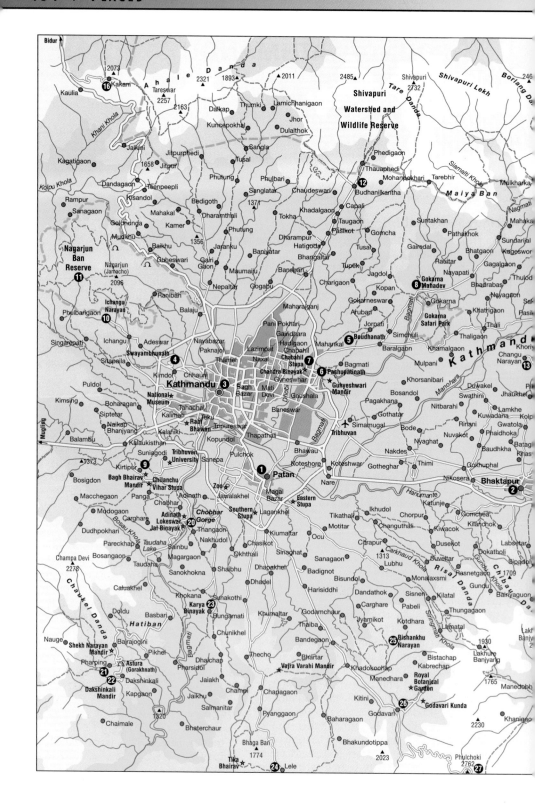

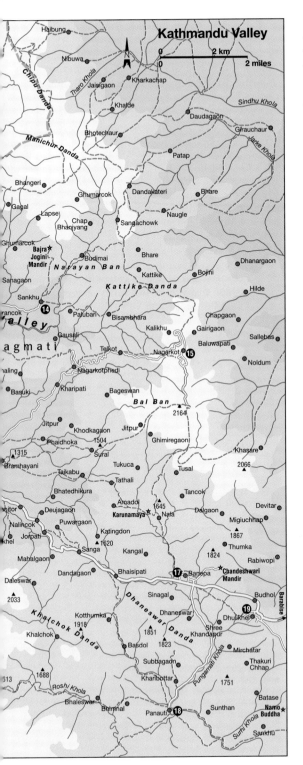

Kathmandu Valley

If you begin to feel slightly overwhelmed by all the religious fervour, turn around and look out, instead, across the spectacular scenery of the valley.

Approximately 15 minutes' leisurely walk south of Swayambhunath, the **National Museum** in Chhauni (open Wed–Mon 10am–5pm, until 2.30pm on Friday; entrance fee) features local treasures, including ancient stone sculptures, paintings, woodwork and metal sculpture. Medieval treasures include delicately rendered images of Buddhist deities.

Boudhanath's beauty

The largest stupa in the whole of Nepal is **Boudhanath** ❺, located on flat land 5 km (3 miles) northeast of Kathmandu and encircled by pastel-painted facades of houses.

Boudhanath shelters the largest community of the 16,000 Tibetans who have made Nepal their home since 1959 (see page 46). The many new monasteries and the Rinpoches who reside here have established Boudhanath as one of the most flourishing centres of Tibetan Buddhism in the world and there are few places, outside Tibet itself, that offer such an insight into their culture.

The huge white dome is surmounted by penetrating red, yellow and blue painted all-seeing eyes of the primordial Buddha and is set on concentric, ascending terraces in the powerful pattern of a *mandala* (meditation). Around the base of this enormous and strikingly simple stupa is a ring of 108 images of Buddhist deities and 147 insets containing prayer wheels. Boudhanath is more accessible than Swayambhunath – it is possible to climb up onto the base of the stupa and take a peaceful (clockwise) stroll amid the monks and the devout.

Poles are hung with prayer flags, renewed and blessed with fragrant juniper incense at the Losar Tibetan New Year festival between February and March. As hundreds of Tibetans gather in their best clothes and jewellery, a portrait of their spiritual leader, the Dalai Lama, is processed under silk umbrellas accompanied by the growls of horns.

Masked dancing completes the celebrations on this most happy and picturesque day in the valley *(see page 85)*.

Around the stupa the area is always bustling: pilgrims prostrating themselves around the dome *(kora)* mingle easily with stands of butter candles, souvenir stalls and tourists, accompanied by Tibetan music emanating from the surrounding buildings.

Pashupatinath

Shiva is both the Destroyer and Creator, at once the end of things and the beginning of new ones. Among other identities, he is Bhairav "The Cruel", Mahadeva "The Great God" or Pashupati "Lord of the Beasts". Shiva is usually represented as a light-skinned man with a blue throat, five faces, four arms and three eyes. He holds a trident (the symbol of his threefold identity: creator, keeper, destroyer), a sword, a bow and a skull. His vehicle, the bull, is an ancient symbol of fecundity. Together with his elephant-headed son, Ganesh, he is the most helpful god in the valley – and also the most awesome.

Sometimes Shiva is seen as an ascetic holy man, and many of his sadhu (holy man) followers, covered with sackcloth, dust and ashes, swarm to **Pashupatinath** ❻ between February and March to celebrate his birthday. Shivaratri is one of the great Hindu festivals of the valley, attracting thousands of pilgrims to one of the four most important Shiva shrines in the entire subcontinent *(see page 86)*.

Throughout the year, Shiva is worshipped at Pashupatinath as a *lingam* (phallus) in his incarnation as the Lord Pashupati. Don't be too taken in by the dreadlocked sadhus that surround the temple – while some are undoubtedly genuine,

Shiva is generally credited with having discovered the powers of ganja *(cannabis), which is why sadhus are often under the influence, regularly smoking hashish through their* chilam *(clay pipe).*

BELOW:
Hindu shrine at Pashupatinath Temple.

many are fakes dressed up to earn money from the relentless tourist photographs.

The great temple complex is 5 km (3 miles) east of central Kathmandu. The easiest way to reach it is to walk from the Bagmati Bridge, near the Royal Nepal Golf Club.

Entrance to the temple precinct is forbidden to non-Hindus. The best view is from the terrace on the wooded hill across the river. The large, gilded, triple-roofed temple was built in 1696, though 300 years earlier there was a structure on this site. The Bagmati River is lined with *dharmsalas* (pilgrim resthouses) and cremation ghats, including a royal ghat reserved exclusively for members of the royal family. There is usually a cremation in progress on one of the platforms by the river. The ashes will be scattered in the river, regarded as holy as it flows into the sacred Ganges, despite its polluted water and seasonal low flows. If you have the stomach for it, tourists are free to watch cremations from above, but photography is generally discouraged as a sign of respect.

The tradition of *sati*, when wives burned themselves alive on their husband's funeral pyre, has not been permitted since the early 20th century, but many married couples still bathe together in the water in the belief that this will lead to their reunification in the next life. There are also many other occasions when the faithful take ritual purificatory baths in the river. One of the most colourful is the three-day women's festival of Teej between August and September when, dressed in their finest red and gold saris, hundreds of women, laughing and singing, converge on Pashupatinath. At other times of the year, the ghats are a mixture of the devout washing and laughing children splashing about irreverently in the water.

Map on page 194–5

Tika colouring powder on sale at Pashupatinath.

BELOW: sadhu on the temple steps at Pashupatinath.

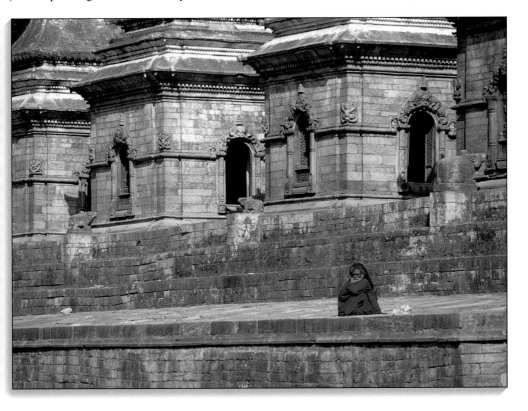

Chabahil stupa stands proud amid the traffic.

If you continue up the hill, the path leads through the trees to the brick structure of the Gorakhnath Shikhara, flanked by the brass trident of Shiva and surrounded by resthouses and *lingas* on a wide platform.

Down the hill on the other side is the Guhyeshwari Temple dedicated to Shiva's *shakti* (consort) in her manifestation as Kali. Female Hindu deities sometimes take on ferocious, fierce and bloodthirsty appearances. One of the most important goddesses is the dominating and sexual *shakti* Maha Devi. She can take thousands of names and incarnations. She is the black goddess Kali "the Dark One" and Durga "The Terrible of Many Names". She is forever giving birth but her stomach can never be filled and her craving for blood is insatiable. Sacrifices are characteristic of her worship, particularly popular in Nepal.

This riverside shrine is, like so many others, forbidden to non-Hindus, although Buddhists also revere this as a sacred site and the seed from which the Swayambhunath lotus grew.

The ancient stupa of **Chabahil ❼** is at a busy crossroads north of Pashupatinath and marks an early Licchavi settlement. It is a relatively primitive stupa but does have some interesting early sculptures and *chaityas*. The Chandra Binayak is in the middle of the village of Chabahil, 200 metres (650 ft) behind the stupa. This small Ganesh shrine features rich brasswork and is believed to cure diseases and external bodily injuries.

Gokarna Mahadev and Tika Bhairav

BELOW: sadhus gathered at Pashupatinath.

Beyond Pashupatinath, past the Hyatt Regency Hotel and Boudhanath, take the road left for 4 km (2½ miles) to the important Shiva shrine, the **Gokarna Mahadev ❽**, on the banks of the Bagmati River in the small village of Gokarna.

The ochre-coloured three-roofed temple was built in 1582. The fine wood-carvings around the doors and roof have been restored to their original pure beauty and the golden roofs glisten in the sun, framed against the dark forest across the river.

The temple is not accessible to non-Hindus. Irregular stone steps descend the river bank, where Shiva lies on a stone bed of cobras. In August and September at Gokarna Aunshi, or Fathers' Day, those whose fathers have died during the previous year must come and ritually bathe here at the Mahadev temple by the river at Gokarna *(see page 89)*.

Early sculptures surround this scenic shrine, including one of Brahma, but none are more beautiful than the 8th-century statue of Parvati, the oldest image at Gokarna, now protected by clothes inside a small shrine, set between the main temple and the road.

Map on page 194–5

Terrible Shiva's shrine

A Shiva shrine of an altogether different register is located at Tika Bhairav near Lele *(see page 215)*, where Shiva is portrayed in his terrible form as Bhairav. To reach this unusual shrine, you have to travel outside the Kathmandu Valley towards the adjoining Lele Valley, to the south of the capital, and turn sharply left, descending to the confluence of the rivers. Do not look out for a conventional temple, however. This monumental, multi-coloured fresco is an abstract close-up of Bhairav's face painted on a huge brick wall, under the spartan shelter provided by a tin roof. For those travellers who keen on cycling among beautiful unspoiled scenery, this also makes for a very pleasant mountain-biking route. ❏

BELOW:
marigold offering at one of the valley's many temples.

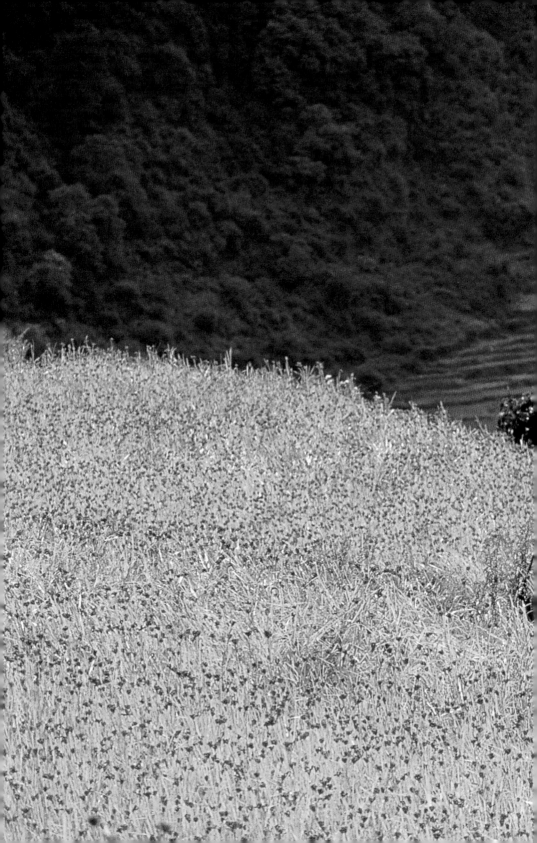

KATHMANDU VALLEY

Most visitors to Nepal concentrate on the Kathmandu Valley and it is easy to see why: the abundance of ancient architecture and mountain views offers an unbeatable combination

Map on page 194–5

Kathmandu

The rich fabric of the cultural and artistic heritage of Nepal is at its most visible in the Kathmandu Valley. Successive dynasties have left their mark in the stupendous palaces and temples, sculptures and carvings to be found throughout the valley. According to one myth, Kathmandu was built on a sacred lake; the god Manjushri created a river with one blow of his sword and thus drained the valley. It is said there are more gods than people in the Kathmandu Valley and this is not hard to believe. At every corner there is a shrine and many are still the object of daily devotions. Flower petals, vermilion powder and rice are offered daily on brass trays and it is not unusual to pass a colourful festival procession in the streets.

Perhaps nowhere else on earth is there such a concentration of important monuments which are still active and part of everyday life. There are beautiful shrines, both Buddhist and Hindu, and it is easy to get off the beaten track to explore the more remote temples, unchanged settlements and pilgrimage sites. This cultural wonderland is set against a backdrop of rural tranquillity, with fertile green hills offering wonderful trekking opportunities. Indeed for the more adventurous visitor the best way to explore is on foot or bicycle. Within minutes of leaving the main roads, you can still return to the spiritual atmosphere of the old Nepal, where villagers tend their terraced fields and scarlet chillis dry in the sun. At every turn natural wonders are evident; the towering white Himalaya glimpsed to the north, the emerald of young rice or the shimmering gold of a field of mustard.

The Kathmandu Valley is compact and relatively flat. Drained by the sacred Bagmati River which flows into the Ganges, it is almost as broad as it is wide and covers an area of some 570 sq. km (220 sq. miles). Set at an altitude of between 1,200 and 1,500 metres (4,000–5,000 ft) above sea level in the midlands of Nepal's Mahabharat range, the fertile alluvial soil is ideal for the cultivation of rice, the staple diet.

PRECEDING PAGES: verdant hillside on the edge of the Kathmandu Valley. **LEFT:** rural houses in the Kathmandu Valley. **BELOW:** *chaitya* (small Buddhist stupa).

Kirtipur

The rocky ridgetop city of **Kirtipur ❾**, lying to the west of the Bagmati River, is a magnificent exception to the usual Newari settlements that are built on plateaux. Perched on twin hillocks and clinging to a saddle about 5 km (3 miles) southwest of Kathmandu, Kirtipur has two satellite hamlets of Panga and Nagaon, located to the south.

First established as a kind of outpost of Patan in the 12th century, it became an independent kingdom and was the last stronghold of the Mallas, only falling to King Prithvi Narayan Shah in 1769, after a prolonged and terrible siege. After the conquest it is said the vengeful Gorkha ruler had the noses and lips of all

TIP

To reach Kirtipur, hire a taxi or catch a bus from the City Bus Park in Kathmandu. It is a 10-minute walk up to the village from the marketplace where the bus stops.

the men in the town cut off, sparing only players of wind instruments. In memory of this atrocity, residents of Kirtipur still forbid the monarchy to enter their village. Remains of the fortified wall and part of the original 12 gates can still be seen.

Most of the 20,000 inhabitants of Kirtipur are farmers and merchants and many commute daily to office jobs in Kathmandu. The nearby campus of the Tribhuvan University occupies portions of Kirtipur's former farmlands. The traditional occupation of spinning and weaving produces handloom fabric for sale in Kathmandu. The thud of the looms in the houses can be heard when walking down the narrow streets.

New houses and a few monasteries are growing up around Kirtipur, but the old centre has a neglected feel, and to visit this is almost like stepping back in time. The brick-built homes are set on stepped terraces linked by steep paths, milling with villagers, cows and dogs. A long flight of steps leads up to Kirtipur from the valley floor and a road switchbacks halfway up the hill, although no cars are able to drive into the village itself.

The southern hill is surmounted by the **Chilanchu Vihar**, a central stupa surrounded by four similar stupas at cardinal directions. The paved area of this former monastery is still used for drying crops. The higher northern hill is inhabited by Hindus who surround the **Uma Maheshwar Mandir**. The approach up stone steps is flanked by a pair of fine stone elephants; from the temples there is a stunning view of Kathmandu and the striking patchwork of the valley and the mountains beyond.

In the middle of Kirtipur, where the two hills meet north of the tank, stands the famous **Bagh Bhairav Mandir**. This three-roofed temple is enclosed within

BELOW: the centre of Kirtipur.

a courtyard and contains an image of Bhairav in his tiger form. The shields and swords were presented by the Newari troops after Prithvi Narayan Shah's conquest. In an upper room is an image of the goddess Indrayani, who is paraded through the streets during the village's largest festival between November and December *(see page 90)*.

Map on page 194–5

Ichangu Narayan and Budhanilkantha

Part of the Hindu trinity of Brahma, Vishnu and Shiva, Vishnu is revered by many Hindus as the highest deity, as the creator and keeper of the world. He is a god with a thousand names, and comes in a variety of forms or incarnations (*avataras*). As the god Narayana he is most often depicted resting atop a bed of snakes afloat in the cosmic ocean; as Krishna he is a youthful god frolicking with *gopis* (milkmaids). Once a year, in either October or November, a day's pilgrimage requires devotees to visit the four great Narayan shrines *(see page 89)*; no mean feat as they lie far apart. In addition to Changu Narayan *(see page 207)*, the other three are found in rural village settings.

Shiva lingam *at Budhanilkantha.*

Worshippers start at **Ichangu Narayan ⑩**, an ancient site thought to have been founded by King Hari Datta in the 6th century AD. The little temple complex is set in a clump of trees just beyond the village of Ichangu, a pleasant half-hour walk west from the ring road crossroads opposite the temple of Swayambhunath *(see page 193)*.

To the northwest, the "Queen's Forest" reserve of **Nagarjun Ban ⑪** (open daily 7am–10pm; entrance fee) is a beautiful walled hill topped with a Buddhist *chaitya* (small stupa), where the Lord Buddha is believed to have

BELOW:
Budhanilkantha.

meditated, and it is a favoured place for joggers, walkers and picnickers who enjoy this rural haven. There are two sacred caves and pheasant, deer and monkeys can still sometimes be seen here.

There are also spectacular views of the valley and the Langtang region. The main entrance gate into the forest is just to the north of **Balaju**. In Balaju itself is a Sleeping Vishnu statue, which dates from the same time as the larger and more famous image at Budhanilkantha *(see below)*. The Balaju Vishnu reclines in a shady park known as the Water Garden, a popular weekend picnic spot. In the same park are the 22 carved stone water spouts of the Balaju Hiti, more than any other *hiti* in the Kathmandu Valley and an oasis amid the surrounding urban sprawl and the "Balaju Industrial Estate".

Budhanilkantha ⑫, 9 km (6 miles) north of Kathmandu, with its monumental reclining Vishnu, is a modest village on the north side of the valley near an early Licchavi settlement. It nestles at the foot of the 2,732-metre (8,963-ft) Shivapuri Hill, the summit of the Shivapuri Watershed and Wildlife Reserve *(see page 107)*, a favourite trekking, birdwatching and picnicking area. The massive black statue of the reclining Vishnu lies comfortably half-submerged in the primeval ocean, resting on a bed of snakes.

Nowhere else have the Licchavi sculptors translated the ancient image into stone so powerfully or so literally. Some 1,500 years ago man had apparently dragged the 5-metre (16-ft) rock from outside the valley and placed the "creator of life" in this small pond at the foot of the Shivapuri hills. Worshippers cover the sleeping Vishnu with offerings of flower petals and rice. A forecast of death forbids the kings of Nepal from looking on Budhanilkantha's monumental sculpture.

BELOW: ancient temple of Changu Narayan.

Changu Narayan

Since the 14th century, the successive rulers of Nepal have been considered incarnations of Vishnu. Every former royal palace has its Vishnu shrine and there are several more scattered throughout the valley. None is richer in spectacular Licchavi sculpture than the hilltop temple of **Changu Narayan ⑬**.

Map on page 194–5

The road access to Changu Narayan, 12 km (7 miles) east of Kathmandu, is from the north side of Bhaktapur. Alternatively the temple can be reached by a 45-minute walk up from the Sankhu road, across the Manohara River, using the old pilgrim's route; or a pleasant half-day hike along the ridge from Nagarkot on the eastern valley rim. Local guides from the village are available.

The lavishly decorated two-tiered temple was rebuilt after a fire in 1702, but the earliest inscription in the valley dated AD 464 testifies to the considerable talents of the Licchavi King Manadeva I, Nepal's first great historical figure. The temple stands in a spacious courtyard, littered with priceless stone sculptures from the 4th to the 9th centuries AD, the Licchavi period. This golden age of classical Newari art produced masterpieces that were entirely religious in character. Note especially the lion-headed Vishnu Narasimha, dismembering the king of the demons; Vishnu with ten heads and ten arms going through the different layers of the universe; Vishnu Vikrantha, a dwarf with six arms. A 5th-century stone sculpture of Vishnu is also kept inside the temple but is accessible only to the priests.

Carved detail on Changu Narayan temple.

Beside the stele with the oldest inscription, which is set in front of the temple, is an image of a Garuda, the mythical bird that serves as Vishnu's heavenly vehicle. Graceful statues of King Bupathindra Malla and his queen sit in a gilded cage.

BELOW: hills and houses near Nagarkot.

Views from the valley rim

Vestiges of Nepal's glorious past are conveniently concentrated in the Kathmandu Valley, but sometimes their profusion is overwhelming or the urban environment distracting. To experience rustic Nepal, one must go into the countryside. Fortunately for the non-trekker, there are a number of viewpoints with clean and comfortable accommodation and easy day-trips to interesting villages or historic and sacred sites. The sedentary connoisseur of fine mountain scenery can enjoy it all from the comfort of a deckchair.

Hills surround the sleepy village of **Sankhu ⑭**, once on the trade route east to Helambu. It is now reached by driving beyond Boudhanath and the new Le Meridien Kathmandu hotel with its 18-hole Gleneagles-inspired golf course set amid the virgin forests of Gokarna.

Trees above the village of Sankhu hide an important temple to the Tantric goddess, Bajra Jogini. Follow the wide stone path north of the village and climb up the steps to the temple, flanked with smaller shrines, stupas and statues. The main structure dates from the 17th century and has a fine golden *torana* above the door. Behind the temple you will find various other shrines and sculptures.

Further east, the settlement of **Nagarkot ⑮** clings to a 1,985-metre (6,512-ft) hilltop, far removed from

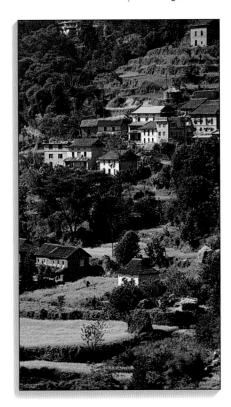

Buddhist prayer wheels are spun to "release" prayers to the gods.

BELOW: temples of Panauti, set on the confluence of two rivers.

noise and traffic pollution. A one-hour drive up the winding road from Bhaktapur greets the fresh hill breezes and valley views east and west, eclipsed by one of the best close-range Himalayan vantage points from anywhere on the Kathmandu Valley rim. From the Annapurnas to Everest, the peaks seem no more than a day's walk away. The increasingly up-market accommodation at Nagarkot attracts foreign, Indian and Nepalese overnight visitors who come to see the sun rise and set over the mountains. These include the dominating Club Himalaya and the more modest Fort. The Vajra Farmhouse, not far away past the main cluster of resorts, offers extra peace and quiet, a pretty garden and pleasant rooms built around a converted old Newari farmhouse. Travel agents in Kathmandu can arrange overnight private taxi services or guided tours for viewing the sunset or sunrise. Tourist minibuses run daily between Thamel and Nagarkot. The more active-spirited traveller might hitch a ride up to Nagarkot and walk down via any of several routes. Mountain bikers can enjoy a fun, zigzag descent to Sankhu on a dirt road.

On the opposite, western rim of the Kathmandu Valley, the road northwest to Trisuli and the fort at Nuwakot *(see page 221)* leaves the valley near the viewpoint village of **Kakani** ⑯, at a height of 2,073 metres (6,801 ft). An old retreat of the British envoys to Nepal since the mid-19th century, a delightful Raj-style cottage at Kakani still belongs to successive British ambassadors to Nepal. Taragaon Resort is shared by the British ambassador's private residence and a police training academy. From the hotel terrace, Ganesh Himal and Langtang Lirung dominate the centrestage with Annapurna II and Himal Chuli, Lenpogang (Great White Peak) and Gauri Shankar in the left and right wings. Several day hikes and valley rim treks begin or end at Kakani. Nearby is the

bungalow built by the British Gurkhas and a well-maintained park built to commemorate victims of the 1992 plane crash in the area.

Map on page 194–5

Banepa Valley and Panauti

The "Chinese Road" or Arniko Raj Marg skirts Bhaktapur and leaves the rim of the Kathmandu Valley at the village of Sanga before descending into the Banepa Valley. The busy and charmless trading town of **Banepa** ⓱ was once the capital of a 14th-century kingdom which boasted diplomatic relations with China's Ming emperors. Turn right at the Tribhuvan statue to reach Panauti. To the northwest of Banepa a track runs through terraced rice fields to **Nala**, another former outpost of Bhaktapur. Seldom visited by tourists, the Newari town retains a medieval atmosphere. In the centre of the village is a beautifully proportioned temple dedicated to the great goddess Bhagvati, built in 1647.

A treasure trove of art and architecture, **Panauti** ⓲ is set south of Banepa at the confluence of the Pungamati and Roshi rivers. Once an important staging post on the Tibet trade route with pre-Licchavi origins, Panauti boasts one of the only two known pre-Malla structures, the Indreshwar Mahadev Temple. Contemporary with the 12th-century Kasthamandap and of the finest proportions with exquisite woodcarvings – especially the simple but beautiful roof struts – this important temple was damaged in the 1988 earthquake and has been recently restored with French assistance.

At the confluence itself is a pleasing jumble of small temples, shrines, *lingas* and a cremation ghat. Across the river is the 17th-century Brahmayani Temple with superb Newari paintings or *paubha*. Apart from these attractions, it's a pleasure to simply wander the town's brick-paved streets, admiring the finely

BELOW:
Dhulikhel offers spectacular views.

carved resthouses, stupas and stone water taps, perhaps stopping to observe a traditional gold- or silversmith at work.

Over the rim of the valley from Banepa is the **Chandeshwari Mandir**. A track leads northeast past the Adventist Hospital to the temple on the bank of a forested gorge. Legend says that this entire valley was once crowded with wild beasts, regarded locally as demons. The temple is dedicated to Parvati, whom they called upon to slay Chand, the most fearsome of these demons. It thus became known as Chandeshwari, "The Slayer of Chand". The main attraction is a remarkable fresco of Bhairav, painted on the western wall of the main structure. The *torana* and struts of the three-tiered temple are richly carved with the eight Astha Matrikas, or "Mother Goddesses", as well as eight Bhairavs.

Bhairav fresco at Chandeshwari shrine.

A gilded trade post

A short distance east from Banepa on the Arniko Raj Marg is the town of **Dhulikhel** , set on a hilltop overlooking fields and terraces. Dhulikhel was an important trade post and duty collected on gold and riches destined for the *rajas* of Kathmandu financed the elegant woodcarvings on some of its handsome buildings. Its strategic importance continues as the new Sindhuli highway to the Terai, when completed, will lead from here to Janakpur *(see page 297)*.

The ancient art of Newari woodcraft is kept alive at several charming resorts around Dhulikhel. The Dhulikhel Mountain Resort, Himalayan Horizon Hotel and Mirabel Resort all incorporate indigenous styles of architecture but with modern amenities of high tourist standards. From garden patios and bedroom windows, an impressive vista of the snowy central Himalaya makes an incongruous backdrop to the gentle hills and temperate climate.

BELOW: the plaque at Namo Buddha depicts the legend of Buddha's sacrifice to the starving tigress.

Dhulikhel is central to a number of day excursions, beginning with an early morning 30-minute hike up to the Bhagvati Temple for an unforgettable sunrise over the Himalaya. Trails lead along the ridge north of town, self-evident or invariably guided by schoolchildren eager to practise their English.

South of Dhulikhel, the **Namo Buddha** (meaning "Hail to the Buddha") is a sacred site which for untold centuries has drawn reverent pilgrims. Legend tells that the Buddha sacrificed his body here to feed a starving tigress and her cubs. A carved stone slab on the top of the hill depicts the moving story, a lesson in compassion and selfless giving. Clustered around the main stupa are tea shops selling *chiya*, *alu daam* and *chiura* (tea, potato curry and beaten rice) and a huge prayer wheel; on the hilltop above are several Buddhist retreats and monasteries, ringed with prayer flags and a line of nine white stupas.

A dirt road travelled by increasing numbers of vehicles (though only really suitable for 4WDs) reaches Namo Buddha from Dhulikhel via Kavre, and is a pleasant round-trip walk of eight hours. From the stupa still another road drops west downhill through a sacred forest and across a wide valley for a two-hour walk or a half-hour drive to Panauti. Check the prevailing road condition before you attempt to drive. The main road continues to the Chinese border and eventually to Lhasa, the Tibetan capital, provided it is not obstructed by snow or landslides *(see page 288)*.

Map on page 194–5

Patan to Pharping and Dakshinkali

South of Patan, various road and trails link settlements and sacred sites to the one-time capital. There is a road to Pharping and Dakshinkali, another to

BELOW: rural houses in Pharping.

Lele via Chapagaon, and another leads through some pretty villages to the botanical gardens at Godavari.

The road to Pharping follows the serpentine twists and turns of the Bagmati River, passing one of the most celebrated natural sites of the valley, the **Chobhar Gorge ⑳**. This is where, legend tells us, the patriarch Manjushri released the waters of the lake with his mighty sword and the Chobhar Hill is indeed sliced in two by the waters of the Bagmati River. Now much disfigured with a massive cement factory, this sacred spot is marked with the Adinath Lokeshwar temple on the top of the Chobhar Hill. This temple, built in 1640, is decorated with household utensils.

Those seeking strength of character go to worship Ganesh at **Jal Binayak**, just beyond the Chobhar Gorge. A beautiful brass rat, the vehicle of Ganesh, faces the rock that represents the elephant-headed god in this recently restored triple-roofed temple – which was originally constructed in 1602. A steel suspension bridge imported from Scotland in 1903 crosses the river near the Jal Binayak shrine. Just beyond the gorge is the pretty and sacred Taudaha Lake which, according to legend, was created by Manjushri himself for the *nagas* (serpents) who were stranded when the valley lake was drained.

En route to Pharping, the road passes through the pine forest of **Hatiban**, which shelters the pleasant Hatiban Himalayan Heights Resort. There are stunning views across the valley from part of the way up Champa Devi Hill, which rises to the right.

Pharping ㉑ is the largest village in this historic corner of the Kathmandu Valley and an important centre for Tibetan Buddhism. The mysterious 17th-century Tantric Bajra Jogini Temple is still closed to foreigners, but next to the

BELOW:
Bungamati, winter home of Rato Machhendranath, deity of Patan.

temple steps lead up the hill to the **Astura Cave**. The cave is sacred to the great Tibetan saint Guru Rinpoche (Padmasambhava), as it is believed to bear the marks of his head- and hand-prints, although Hindus attribute these to Gorakhnath. The cave has become an important pilgrimage site, and has encouraged the spread of new monasteries and meditation centres around Pharping, which attract foreign and local Buddhists. Nearby is the **Shekh Narayan Mandir**, dedicated to an incarnation of Vishnu as the dwarf Vamana. Adjacent to the temple is another important Buddhist cave, known as Yanglesho, where Guru Rinpoche is said to have turned a group of *naga* (snakes) to stone. He is also believed to have attained his realisation of the Mahamudra teachings at this spot.

Map on page 194–5

Located in a dark valley at the confluence of two streams, **Dakshinkali** ㉒ is renowned for its twice-weekly sacrifices on Tuesdays and Saturdays. This sinister shrine is the most spectacular of all the Kali temples attracting hundreds of thousands of visitors annually. Only male animals are sacrificed in Nepal, usually buffaloes, goats or chickens. Women line up on one side and men on the other, carrying their animals to the priest who will ritually decapitate them with a *khukri* knife and bathe the black stone image of Kali in blood. Surprisingly or not, this is one of the valley's most popular picnic spots; there are cooking facilities in the managed park area of the shrine.

Shiva lingam *at Bungamati.*

Patan to Lele

The twin villages of **Khokana** and **Bungamati** date from the 16th century and are located down a road dotted with *chaityas*, appropriate for an ancient processional route. Bungamati is famous as the winter home of the Rato Machhendranath god of Patan *(see page 181)* who resides every winter in a *shikhara*-style temple. Khokana is slightly bigger than Bungamati and is known for its manufacture of mustard-oil. The oil presses can be seen in operation in the houses of the village. UNESCO has now identified these two ancient villages as being of both historic and architectural importance worthy of restoration.

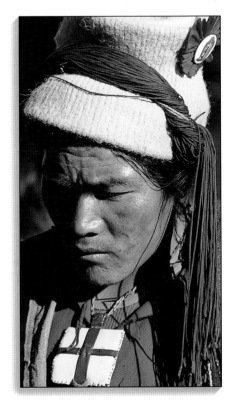

BELOW: shaman with a talisman around his neck

The shrine of **Karya Binayak** ㉓ is located between Khokana and Bungamati, in a forest preserve. From the road linking the hamlets, a path leads up to a beautiful clearing and the walled compound of the shrine. Here Ganesh is the centrepiece of the shrine and is believed to help complete difficult tasks

The road from Patan to Lele passes some beautiful countryside with terraced mustard fields and bamboo stands drenched in sunlight. Drive through the 16th-century brick-built towns of **Sunakothi** and **Thecho**, with fine examples of Newari temple architecture. A short distance to the south of Sunakothi, a path leads west to Bungamati and the shrine at Karya Binayak. Just before you reach Chapagaon, where the surfaced road comes to an end, take the path east to the important Tantric temple of **Vajra Varahi**, located in a sacred grove of trees. Although built in 1665, the site itself is much older and various natural sculpted stones are regarded as images of Ganesh, Bhairav and the Ashta Matrikas. The Vajra Varahi is a Tantric manefestation of Kali; the stone statue of the deity is a replacement for the ancient image which was stolen. It has since been recovered and is on display at the National Museum in Chhauni *(see page 195)*.

There is an holy *kunda* pool in the dusty Lele Valley, a bumpy trip south only made by the more intrepid tourists. Leaving the Kathmandu Valley, the track winds its way steeply downhill through intricately terraced fields and reddish-brown soil to the ancient Licchavi village of **Lele 24**. The Saraswati *kunda* is beyond the village and marked by a shrine built in 1668 and other temples. Turn right before Lele and the park commemorating the 1992 Pakistan Airlines disaster, to the confluence village of **Tika Bhairav** famed for its painted fresco beside the river *(see page 199)*. Unfortunately there is a large quarry nearby, and heavy lorries can make the road rather noisy and dusty. Further on down this rough road is the lovely Malla Alpine Resort with commanding views, while the minor tracks heading into the hills south of the Lele Valley are popular with trekkers and mountain bikers.

Godavari and Phulchoki

The tree-lined road running southeast to Godavari from Kathmandu passes through the pleasant country towns of Harisiddhi, Thaiba and Bandegaon, where the road branches to **Bishankhu Narayan 25**, one of the most celebrated Vishnu shrines in the valley. This cave temple marks the site where Vishnu is believed to have thwarted the evil intentions of the demon Bhamasur. Those able to squeeze through the narrow rock fissure to reach the shrine, marked with statues of Vishnu and Hanuman, are reputedly atoned for all their sins.

BELOW:
consecration at
Godavari stupa.

The verdant village of **Godavari** ❻ lies further to the south. St Xavier's School is located here; run by the Jesuits, this was the first Catholic school to open in Nepal following the expulsion of missionaries in 1768. The Royal Botanical Garden (open daily 10am–4pm; entrance fee), with its Department of Medicinal Plants, is to the north. This is a pleasant spot with its rushing streams and shady meadows and is popular for picnics and as a location for the filming of Hindi film sequences. A greenhouse on the hill above has a collection of orchids and ferns. From here a quiet path leads on to the Godavari *kunda*, a sacred pool where the waters of the Godavari River pour from the mountains. Beyond this is a newly constructed Buddhist stupa, a government fish farm and a small deer park.

Phulchoki ❼, the "flower-covered hill", is the highest on the valley rim at 2,762 metres (9,062 ft) and a rewarding area for hikers and birdwatchers. The triple-peaked hill is 20 km (13 miles) southeast of Kathmandu, and a road winds its way to the top where a small shrine has been built to the "mother of the forest", Phulchoki Mai – the hill is swathed in beautiful forest, something of a rarity in the area these days. Another small Phulchoki shrine is found at the bottom of the hill, near the disfiguring marble quarry. Spring is a spectacular time to see the flowers – rhododendrons, orchids and morning glories, as well as many beautiful butterflies. Several excellent walks start from here *(see page 217)*, with tremendous views of the Kathmandu Valley and the Himalayan peaks beyond.

A road leads southeast from Patan to the villages of Sanagaon and Lubhu, from where a track can be followed all the way to Panauti *(see page 209)*, a rewarding trip for mountain bikes. ❑

Map on page 194–5

white scarves at Godavari stupa during the consecration ceremony.

BELOW: rice planting in the Kathmandu Valley.

Hikes in Kathmandu Valley

The Kathmandu Valley has many enjoyable day hikes or mini-treks that offer the rewards of wandering further afield: serenity, an introduction to Nepalese hill life and dramatic mountain views. A Schneider Valley map is helpful for navigating the trails and hills that ring the perimeter of the valley. A guide can be valuable where trails evaporate or multiply, and you may consider porters if you want to hike without gear on your back.

Commanding the eastern rim, Nagarkot (1,985 metres/6,512 ft) is a good place to begin several day hikes or a longer northern rim trek (*see page 208*). A three-hour walk descends westward to Changu Narayan (1,541 metres/5,055 ft), passing through corn terraces and thatched-roof villages, crossing the road at a sharp bend and heading along the ridge to the temple's gilded roofs (*see page 207*). A staircase leads down

to a fork in the trail, left to Bhaktapur and right descending to rice paddies and across a stream to the Sankhu road.

A dirt road winds down from Nagarkot to Sankhu, but its graded track is more fun for mountain biking or motorcycling. An alternative route heads north to the Kattike Dara ridge, curves west, descends south on the Sankhu to Helambu trail then climbs to the Bajra Jogini temple. A third route drops to the north from the first sharp bend in the Nagarkot road and reaches Sankhu.

Descending southeast from Nagarkot to Banepa is another pleasant excursion. The trail begins below the view tower within the military area. Two tracks lead south through terraced fields to Nala, an old village with splendid temples, en route to reaching Banepa in five to six hours. Walk through old Banepa and ask directions to the temple of the Newar mother goddess, Chandeshwari.

A two-day hike from Nagarkot to Shivapuri or a day-and-a-half to Sundarijal share the same trail for the first eight hours. It follows a dirt road north towards Manicur Dara, then stays high on the ridge to Burlang Bhanjyang (2,438 metres/8,000 ft) where food and lodging are available. For those unfamiliar with the area a guide is essential.

The way to Shivapuri continues west through oak and rhododendron forests along the ridge for about four hours, without water, before mounting the final knoll (2,732 metres/8,963 ft) for a 360-degree view of the Himalaya and Kathmandu Valley. You can stay in the Shivapuri Village resort on the north side of the valley rim. The walk is three to four hours from the summit down forested slopes but arrange a guide from the lodge.

For a longer, six-hour walk, retrace your steps east from the summit for one hour and descend to the right, down to the Buddhist monastery and retreat of Nagi Gompa, then further down to the loop road. Turn left, head through Tamang villages, and follow the Thana Dara ridge that overlooks Phulbari and Kopan monasteries and Boudhanath (*see page 195*) before angling east to the Shivaite temple, Gokarneswar.

You can return to Kathmandu from Shivapuri by walking west past the army barracks to the first main trail on the left. Alternatively, turn right on the loop road below Nagi

Gompa, walk for one hour and exit left via the gate to the Shivapuri Reserve and down to Budhanilkantha, serviced by taxi and bus.

The rim trek continues west, reaching Kakani (2,073 metres/6,801 ft) in eight to ten hours. The westward path off the summit meets the dirt loop road and you can take either the south or north path. With a guide you can follow a forest ridge trail, crossing the Kathmandu to Likkhu Khola trail (a possible campsite) and continuing toward two hills from where Kakani's white lodge is visible. A bus to Kathmandu can be stopped on the Trisuli road. Or the next day, descend towards the northwest of the valley for an easy half-day hike along the hillside above the Kakani road, using Nagarjun's white stupa as a landmark. Meet the road at Teen-peepli where you can catch a bus to Kathmandu or walk the dirt road to Dharamthali and on to Kathmandu.

The forested hill west of Kathmandu is Nagarjun, also called Jamacho. A modest entry fee is requested at the main gate, 1 km (half a mile) up the Trisuli road from Balaju. A dirt road winds to the top (2,096 metres/6,877 ft), while hikers can walk for two hours on a footpath. At the top is a Buddhist stupa and a view of Ganesh Himal, Langtang and the Kathmandu Valley. A return trail descends southwest to Ichangu Narayan. There is no easy route in this area. A few Nepali phrases or a guide will help.

From the Thankot police checkpost you can walk local trails that link Bagwati, Shiva, Matatirtha and Maccha Narayan temples en route to Kirtipur (see page 204). South of Kirtipur the Chandragiri Ridge runs parallel to the Kathmandu-Pokhara highway, as far as the Nagdhunga Pass. Champa Devi (2,278 metres/7,474 ft), the highest peak on the ridge, affords a panoramic view of the valley backdropped by the Himalaya.

Day hikes to Champa Devi also start from Pikhel, on the Chobhar-Dakshinkali road. A road leads up through Haatiban (Elephant's Forest) to the Himalayan Heights Resort, with good views. The easy grade turns steep and the path peters out, leaving a scramble up

the rocky slope to a white stupa and a Hindu shrine marking the Champa Devi summit. Several return routes are possible; close to the ridge continuing west a trail descends from the second saddle to Kirtipur. From the third saddle the trail reaches Kisipidi.

There is no main trail connecting Chobhar or Pharping to Phulchoki, the highest hill on the valley rim (2,762 metres/ 9,062 ft). An easier approach is from Godavari. Two trails lead to the top in about four hours, one climbing up from the temple across from the marble quarry, the other ascending along the next ridge north. Both enjoy rhododendron forests and breathtaking views: Himal Chuli, Everest, Kathmandu Valley and the Terai.

The last leg of the perimeter trek links Phulchoki to Panauti. It is not an easy descent to the Roshi Khola, but once there a trail follows the stream most of the way. From Panauti it is four hours to Dhulikhel with its comfortable lodges, or six hours via the Buddhist site of Namo Buddha. ❑

● *For details of trekking guides, see the trekking agencies on page 330.*

LEFT: trekking in Kathmandu Valley offers rewarding and spectacular views.
RIGHT: country life in the heart of the valley.

KATHMANDU TO POKHARA

Map on page 222

Historic fortresses, ancient temples and striking mountain views make the journey from Kathmandu to Pokhara memorable, whether travelling on foot or by road

Thirty years ago, anyone wishing to get to Pokhara from Kathmandu had two choices: to fly or to walk. Most Nepalese walked, covering the distance in four or five days. In 1974, the 200-km (124-mile) Prithvi Raj Marg connecting the two cities was completed with Chinese aid, speeding travel time to seven or eight hours, depending on road reconstruction delays. But the old pedestrian "highway" remains a worthwhile journey, heavily plied by locals who delight in seeing and sharing a meal with a stranger from another land. For *bideshis* (foreigners), the eight- to nine-day walk is an excellent introduction to trekking in Nepal, with relatively low passes – a maximum of 1,300 metres (4,250 ft) – tea houses and several exit spots should the experience prove tiring. It is best to do the trek in winter, otherwise the lowland heat can be draining.

PRECEDING PAGES: Bhagvati Mandir, Manakamana. **LEFT:** old-style carousel in Gorkha. **BELOW:** village children in the Gorka region.

The Pokhara trail

The trail begins at Trisuli, at the end of a twisting 80-km (50-mile) road from Kathmandu. Prithvi Narayan Shah's old fortress of **Nuwakot** ❶ stands an hour's climb above the little bazaar town. The warrior prince captured Nuwakot in 1744, thereby cutting off one of the valley's primary supply routes, then launched his heroic siege while based here *(see page 32)*. The seven-storey palace fortress stands little marred by time despite a history of attacks by Malla and later Chinese forces. Basic lodging is available in Trisuli, or a day-trip can be made from Kathmandu or Kakani.

Highlights along the Pokhara trail include numerous stream crossings availing a dunk in the rushing waters, and superb views of the Central Himalaya: Ganesh Himal, Himal Chuli, Ngadi Chuli, Manaslu and the Annapurnas. A side trip can be made to the pleasant bazaar town of Ampipal, with its project hospital and primary school. Newars, Brahmans, Chhetris, Tamangs, Gurungs and Magars populate this corridor *(see page 43)*. Old men sit cross-legged sucking tobacco smoke through a *hookah* (water pipe); schoolrooms full of boys and girls pronounce their lessons aloud; women weave on looms stretched taut across their backs – memorable scenes abound. The trail ends at the peaceful lake of Begnas Tal in the Pokhara Valley, from where buses run to Pokhara *(see page 229)*.

Most travellers, of course, will choose the ease of modern transport, driving or flying from Kathmandu to Pokhara. Depending on road conditions, it's a five- to eight-hour journey by road. The highway climbs out of the Kathmandu Valley, exiting at Thankot, then drops in a series of hairpin curves down to Naubise. From here on the road follows the course of the Trisuli River, the most popular stretch of whitewater rafting in Nepal *(see page 143)*. En route to Pokhara, lunch is usually had at **Mugling**, locally known as "Daal Bhaat Bazaar" for the quantity of local eateries lined up along the highway. Mugling marks the journey's halfway point. Shortly after is the small town of Abu Khaireni, and the turn off to Gorkha. A little further is **Dumre**, a dusty roadside stop marking the turnoff for the Manang trek and the eastern side of the Annapurna Circuit. The old Newar town of Bandipur, once a major rural trading centre, is a two-hour climb from Dumre. Next is the district headquarters of Damauli, set at the confluence of the Madi and Seti rivers, which offer good swimming. The highway ends at the statue of Prithvi Narayan Shah near Pokhara's main bus park.

Hill stations and cable cars

The Tribhuvan Raj Path, Nepal's first road link to India, branches off from the main highway near Naubise and leads through the viewpoint town of **Daman ❷**. Daman is visited mainly by hard-core bikers who have snaked up the 2,100-metre (6,900-ft) hill from Hetauda. The town remains an underrated hill station with the broadest Himalayan views of all. From its 2,400-metre (7,874-ft) vantage point, enhanced by a circular view tower, a full 400 km (250 miles) of ice-cast peaks are visible, from Dhaulagiri to Everest and beyond. Several new tourist hotels built nearby offer a higher standard of accommodation, but the town itself, a mainly Sherpa community, remains a tiny huddle of shops and tea stalls serving as an overnight halt for lorry drivers who ply the Tribhuvan Raj Path between Kathmandu and Birganj on the Indian border. One can hitch a ride on a lorry or hire a private car and driver in Kathmandu for the winding three-hour drive. Travellers en route to or from Royal Chitwan National Park *(see page 301)* can request the driver to take this

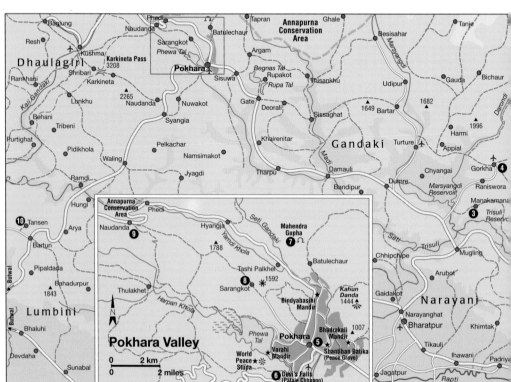

longer route as an alternative to the faster and more familiar road via Mugling.

From Daman's often windy, pine-forested hill the lovely Palung Valley, with its jigsaw-patterned terraces, stretches to the north and west. A small Buddhist *gompa* tended by monks and nuns from Bhutan can be reached in an hour's walk from the tower, down a marked trail through the forest.

Perched on a hilltop a four-hour hike from Gorkha is the famous wish-fulfilling temple at **Manakamana** ❸ (1,713 metres/5,620 ft), one of Nepal's most popular shrines. The devout pray at this temple, the **Bhagwati Mandir**, for male offspring or before setting out on any major venture – physical, spiritual or commercial. The journey has been eased by the construction of a cable car from Cheres, a small town midway between Mugling and Kuringhat on the Kathmandu-Pokhara highway.

Only 22 km (14 miles) off the main highway, the historic town of **Gorkha** ❹, the ancestral home of the Shah kings, makes an interesting side trip. Basic to medium-standard accommodation is available. A number of treks begin from here as well *(see page 251)*. Gorkha's old bazaar is a typical hill centre purveying a jumble of rice, gold, pots, pans and bangles. The town is dominated by the old Shah palace, Upallo Durbar, perched on a ridgetop some 300 metres (1,000 ft) above. It's a long climb up a stone stairway, but the crest rewards with lovely views of Baudha, Himal Chuli and Manaslu. The palace itself has been impeccably restored, and its stone-block construction and detailed woodwork is exceptional even by Nepalese standards. The inner sanctum is guarded by soldiers and contains a Kali image which demands a prodigious number of animal sacrifices, particularly during Dasain, when the compound runs red with the blood of hundreds of buffaloes, goats and chickens *(see page 89)*. ❑

Map on page 222

Cable car to Manakamana and the Bhagwati Mandir.

BELOW:
Upallo Durbar palace in Gorkha.

Kathmandu to Pokhara

0   10 km

0   10 miles

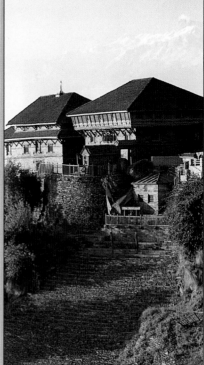

Gurkhas: Bravest of the Brave

Rare is the person today who has not heard of the Gurkha soldiers, the brave troops from Nepal's isolated hills who bolster the forces of the British and Indian armies. Famed for their tenacity and loyalty in warfare since the late 18th century, these *khukri*-wielding soldiers have played a key role in numerous wars.

The original Gurkha troops were from Gorkha, the small principality in central Nepal from which Prithvi Narayan Shah conquered the Kathmandu Valley in 1769 and unified the land of Nepal (*see page 32*). Composed largely of Thakuri, Magar and Gurung men, by 1814 these forces had swept their long *khukri* knives across the central Himalaya.

The first two regular Gorkhali battalions were raised in 1763. Known as the Sri Nath and Purano Gorakh, they fought together against the British in 1769 and saw separate

action against Tibet and in the Anglo-Nepal war of 1814–16. It was the latter that first cast the legend of Gurkha bravery, with their motto "Better to die than be a coward".

Impressed by what they had seen, the British began recruiting Gurkhas into their service, but this was not formalised until 1886, by which time India already had eight Gurkha Rifles units. The men were drawn largely from the Magar and Gurung tribes, but also from the Rais, Limbus and Sunuwars of the east hills and the Khasas of the west.

At first, given their past hostilities, the relationship between the British and Nepalese was uneasy, but by the time of the Rana regime in 1846 and the subsequent visit to England of Jung Bahadur Rana, there was no question of the Gurkhas' allegiance. During the Indian mutiny of 1857, the British Gurkha regiments were joined by 12,000 of Jung Bahadur's own troops, with decisive results. Over the next 50 years, Gurkhas fought all over south Asia, from Afghanistan to Malaya, and even African Somaliland in 1903.

When they were not fighting, they were climbing. Long before the Sherpas achieved fame as mountain guides, Gurkhas were climbing Himalayan peaks. In the Alps in 1894 two Gurkhas, Amar Singh Thapa and Karbir Burathoki, travelled 1,600 km (1,000 miles) in 86 days, crossing 39 passes and scaling 21 peaks. They named a Swiss peak Piz Gurkha after being the first to scale its 3,063 metres (10,049 ft); a col was named Gurkha Pass. In 1907 Burathoki and Englishman Tom Longstaff made the first major ascent of a Himalayan peak, Trisul (7,120 metres/23,360 ft). Gurkhas joined five Everest expeditions between 1921 and 1937.

With the advent of World War I, Gurkhas were called on in even greater numbers. More than 114,000 Gurkhas went into active service in Givenchy, Ypres, Gallipoli, Palestine, Mesopotamia, Suez and Persia. Another 200,000 of these fearless fighters were mobilised in the Indian army. Two Gurkhas, Kulbir Thapa (France, 1915) and Karna Bahadur Rana (Palestine, 1918), were awarded the Victoria Cross for gallantry.

LEFT: Gurkha soldier in the 19th century.
RIGHT: physical and medical records are tested and checked; celebrating being selected.

During World War II Gurkha strength was expanded to 45 battalions, seeing action in Iraq, Persia, Cyprus, Tunisia, Italy, Greece, Burma, Malaya and Indonesia; 10 Victoria Crosses were awarded. Two of the battalions were paratroopers. As the tale is told today, the British were seeking Gurkha volunteers for a risky 300-metre (1,000-ft) airdrop behind enemy lines. About half of the troops stepped forward. The regiment leader proceeded to explain the troops' role in the drop, when a surprised voice queried: "Oh, you mean we can use parachutes?" Every remaining Gurkha promptly volunteered.

In 1947, with Indian independence, the Gurkha regiments were divided: six of the ten became the Indian Gurkha Rifles; the remaining four – the 2nd, 6th, 7th and 10th – remained the British Brigade of Gurkhas. In India, the troops plunged into the India-Pakistan conflict over Kashmir; later came the Sino-Indian war of 1962 and further battles between India and Pakistan in 1965 and 1971. The British Brigade served in Malaya, Indonesia, Brunei and Cyprus.

Another Victoria Cross was presented to Lance Corporal Ram Bahadur Limbu for heroism in Sarawak in 1965.

Gurkhas are still regularly called upon to assist in world conflicts. During the Falklands War in 1982 between Britain and Argentina, their legendary fighting prowess appeared to terrify the South American troops, who "turned and fled" according to a British newspaper report. More recently, they have been employed to protect routes into Kosovo during the NATO crisis, and to guard aid being sent to East Timorese refugees in Indonesia.

Being a Gurkha soldier is a position of great status in Nepal. Men are recruited as teenagers of 17 or 18 from their villages after passing strict medical tests. They are given uniforms, good food and ten months' schooling and basic training. On their first home leave they are invariably treated as heroes. Many spend their entire careers in the Gurkhas and Gurkha salaries, pensions and related services provide a significant contribution to the national economy – only tourism earns more. ❑

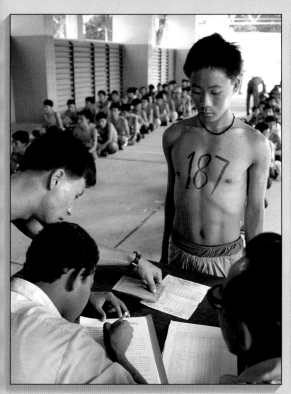

POKHARA AND
POKHARA VALLEY

*As a starting point for treks into the Annapurnas, Pokhara has
become a thriving centre for the trekking industry, while its
surrounding countryside is littered with traditional villages*

Maps:
Area 222
City 230

Nestled beneath the snow-crested Annapurna Massif 200 km (125 miles)
west of Kathmandu, the lush Pokhara Valley has quietly won the hearts
of travellers from around the world. Many visitors find that their most lasting impression of Nepal is Machhapuchhre's razor-edged "Fish Tail" peak
piercing the skyline or reflected in the still waters of Phewa Lake. The anti-
thesis of Kathmandu's flurry of cars, concrete and temples, Pokhara is a laid-
back and spread-out bazaar town where farmhouses nudge against tourist lodges
and a New Age T-shirt is *haute couture* for even the best hotels.

Fertile valley

Pokhara ❺ is Nepal's second most popular tourist destination. A quarter of all
visitors travel here, many on their way to trekking in the Annapurnas *(see page
237)*, or to enjoy a relaxing holiday at the very foot of the Himalaya. The
124 sq. km (48 sq. mile) valley remains largely farmland, its fields an intensely
vivid green during the monsoon with newly planted rice shoots. Lazy water
buffalo amble down back lanes, followed by women carrying fodder.

Pokhara's lush natural beauty contrasts with mountain views of epic proportions. The peaks seem closer
here than almost anywhere else; Annapurna I, crowning a 140-km (87-mile) horizon stretching from
Dhaulagiri to Himal Chuli, lies just 48 km (30 miles)
from the lake's edge as the crow flies. Machhapuchhre, just 30 km (19 miles) away, seemingly erupts
from the valley. The elevational differences are
equally impressive; 7,000 metres (23,500 ft) from the
valley floor to the tip of Annapurna I, tenth highest
mountain in the world at 8,091 metres (26,545 ft)
above sea level.

Pokhara sits at about 900 metres (3,000 ft) elevation, significantly lower than Kathmandu and generally several degrees warmer. The fertile valley and an
annual rainfall of 4,000 millimetres (157 inches) produce a landscape of subtropical flora. Flowering cacti,
poinsettias, citrus and banana trees line the rice and
mustard fields; garden walls are hedged with thorny
spurge spiked with red blossoms and the gnarled roots
of pipal and banyan trees burst from stone *chautaras*
(resting platforms). A lakeside forest of mixed oak
and evergreen conifers borders the extensively cultivated Mahabharat hills to the south.

Located in the geographical centre of Nepal on a
main highway from Kathmandu, Pokhara is accessible by tourist bus or private taxi via a five- to
eight-hour drive through a scenic cross-section of

PRECEDING PAGES:
Sarangkot,
above Pokhara.
LEFT: Phewa Tal,
Pokhara's
beautiful lake.
BELOW: the lush
Pokhara valley.

*Statue of King
Prithvi Narayan
Shah overlooking
Pokhara.*

BELOW: German
bakery at Lakeside.

Nepal's middle hills. Like most Nepalese highways this one suffers annual damage from monsoon rains. Due to ongoing road construction, the ride can be slow or delayed. Local airlines ferry passengers several times daily from Kathmandu with panoramic views of the Annapurnas and the Central Himalaya.

A trip to Pokhara blends well with visits to other Nepalese attractions: Royal Chitwan National Park, Lumbini and Tansen are all accessible by road from here, as are several whitewater rafting runs, including the popular float down the relatively calm Trisuli River *(see page 143)*.

Exploring Pokhara

Until a quarter of a century ago, Pokhara was a quiet Newar and Gurung farming community which came alive only during winter when caravans from Mustang – announced by the jingle of mule bells – and heavily laden porters from Butwal congregated to exchange goods. The wheel was not yet in use when the first airplane landed at Pokhara in 1952. Six years later, the first jeep flew in by plane even before the primitive wooden bullock cart arrived by the same means in 1961. The eradication of malaria in the late 1950s, the commissioning of hydroelectric power in 1968 and the completion of the Kathmandu-Pokhara and Pokhara-Sonauli highways in the early 1970s rocketed Pokhara into the 20th century – but without much planning.

Modern Pokhara is an important regional centre of government, education and commerce, but it retains its laid-back feel. The town is sprawled out over a surprisingly large area. To the north is the old town, an area called Bagar, a clutter of small shops selling traditional goods. North of here is **Shining Hospital Ⓐ**, named for the way the sun glinted off the original corrugated metal roof. The

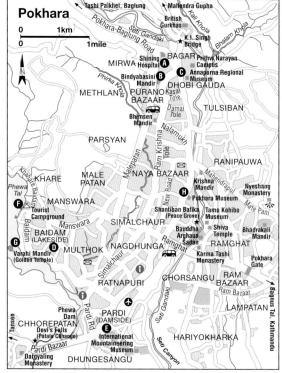

hilltop **Bindyabasini Mandir**  is dedicated to a form of the goddess Bhagvati and is frequented by devotees dragging up goats and chickens for sacrifice. East of here is **Prithvi Narayan Campus**, where the **Annapurna Regional Museum** ⓒ (open Wed–Mon 9am–4pm; free) displays exhibits on local flora and fauna, including an extensive butterfly collection.

Five minutes' taxi ride past the Immigration Office is serene **Phewa Tal**, the largest of the Pokhara Valley's eight lakes. On its eastern and southern shore stretch the tourist quarters of **Lakeside (Baidam)** ⓓ and **Damside (Pardi)** ⓔ. Inexpensive lodges, restaurants and shops selling Tibetan jewellery and artefacts, carpets, clothes, books and trekking equipment line the lanes. It's easy to while away the day strolling the peaceful streets. Unlike Kathmandu, Pokhara has not yet been submerged by motorcycles, taxis and *tempos*. The best lake views come at the southern end, around Gauri Ghat. Also on the lake is the **Tourist Campground** ⓕ which has hot showers and cooking facilities.

Lazy Pokhara life is best experienced with a serene float on the placid waters of the 2.5-km (1-mile) long Phewa Tal. Brightly painted rowing boats can be rented at several locations. The pretty **Golden Temple of Varahi** ⓖ on a tiny shaded island draws pilgrims and romantics. Just opposite is the modest winter palace of King Birendra. The lake's opposite shore makes a worthy destination, with a few simple restaurants and a growing number of resorts. Trails lead from the shore up to the ridgetop, crowned with a Japanese-built Buddhist monastery. Damside is an easy paddle to the south.

A long paved road leads from here through the modern bazaar area around Mahendra Phul and down to the local Bus Park at the eastern entrance to town. The **Pokhara Museum** ⓗ (open Wed–Mon 10am–5pm, until 3pm on Friday;

Maps:
Area 222
City 230

BELOW:
Machhapuchhre, the fish-tail peak, towers above Pokhara.

Golden light on Phewa Tal.

entrance fee) displays typical costumes, implements and ritual items of some of the many ethnic groups inhabiting the region around Pokhara, with a special exhibit on Upper Mustang. Not far from the bus park is Pokhara Airport, fronted by a government **Tourist Information Centre**, several medium-priced hotels and trekking agencies.

Fish Tail Lodge, one of Pokhara's nicest hotels, is set on a lakeside island peninsula. Part of its charm is that it is accessible only by rope-drawn raft. The lake's edge just beyond the hotel grounds is the best vantage point for photographing Machhapuchhre's reflection in the clear morning light. The hotel with the best close-up mountain views, however, is the new, deluxe **Tiger Mountain Pokhara Village**, located on a ridge northeast of Pokhara, a half-hour's drive from town. Stone bungalows cluster around private hot tubs in a garden setting. The Dusit Thani Fulbari Spa Resort rounds out Pokhara's recent surge in luxury accommodation, with a health club, pool and tennis courts.

Lakes and caves

Most of the remaining seven lakes of the Pokhara Valley are minor, but the twin lakes of Rupa and Begnas Tal make a pleasant destination for a day hike or a picnic. They are located about 15 km (9 miles) east of Pokhara by road. Begnas Tal, with its long line of rowing boats for rent, is tucked behind the village of Sisuwa, with its extensive fisheries project and a few simple tourist lodges. The forested ridge of Panchbhaiya Danda divides Begnas Tal from Rupa Tal. An hour-long hike up the ridge to the viewpoint of Sundari Danda rewards with sweeping views of peaks and lakes.

Another minor natural wonder can be seen 2 km (1 mile) south down the Siddhartha Rajmarg, an easy walk from Damside, where the Pardi Khola drops into a deep sinkhole called **Devi's Falls ⑥**. A local high school has taken over the site and charges a small admission fee to view the torrent – impressive in the rainy season but unspectacular in the winter. Friendly vendors sell tourist trinkets and souvenirs with their own particular brand of aggressive Tibetan charm.

BELOW: Tibetan monastery banners flying in Pokhara.

Across from Devi's Falls is the Tibetan settlement of Tashi Ling, one of three former refugee camps in the Pokhara Valley. The biggest and most interesting of the trio is Tashi Palkhel near Hyangja, 4 km (2 miles) west of town along the Baglung Highway. The whitewashed houses strung with fluttering prayer flags house around 1,000 Tibetans, many employed in the local carpet factory. Cottage industries abound here. A small monastery, a few simple restaurants and a basic guesthouse can all be found on the grounds.

At the village of Batulechaur, north of Pokhara Bazaar, ancient subsurface lakes have left limestone caverns large enough to walk through at **Mahendra Gupha ⑦**. There is a small admission fee to the cave, dimly lit by a generator. For a few more rupees, young boys with flashlights will provide a guided tour, pointing out stalactite and stalagmite features which locals interpret as images of deities. The local name for the cavern is Chamero Odhaar, "House of Bats".

The Pokhara region's fascinating geology is also visible at the deep gorge of the Seti Gandaki, visible from the Mahendra Phul bridge near the airport. Here the river rushes 30 metres (100 ft) below in a 9-metre (30-ft) wide gap in the earth, carved as the river winds its way through the valley's soft soil.

Maps:
Area 222
City 230

Excursions from Pokhara

Numerous trails lead into the hills surrounding Pokhara, making it a superb trekking headquarters. A day hike to the hilltop viewpoint of **Sarangkot** ❽, at 1,592 metres (5,271 ft), is popular despite the steep ascent of two to four hours. Climbers are rewarded with stunning mountain and lake views, while several restaurants and lodges at the top cater to visitors. Try to take the walk in the early morning to watch the sun rise slowly over the mountains, changing their colours from pink to gold. For non-hikers or those with less time, a road leads up to a cluster of tea stalls some 15 minutes below the summit. From Sarangkot a trail leads westward along the ridge to the old fortress of Kaski and follows on to the village of **Naudanda** ❾, now on the Pokhara-Baglung Highway and another base for treks into the Annapurnas.

On the east side of Pokhara, the slightly lower vantage point of Kahun Danda (1,443 metres/4,778 ft) is a shorter, easier and less crowded way of obtaining mountain views. The Manangi Gompa at the foot of the hill, sponsored by wealthy Buddhists from the Central Nepal region of Manang, displays typical Buddhist implements in a modern setting.

Another scenic excursion involves a drive west along the Siddhartha Rajmarg to Kubhinde Pass for a spectacular sunrise over the Annapurna massif. Like the fortress ruins site at Sarangkot, Nuwakot, located 15 km (9 miles) south of

BELOW: a local family watching the world go by.

Nepali buses are colourful, overcrowded and extremely cheap.

Pokhara, served as a lookout for Kaski kings prior to conquest by Prithvi Narayan Shah *(see page 221)*. The new 72-km (45-mile) highway joining Pokhara with Baglung to the west has improved access into countryside once considered remote, chopping several days off many treks. It's a pleasant two-hour drive to the roadside tea stalls at Naya Phul, the jumping-off point for many treks, including up the Kali Gandaki River to Jomsom *(see page 242)*. The pretty riverside town of Birethanti is only a half-hour walk from here.

Travel agents in Pokhara also arrange pony treks along the lakes. River-rafting trips in the region include a moderate float on the Seti Gandaki from Damauli to Narayanghat, the Kali Gandaki and the Marsyangdi. Some companies hold kayaking clinics, beginning with an easy day on Phewa Tal and concluding with a whitewater passage down the Seti Gandaki *(see page 143)*. The **Himalayan Golf Course** (tel. 61 27204) at Majeri Patan, 7 km (4½ miles) outside Pokhara, offers the opportunity to tee off beneath Himalayan views. Green fees are around US$60, including lunch and hotel pickup. For the more adventurous, Avia Club Nepal (tel. 61 25192) offers flights over the Pokhara Valley in single passenger ultra-light aircraft, for 10 minutes to one hour.

Tansen's quiet pleasures

BELOW: Brahman and Chhetri villages in the hills around Pokhara.

A half-day's drive from Pokhara along the bumpy Siddartha Rajmarg linking Pokhara and Butwal reaches the enchanting trading town of **Tansen ⑩**, at an elevation of 1,400 metres (4,600 ft). Daily flights from Kathmandu to Siddharthanagar shorten this trip to less than two hours.

Few tourists have discovered Tansen's secluded serenity and the atmosphere only adds to the simple pleasures of a visit here. A huddle of red-brick houses

perched on a steep hillside, Tansen is an old Newari trading settlement, one of the largest scattered across Nepal's central hills. This town of 16,000 people was the former capital of the Kingdom of Palpa until a final subjection by the Shah kings in 1806. Many people, however, still refer to the town as Palpa.

Steep old cobbled streets lead up through small bazaars famed for their colourful *topis* (traditional men's hats) and handcrafted metalware. The clack of wooden looms reminds the visitor that handwoven *dhaka* cloth is a local speciality. Other sights include Baggi Dhokha, the northern gate to rambling old **Tansen Durbar**, a former residence for Rana governors which now houses government offices. The 19th-century **Amir Narayan Temple** on the eastern side of town has a glittering facade of beaten metal. Nearby is the town's parade ground or Tundikhel, overlooking the green Madi Valley far below.

From the wooded hilltop viewpoint of Srinagar Danda rising up behind the town, the Himalaya are visible from Dhaulagiri to Gauri Shankar. To the south, the Tinau River cuts through the Mahabharat range; beyond, the Siwalik hills rise from the Terai. On winter mornings the valleys are swathed in white mist.

The countryside surrounding Tansen offers lovely rambles for the day hiker or trekker, such as the Magar village of Chilangdi, an hour's walk from town, or the potters' village of Ghorabanda Bazaar, 3 km (2 miles) north off the highway. **Ridi Bazaar**, a Newar settlement with an important Vishnu temple, lies 10 km (6 miles) down an unpaved road with a minibus service. Most intriguing is the 14-km (8-mile) hike up the Kali Gandaki to the crumbling riverside palace of Rani Ghat, an imposing Rana-era edifice. Longer trips include a Pokhara-Dhorpatan-Tansen circuit, a four-day hike along the Kali Gandaki to Beni, or a week's walk along Panchase Lekh to Pokhara. ❑

Map on page 222

LEFT: the Buddhist monastery in Tansen.
BELOW: Pokhara is a popular starting point for treks.

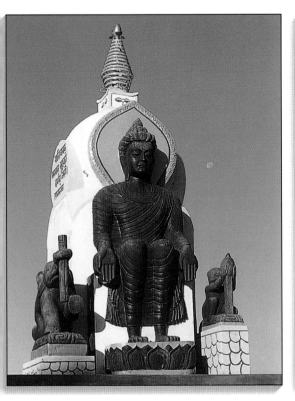

TREKKING IN THE ANNAPURNAS

Map on page 238

The Annapurna region is consistently popular with trekkers visiting Nepal, with a wide choice of routes of variable degrees of difficulty, allowing breathtaking mountain views whatever your abilities

Kathmandu

Dawn's rays gild Annapurna I before any of her sister peaks in the majestic Annapurna Himal. At 8,091 metres (26,545 ft), she crowns a range which scarcely dips below 6,000 metres (20,000 ft). This is a land of astonishing altitudinal variation and ecological diversity, extending from the subtropical Pokhara Valley to the frozen tips of the some of the world's highest peaks – a region brimming with natural beauty that is the most popular trekking area in Nepal.

Marking a convergence of biogeographical zones east and west, the Annapurnas host a wide assortment of flora and fauna. The massif's southern flanks are blanketed in lush deciduous forests, watered by plentiful rainfall. Fir, pine and juniper cluster on upper slopes, while the mountains' rainshadow effect keeps high valleys brown and barren. Wildlife once abounded in every habitat, but has been driven to remote corners by widespread land clearing. The remaining populations of rhesus and langur monkeys, jungle cats and wild boar give way to mid-elevation black bear, musk deer and yellow-throated marten. Long-haired *tahr* (mountain goat), *bharal* (blue sheep) and snow leopard prowl the loftiest reaches. Among the 440 recorded bird species are the monal and Impeyan pheasants, and some 40 migratory varieties which take refuge here en route to and from Tibet.

The region's human population, numbering over 40,000, is a melting pot as well. Seven ethnic groups live side by side, each wearing their own distinctive dress, revering different deities and speaking their own languages. Lowland valleys are inhabited primarily by Hindus: high-caste Brahmans and Chhetris, Newars, and the occupational castes of Kamis (blacksmiths), Damais (tailors) and Sarkis (shoemakers). Hill peoples include the Gurungs, Magars and Thakalis. Most follow the Buddhist doctrine or a syncretism of Hinduism and Buddhism. In higher terrain closer to the border are peoples more recently migrated from Tibet, such as the Lopa of Kagbeni, who practice the Bön religion *(see page 60)*, or the Manangis, whose career as skilled traders began in the 18th century with a royal edict exempting them from customs regulations.

A magnet for trekkers

More than 50,000 trekkers visit the Annapurna area each year, three times the number who hike in the Everest region. This figure, combined with a growing native population, has contributed to environmental problems such as deforestation, poor

LEFT: the classic view of Machhapuchhre from the Annapurna Sanctuary.
BELOW: highland Tibetan man.

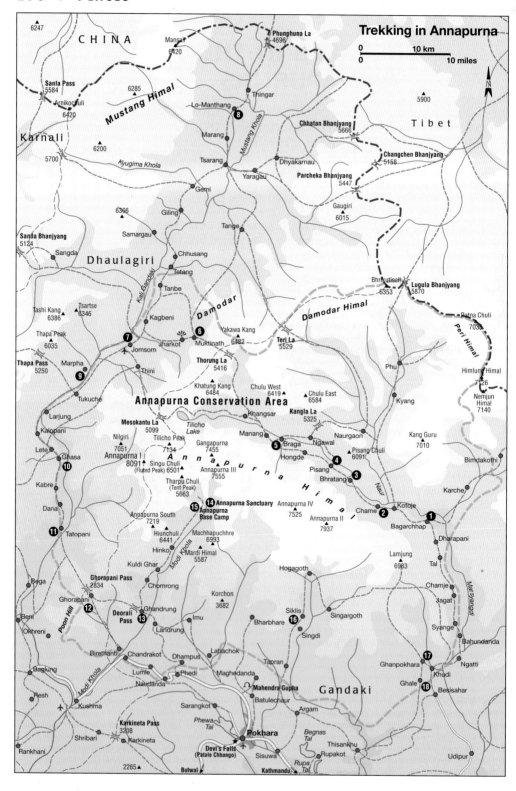

sanitation, littering and water pollution. Since 1986, the non-governmental Annapurna Conservation Area Project (**ACAP**) has been organising villagers to take up measures of resource management, low-tech conservation, alternative energy schemes and community development programmes. The results are inspiring *(see page 119)*.

Map on page 238

The **Annapurna Circuit**, a walk of almost one month's duration around the Annapurna massif, is widely considered to be the classic Nepal trek. The route circles the Annapurna and Lamjung Himals (6,983 metres/22,910 ft), including **Annapurna I**, the tenth-highest peak in the world, **Annapurna II** (7,937 metres/ 26,040 ft), **Annapurna IV** (7,525 metres/24,688 ft), **Annapurna III** (7,555 metres/24,787 ft) and Gangapurna (7,455 metres/24,458 ft). On the eastern front, it traces the Marsyangdi River up and over the Thorung La pass (5,416 metres/17,769 ft) then descends the long gorge of the Kali Gandaki River to the west. The trek can be done in reverse but requires a greater one-day elevation gain to get over the pass. Lodges catering to independent trekkers line the trail, providing nightly lodging, meals and snack stops.

The trek commonly begins in Dumre *(see page 222)*. Trucks and jeeps run from here along an unpaved seasonal road to the pleasant trailhead village of Besisahar. Alternatively, the trail enters the Marsyangdi valley at Tarkughat, two days west of Gorkha *(see page 223)*, or at Khudi, a slightly longer walk from Pokhara. These less-travelled sections give a taste of hill life unadulterated by tourist-catering entrepreneurs.

Weaving ropes for porters' baskets, Syalung area.

The first day's walk up the Marsyangdi River affords excellent and ever-changing views of the high Himalaya. To the north and west loom **Machhapuchhre** (6,993 metres/22,937 ft) and Annapurnas II to IV. Dominating the eastern skyline are **Manaslu** (8,163 metres/26,781 ft), the world's eighth highest peak, **Himal Chuli** (7,893 metres/25,895 ft), Peak 29 (7,835 metres/25,705 ft) and Baudha Himal (6,672 metres/21,890 ft).

BELOW: local children at Chame on the Annapurna Circuit.

The trail climbs gently through banana palms and rice fields, shaded by welcome *chautaras* beneath the sprawling limbs of aged pipal and banyan trees. Sometimes the two types of trees are joined, symbolising a male-female union. At Bahundanda (1,310 metres/4,300 ft), Hindu communities give way to Gurung and Magar villages. Typical two-toned ochre and white-washed houses mirror the amalgamation of two cultures and ecological zones. Here, the wide valley squeezes into a rock-bound cleft, millet replaces rice and oak-rhododendron cover the slopes.

At the little settlement of Tal, tourist inns outshine the dark, cramped quarters previously shared with herdsmen and traders. The bazaar town of **Bagarchhap** ❶, a half-day's walk further, suffered a massive landslide in 1995 that killed several trekkers and villagers. Here the valley swerves due west to enter the 24-km (15-mile) long Manang Valley. A new trail blasted out of solid rock avoids a section once considered too dangerous even for pack animals. In earlier times, the only southern entry into the Marsyangdi Gorge was a high trail over the treacherous Namun Bhanjyang pass (4,890 metres/16,039 ft) to Ghanpokhara, Khudi or west to the Modi Khola.

A traditional street in the Thakali village of Marpha in the Kali Gandaki valley.

As the climate cools, forests turn to pine. **Chame ❷** (2,655 metres/8,710 ft) is the district headquarters and checkpost for Manang, with electricity and natural hot springs (as at Bahundanda). The Naur Valley, requiring a special permit to visit, enters here from the north. The people of **Naur** and **Phu** villages were originally from Tibet and, like those of Dolpo *(see page 319)*, remain largely isolated. In such a high, cold environment only barley, buckwheat and potatoes grow, supplemented with summer greens, yak meat and dairy products.

One km (half a mile) beyond **Bhratang ❸**, a sweeping rock face of dark limestone spans two promontory points some 1,650 metres (5,413 ft) above the river. Known as "Ghost Rock", it represents the arduous route to heaven for local Gurungs. The main trail continues up through thinning pine forest and enters the broad valley of Nyeshang, or upper Manang.

Traditional villages

With their clusters of flat-roofed stone buildings huddled against eroding cliffs, the villages of **Pisang ❹** and **Braga ❺** are reminiscent of Native American communities. Buddhist prayer flags flying from the houses' corners, and the northern flanks of Annapurna II, IV, and further up Annapurna III, Gangapurna, Tarkekang (7,193 metres/23,599 ft) and Tilicho Peak (7,134 metres/23,405 ft) confirm the geographic location. A high trail connects Pisang to Braga through the traditional villages of Ghyaru and Ngawal. This route is longer but more interesting, offering mountain views of Pisang Chuli (6,091 metres/19,983 ft), Chulu East (6,059 metres/19,875 ft), and Chulu West (6,548 metres/21,477 ft). There is much to see in the upper valley warranting a rest-day at Braga or Manang, which can also help acclimatisation.

BELOW: Braga village in the Manang Valley.

Braga's 500-year-old *gompa* is one of the cultural highlights of the valley. Terracotta statues of the Kargyu *lama* lineage lines its walls, which are painted with vivid frescoes. Manang village (3,535 metres/11,600 ft), the largest and last significant settlement in the valley, has its own, simpler monastery. The region's most active Buddhist centre is Bodzo Gompa, perched on a ridgetop between the two towns. It is customary to make a small donation to help with its upkeep.

Day hikes to higher elevations help with acclimatisation. One trip reaches a forested plateau overlooking the Gangapurna ice waterfall which feeds a stunning glacial lake. Another ascends to **Khangsar**, a Tibetan-influenced village along the difficult 18-km (11-mile) track to the restricted area of Tilicho Lake (4,919 metres/16,138 ft).

Trekkers number upward of 300 per day through Manang during peak season. Flights from Pokhara to the airstrip at Hongde, south of Braga, bring others not so well acclimatised. The Himalayan Rescue Association (HRA) Trekkers' Aid Post, which is seasonally staffed by volunteer Western physicians, treats trekkers and villagers. The Manang Mountaineering School, built in 1979 by Yugoslavians to honour a Sherpa killed on Everest, offers summer classes in climbing techniques and safety.

Proceeding slowly up from Manang, a night at Lattar and another at Phedi (4,404 metres/14,449 ft) bodes well for crossing the Thorung La (5,416 metres/ 17,764 ft), the highest point on the circuit. The first part of the pass is the steepest, levelling off in a series of false summits before the top, which is unmistakably marked with stone cairns and wind-whipped prayer flags. Magnificent views unfold all around. The icy trail descends to Muktinath (3,810 metres/12,500 ft), completing an eight- to ten- hour hike from Phedi.

Map on page 238

BELOW: the Thorung La Pass.

Muktinath is sacred to both Hindus and Buddhists.

Place of a Hundred Springs

Along with Pashupatinath temple in the Kathmandu Valley, **Muktinath ❻** is the most sacred Hindu site in Nepal. Pilgrims come to bathe in the pure spring waters that gush from 108 water spouts shaped as cows' heads. Buddhists come to pay homage at a shrine enclosing a blue flame of natural gas which burns eternally above a trickle of water, a wondrous union of fire, air and water. Ammonite fossils called *shaligrams* – evidence of the Himalaya's former position beneath the Tethys Sea – are revered as embodiments of Vishnu. Full moon is a propitious time to visit Muktinath, and, during August and September, to witness a rowdy festival called Yartung wherein local Tibetans hold horse races amid much wild drinking, gambling and dancing.

The trail descends through a lovely high valley dominated by the ruined fortress of Jharkot. En route to Jomsom, it's well worth taking a short detour through the fascinating old citadel town of Kagbeni. Close-packed mudwalled houses, their flat roofs stacked with firewood, lend a medieval feeling to the narrow streets. The local monastery is open to visitors. Near Kagbeni, the trail divides in four directions; north into Mustang, one of the few remaining Tibetan dominions ruled by ancestral nobility; south down the Kali Gandaki, dividing the Dhaulagiri Himal from the Annapurnas; west to Dangar Dzong and Dolpo; and east from Muktinath.

The district headquarters of **Jomsom ❼** is a busy cluster of government offices, hotels, shops and a hospital. Several airlines service the local airstrip with flights from Pokhara and Kathmandu. The Jomsom Eco-Museum (open daily; entrance fee) on the town's southern outskirts features displays of local ethnic groups and geography.

BELOW:
pack mule on the
Annapurna Circuit.

MULE TRAINS

Jingling, clopping mule trains are unique to the Annapurna region, a long-standing tradition dating back thousands of years. Trans-Himalayan trade of this type is described in historical records dating back to the 4th century and no doubt predates these. For millennia people have ferried goods up and down the river valleys carved through the mountains, exchanging highland necessities for lowland ones, traditionally by barter. The old salt trade is a typical example, involving two vital goods – highland salt gathered from Tibet's vast lakes, and rice which grows in abundance on the lower slopes of the Himalaya.

Traditionally Thakali people operate the caravans of sturdy mules, a sterile hybrid of donkeys and horses. Sure-footed and calm-tempered, the mules are well built for narrow, rocky Himalayan trails. Wooden packsaddles are laden with goods that vary depending on the direction: wool, salt and turquoise from Tibet on the downward journey; Nepalese rice, cloth and cigarettes for the upward return. Modern selections have been updated to include Chinese shoes, fabric and thermos flasks. The animals are adorned with harnesses of bells and headdresses of colourful plumes. Lead mules may wear a headpiece inset with a piece woven in the same fashion as Tibetan carpets.

Unknown Mustang

Hidden within the Inner Himalaya, Mustang was only opened to foreign trekkers in 1992, and access is limited to group travellers who must pay substantial fees, be accompanied by an official and adhere to the strictest environmental regulations. Because Mustang is rain-sheltered by the Himalaya, it has no monsoon season and can be visited during the summer.

The trek starts in Jomsom (2,750 metres/ 9,020 ft). *Chortens*, prayer flags and *mani* walls show the religious importance of the route leading north from here. The first leg of the journey (five to six hours) ends at Muktinath. The long haul via Kagbeni is well worth the effort. After a good night's rest the trek leads into the land of the Lopas, a tribe whose language, religion and clothes all signal they are essentially Tibetans. The women wear colourful aprons and the men display plaited ponytails and heavy turquoise earrings.

Several mountain passes up to 4,300 metres (14,104 ft) cross impressive steppes and deserts with small watering holes. All around are the grand 6,000-metre (19,680ft) mountains of the Damodar Himal. Eight hours of trekking come to a deserved halt in a Champa village at 4,100 metres (13,448 ft).

The next day is filled with a seven-hour hike across several passes (up to 4,600 metres/15,088 ft) to the meadows of Pee (4,100 metres/13,448 ft) where a spring invites the traveller to take a rest. The destinations for the following day are the villages of Tange and Dri (3,350 metres/10,988 ft). From there the path leads to the 600-year-old Mustang capital of **Lo-Manthang 8**. The flat-roofed houses and numerous art treasures of this town are surrounded by a mighty wall: the Maharajah Palace, the ancient town temple, the giant statue of Buddha Maitreya and several monasteries are all waiting to be explored.

Map on page 238

BELOW: Lo-Manthang in the Mustang region.

Thak Khola

The upper Kali Gandaki region south of Jomsom is known as the Thak Khola, home of the Thakali people whose *bhattis* (lodges) are legendary among trekkers for their cleanliness and unbeatable *dal bhaat*. The turbulent river flows between incredibly high peaks, creating the deepest river gorge on earth. **Dhaulagiri I** (8,167 metres/26,795 ft) and Annapurna I tower nearly 7 km (4 miles) above the river at some points, separated by a distance of less than 20 km (12 miles). A stiff wind created by the temperature differential and the deep gorge blows through here daily, gusting up to 40 kmph (25 mph).

A trip strictly for hardy trekkers encircles the Dhaulagiri Himal, comprising Dhaulagiri I–VI all over 7,260 metres (23,800 ft), through partially restricted, semi-wild territory. A month-long trek heads west from Dangar Dzong, crossing two high passes and continuing on to Tarakot in Dolpo, returning to Pokhara via Dhorpatan. A short-cut itinerary climbs out of the Kali Gandaki and over Dhampus and French Passes via Hidden Valley, then turns southeast to follow the Mayangdi Khola to **Beni**, west of Pokhara.

Marpha ❾ is a gastronomic delight with garden vegetables and juicy apples, apricots and peaches sold fresh, dry and as robust *rakshi* (distilled liquor). Both Marpha and **Tukuche** (2,590 metres/8,480 ft) have retained their indigenous charm despite electrification.

Traces of forest appear on the hillsides as the trail leaves behind the dry moonscape for wetter, lower regions. The spectacular waterfall at Rupse Chhaharo cascades into the swirling Kali Gandaki. Exploratory trips such as up the Dhaulagiri Icefall reward those with a flexible schedule. A seven-day hike up to Annapurna Base Camp and back follows the spectacular route discovered by

French climbers with Maurice Herzog in 1950 *(see page 138)* on the first-ever ascent of an 8,000-metre peak (Annapurna I).

Below the Thakali town of **Ghasa** ❿ the Kali Gandaki plunges through a narrow chasm, and the transition from pines to broadleaf, deciduous trees marks the lower reaches of Thakali *bhattis* and Tibetan Buddhist influence. At **Tatopani** ⓫ (1,189 metres/3,900 ft), whose name means "hot springs", lodge-keepers capitalise on natural hot springs and a balmy, floral setting, tempting trekkers with hydro-generated videos and oven-baked pizza. The long climb up through rhododendron and oak forests to Ghorapani Pass regains 1,660 metres (5,450 ft), with views back to Dhaulagiri I.

Sunrise from Poon Hill

Ghorapani ⓬ ("horse water"), a jumble of trekker lodges literally carved out of a denuded landscape, was once a film-set tradepost. Now it is an easy destination for trekkers, boasting glorious views of Annapurna South (7,219 metres/ 23,684 ft), Hiunchuli (6,441 metres/21,130 ft) and from the top of Poon Hill (approximately 3,200 metres/10,500 ft) an unforgettable sunrise over Machhapuchhre. Inspired by an Australian conservation project, lodge-keepers have installed fuel-efficient stoves and composting toilets, and have removed lodges from Poon Hill (named for a Magar clan), establishing it as a protected area.

From Ghorapani there are two main return routes to Pokhara, each taking four to five days. One follows the donkey trains down some 3,700 steps from Ulleri to Tirkhedhunga (1,577 metres/5,175 ft) and on to **Birethanti**'s riverside lodges in a long day. The roadside stop of Naya Phul on the Pokhara-Baglung Highway is an easy half-hour walk from here. The old trail continues

Map on page 238

Labourer at Ghandrung on the Annapurna Sanctuary trek.

BELOW: rhododendron forest flanked by Annapurna South.

Cooking dal bhaat *on an environmentally-friendly low-wattage stove.*

BELOW: rice terraces on the Annapurna foothills.

up to Chandrakot and contours through Lumle where it meets the highway again near Khare and Naudanda. An alternative skirts to the next ridge south via Jhobang and Bhadauri before descending to the Harpan Khola flowing out of Phewa Tal. The journey culminates with a boat ride across the lake into Pokhara.

Many trekkers make a six- to eight-day Pokhara-Ghorapani-Ghandruk loop, beginning at Naya Phul and ascending up to Poon Hill for mountain views. This loop has the advantage of low altitude, which makes it less challenging than many and also feasible even in winter months. The walk from Ghorapani (2,853 metres/9,360 ft) to **Ghandrung** ⓭ – also known as Ghandruk – was only recently adopted by trekkers and tunnels through virgin forest and lush jungle. The trail passes through an incredible rhododendron forest whose bronze twisted limbs might have inspired Tolkien in *The Lord of the Rings*. During March and April, the Annapurna forests, as throughout much of Nepal's mid-region, are smothered with laligurans (rhododendron) trees ablaze with ivory, rose, apricot and crimson bouquets. The little settlement of Tadapani provides food and lodging along the route, although it's possible to hike from Ghorapani to Ghandrung in a single long day. Ghandrung's sprawling split-level town is one of the biggest Gurung settlements in Nepal. A day is well spent roaming its maze of stone-paved paths among handsome slate-roofed houses. The community prospers, as do others in the region, from its young men serving in Gurkha regiments.

The Annapurna Conservation Area headquarters, with a museum and informative staff, sits on a promontory behind the health post. The site provides an unbeatable photo opportunity taking in Annapurna South, Hiunchuli, Machhapuchhre and the steep-sided Modi Khola valley leading into the Annapurna Sanctuary.

The Annapurna Sanctuary

Long before trekkers came flocking to the Himalaya, Deothal, as the Gurungs know it, was a place of refuge and spiritual renewal, where nothing should be slaughtered nor meat eaten. Lt. Col. Jimmy Roberts christened it the **Annapurna Sanctuary** ⑭ during his 1956 unsuccessful attempt to climb Machhapuchhre, itself a sacred summit that is closed to expeditions.

A natural amphitheatre surrounded by 11 peaks over 6,400 metres (21,000 ft), the Sanctuary affords trekkers a high usually reserved for mountaineers. **Annapurna Base Camp** ⑮ (4,070 metres/13,550 ft), a large snow-covered meadow with several small lodges, is only a week's walk from Pokhara, through Dhampus and Landrung in one direction and Ghandrung and Itinku in the other.

Along the trail's lower reaches, tea houses provide some of the highest standard trek lodging in Nepal. The ACAP "demonstration" lodge at Kuldi Ghar features fresh garden vegetables and a hot shower heated by the efficient back-boiler system. In order to save trees, ACAP regulations prohibit fires in the Sanctuary. Kerosene can be purchased and stoves rented in Chomrong, an idyllic little Alpine village. While the Sanctuary's route is straightforward, following the course of the Modi Khola River, weather is fickle and the Modi valley gorge is susceptible to avalanches and early snow. Non-expedition climbers can try out Tharpu Chuli (Tent Peak, 5,663 metres/18,550 ft) with a permit.

Historic hill treks

Siklis ⑯, one of the early southern Gurung settlements, retains an aura of olden times where traditions run strong. The local *jhankri* (shaman) and *lama* (priest) each have a place in the Buddhist community. Village elders oversee an effective forest management system whereby the entire year's wood supply is cut during three frenzied days, culminating in a celebration.

Built on an east-facing slope above the Modi Khola at 1,981 metres (6,500 ft), Siklis looks north onto Annapurna IV and east to Annapurna II and Lamjung Himal. From Pokhara, a two-day trek to Siklis continues west to the Piper Pheasant Reserve where hunting is permitted. A seven- to ten-day trek returns along the Modi Khola southeast from Siklis, climbs to Kalikathan and Syaglung on a ridge parallelling the east-west Annapurna Himal, and descends to the lakes of Rupa Tal and Begnas Tal in the Pokhara Valley.

The Annapurna hills are alive with tales of battles between rival kings from the days of fierce trade feuds and territorial skirmishes. The faded glory of **Ghanpokhara** ⑰ tells its story as controller of the Marsyangdi salt trade. A prominent hilltop position (2,165 metres/ 7,100 ft) grants it sweeping views of Lamjung, Manaslu and Gorkha Himals. Stone ramparts of the old Lamjung Durbar royal fort residence of **Ghale** ⑱ remain from this lineage which in 1559 conquered Gorkha and gave birth to the kingdom of Nepal. Today, Gurungs raise sheep and goats for wool which the women weave into striped blankets *(baakhu),* shawls and jackets.

Climbing to the west of Pokhara gains excellent views of the Annapurnas and Machhapuchhre. Above

Map on page 238

Prince Charles tramped in the Siklis area in 1980, calling on Gurkha recruits' home hamlets. A four-day "Royal Trek" retracing his route takes in village life and striking mountain panoramas.

BELOW:
haute cuisine at Annapurna Base Camp.

Map
on page
238

Bamboo bridge over the swirling waters of the Marsyangdi Khola.

BELOW:

descending from a mountaineering expedition.

Phewa Tal's southern rim are picturesque Pumdi and Bumdi, with their old-style oval houses of red clay. In earlier times, evil spirits were thought to dwell in corners, hence the rounded walls.

Annapurna Himal Trekking Peaks

The lofty summits of the Annapurna Himal lie north of Pokhara, between the valleys of the Marsyangdi Khola in the east and the Kali Gandaki, the world's deepest valley, in the west. The Annapurna massif is the focal point of two distinct groups of trekking peaks; those of the Annapurna Sanctuary and Manang Himal. Within the Annapurna Sanctuary are four trekking peaks.

Mardi Himal (5,587 metres/18,330 ft, Group B) is only 24 km (15 miles) north of Pokhara and is somewhat overshadowed by Machhapuchhre. It forms a distinct knot of aretes and glaciers on its southwest ridge. First identified by Basil Goodfellow in 1953, it was not climbed until 1961, when Jimmy Roberts reached the summit via the east flank. Mardi Himal is seldom climbed today.

Hiunchuli (6,441 metres/ 21,132 ft Group A) is a difficult mountain, despite its apparently accessible location. A guardian at the entrance to the Sanctuary, it looms due north of Chomrong. All of its approaches are challenging, protected by rock slabs and hanging ice. First climbed in 1971 by an American Peace Corps Expedition, it has seen few ascents since.

Tharpu Chule (Tent Peak) (5,663 metres/18,580 ft, Group B) was named by Jimmy Roberts for obvious reasons. The peak stands opposite the lodges near the Annapurna South Base Camp on the north side of the South Annapurna glacier. Several routes have been done on the mountain but the normal route is the northwest ridge, first climbed in 1965 by Gunter Hauser and party. **Singu Chuli (Fluted Peak)** (6,501 metres/21,329 ft, Group A) rises north of Tent Peak and is part of the same ridgeline. First climbed in 1957 by Wilfred Noyce and David Cox, following a route on the northeast face, the mountain has resisted most later attempts.

The arid landscape of Manang lies north of the Great Himalayan Range at the head of the Marsyangdi Valley and was first explored by Tilman and Roberts in 1950. North of the Manang Valley is a line of peaks that include the following summits: **Pisang Chuli** (6,091 metres/19,983 ft, Group A) is popular with trekking groups and rises from the meadows above Pisang. First climbed by J. Wellenkamp in 1955 by the southwest face and ridge, this route remains the only reported climb on the mountain, despite it having a striking west flank. **Chulu Gundang (East)** (6,584 metres/21,601 ft, Group A) lies north of Ongre at the head of the Chegagji Khola, where it forms an icy pyramid. It was first climbed by the German Annapurna Expedition in 1955, probably by the south ridge. The northeast ridge, however, provides a route of moderate difficulty, first climbed by Isherwood and Noble in 1979. **Chulu West** (6,419 metres/21,560 ft Group A) is along the main crest of the Manang Himal and southeast is **Chulu Central** (6,429 metres/21,505 ft). Both can be climbed on the same permit. Chulu West was first climbed in 1978 by Larry Zaroff and Peter Lev via the northwest ridge. ❏

A Day in the Life of a Gurung Hillwoman

Sun Kumari and her husband have been up since dawn, he reciting the morning prayers to a medley of Hindu and Buddhist gods, she stoking the coals of last night's fire to brew a fresh pot of tea. "Kaanchi! Oh Kaanchi!" she calls to her youngest daughter into the dim light of the coming day.

Kaanchi arises from a shapeless pile of children and goat-hair blankets and sleepily adjusts the *naamlo* (rope headstrap) and jug that are her tools for fetching water, the first chore of the day. Barefoot, she enters the mist, her small callused feet padding silently down the slate steps that overlook the precipitous canyon walls of the Modi Khola.

Sunlight filters through the glassless windows of the tidy stone house, piercing the smoky interior and spotlighting an assortment of copper pots and utensils. The other children rise and drink tea as their grandmother, the Bajai, sits up and, with a toothless grin, lights a Yak brand cigarette. Sun Kumari squats by the doorway and spreads a layer of fresh ochre-coloured mud on the inside floor, a daily ritual performed by Gurung women to cleanse their homes of malevolent spirits. The day comes to life punctuated by laughter, good-natured teasing and the scratchy sounds of Radio Nepal.

After the morning meal of *dhero*, a gruel of ground, boiled millet, accompanied by venison curry, the older children go to school, the younger ones wander into the forest to collect firewood and fodder, and the adults migrate to the sunny stone courtyard. Sun Kumari beats and winnows rice to be distilled into *rakshi* or cooked as *dhal bhaat*. Her husband weaves a bamboo basket and Bajai soaks up the sun, her pendulous golden earrings glistening like ice crystals.

The hard work of the harvest is over; the corn and chillis hang in colourful clumps on the drying racks, the sheep and goats graze on the Pokhara lowlands, and Sun Kumari spends her afternoons spinning wool and weaving carpets. Today some neighbour women drop by for an impromptu weaving and gossip session that lasts well into the night. Their usual light-hearted exchange grows uneasy as one recounts a story about several young village men who were caught fighting with a gang from over the hill. Once before they were reportedly drunk and watching lurid videos in Pokhara.

Times are changing; young people's behaviour is unprecedented and bewildering, causing disruption in the peaceful village. The youth are losing respect for Gurung ways; they seem angry and dissatisfied. If they go, who will run the village after the old folks die? Who will look after the fields and animals, and weave the baskets and blankets? Sun Kumari pauses for a moment to ponder the situation and says a quiet prayer of thanks that this destructive spirit has not afflicted her family. She weaves a band of soft brown wool into a new *baakhu*, a blanket for her son, and turns her thoughts to tomorrow's morning meal. ❑

RIGHT: a Gurung ethnic photographed near Manaslu Himal.

TREKKING IN LANGTANG-GOSAINKUND-HELAMBU

Map on page 252

The areas around the Langtang Valley, Helambu and the sacred Gosainkund Lakes offer some of the best walking for both experienced and novice trekkers, within easy reach of Kathmandu

The Langtang-Gosainkund-Helambu area to the north of Kathmandu offers wonderful trekking, yet is less popular than the Annapurna or Everest regions, despite its fantastic scenery, easy access and extensive network of trails. Adjoining areas are even more unspoiled; few trekking agents promote the Manaslu, Ganesh or Jugal Himal, which flank the Langtang range west and east. The custom-outfitted group and the independent trekker willing to sleep in smoky homes and carry a few days' food supplies, however, will discover an environment unchanged in centuries.

Kathmandu

Gorkha treks

In the mid-1700s, Nepal was politically divided into 80 principalities. They were in constant flux, with borders changing, contracts dissolving and the *rajas* – heads of state, mostly emigrant Rajputs – spent precious resources defending their territories against neighbouring states. The state of Gorkha, centring on the present-day town of **Gorkha** *(see page 223)* halfway between Kathmandu and Pokhara, was neither the largest nor the strongest force. Its manpower was no more than 15,000 to 20,000, a figure later extrapolated from a recorded "12,000 roofs". But its leader, Prithvi Narayan Shah, was the most able and determined and he led a campaign to conquer the Kathmandu Valley and form a unified kingdom. His palace still stands on the hilltop above Gorkha.

A number of short and long treks begin in the town of Gorkha, making concentric loops into the Himalaya which end at Dumre or the Gorkha access road. From almost any point it is possible to see the stalwart ramparts of Manaslu (8,463 metres/27,766 ft), Himal Chuli (7,893 metres/25,895 ft), Baudha (6,672 metres/21,890 ft) or Ganesh Himal (7,406 metres/ 24,298 ft). After the half-day drive from Kathmandu, most trekkers stay in Gorkha itself or camp nearby.

The main trekking path out of Gorkha descends west to the Darondi Khola down a slippery forested hillside, where a trail sets off to the northeast, riding a corrugated ridgeline between the Darondi and Buri Gandaki rivers. By day three on this route the lush millet terraces are left behind and camp is made in the forest on top of bulky Darchya (3,048 metres/ 10,000 ft), from where the Himalaya appear in their snowy finery.

The route then splits in three directions. The eastward trail descends to the village of **Laprak ❶**, facing a waterfall as it plummets to a tributary stream of the Buri Gandaki. The westward route winds down

LEFT: monk dancing at a monastery festival in Helambu.
BELOW: waterfall on the Buri Gandaki River.

through rhododendron forests to the pleasant Gurung town of Barpak, with its flagstone walkways and smells of freshly distilled millet *rakshi*. Continuing westward, a steep descent into the valley meets a pedestrian highway that parallels the gentle Darondi down to Khoplang and back to Gorkha, completing a week-long trek.

The northern path leads to Rupina La (4,600 metres/15,100 ft) which connects the headwaters of the Darondi and Buri Gandaki rivers. Beyond the cairn-marked summit, a sketchy trail skirts the Chhuling Glacier and eventually joins the Buri Gandaki at Ngyak.

Around Manaslu

A challenging trek reaches north of the Himalaya circling the Manaslu-Himal Chuli-Baudha massif via Larkya La (5,135 metres/16,846 ft). The 18- to 21-day trip can begin from either **Besisahar** on the Marsyangdi or Gorkha. From Thonche, above the Marsyangdi, to Nyak in the upper the Buri Gandaki, travel is permitted only to holders of trekking or expedition permits organised by a trekking agency. Tents and food for at least a week and a guide are essential.

Larkya La ②, guarded by the northern flanks of **Manaslu** and **Larkya Himal**, is within 10 km (6 miles) of the Tibetan border. On the east side, descendants of Tibetan immigrants have settled in hamlets such as Sama and Lho. Stone images of Milarepa, an 11th-century Tibetan teacher of Buddhism, record his visits to the region for meditation. At Ngyak, the Buri Gandaki heads south through a gorge to Arughat (488 metres/ 1,601 ft), after which the route climbs westward onto the ridge via Khanchok to Gorkha.

The 16- to 18-day Gorkha-to-Trisuli trek traverses undulating ridges at the

Tibetan Buddhists live in the Langtang region, close to the Tibetan border.

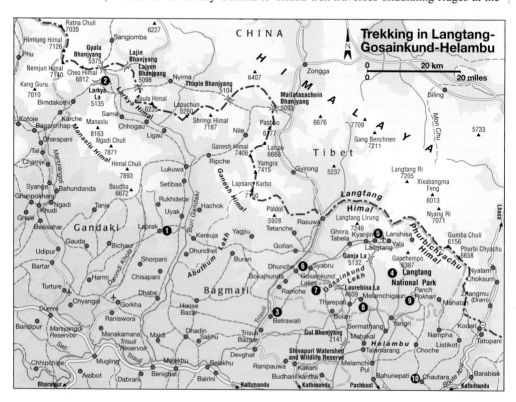

base of Ganesh Himal. From the upper Buri Gandaki the route heads northeast to Tirudanda, ending either at **Betrawati** ❸ on the Trisuli River or at Syabrubensi, where the Langtang River enters the Bhote Kosi valley giving birth to the mighty Trisuli River. Tamangs, the predominant hill people across Nepal, populate these slopes and ridges. Their Tibetan heritage is evident by Mongoloid features and an adherence to Buddhism. They marry young, usually in an arranged union, entitling the young man's family to his wife's labours *(see page 46)*.

Map on page 252

The Langtang Valley

From downtown Kathmandu the massif of Langtang Himal, crowned by a snow-capped **Langtang Lirung** (7,246 metres/23,771 ft), can be seen on a clear day jutting above the Shivapuri summit. Some 30 km (19 miles) away, the long glaciated valley known as Langtang divides the northern range from **Gosainkund Lekh** (4,590 metres/15,060 ft) and the Jugal Himal.

Langtang is easily accessible from Kathmandu: a tarmac road connects the capital to Trisuli and **Dhunche**, entrance to **Langtang National Park** ❹ (entrance fee) and take-off point for treks into Langtang and to the Gosainkund Lakes. This road linkage is being pushed through to the historic Tibetan valley of Khirong and future cross-border treks are being discussed.

In 1976, Langtang became Nepal's second largest national park *(see page 106)*. Healthy forests of rhododendron, fir, birch, and blue and chir pine stand out amid central Nepal's cultivated hillsides. Wildlife of the park includes leopard, musk deer, Himalayan black bear, rhesus and langur monkeys and the endangered red panda. The Bhote Kosi-Trisuli River is an important migratory

BELOW: village dwarfed by its surroundings in Langtang Valley.

Legend tells that the upper Langtang Valley was discovered by a man in search of his yak, hence the name which means "in pursuit of a yak". The people are thought to be descendants of Tibetans who intermingled with Tamangs from Helambu. They are mainly sheep and yak herders, but grow buckwheat, potatoes and barley as well.

BELOW: a porter pauses by the Gosainkund lakes.

route for birds travelling between India and Tibet. A national park information centre at Dhunche introduces the park's ecology.

Two main tracks enter the Langtang Valley, each with lodging as far as Kyanjin Gompa. The longer route goes through Syabru (2,330 metres/7,642 ft), clinging to the steep, dry hillside in contrast to thick forests on the opposite side. At Ghora Tabela ("Horse Stable") high cliffs rim the meadows.

Langtang village (3,300 metres/10,850 ft) is the largest and last permanent settlement. Beyond is **Kyanjin ❺**, a cluster of stone huts surrounded by potato and turnip fields, with a small Buddhist *gompa* and a Swiss-initiated government cheese factory. Kyanjin can be reached in three fast days from Dhunche, but at 3,750 metres (12,300 ft) a slower pace is advised. This is as far as most trekkers go, but beyond here several day-hikes are possible. For the self-sufficient hiker, there are possibilities for exploring the upper valley to Langshisa (4,080 metres/13,400 ft) and Tilman's Col – a difficult crossing (named after Bill Tilman, the first westerner to visit Langtang in 1949), which leads east to Panch Pokhari. The Ganja La, a snowy and often cloudy 5,132-metre (16,833-ft) pass which requires alpine equipment, leads south to Helambu. Hikers with experience, tents and a guide can reach Tarke Ghyang on the other side in three to four days.

The easiest return route from upper Langtang is back down the valley. Below Ghora Tabela, the path scrambles south up a landslide to **Syabru ❻**, its single row of timber houses stretched far down the ridgeline.

A Shiva pilgrimage

Langtang National Park also includes the sacred **Gosainkund Lakes ❼**, a pilgrimage site for thousands of Shiva devotees during the July-August full-

moon festival of Janai Purnima. Hindus throng to bathe in the lakes' holy waters; males change a string worn around one shoulder renewing their devotion to Shiva, god of reproduction and destruction. *Jhankris* (shamans) dance in an induced trance to all-night singing and drum-beating. According to legend, Shiva formed the lakes by thrusting his *trisul* (trident) into the mountainside, creating three gushing springs and giving the Trisuli River its name.

The trail to **Gosainkund** (4,312 metres/14,144 ft) climbs from either Dhunche or Syabru through lush rhododendron hillsides to Sing Gompa, where there is another cheese factory. The 2,400-metre (7,800-ft) elevation gain from Dhunche requires three days for proper acclimatisation. Food and lodging are available at the lakes during trekking season.

Map on page 252

East of the lakes Laurebina La (4,609 metres/15,121 ft) leads to the **Helambu** region. Scores of rock piles left by pilgrims seeking good fortune dot the treeless landscape. The path descends to a cluster of shepherds' huts at Tharepati, where it divides into two return routes to Kathmandu. The shorter way rides the ridge south through cool rhododendron forests (crawling with leeches during monsoon season) passing several Tamang villages, and crests the Kathmandu Valley rim at Buriang Bhanjyang, some 1,100 metres (3,600 ft) above Sundarijal. This ridge forms the divide between two of Nepal's major river systems; the Gandaki, which extends west to Dhaulagiri, and the Sapt Kosi whose tributaries extend east to Kanchenjunga on the border with Sikkim.

Guardian effigy outside a Sherpa village in Helambu.

The other trail from Tharepati climbs east and then plunges 1,000 metres (3,300 ft) to a tributary of the Melamchi Khola and above it the village of **Melamchigaun ❽**. Stone houses scatter across the terraced fields above an old *gompa* dressed with tall prayer flags. The people of Helambu call them-

BELOW: Sherpa tea house in Helambu.

TIP

If visiting the Helambu in late summer, don't fail to try the local apples which are a treat, as is spring's flower show of laligurans and purple irises.

selves Sherpas but their link with the Sherpas of Solu Khumbu is distant, underlined by different dialects, clothes and family lines. Inside the heavy timber homes of Tarkeghyang and Sermathang, rows of polished copper cauldrons and brass plates line the sitting room. A *gompa* set on the ridge above Tarkeghyang commands excellent views of the Himalaya, looking north toward Ganja La and Dorje Lakpa (6,990 metres/ 22,927 ft) and a cluster of peaks over 6,000 metres (20,000 ft).

The trail descends into the Melamchi Khola valley, the village of Talamarang and the rice paddies of Melamchi Pul from where the route to Kathmandu follows the dirt road south to Panchkaal. A more scenic alternative climbs west from Talamarang back up to 1,890 metres (6,200 ft) via Pati Bhanjyang on the way to Sundarijal.

Sacred lakes

The Nepalese invest sacred meaning in nature, particularly water and high points, expressed by strings of prayer flags and *mani* stone piles. Many high lakes are important places of pilgrimage.

Dudh Pokhari (Milk Lake) lies at 4,270 metres (14,000 ft) on the ridge west of the Darondi, a two-week trek north from Gorkha via Darchya and Barpak. Days above permanent settlements, only shepherds or devotees are encountered on the trail. This trek should be attempted only with the help of a guide and staff to carry supplies. The return route stays high along Sirandanda ridge and exits east to the Gorkha road or west via the Chepe Khola to Dumre.

A five-day round trip to Bara Pokhari (3,110 metres/10,200 ft) trails east from Phalesangu and Ngadi on the lower Marsyangdi. Paths also connect with

BELOW:
Sherpanis dancing at Tarkeghyang in Helambu.

Sirandanda, three to four days away. The lake often has snow until spring.

Another set of sacred lakes in the east of Langtang National Park called **Panch Pokhari ❾** (Five Lakes) introduces trekkers to the saw-toothed Jugal Himal. The trek from Tarkeghyang crosses the Indrawati Khola, brown with the hills' red clay which it carries to the Sun Kosi, and mounts a 3,600-metre (12,000-ft) ridge to the lakes. The shortest exit route heads straight down the ridge to **Chautara ❿**, a large bazaar connected to the Kathmandu-Kodari road by jeep or bus.

Map on page 252

Trekking Peaks of Langtang, Jugal and Ganesh Himal

Langtang and Jugal, being only 50 km (30 miles) north of Kathmandu, are readily accessible to visitors, yet despite the extent of this area there is only one trekking peak. Formerly known as Ganja La Chuli, Naya Kanga (5,844 metres/19,180 ft) is west of the Ganja La pass which separates the Langtang Valley from Helambu.

The normal route climbs from Kyanjin Gompa towards the Ganja La and ascends the northeast face and north ridge. No record of a first ascent has been traced. South side routes have been made but are more difficult.

To the west, the icy pyramids of Ganesh Himal make a stunning panorama from the Kathmandu Valley. Set between the Buri Gandaki and the Bhote Kosi, they provide an enjoyable trekking peak climb for able mountaineers. Paldor (5,896 metres/19,344 ft) can be approached from the Trisuli Valley and thence the Chilime Khola to Gatlang. Base camp is best placed at the head of the Mailung Khola from where several small peaks offer training climbs. The northeast ridge, known as Tilman's Ridge, provides a fine route of ascent. ❑

The fast-flowing Buri Gandaki River.

BELOW: Langtang Lirung just shows behind Yala Peak.

THE EVEREST REGION

Mount Everest, the highest mountain on earth, is undoubtedly Nepal's most ubiquitous image; the surrounding region is also fascinating for its village life and religious traditions

Kathmandu

Eastern Nepal epitomises the original meaning of the name Himalaya: "Abode of the Gods". Five of the world's 10 highest peaks, including Mount Everest at 8,850 metres (29,035 ft) – known as Sagarmatha to the Nepalese and Chomolungma to the Tibetans – preside over a region of enormous geographical and cultural contrasts. In ancient Tibetan literature, valleys such as Khumbu and Rolwaling are sanctified as *beyuls*, hidden places of refuge for troubled times. A wide variety of Himalayan wildlife find the eastern hills a hospitable environment, and because the annual monsoon rains arrive earlier and stay later, the region as a whole is greener and lusher than the rest of Nepal. It is also friendly, relaxed and relatively prosperous.

The first people known to inhabit east Nepal were the Kiratis, a Mongolian tribal people. In the 7th or 8th centuries BC they invaded the Kathmandu Valley and established a thriving kingdom which ruled until about AD 300. Their descendants, the Rais and Limbus, are still living in the east and have carried on their military tradition by serving as valued recruits in the British and Indian Gurkha regiments *(see page 224).*

Eastern Nepal is home to at least a dozen ethnic hill peoples including the celebrated Sherpas of mountaineering fame *(see page 50).* The Sherpas, whose name "people from the east" denotes their original home in the Eastern Tibetan province of Kham, settled in the Everest region around 1533. They kept their connection to their homeland by continuing to trade over the Nangpa La pass, bringing salt, wool, carpets, Tibetan artifacts and mastiff dogs south from Tibet and grains, raw iron, paper, cotton cloth and *dzo* (a cross-breed of cattle and yak) north from the lowlands. When trans-Himalayan trade subsided in the early 1960s, the Sherpas had already proven adept as mountain guides and high-altitude porters. Turning their energies to the new trekking business, they have prospered from tourism more than any other ethnic group, both as lodgekeepers in Khumbu and through employment in the Kathmandu-based trekking industry. Sherpa life is changing with the influx of visitors and money, but most observers agree they have managed to maintain the core of their identity, successfully combining newfound prosperity with traditional values.

Trekking in Eastern Nepal offers a wide range of wilderness and cultural encounters. Most first-timers choose to live out their dreams of standing at the foot of Mount Everest, though Upper Khumbu offers a number of other routes. Others prefer less-tramelled areas east of Khumbu, including the Kanchenjunga region *(see page 285).* A middle-altitude region such as Solu rewards with pleasant walking and a moderate climate year-round.

PRECEDING PAGES: Mount Everest and Nuptse. **LEFT:** yak at Gokyo Lake. **BELOW:** a Sherpa woman in traditional costume.

The land of milk and honey

The region of Solu, or Sho Rung as the Sherpas know it, lies between 2,600 and 3,200 metres (8,500–10,500 ft) elevation, extending from Jiri east to the Dudh Kosi (Milk River). It is a land blessed with a temperate climate, well-watered forests and pasturelands, and rolling farmlands cultivated in maize, wheat, barley and apples. Buddhist monks and nuns led by *rinpoches* serve the predominantly Sherpa communities from *gompas* or monasteries patterned after those built by their ancestors in Tibet. Communities such as **Junbesi** tempt trekkers with the promise of fresh-baked apple pies served in homey lodges. The cheese factory at Tragsindhu is another favourite stop.

This land of milk and honey is ideal for trekkers without a particular destination in mind. Much more than a path to Khumbu's high country, Solu invites a leisurely pace. Detour for a retreat at the fascinating Thupten Choling monastery a few hours walk above Junbesi. Relocated from Rongbuk Monastery on the Tibetan side of Mount Everest, the monastery is the focal point of a large community of monastic and lay practitioners. Chiwong Gompa near Phaplu is another vibrant Buddhist community: ritual *Mani Rimdu* dances are performed here every autumn. Trekkers come also to photograph the spring rhododendron and magnolia blooms that are more profuse in Solu's forests than almost anywhere in Nepal.

The mountains are, of course, present as well: a wilderness trek north from Junbesi to the pilgrimage site of Dudh Kunda reaches the base of Numbur (6,959 metres/22,829 ft), Solu's sacred peak, locally known as Shorung Yul Lha. Everest and the Khumbu range rise to the east, while Gauri Shanker (7,146 metres/23,444 ft) and Menlungtse (7,181 metres/23,560 ft) tower to the north.

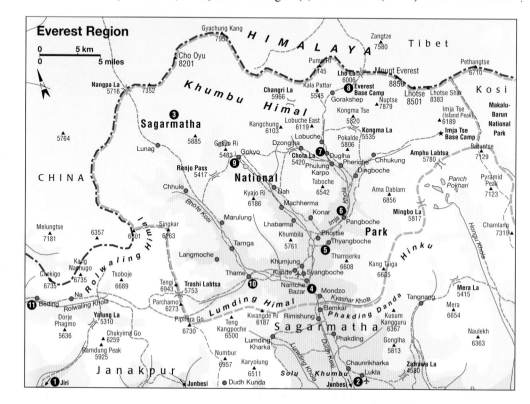

Most treks through Solu follow the route used by early Everest expeditions. Nowadays the trail begins at the roadhead town of **Jiri ❶** at 1,905 metres (6,250 ft), a day's bus ride from Kathmandu, cutting several days off the old trail from Lamosangu. Solu's mid-elevation does not signal an easy trek, however, for the terrain is relentlessly up and down. On the nine- to ten-day hike to Namche Bazar, the gateway to Khumbu, the track crosses seven ridges, three of them 3,000 metres (9,850 ft) or higher. Frequent lodges allow the independent trekker to travel light. Air service to mid-elevation airstrips at Phaplu and Lukla reduce travel time from Kathmandu. Airstrips at less-visited lowland sites such as Ramechhap, Okhaldhunga/Rumjatar, and Lamidanda in eastern Nepal provide other entry and exit options.

Map on page 262

Aircraft used on mountain flights (DHC-6 Twin Otter).

Trekking in Khumbu

Khumbu is too beautiful and too friendly a place to hurry through. Besides, at such elevations, it can be dangerous to trek too high too fast *(see page 138)*. Fortunately for trekkers, there are two medical stations in Khumbu staffed by Western doctors during the trekking seasons: a small hospital at Kunde developed with assistance from Sir Edmund Hillary's Himalayan Trust, and the Trekkers' Aid Post at Pheriche, operates under the auspices of the Himalayan Rescue Association. The Trust has assisted in building numerous schools, health posts, bridges, roads and water pipelines throughout Solu-Khumbu.

For visitors with limited time, the best way to approach Khumbu is to fly to **Lukla ❷** (2,866 metres/9,403 ft). The 40-minute flight gives a thrill of a lifetime as the little plane descends below the peaks into the Dudh Kosi gorge and bounces up the gravel runway which ends in a mountain face. Forty years ago Lukla was the "sheep place" its name implies: today it's a bustling little community of lodges and restaurants serving cinnamon rolls and coffee to trekkers awaiting their morning flight. Erratic scheduling and windpatterns often result in delays or cancellations. From Lukla, the trail climbs gradually up the steep-sided Dudh Kosi Valley, weaving from side to side as it passes through forests of blue pine, fir, juniper, rhododendron, birch and oak. Many villages, particularly Phakding, the standard first night's stop, cater to trekkers with western food and dormitory lodging.

BELOW: trekking in the Solu-Khumbu region.

Narrow bench-lands are cultivated in wheat, potatoes, spinach, onions and radishes. Piled stone walls and huge boulders are carved with the Buddhist mantra *"Om mani padme hum"*. On Fridays, hundreds of barefoot porters line the trail, toting food and wares up the mountainside to Namche Bazar's market.

All of Khumbu falls within **Sagarmatha National Park ❸**, established with help from the government of New Zealand, Sir Edmund Hillary's native country *(see page 141)*. In 1979 Khumbu was recognised as a World Heritage Site. The entrance fee for the park can be paid at Mondzo (2,845 metres/9,332 ft).

Crampons and canned pâté

At the confluence of the Dudh Kosi and Bhote Kosi (a river named for its Tibetan origins), the trail crosses a high, sturdy bridge and begins a gruelling ascent to

TIP

Atop a hill east of Namche Bazar, the Visitor's Centre at Sagarmatha National Park headquarters offers informative displays on local customs, flora and fauna, as well as stunning mountain views up the valley.

BELOW:
the thriving town of Namche Bazar.

Namche Bazar (3,446 metres/11,300 ft). On the way, the first glimpses of Everest and Lhotse (8,501 metres/27,890 ft) are revealed. The Bhote Kosi leads northwest to Thame and over the Nangpa La (5,716 metres/18,753 ft) to Tibet.

The prosperous town of **Namche Bazar ❹**, with its two- and three-storey houses-cum-lodges, a bank and post office, sits in a U-shaped west-facing valley, with the sacred mountain Khumbila (5,761 metres/18,900 ft) to the north, Thamserku (6,608 metres/21,680 ft) to the east and Kwangde Ri (6,187 metres/20,298 ft) to the west. Stone-paved lanes are lined with shops filled with an amazing selection of mountaineering ware and gourmet expedition food. Swiss chocolate and French pâté stand alongside Russian sardines and Italian sausage; other shops rent crampons, mountaineering boots and sleeping bags, or sell small libraries of paperback novels and Tibetan jewellery imported from Kathmandu.

High-quality lodges proffer videos, hot showers, and fresh-baked pastries. Namche's weekly Saturday market or *haat bajaar* is a fascinating example of this local means of trade typical of Nepal's eastern hills. Porters, merchants and locals gather together for a busy morning of commerce; afterwards, they filter into local tea- and *chhang*-shops to exchange the week's gossip.

Above Namche, the ridge hamlet of Syangboche clusters around an airstrip serving the deluxe Japanese-operated Hotel Everest View. Tucked into a lovely valley a half-hour walk beyond, the two traditional villages of Khumjung and Kunde provide a counterpoint to Namche's commercial excess. Rock walls separate potato fields where entire families can be seen digging or ploughing in season. The local landscape has been immortalised by Sherpa painters in whimsical artwork which portrays yetis and trekkers amid the Khumbu village-scape

in primitive Tibetan mural style. The introduction of the potato in the 18th century revolutionised Khumbu's economy, allowing the barren terrain to support a much higher population.

The trail to Everest Base Camp

By far the most travelled trail in Khumbu leads to Everest Base Camp. Most trekkers take at least six days from Namche Bazar, including time for acclimatisation. But with side trips and days to simply soak in the mountains' wonders, two, or preferably three, weeks are needed to see this area of Khumbu and more without rushing.

The monastery of **Thyangboche** ❺, rebuilt after a fire destroyed the original buildings in 1989, is one of Khumbu's most important and beautiful cultural centres. Thanks to donations from the Sherpa and international communities, the monastery has been faithfully rebuilt in an almost identical style to its predecessor. The monastery site is perched on a high forested promontory at 3,867 metres (12,684 ft). From here Ama Dablam (6,856 metres/22,493 ft), Everest, Nuptse (7,879 metres/25,850 ft) and Lhotse (8,501 metres/27,890 ft) make a perfect picture to the north. A Sherpa Cultural Centre, with informative displays explaining the religious and home lives of Sherpas, and several lodges share the meadow site, which is a popular campsite for group treks.

Thyangboche is the best-known location of the annual Mani Rimdu festival, a dance-drama in which monks dressed in brilliantly painted masks and silk robes perform ritual dances depicting Buddhism's subjugation of the ancient Bön religion *(see page 60)*.

Thyangboche Rinpoche, *backed by Tamserku.*

BELOW: Thyangboche buried in a blizzard.

The forest surrounding Thyangboche is considered sacred and species such as the "fanged" musk deer and iridescent *danphe* thrive here. The trail wanders down through the forest and crosses the Imja Khola's seething waters on a plank bridge. The climb to **Pangboche** ❻, site of Khumbu's oldest *gompa* where a yeti scalp and hand relic are displayed, passes by skilfully etched *mani* stones and the last scattered trees below timberline.

Soon the canyon widens into Alpine meadows, and the river and trail divide. The Imja Khola leads east toward the high, uncommercialised settlements of Dingboche and Chhukung. The mountain viewpoint of Chukkung Ri (5,043 metres/16,588 ft) provides superb views of the ice-draped southern face of the Lhotse-Nuptse massif. At Chhukung (4,753 metres/15,594 ft), five glaciers descend; a path edging Imja and Lhotse glaciers passes a lake on the way to Island Peak (Imja Tse) Base Camp. To the south, the Amphu Labtsa Pass (5,780 metres/18,963 ft) leads to the wild and rugged Hongu Basin. Within this huge glacial cirque nestle five small lakes (Panch Pokhari) amid a number of peaks over 6,000 metres (19,685 ft). Hongu can also be reached via the Mingbo La (5,817 metres/19,084 ft) on the southeast ridge of Ama Dablam, the high but gentle Mera La (5,415 metres/17,766 ft), accessed from Lukla or from the Salpa Pass trail leading into Khumbu from the east.

From the confluence of the Imja and Lobuche Kholas, the left-hand trail climbs gradually to Pheriche, an unimpressive settlement with tea shops and a trekkers' medical post midway up a windswept valley. Yak trains carrying goods whose prices increase incrementally with elevation plod up the eroded slope to **Duglha** ❼ and over the crest where a line of stone *chortens* remember climbers killed on Everest.

Stone carving at Pangboche Gompa.

BELOW: mani symbols in the moss, Everest trail.

Map on page 262

Lobuche's clustered lodges, set at the edge of the Khumbu Glacier (4,930 metres/16,171 ft), are the staging ground for higher forays to Kala Pattar (Black Rock), Everest Base Camp and climbs on the trekking peak Lobuche Peak. A two-hour hike through a morass of boulders reaches Gorak Shep, where there are a few small lodges. The climb to Kala Pattar (5,545 metres/18,192 ft) takes one to two further hours and is worth every step for the views of Everest's distinctive black triangle. During winter, high-level winds from the west blast all snow off Everest's towering face and produces the characteristic plume from its summit. Summer winds from the east leave its white mantle intact.

Pumo Ri (7,145 metres/23,442 ft) looms immediately to the rear of Kala Pattar, while Nuptse shows its vast marbled face directly in front. Base Camp and the unforgiving Khumbu Icefall stretch across the foreground, while less than 6 km (3½ miles) away across the **Lho La** (6,006 metres/19,704 ft) lies the Rongbuk Glacier and Tibet. If only we had wings!

A few sherpas have summited Everest on more than one occasion. Ang Rita Sherpa, who has reached Earth's highest point on six occasions, is now a Nepalese hero.

Tourism's two sides

The trail to **Everest Base Camp** ❽ (5,357 metres/17,575 ft) crosses the glacier amid ice seracs, some topped with boulders. Hikers are often disappointed with Base Camp, from where Everest is not even visible. Piles of garbage further spoil the illusion, emblematic of the nation's environmental woes compounded by tourism *(see page 109)*. Efforts are periodically mounted to clear away expedition litter, but the ultimate solution lies in the mountaineers themselves. Every expedition must now pay a $2,000 "garbage deposit" in Kathmandu. Non-combustible rubbish must be brought back to the tip in Kathmandu or else the deposit will be retained.

BELOW: yaks are vital to high mountain life.

Everest Dates

The summit of Mount Everest is 8,850 metres (29,035 ft) above sea level. Listed below are some landmarks in man's struggle to reach the top:

1921: The first expedition, headed by C.K. Howard-Bury, on the north face. During the expedition seven Sherpas from India die in an avalanche, the first fatalities recorded on Everest.

1922: The second expedition with C.G. Bruce starts again from the northern side.

1924: Third British expedition, headed by C.G. Bruce but replaced by E.F. Norton. Andrew Irvine and George Mallory are last seen at 8,500 metres (27,890 ft).

1953: Edmund Hillary and Tenzing Norgay Sherpa become the first to reach the summit, via the south ridge *(see page 141)*.

1963: Americans Willi Unsoeld and Tom Hornbein, guided by N. Oyrenfurth, become the first to ascend by one route (west ridge) and descend by another (southeast ridge).

1965: Nawang Gombu Sherpa of India becomes the first person to scale Everest twice by the southeast ridge.

1975: Junko Tabei is the first woman to reach the summit by the southern approach.

1978: Everest is scaled for the first time without the use of artificial oxygen by Reinhold Messner and Peter Habeler, by the southern approach *(see page 141)*. The first German to summit is part of this party: Reinhard Karl.

1979: Ang Phu Sherpa becomes the first person to scale the mountain by two different routes (southeast ridge, 1970, and west ridge, 1979); a Yugoslavian group is the first to ascend and descend by the west ridge – still the most difficult route today.

1980: Leszek Cichy and Krzystof Wielcki of Poland make the first winter ascent; complete ascent and descent via the northern face (Japan) and first ascent via the southern peak (Poland); Messner makes the first solo ascent, without bottled oxygen, and, in August, the first summer ascent.

1982: Yasuo Kato of Japan is the first person to reach the summit in different seasons (spring, autumn, winter). He dies in a storm.

1983: Several summits by various routes: eastern ridge (Mexican), southern peak and southeastern ridge (Japan).

1985: At 55, American Dick Bass becomes the oldest person to scale Everest.

1988: A huge Chinese-Japanese-Nepalese group scales the first north-south and south-north traverses simultaneously.

1988: Marc Betard of France sets a speed record in an ascent of 22½ hours up the southeast ridge.

1990: Ang Rita Sherpa of Nepal becomes the first to scale the mountain six times.

1996: Eight climbers perish in a storm on May 11, including British climber Rob Hall. The disaster becomes the subject of the bestseller *Into Thin Air*, by survivor Jon Krakauer. David Breashears and Ed Viesturs are on the mountain the same week to capture the ascent on a 65-mm IMAX format film *(see page 138)*.

1999: George Mallory's body is discovered *(see page 276)*. ❏

LEFT: Sir Edmund Hillary, honoured by the Sherpas with silk *khatas* (scarves).

The effects of mountain tourism on the local environment, both social and natural, are hard to overlook in Khumbu. Much of the area's forest had disappeared by the time national-park regulations stopped tree-cutting for fuel and construction use, and it takes 60 years at such elevations for trees to grow back. Now trekking groups are required to be self-sufficient in kerosene for their clients' cooking needs. Individual trekkers stay in Sherpa lodges, where the cooking hearth has traditionally been a congenial gathering spot, and large amounts of wood are needed to feed hungry foreigners. Recent innovations to save firewood include a "back boiler" system that heats water via a pipe through the hearth. Mini-hydroelectric projects are becoming more common, but these primarily provide power for lighting, not cooking. And whereas Khumbu Sherpas have certainly benefited economically from the popularity of trekking, ever-increasing contact with Westerners undeniably accelerates cultural change, which penetrates even the most remote villages of the region.

Lodges for trekkers at Gokyo.

The Gokyo Valley

The return trip to Namche Bazar can be accomplished much more quickly by following the same route, but hardy trekkers take the time to explore side valleys such as **Gokyo** ❾. Churning with glaciers that melt into turquoise lakes, and rimmed with savage mountain scenery, the Gokyo Valley is veteran trekkers' favourite side of Khumbu. Trails cling to both sides of the steep Dudh Kosi gorge, joining at the toe of the giant Ngozumpa Glacier, and continuing up its lateral moraine past half-frozen lakes to a cluster of lodges at the small lake of Gokyo. The west side's trail passes lodges at Dole, Lhabarma, Luza and Machherma. The opposite trail is visibly unpopulated except for a single tea shop at Thare. For proper acclimatisation, the whole journey from Namche or Khumjung should take four half-days (or three full days with one day's rest).

BELOW: ascending Gokyo Peak.

Himalayan *tahr* are often seen grazing on narrow ledges in the lower reaches, their long golden-brown hair barely visible against similarly coloured grasses. Below Dole, the trail winds up through rhododendron, poplar and birch, its thin smooth bark, like brown mylar, peeling off layers at a time.

The entire Gokyo Valley is sparsely populated, with shelter found only at summer yak-herding settlements where trekking lodges have also been established. There is no food or lodging from Machherma to Gokyo. This altitude is well above treeline, and only scrub rhododendron, azalea and hardy grasses can survive. Around the lakes, the ground is snow-covered for much of the year, except during the monsoon when buttercups, asters, edelweiss and gentians bloom.

Gokyo, with several surprisingly deluxe lodges, sits on the shore of the third lake, Dudh Pokhari, at 4,750 metres (15,580 ft). Rising above it is the easily climbable Gokyo Ri (5,483 metres/17,984 ft). From the top, a panoply of peaks loom on every horizon. To the north, **Cho Oyu**, at 8,201 metres (26,906 ft), the sixth highest in the world, and Gyachung Kang (7,952 metres/25,991 ft) grow out of the corrugated ice folds which tumble to the glacier. Pumo Ri, **Changtse**, Everest, Nuptse, Makalu (at 8,463 metres/27,766 ft,

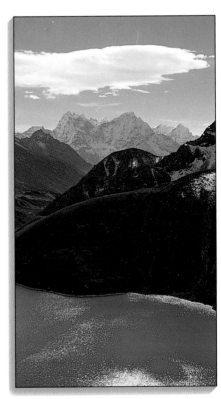

*Mani stones on the
Everest trail.*

the world's fifth highest), Ama Dablam and Thamserku stretch to the east and south. Beyond a 5,900-metre (19,360-ft) ridge to the west lies the Bhote Kosi valley leading to the Nangpa La.

Day hikes from Gokyo along the lateral moraine lead past several more lakes and the mountaineering touchpoint of Cho Oyu Base Camp. For those combining Gokyo with a trip to Everest Base Camp, it's possible to save two days' walk by taking a short cut crossing Chola La (5,420 metres/17,782 ft). The eastern side skirts the small mountain lake of Tshola Tsho and crosses the moraines between Cholatse and Taboche (6,542 metres/21,462 ft), emerging above the village of Pheriche. Another shortcut from Gokyo can be done without a tent: trekkers can stay overnight with Sherpas in Dragnag (4,680 metres/ 15,351 ft) and travel in one long day (12–14 hours) to Lobuche.

Locals walk from Gokyo down to Namche on the Machherma-Dole trail in a single day, but a more moderate pace requires two to three days. If heading to Pangboche, the Dudh Kosi's east side trail via Phortse offers an unparalleled perspective on Khumbila, Thamserku, Kang Taiga (6,685 metres/21,932 ft) and Ama Dablam. Set above a steep ravine facing Thyangboche to the west, Phortse is a peaceful farming community. Potato fields stretch to the cliff's edge, marked by 300-year-old stone *chortens* and a fringe of birch forest. The three-hour walk to Pangboche is memorable for its vantage over the Imja Khola.

Quiet Thame

BELOW: Sherpas
in Namche Bazar.

A relatively easy three- to four- hour walk up the Bhote Kosi from Namche Bazar reaches the settlement of **Thame** ❿. Its mud-walled, Sherpa-style houses surrounded by potato fields reveal little of the 20th century. Here is the perfect

Map on page 262

antidote to noisy trekker lodges. Thame's monastery clings to the ridge above, with views of waterfalls cascading down Kwangde Ri. The *gompa* looks up valley toward Nangpa La leading into Tibet, territory that is closed to trekkers. Guests at the monastery may be offered a cup of Tibetan butter tea – a mild black tea churned in a wooden cylinder with yak butter and salt, often unappealing to the naive tongue.

Crowning the tributary valley west of Thame is the infamous Trashi Labtsa pass (5,753 metres/18,875 ft) leading into the Rolwaling Valley. Trekkers have died from rock falls and sudden avalanches on this extremely rugged route, now restricted to organised groups. Ice axe, crampons, rope and a blessing from the Thame *lama* are advised. Most mountaineering expeditions in Khumbu follow the Sherpa practice of making a *puja*, an offering, to the mountain deities before beginning a climb.

Khumbu Trekking Peaks

Home of the world's highest mountains, the Khumbu region provides a profusion of lesser peaks accessible to serious mountaineers who may not be ready for an ascent of one of its true giants.

Island Peak (Imja Tse) (6,189 metres/20,305 ft, Group A) is the most popular and one of the more accessible Trekking Peaks, lying between the Imja and Lhotse Glaciers up the Chhukung Valley. It is dwarfed by the massive south face of Lhotse and Baruntse and Ama Dablam. Its south face rears up as a rocky black triangle, the end of a truncated ridge thrown down from Lhotse Shar, from which it is separated by a snowy col at 5,700 metres (18,700 ft). Its name comes from a 1952 expedition led by Eric Shipton, who described an isolated mountain "resembling an island in a sea of ice". Island Peak was first climbed in 1953 by a party that included Tenzing Norgay. Their initial route, from a camp at Pareshaya Gyab up the southeast flank and the south ridge, remains the standard route.

Pokalde (Dolma Ri) (5,806 metres/19,049 ft, Group B) is a relatively undistinguished peak, the culmination of a rocky pinnacled ridge beyond the huge lateral moraines of Pheriche. In many ways it can be regarded as the final bony knuckle on the long-fingered ridge that extends southward from Nuptse, bounding the east bank of the Khumbu Glacier. To the Sherpas, Pokalde is immensely important as the home of a major deity and the object of a monsoon pilgrimage during which the devout walk clockwise around the mountain. The straightforward route from the east was probably pioneered by Sherpas to place prayer flags on the summit. The first western ascent was recorded in 1953 by a group from the Everest Expedition that included John Hunt, Wilfred Noyce, Tom Bourdillon and Mike Ward. They climbed the north ridge direct from the Kongma La. Everest and Makalu rear above the clouds like two great fangs.

Pokalde is best approached from the lodges of Lobuche and can be climbed in a day. A well-marked trail leads across the Khumbu Glacier and climbs to the pass in about three hours. The cluster of tiny lakes on the east side provides an ideal high camp.

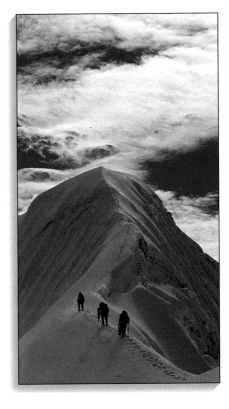

BELOW: Island Peak (Imja Tse) is one of the most popular Trekking Peaks.

Himalayan tahr *in Sagarmatha National Park.*

Kongma Tse (5,820 metres/19,094 ft, Group B) was originally listed as Mehra Peak but was renamed to avoid confusion with Mera Peak further south. Twinned with Pokalde, Kongma Tse rises to the north of the Kongma La. *Kongma* is the Sherpa word for the snow cock, a large bird which abounds in this area. Viewed from Gorak Shep, the mountain sports fine glaciers that hang suspended above the west face. The normal route is from the lakes below the Kongma La via the south-face glacier.

Lobuche East (6,119 metres/20,075 ft, Group A), west of the town, has a rocky east face which stands sentinel over the route to Everest Base Camp. Named after a Sherpa god, the true summit has proved an elusive goal. The rocky outliers of the peak were first climbed by the Swiss in 1952. Numerous subsequent attempts have fallen short of the actual summit, which rises above a deep notch at the far end of a long aligned ridge. It is possible the first ascent was not until April 1984, when the south ridge was climbed to the main ridge and followed over several false crests to the true summit. The east face of the mountain, easily accessible from Lobuche village, has attracted strong teams. Jeff Lowe, a pioneer on many Trekking Peaks, led a difficult route up an icy couloir, while the obvious but still difficult east ridge was climbed by Todd Biblier and Catherine Freer. A host of challenging possible lines remain.

Kwangde Ri (6,187 metres/20,298 ft, Group A) is a stunning peak visible from Namche Bazar, forming a long east-west ridge bounding the Bhote Kosi. Although included in Khumbu, Kwangde is the northern limit of the Lumding Himal. Kwangde has several summits, all of which are permissible on a single permit. The main summit, Kwangde Lho, has a formidable north face that was first climbed by Jeff Lowe and David Breashears in 1982.

BELOW:
porters trekking
in the snow.

Far less formidable from the north is the curving main ridge thrown towards the Bhote Kosi from Kwangde Shar. This fine northeast ridge offers a less difficult route and was first climbed Alpine-style in 1978 by Lindsay Griffin and Roger Everett.

More exacting, and perhaps more interesting, is the approach to Kwangde from the south. The high, uninhabited Lumding Valley was first explored by Jimmy Roberts and Sen Tenzing in 1953. A year later, American Fred Becky entered the valley, crossing the Moro La from the east before going on to discover the Lumding Tsho Teng, one of the highest lakes in the world. The south ridge of Kwangde Lho has become the normal, albeit difficult, ascent and was first climbed in 1975 by a Nepalese team.

Kusum Kangguru (6,367 metres/20,889 ft, Group A), more than any of the other Trekking Peaks, epitomises the dilemma inherent in the name. As its Tibetan name implies, this shapely citadel of rock and ice has "three snowy summits" that have provided a difficult and adventurous challenge. Found at the southern end of Charpati Himal, Kusum Kangguru rises between the Dudh Kosi and the uninhabited river drainage of Hinku Drangka. Rising close to Lukla, it is perhaps the easiest Trekking Peak to approach and the hardest to climb. Kusum Kangguru offers nothing for the incompetent and little for the merely skilful. Even by its easiest route, the east face above the Lungsamba Glacier, the mountain is technically demanding. The peak has attracted the élite of the mountaineering world and boasts more routes than any other peak on the list. Of the many climbs on its numerous faces and ridges, perhaps the most daring exploit was that of New Zealander Bill Denz who in 1981 completed a solo traverse of the mountain.

Map on page 262

BELOW: trekking rewards with spectacular views.

Mera Peak (6,654 metres/21,830 ft, Group A) is the highest of the Trekking Peaks, It forms a heavily glaciated mass between the Hinku and Hongu valleys, east of Lukla and almost due south of Everest. First climbed in 1953 by Jimmy Roberts and Sen Tenzing, it has in the last few years become one of the most frequently climbed mountains on the list. Its popularity is undoubtedly due to both its altitude and technical simplicity. As there are no lodges in either the Hinku or Hongu valleys, parties need to be self-contained, which makes it even more attractive to those in search of a mountaineering adventure.

The quickest approach is the Zatrawa La, east of Lukla. Parties approaching from Jiri can reach the mountain from the south via the Hindu Drangka and Pangkongma. The normal route of ascent is via the Mera La and the wide, gently sloping glaciers that fall from the summit's north face.

Rolwaling's hidden valley

The Rolwaling Valley is considered one of the eight "hidden lands" of Tibetan Buddhism and to this day animal slaughter is not permitted here. The valley's northern flank is dominated by Gauri Shankar (7,146 metres/23,439 ft), at one point thought to be the highest peak in the world. It resisted all mountaineering attempts until a Nepalese-American team scaled it in 1979. Three smaller peaks in this region are open as Trekking Peaks.

Trekking access to Rolwaling is from Charikot (1,998 metres/6,554 ft) on the Lamosangu-Jiri road. Several days' walk up the Bhote Kosi is Simigaon (2,019 metres/6,623 ft), where the Rolwaling Khola enters from the east. **Beding ⓫** (3,693 metres/12,113 ft) the last permanent settlement in upper Rolwaling, is grey and barren save for the brightly painted red, blue and yellow window

BELOW: high camp on Mera Peak.

shutters of the stone houses and a *gompa*. Beyond is the summer yak herders' settlement of Na (4,183 metres/13,720 ft), and, still further, the stark beauty of glaciers and glazed ice slopes. To trek this far and return down the valley is worthwhile for the high-altitude experience and the serenity of a silent white world.

From the lower Bhote Kosi, an alternative trail heads west up the Sangawa Khola and climbs to Bigu Gompa (2,512 metres/8,240 ft) with its sheltered convent tucked in a juniper forest. The path continues upward beyond all habitation, passing numerous potential campsites, to cross Tinsang La (3,319 metres/10,890 ft) and descend to the roadside town of Barabise. Another follows the ridge north past Deodunga ("God's Rock") almost to the Tibetan border, where the trail turns west to meet the Kodari-Kathmandu road.

Closed to Westerners for much of the 1980s and only reopened in 1989, Rolwaling offers several Trekking Peaks. **Ramdung** (5,925 metres/19,439 ft, Group A) is one of several appealing small peaks south of Na, best approached by crossing the Yalung La. These peaks were first climbed in 1952 by the Scottish Himalayan Expedition led by W.H. Murray. Although not a high peak, the approach is quite long and for most parties two camps above Kyiduk will be required. A second high camp on the Ramdung Glacier is usual if climbing the normal route, the northeast face from the Yalung La. In recent years groups have favoured an approach around the west side of the mountain.

Parchamo (6,273 metres/20,580 ft, Group A) is a lovely glacier peak at the eastern end of the Rolwaling Himal. Shipton, Gregory and Evans first attempted it in 1951, following the north ridge until they were stopped by difficult terrain and lack of crampons. Parchamo was not climbed until 1955, when Dennis Davis and Phil Boultbee finished the north ridge. ❑

The sheer wall of rock that is Ama Dablam.

BELOW: Thyangboche *Rinpoche* officiates at a cremation.

The Legend of Mallory and Irvine

On 8 June 1924 on the Tibetan side of Mount Everest, two British climbers apparently disappeared into the mists high on this huge mountain and thereby entered the realm of speculation and legend. Their names were George Leigh Mallory and Andrew Irvine.

Mallory, at the age of 38, had already become a well-known mountaineering figure. He had been a leading participant in the first reconnaissance ever made of Everest in 1921, and in the first attempt to scale the vast mountain the following year, both approached from its northern flanks in an unexplored area of Tibet. When he returned to the north side of Everest in 1924 and disappeared into the clouds on his way to the top of the world, Mallory caught the imagination of a British public demoralised by the carnage of World War I.

Handsome, a skilled Alpinist, talented writer and schoolmaster, Mallory had also become known for his pithy response to a query as to why anyone would try to climb Everest. It was he who answered with the classic line: "Because it is there". Among fellow mountaineers, Mallory was often quoted for another remark, in which he rejected the common use of the term "conquest" when a summit is reached. "Have we vanquished an enemy? None but ourselves."

Andrew Irvine was much younger, only 22, and much less experienced but he was selected by Mallory to accompany him on the push for the summit. Thus he also vanished into legend with his mountain leader.

Clad only in thick tweeds and carrying such essentials as wind-up gramophones to Base Camp, these early attempts were very different from the high-tech, super light-weight expeditions of today. There was no communication between the climbing team and Base Camp; those on the mountain were on their own to do or die. Burdened by hefty metal oxygen cylinders and layer upon layer of non-waterproof clothing, climbers faced minimal odds in a ground-breaking venture that exceeded all known heights. European mountaineers, well acclimatised to Mont Blanc's 4,810-metre (15,781-ft) summit, had no idea what elevations of nearly twice this figure would do to their bodies. But the excitement and challenge of the attempt is clear in Mallory's description of his first sight of Everest: "We paused, in sheer astonishment. The sight of it banished every thought; we asked no questions and made no comment, but simply looked ..."

The disappearance of these two men has led to numerous unanswered questions that fascinates the mountaineering world to this day. Did they reach the summit of the world's highest mountain before they perished? Why did they not manage to return to waiting teammates below? Did one of them fall and pull the other with him? Or did they become too exhausted to descend to the shelter of their tent and so died of exposure? No one yet knows. Although Irvine's ice pick,

LEFT: Sir George Mallory.
RIGHT: Mallory and Irvine's fated Everest expedition.

distinctively marked with three notches on the handle, was found in 1933, it would be more than 40 years before a body was sighted and a further 22 years before it was identified as Mallory.

In 1999 a research team, led by climber Eric Simonson and including historians and glaciologists, as well as film-makers, set off on an expedition to try to solve the mystery. In 1975 a Chinese climber on the northeast ridge claimed to have sighted an "old English dead", but died himself before clearly indicating the body's location. Piecing together information of the Chinese climber's route, the team began their search of the area's infamous "steps". On 3 May they made the remarkable discovery: Mallory's body, still clothed in his vintage tweeds, 600 metres (2,000 ft) below the summit.

The plight and bravery of these two men still inspires the world's greatest mountaineers. "I regard Mallory as the man of Everest of all generations," says Sir Edmund Hillary. "He was the man who really brought Everest to the public mind and was... the inspiration for all of us who followed... If anyone deserved to get to the top, he would have. But I have no idea whether he did."

Another of the world's finest climbers, Reinhold Messner, has analysed what happened based on his experience. "They went up towards the summit from their camp and surely climbed the first step (a rock feature at 8,535 metres/28,000 ft) but surely not the second step (a greater barrier not far above the first). At the first step they were already late for getting to the summit. They arrived below the second step, and in 15 minutes they could see it was impossible... They slowly went back towards their camp in the middle of the afternoon, on the way they died. Maybe one fell and pulled the other off. Maybe both fell. I don't know. Anyhow I'm sure they didn't reach the summit."

Or did they? Whether they equalled the achievements of Hillary and Sherpa Tenzing (*see page 141*) remains unknown. The team are still searching for their camera, hoping this may provide evidence of their summit success – or not, as the case may be. ❏

GOMPAS: SHERPA MONASTERIES

Gompas are the spiritual centres of the Sherpa communities of Solu Khumbu and serve as the focus of all religious and cultural activities.

Sherpas follow the Mahayana Buddhist practice known as Nyingma and worship in monasteries known as gompas. The first gompas at Pangboche and Thame were established by Lama Sanga Dorje between 300–400 years ago. In 1916 the first celibate monastery was established for religious study.

Sherpa gompas follow a traditional pattern of construction. At the front are three statues: the centre is Buddha who lived 2,500 years ago and taught a means for developing spiritual potential; the right is Guru Rinpoche, an Indian mystic who established Buddhism in Tibet about AD 730; the left is the god embodying compassion.

THE GOMPA COMMUNITY

Villagers take turns as the gompa custodian while lamas and celibate monks fill the religious roles. Monks devote their lives to studying, teaching and performing religious rites for the Sherpa community but they may also be stewards, custodians, artists or prayer leaders. Monks and nuns are supported by their relatives, who consider it an honour to the family. Both are free to leave and return to lay life without discredit.

Students enter monastery schools at age seven. They study the Tibetan language, religion, history, grammar, psychology and medicine. Students may take vows of commitment to monastic life but to take the final Gelung vows, a man must be celibate and at least 20 years old.

▷ **FEMALE FAITH**
Women may take vows to become nuns and live within female religious communities.

◁ **MOUNTAIN TEMPLES**
Many gompas, such as Thyangboche in the Khumbu Region, are located high in the Himalaya.

△ **GOLDEN SHRINES**
Many gompas have ornate altars to the Lord Buddha, as seen here at Sakyapa Gompa, Kathmandu.

◁ **DOMESTIC SCENE**
As well as their religious and science studies, young student monks take part in the monastery's communal life, including kitchen work.

▽ **PERFORMANCE RITES**
The Mani Rimdu festival at Thyangboche Gompa takes place in the autumn, a spectacular masked dance event *(see page 90)*.

◁ **HOLY BOOKS**
Books of Sherpa history and religious teachings are kept with much care in the gompa, as in this monastery library in Thame.

▷ **SPINNING WHEEL**
Many Nepalese devoutly attend gompas and temples to spin prayer wheels, releasing words of faith into the air with each turn.

LAMAS: RELIGIOUS TEACHERS

The title "lama" is reserved for religious teachers, whether or not they have taken vows of celibacy. They have studied the Sherpa beliefs, can read the scriptures, perform rituals and teach Buddhist principles.

A lama who has attained the highest level of spiritual achievement is called Rinpoche, meaning "precious one." He may earn this respected title through study and wisdom attained in this lifetime or by being recognised as the incarnation of a previous lama. The reincarnate's identity is determined when as a child he exhibits the characteristics of the late Rinpoche and can identify the deceased's belongings. The young lama is then raised in the monastery and given a religious and secular education.

Previously, students of higher level Buddhist teachings went to Tibet to study with the most respected Rinpoches. Today a spiritual education is more accessible, in Nepal and India as well as the West, as interest in Tibetan Buddhism is growing.

MOUNTAIN FLIGHT

Nearly everyone who comes to Nepal wants to see Mount Everest, one of the world's greatest spectacles, and one of the best ways to achieve this is to take a short flight over the Himalaya

A short mountain flight over the Himalaya is one of the best ways to see these spectacular mountains at close range, particularly for those without the fitness, skill or time to trek on the mountains by foot.

Four carriers arrange a daily one-hour mountain flight east from Kathmandu to see Mount Everest and 13 other white craggy peaks that define the central and eastern Himalayan range. Flying at altitudes of approximately 7,500 to 8,500 metres (25,000 to 28,000 ft) – eye level with the peaks at some 22 km (14 miles) distance – passengers get a magnificent close-up perspective. The flight route parallels the mountains for 160 km (100 miles) east of Kathmandu, and then turns around to give the view to both sides.

This one hour "fly past" of the world's greatest peaks is offered by Buddha Air, Gorkha Air, NECON Air Ltd. and Royal Nepal Airlines Corporation (RNAC), the Nepalese flag carrier. Buddha Air flies a new Beechcraft, with 16 seats, all with window views. Its cabin is pressurised, allowing it to fly higher (7,620–9,150 metres/25–30,000 ft), and offer face-to-face views, but at faster speed, cutting the circuit flight to 45 minutes. This is also expected to be the case for a new airline, Mountain Air, soon to be starting mountain flights in a Beechcraft. Gorkha Air flies a new Donier, with 17 seats in an unpressurised cabin. Their 3,350-metre (11,000-ft) cruising height views the mountains from a lower angle but makes the passing at an enjoyably slower speed. RNAC and NECON both fly AVROS, which are older planes no longer commonly flown in the West. Unpressurised, they also fly lower and slower. They sell 32 seats, but with double seating, half of the passengers that were not early arrivals must rely on a cooperative window-seat companion.

All flights are in the morning, when the weather is most likely to be clear. Boarding is at the Domestic Terminal of Tribhuvan Airport, with daily departure times (variable by season, demand and company) ranging from 6.30 to 9am. All the carriers run the flight year-round, including during the monsoon season, and crystal-clear views might be caught at any time. However, the best time for prime views is from late September to mid-December, after the rains, but before the fog of the winter months and the haze of the pre-monsoon season.

The mountain flight route has a perfect safety record, with no accidents to date. The safety records of other domestic routes have been less pristine, however. Buddha Air is currently considered top in safety and correspondingly, it is booked up first in the busy autumn season, sometimes months in advance. In response, they have started offering up to nine flights per morning at this time of year. For the

BELOW:
the awe-inspiring
Mount Everest.

other airlines one to two weeks' advance booking is recommended, but seats may be available with shorter notice. Between May and August seats can be found on most airlines with only a few days' notice. If the weather is not suitable for flying, all the airlines give full refunds or fly you the next day – unless you have booked with an agency, in which case the flight is not paid for until it has been completed.

Flights can also be chartered for the eastern range or the Annapurna area *(see page 237)* on Buddha Air and Shangri-La Air Pvt. Ltd. The Annapurna flight covers five magnificent peaks over 7,000 metres (23,000 ft). For a smaller group, chartering a private plane is possible, but book one month in advance.

Almost as spectacular as the awesome white mountain peaks are the middle hills of Nepal with their intricate cobwebs of green and yellow terraces and fairytale villages clinging to ridge tops, dissected with great grey-green rivers snaking through their narrow valleys *(see page 293)*. Lofty views of the earth's own textures extend far north onto the Tibetan plateau and far to the south over the Terai and the plains of northern India.

The sheer magnitude of the Himalaya is intimidating but, in addition to the well-known giants such as Everest and the Annapurna Range, there are a large number of "smaller" peaks – most of them considerably higher than any of the summits of Europe or the Americas – which march range after range across the northern reaches of this small nation. Indeed, Nepal's base camps at the foot of a mountain generally lie at about 5,500 metres (18,000 ft) elevation, higher than any mountain in Europe. The time and effort expended just trekking to reach them is for most people a once-in-a-lifetime adventure. But a mountain flight is an equally thrilling opportunity to see them at close range. ❑

TIP

The approximate cost for a one-hour mountain flight is US$100. Airport tax is NRS100.

BELOW: view of the Himalaya from the Everest flight.

EAST OF EVEREST

Though less visited than the Everest region, the appeal of east Nepal is the mighty face of Kanchenjunga and the changing face of the people as the Tibetan border approaches

Map on page 284

Kathmandu

L ike Nepal's far west, the region to the east of Everest is seldom visited by foreigners, but the similarities stop there. The east is far more populated than the west, in part due to a wetter climate; it is also narrower from north to south, is more accessible and its people are generally better off, having benefited from geography as well as participation in the Gurkha regiments *(see page 224)*. The east is a fascinating area in which to trek, enlivened by open-air markets attracting a carnival of costumed peoples. Naturalists rate the eastern Himalaya highly, especially birdwatchers who can rack up scores of new sightings.

The Arun Valley

The mighty Arun, one of Nepal's two largest rivers, flows from Tibet through a narrow gorge which is thought to pre-date the rise of the Himalayan massif. At its uppermost reaches within Nepal it receives melt-waters from the Barun Glacier off the slopes of Baruntse (7,129 metres/23,389 ft), Makalu and Lhotse Shar (8,383 metres/27,503 ft), and then heads south to join the Sapt Kosi.

A little-known trail which leaves the crowds of Khumbu behind follows an up and down trade route east over Salpa Pass (3,414 metres/11,200 ft). This seven-to eight-day walk from Kharte on the Dudh Kosi to **Tumlingtar ❶** on the Arun crosses three ridges and two main rivers, the Hinku and Hongu Kholas; trails connect to the bazaar towns of Hille and Dhankuta north of Biratnagar. Food and shelter are sporadically available at Sherpa and Rai villages along the Salpa trail but trekkers are advised to take food for a few days and a knowledgeable guide. This trail also provides southern access into the upper Hongu Basin where well-equipped trekkers might venture. Another approach to the Arun is via **Bhojpur**, famed for its hardened steel *khukri* knives wielded by the Gurkhas. The Tumlingtar airstrip or the Hille border crossing are the most convenient entry points to the Arun Valley.

The people of Tumlingtar are mostly *Kumals* (potters) who live in elevated bamboo houses and cultivate dry crops such as black lentil *(dal)* and sesame. Bulbous clay pots like those sold nearby at Khandbari are used for carrying water or storing millet as it ferments into *tongba*. Virtually all of east Nepal (and Sikkim) drinks *tongba*, a tasty brew made by pouring boiling water into a bamboo or wooden cylinder filled with fermented millet. The liquid is drunk through a straw sieved to keep out the millet kernels. The Sherpas and Bhotias of colder climes appreciate *tongba*'s warming effects. Suntala, similar to Mandarin oranges, are another speciality of the east savoured on warm days from October to March.

The ridge-top bazaar town of **Chainpur ❷**, east of

LEFT: a Limbu girl, Arun Valley.
BELOW: the mighty mahseer.

TIP

From Tumlingtar,
planes fly several
times a week to
Kathmandu;
Biratnagar, in the
eastern Terai, offers
several daily flights
to Kathmandu

Tumlingtar, is well worth a visit, especially for the Friday market. People of the surrounding hills come to sell a variety of goods: tobacco; grains; vegetables; cloth and well-reputed brassware. Tamang porters stop on the trail to rest their loads on wooden T-sticks. Women dressed in brightly flowered skirts, burgundy velveteen blouses and hefty coin necklaces gather in the tea shops and share the week's news. And Newar businessmen display their Dhaka-patterned *topis* (hats) made of hand-woven cotton in geometric designs. Chainpur is a pleasant stop any time with its flagstone walkways and shops spilling over with brass pots sold with a great mark-up in Kathmandu.

Trekking to Makalu Base Camp

Standing in the scorching sunlight on Tumlingtar's red clay airfield at 390 metres (1,280 ft) above sea level, the idea of climbing nearly 4,500 metres (14,800 ft) to the base of Makalu is daunting. Trekking into the upper Arun Valley is a near-expedition undertaking, requiring four weeks to and from

Makalu Base Camp ➌ (5,000 metres/16,400 ft) if the weather cooperates. A vast range in temperatures is confronted, from steamy in the lowlands to serious snow storms on high which can block the route if ill-timed. Weather alone deters most trekkers from the Arun, and dictates others' schedule to a narrow window in March or October to November.

Map on page 284

From Tumlingtar, the trail parallels the river along a ridge to the east, passing through Brahman and Chhetri, then Rai, Limbu, Gurung and Newar villages. Oak and rhododendron forests are teeming with bird and animal life. Precursory views of **Makalu** (8,463 metres/27,766 ft), Baruntse (7,129 metres/ 23,389 ft), Chamlang (7,290 metres/23,917 ft) and the Khumbu peaks open to the west, and Milke Danda, one of the longest ridges in Nepal, rises to the east.

At Num, the trail crosses the Arun and starts up the Kasuwa Khola toward Makalu Base Camp in the upper Barun Valley. This is wild country and should only be attempted with an experienced guide, food for at least 16 days and snow gear. There are no settlements beyond the Sherpa village of Tashigaon, and for nine to ten days the path crosses rugged terrain rising to three passes, including Barun La (4,250 metres/13,940 ft). From the high points there are panoramic views of the eastern Himalaya from Everest to Kanchenjunga and north into Tibet. Camping is possible among alpine meadows and at the base of Makalu's pink face as it reflects dusk's light off the surrounding peaks. Day hikes up the glacier offer more spectacular views. On the way down, the dank, mossy forests make an abrupt contrast to the upper horizons of ice and rock.

Limbu ethnic weaving.

The return to Tumlingtar can be routed along the west side of the Arun, sharing a forested trail with chattering rhesus monkeys and swimming holes with equally boisterous children. Trekkers with a special permit can continue up the Arun from Num into remote reaches populated with Lhomis, most of whom practise the Bön religion *(see page 60)*.

BELOW: primulas and rhododendron forest in east Nepal.

In the 1990s it appeared that much of the Arun Valley was set to be irrevocably changed by the installation of a hydroelectric facility, but the project never went ahead. Parts of the the Barun and Arun watersheds are now protected as the Makalu-Barun National Park and Conservation Area (entrance fee).

Remote Kanchenjunga

Kanchenjunga was opened to foreign trekkers in 1988, at the same time as Dolpo in west Nepal *(see page 319)*. Wary of the potential effects of tourism in such virgin territories, government regulations aimed at preserving the environment and local economies were imposed; the planned Kanchenjunga Conservation Area project will ensure further environmental protection. Individual trekkers have no access to the Kanchenjunga area – all foreigners must go through a registered trekking agency and guarantee self-sufficiency in food and fuel so as not to deplete the native supplies, litter or pollute the area.

The Kanchenjunga trekking region, roughly defined as the Tamur Kosi watershed which drains the west side of Kanchenjunga (8,586 metres/28,169 ft), the world's third highest peak *(see page 134)*, has received more attention than Dolpo, being relatively easier to get to

Bamboo is a valuable resource in eastern Nepal.

BELOW:
Kanchenjunga guards Nepal's eastern frontier.

and topographically more hospitable. Still, a Kanchenjunga trek requires a minimum of three to four weeks' hiking on rough trails crossing ridge and gully to visit the mountain's base either south or north. Pangpema, at close to 5,000 metres (16,000 ft), base camp for Kanchenjunga's northern face, sits on a glacier within 10 km (6 miles) of the Tibet border surrounded by peaks upward of 6,500 metres (21,300 ft). It is a long way from emergency treatment and many trekkers have had to turn back just days short of base camp for lack of acclimatisation time.

Flying in and out of **Taplejung** ❹ saves considerable driving time from Kathmandu (16–20 hours) but as with all mountain airstrips flights are often unreliable. A compromise solution is to fly to and from Biratnagar and drive four to six hours to trailheads at Basantpur (1,790 metres/5,871 ft) via the Dharan/Dhankuta road, or Phidim (1,311 metres/4,300 ft) north of Ilam. Hille sports a lively weekly market on Thursdays and is a good place to start out. Phidim is at the end of a dirt road which traverses Ilam's young tea estates.

Heading northeast out of Hille, the trail climbs through settlements of recent migrants from the Walungchung region, trans-Himalayan yak drivers. Gupha Pokhari (3,150 metres/10,300 ft), the second night's rest, is a lake set on a ridge looking east at the Kanchenjunga massif and west at Makalu and the Khumbu Himal. From here, a shorter trek follows the **Milke Danda** ridge, climbing to 4,700 metres (15,400 ft) into the **Jaljale Himal**, a remote area dotted with lakes and inhabited by Tibetan mountain people. The trail up Milke Danda ridge finds little water and a rocky way often covered in cloud. With a guide who knows the area, the return route can descend east to the Mewa Khola (Papaya River) and on to Taplejung's airfield (two weeks' walk from Hille), or head back down the ridge and turn west via Nundhaki to Chainpur and Tumlingtar.

The main Kanchenjunga trail crosses the Mewa Khola at **Dobhan** ❺, and follows the Tamur Kosi, skirting steep valley walls. The hills are densely forested with rhododendron, oak and pine; waterfalls confirm a copious monsoon. Bamboo gives way to alpine grass and rhododendron. At **Ghunsa** ❻ (3,350 metres/ 10,988 ft), a Tibetan village marked with prayer flags and a *gompa*, two trails from Kanchenjunga's southern flanks join the northbound route.

Now close to 3,500 metres (11,500 ft), full days of trekking may gain elevation too fast. The last three days to Pangpema are increasingly cold but spectacular as mountains close in from both sides of the valley. A small stone hut defines **Lhonak** ❼ and a level snowy pad is Pangpema, where expedition teams spend months as lead climbers make camps far above. Day hikes onto the glacier and higher ground for views of Kanchenjunga can delay departure.

For another perspective on Kanchenjunga and the face of Jannu (7,710 metres/25,300 ft) a 30-day trek visits the southern Yalung Glacier on the return to Pangpema. Two trails head south from Ghunsa. The easterly route scrambles over snow-covered rock to cross higher Lapsang La (5,050 metres/16,564 ft) while the lower alternative traverses three passes, the highest being Sinion La at nearly 4,800 metres (15,750 ft). Both routes require at least a one-night stay at high altitude. Above Ramze Lake, a trail skirts the massive Yalung Glacier up to Oktang for views of Jannu and peaks dividing Nepal and Sikkim.

Starting down the Simbua Khola, the preferred descent diverts south through Yamphudin then either west to Taplejung or south to the subtropical **Kabeli Khola** valley. Like the Arun and other far-reaching areas, the Kanchenjunga trek encounters a vast range of elevations and temperatures, best planned for October–November or March–April, with possible snowfall in any season. ❏

Map on page 284

BELOW: prayer flags flutter in the wind.

The Road to Tibet

Isolated from the outside world for centuries and only recently opened to western travellers, Tibet has gained a reputation as a magical and mysterious realm. Altitude alone sets it apart from other places, creating a land of crisp light and intense colours, bounded by a deep blue sky. Natural beauty is complemented by cultural riches: Tibet is an intensely Buddhist land, and its richly decorated temples and monasteries (gompas) testify to the deep-rooted faith of the Tibetan people.

The capital cities of Kathmandu and Lhasa lie some 1,000 km (600 miles) apart, but their histories and peoples are closely intertwined. Kathmandu's magnificent palaces were built by Newari craftsmen, whose skills were also in demand in Lhasa, and its Buddhist stupas of Boudhanath and Swayambhunath still draw Tibetan devotees (see page 193). Lhasa's massive Potala Palace, the great Drepung and Sera monasteries and the Jokhang Temple all exert a magnetic attraction on Tibetan pilgrims as well as the outsider.

The overland journey from Kathmandu across the Tibetan border is one of the most spectacular road trips on earth, wending its way through Nepal's lush green hills to the barren windswept plains of the Tibetan Plateau. The 114-km (70-mile) Arniko Raj Marg, also known as the Friendship Highway, was built with Chinese assistance in the 1960s and follows the course of the ancient Kathmandu–Lhasa trade route. Mountain bikers favour it for an invigorating four-day trip, while day-trippers choose it for a scenic drive out of Kathmandu. The really spectacular scenery begins only across the Tibetan border, as the highway winds and twists to the very "Roof of the World".

The route begins by climbing eastward over the rim of the Kathmandu Valley, passing Bhaktapur (see page 183) and the tourist resort of Dhulikhel (see page 210). Dropping into the severely deforested Panchkaal Valley, it crosses the braided strands of the Indrawati Khola at Dolalghat. This riverside village is the lowest and hottest point of the trip, at only 634 metres (2,080 ft) altitude. Scattered along the roadside are cottage industries producing handmade paper from the boiled bark of the daphne plant.

From Dolalghat the highway swings north to follow the course of the Sun Kosi, the "River of Gold". As the road climbs, the river gorge deepens and the scenery becomes increasingly dramatic – a taste of what's to come. The turn-off to Jiri, trailhead for the Solu-Khumbu region, is 78 km (48 miles) from Kathmandu. Soon after this is Lamosangu, a sprawling roadside town with a mineral-processing plant. The little village of Barabise lies 8 km (5 miles) further. From this point on, the road situation is touch-and-go. Monsoon landslides regularly wipe out sections of road, which are repaired annually, only to crumble the following summer. Motor transport of some type operates on the functioning sections, and porters are available to carry luggage over any short

LEFT: churning Tibetan salt butter tea.
RIGHT: looking south towards the main Himalaya range from the Lalung La in Tibet.

stretches that must be traversed on foot.

The small town of Tatopani, 23 km (14 miles) past Barabise, is the end of the road for many. Its name comes from its natural hot springs, now channelled through a cement tap-stand that locals favour as a laundry facility. Nepalese customs and immigration is a few kilometres down the road at the tiny settlement of Kodari.

A concrete "Friendship Bridge" spanning the Bhote Kosi marks the border between Nepal and China. Chinese customs and immigration is at Zhangmu, a large town visible high up on the hillside some 8 km (5 miles) away. Also known as Khasa or Dram, it's a bustling settlement where Tibetan, Chinese and Nepalese influences and goods mingle. Nepalese can travel up to this point without a passport or permit; many come to purchase Chinese cloth, thermos flasks, shoes and milk powder.

From Zhangmu the landscape begins its incredible transition, as the road winds its way up a narrow river gorge, its walls lush with greenery and ribboned with waterfalls in the summer monsoon. Travellers usually stop off at the village of Nyalam (4,100 metres/13,450 ft), which marks the dividing point between forest and bare plains. After a few more hours of ascent, the road crests at the 5,050-metre (16,570-ft) Lalung La pass, to emerge onto the Tibetan Plateau, a high, dry and wild realm quite unlike anywhere else on earth.

The north face of Mount Everest is visible slightly further down the road, along with Cho Oyu and a number of other peaks. Lhasa is one-and-a-half days beyond, via a southern route that passes through the pastoral farming village of Gyangtse. The magnificent, multi-roomed Kumbum stupa here was created in the 15th century by Newari craftsmen, who endowed it with a wealth of beautiful frescoes and images.

The next location along the route is Shigatse, Tibet's second largest city, its broad streets lined with whitewashed buildings in the traditional local style. At the centre of town is the great monastery of Tashilunpo, an impressive collection of ochre buildings roofed in glittering gold. ❏

THE TERAI

In contrast to the more familiar mountain images of Nepal, the Terai region is a vast expanse of forests and jungle, home to much of the country's indigenous wildlife

Map on page 294–5

T he name Terai, meaning "land of fever" has long evoked the dangers of this lowland belt of unhealthy jungle and swamps which runs the length of the country. Historically it provided a natural barrier between Nepal and its southern neighbour, India, as successfully as the Himalaya formed an indelible border in the north, but in recent years the two countries have seen their proximity as an advantage rather than a problem and there is a distinct Indian feel to Nepal's southern region.

The Terai is unlike anywhere else in the country, in terms of climate, landscape and vegetation. Although mountains may be the first image that springs to mind when thinking of Nepal, these lush forests and jungles form a sizeable part of the country, east to west, and support a large majority of Nepal's economy through agriculture and industry.

Land of colour

The lowest Himalayan range, the Siwalik hills (also known as the Churia), forms the Terai's northern boundary. Where the hills divide, smaller Inner Terai valleys such as Chitwan, Dang, Deokhuri and Surkhet abut foothills covered with giant sal trees (*Shorea robusta*). Tumbling streams carry stones, gravel and sand from the high mountains and deposit them in rivers which, laden with rich alluvial debris, slow and widen. Swamp and forest merge to create the Terai's beautiful, serene landscape. Giant grasses and trees, such as the khair (*Acacia catechu*), sissu (*Dalbergia sisso*), simal (*Bombax ceiba*) and sal, provide refuge for a wealth of wildlife *(see page 100)*.

During winter, streams dry up leaving wide rocky beds, and large rivers recede to reveal great stretches of white sandy beaches. The climate is pleasant though cold at night. In December morning mist shrouds the landscape, sometimes lasting until mid-day. From April to June mosquitoes invade the towns and a violent, dusty wind parches everything.

The summer monsoon follows, sending water racing into old and new river beds. Greenness, damp-ness and fevers succeed the dust and heat. Despite the floods, which can isolate villages from muddy lanes, the rains give the land its most wild and verdant appearance. Silvery, downy grasses wave on the river banks and young crops flourish in the fields.

In October and November emerald rice plants cover the fields and bright yellow mustard contrasts with the deep blue sky; during February and March the spring flowers emblazon the landscape with splashes of scarlet bougainvillaea, red bombax and the orange flame of the forest. Little wonder, then, that tourism in the Terai is catching on.

PRECEDING PAGES: the Terai is totally different from the rest of Nepal.
LEFT: Janak Mandir in Janakpur.
BELOW: gathering grain in the Terai.

Tharu people make their home in the Terai.

Early settlers

Throughout history Terai dangers repelled invaders, while its fertility attracted migrants. Palaeolithic and Neolithic remains have been found at the foot of the Siwaliks in the Dang valley. The 6th century BC saw a period of great prosperity in the region and it was at this time that the Lord Buddha was born in Lumbini *(see page 311)*. But waves of settlers were soon forced to retreat due to local border conflicts or feudal oppression and the jungle gladly re-established itself. Only a few scattered groups stubbornly remained to tend the rich land in such unhealthy conditions; the most numerous are the Tharu *(see page 49)* and small groups of the Bote, Majhi and Raji, all fishermen and ferrymen, as well as the Kumal potters.

In the 20th century the Terai yielded its virgin forests to settlements of impoverished farmers fleeing the overpopulated middle hills. Cultivation accelerated following the political change of the 1950s and the eradication of malaria in the 1960s. The "land of fever" had now become the granary of Nepal. Its fertile soils are ideal for growing rice and grain as well as oil seeds and, more recently, cash crops such as sugar cane, cotton, jute and a range of vegetables.

Today nearly half of Nepal's people live in the Terai. The population is multiplying faster than that of the country as a whole: 50 percent growth over the last decade compared to 30 percent throughout Nepal.

The eastern Terai is the most densely populated area, particularly Jhapa District where native Tharu, Rajbamsi, Dhimal and people of Indian origin have settled with the more recently arrived Rai and Limbu. In central Terai, Tharu, Kumal and Bote tribes are neighbours with hill peoples such as Brahman, Chhetri and Gurung. Until the 1970s far western Terai was heavily forested but legal and illegal settlers from the western hills, mostly Brahman and Chhetri, have joined the original Tharu tribes of Danguara, Rana and Katharya. Still, the western Terai is sparsely populated – approximately 70 inhabitants per 98 sq. km (38 sq. miles) – and less developed than the east which has received the benefit of foreign aid.

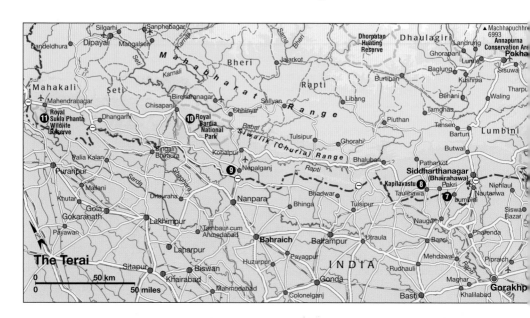

The Terai

Map on page 294–5

Trade and industry

Roads are now being built across the Terai, paving the way for industrial development. Where decades ago there were forests, now there are bustling, Indian-style bazaars; long-distance transport lorries are washed on sandy beaches where ferry boats used to wait all day for a single passenger. The jungle has diminished forever, now confined to scattered patches and tracts protected as national parks and wildlife reserves at Kosi Tappu, Royal Chitwan, Royal Bardia and Royal Sukla Phanta *(see page 106)*.

Though early on an untamed border region, the Terai has also been an unavoidable zone of commercial contact, linking the mountains with the Gangetic plains. Trans-Himalayan trading gave birth to seasonal markets where merchants and villagers swapped news and goods. Bazaars grew into border towns when the British Raj imposed its commercial hegemony and the Indian railways reached southern Nepal.

Terai markets have continued to prosper by their close proximity to India, inevitably Nepal's number one trade partner and financial supporter. Most of Nepal's agriculturally based industries are situated in eastern and central Terai, besides the Kathmandu Valley. Successful sugar mills were opened in Biratnagar in 1946, in Birganj in 1964 and more recently in Siddharthanagar (formerly known as Bhairahawa).

Manufacturing plants produce Nepalese-brand cigarettes and *beedees* (the indigenous smokes), matches and soap. Nepal's first industrial estate with a brewery, tobacco factory, cotton textile and cereal mills was established in **Hetauda**. Although still small, Nepal's industrial sector is growing quickly, introducing not only new products and an increasing number of jobs but an entirely new way of thinking.

Nepal's second city

With a population of more than 200,000, **Biratnagar ❶** is the second largest city in Nepal. Its geographical position near the Indian border has traditionally kept it at the forefront of the country's industrial development – Nepal's very

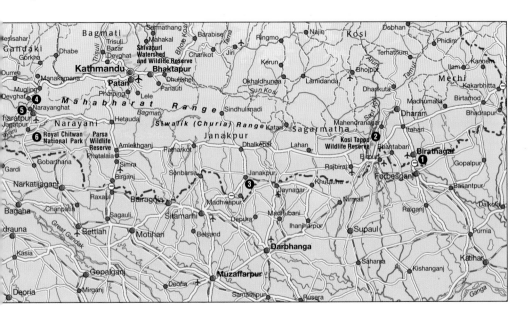

first industry, Biratnagar Jute Mills, was established here in 1936. The Nepal-Indian enterprise prospered with the rise of jute prices following World War II; more mills were opened and jute remains a significant export, although prices have recently gone into decline. Biratnagar's other industries include sugar mills, textile factories and manufacturing of stainless-steel kitchenware.

Aside from its industry, Biratnagar is known as a political centre, having produced four of Nepal's prime ministers.

From a tourist perspective, however, there is little to see here and most visitors use the city as a stopping-off point – Nepal's new private airlines, such as Buddha and Necon, fly between Biratnagar and Kathmandu about ten times a day. Of more interest is the eastern Jhapa District, which has a rich mixture of ethnic groups and an equally varied physical look: wooden houses elevated on high poles stand juxtaposed to charmless concrete structures. At the weekly market of Damak, a diversity of ethnic dress is apparent, such as the Dhimal women who come to shop wearing hand-woven black sarongs tied with red belts, their shoulders naked.

Further east, the recently established tea gardens and processing industry centre around the hilltown of Ilam. The Mahendra Raj Marg leaves Nepal at the eastern border crossing of **Kakarbhitta**, gateway to the Indian hill-station of Darjeeling and Sikkim.

Birdwatchers' paradise

BELOW:
bullock cart.

Beyond the Kosi River Bridge is Itahari, an unremarkable crossroads town midway between Dharan at the foot of the Siwalik hills and Biratnagar, just 6 km (4 miles) from the Indian border. But it is worth continuing west for about one hour along the Mahendra Highway, through scrub jungle, to arrive at the **Kosi Tappu Wildlife Reserve ❷**. On the floodplain of the Sapt Kosi River, the

reserve is famous for its birdlife and wild buffaloes. The reserve is bounded on the east and west by the river embankments and on the south by the barrage (dam) that forms the border with India. The reserve headquarters is at Kusaha but the closest hotel is in Biratnagar, although temporary tented camps can sometimes be arranged.

This little-visited preserve of 175 sq. km (68 sq. miles) is a haven for a superb concentration of waterfowl during the winter months. A total of 280 species of birds have been recorded, including 20 different sorts of ducks and the rare swamp partridge *(Francolinus gularis)*. The migratory birds can be seen between November and March resting at the Kosi barrage and on the main channel. The trail along the east embankment provides a good vantage point.

Kosi Tappu harbours the only remaining wild buffaloes *(Bubalus bubalis)* in Nepal, a population of only about 200. There are also spotted deer, blue bulls *(nilgai)* and wild pigs.

The pleasant hill-style bazaar of **Dharan** was badly damaged in the August 1988 earthquake. Until 1989, it was the headquarters of the British Gurkhas in Nepal, before they moved to Kathmandu. The British Gurkha cantonment has been turned into a major hospital. A British-built road winds from Dharan up into the hills to Dhankuta and Hille, the starting point for Kanchenjunga and many of the other east Nepal treks *(see page 285)*.

Janakpur: birthplace of Sita

Continuing west again along the Mahendra Highway, past Lahan, brings you to Dhalkebar (Lalbiti) bazaar. Here a road leads 20 km (12 miles) south to the sacred town of **Janakpur** ❸, an interesting detour into history.

Map on page 294–5

Giant hornbills at Royal Chitwan National Park.

BELOW:
Brahmany ducks, or Ruddy Sheldrake, winter around the Terai rivers.

Figures re-enacting Ram and Sita's wedding in Janakpur.

BELOW: rickshaw drivers in Janakpur.

Walking along the narrow dusty lanes of Janakpur it is hard to imagine that this town was once Videha, the capital of the fabled kingdom of Mithila that stretches across much of what are now India's northern state of Bihar and the Terai from the Sapt Kosi to the Gandaki. The Maithili language is today spoken by about two million people in India and southern Nepal. Traditional Maithili paintings, passed down from generations of Mithila women, have remained unchanged for centuries with their distinctive styles and colours. They can be found all over the town: on the walls of homes, on pottery and today even on fabric. Recently some of these local women have begun painting for commercial reasons at the Janakpur Women's Development Centre (Kuwa; open Sun–Thur; entrance free).

The Hindu epic *Ramayana* tells the story of "the city of King Janak", Janakpur, as legend has it the birthplace of the king's adopted daughter Sita, whom he found while tilling the soil with a golden plough. Ram, hero of the epic and an incarnation of Vishnu, won Sita in marriage by bending the great bow of Shiva, as no other man could do. The loving couple were then gloriously married in Janakpur.

Janakpur has been an important pilgrimage site since the 16th century when artefacts – holy images of Sita and Ram and a piece of Shiva's sacred bow – were reportedly discovered in the jungle by ascetics. In 1882, a Nepalese-style temple to Ram was built and in 1911 the main temple, the **Janaki Mandir**, was constructed over the spot where Sita's image was found and where she is believed to have lived. It is one of the few buildings in Nepal of Moghul architecture. Try to visit early in the morning or in the evening, to watch the religious chant "Sita Ram" and the priests perform their rituals.

MAITHILI PAINTINGS

The Hindu women of Janakpur (formerly Mithila) have been creating their own style of artwork for almost 3,000 years, passed down from mother to daughter over generations. Young girls are taught the distinctive art style, recognisable by its motifs and bright colours, as well as the Hindu stories behind the images, from an early age. This training culminates in her courtship and marriage, wooing her proposed husband with her paintings, then decorating the wall of the bridal bedroom with a *kohbar*, a fresco that celebrates life and fertility with a number of symbolic images, including bamboo, birds, fish and representations of Krishna and Vishnu. The bride and groom spend four nights beneath this mural, then it is washed away. Visitors to Janakpur between the festival of Diwali in the autumn and New Year in April will also see numerous exterior walls in the town decorated with painted images of wealth, such as peacocks. After New Year the walls are covered over with a fresh layer of mud and the paintings thus destroyed. Tourism, however, has brought with it a demand for more permanent Maithili art and many Janakpur women now work at putting their designs, both religious and secular, on paper, to be sold in gift shops throughout Nepal.

Despite its historical and religious importance, however, few buildings in Janakpur are more than a century old. The majority of the original buildings were razed in the Muslim invasion of northern India in the 15th century.

Two annual festivals in Janakpur attract hundreds of thousands of devotees to bathe in the city's 24 man-made *sagars* (sacred ponds). The most important celebration is Ram Nawami, Ram's birthday, in April. December marks the festival of Biha Panchami, re-enacting Ram and Sita's marriage in a procession of elephants, horses and chariots accompanied by musicians beating on their drums *(see page 90)*.

Janakpur is linked to the sleepy Indian border village of Madhubani by the only railway in Nepal, via numerous ethnic villages. In addition to its religious and historic significance, Janakpur is a modern developing town with a thriving cigarette-manufacturing industry – the Soviet-built factory still churns out "Yak" and other brands of Nepalese cigarettes. The plains around Janakpur have also earned a reputation for aquaculture and supply much of the freshwater fish for the Kathmandu market.

East-West Highway

Until the mid-1950s Nepal had very few motorable roads. Early visitors reached Kathmandu by foot or on horseback from Hetauda. The first road, the Tribhuvan Raj Marg, was completed in 1956 and linked Birganj to Kathmandu. It remained the only gateway to the capital city until the Siddhartha Raj Marg linking **Siddharthanagar** to Pokhara and Kathmandu was completed in 1968. Today few travellers brave the hairpin bends on the road from Hetauda over Daman Pass to Naubise. The main border entry points from India are **Birganj**, close to

Map on page 294–5

TIP

Necon Air flies daily from Kathmandu to Janakpur or there are regular night buses from the capital, with a journey time of about 11 hours.

BELOW: bathing at the festival of Biha Panchami.

the Raxaul railway line, and Siddharthanagar, connected to Nautanwa station. Non-Indian foreigners are only allowed to enter Nepal from India at four border points: at Kakarbhitta, Birganj, Sonauli (near Siddharthanagar), and Nepalganj, but it is advisable to check in advance as regulations are always liable to change.

Transport and communication across the Terai east to west was greatly facilitated with the completion of the 1,030-km (640-mile) Mahendra Raj Marg (Mahendra Highway) in the late 1960s. Part of the Pan-Asian Highway, but more popularly known as the East-West Highway, it was constructed in several phases with assistance from the former Soviet Union, United States, United Kingdom and India. The highway is now complete, and it is possible to drive right across Nepal from east to west from Mahendranagar to Kakarbhitta in about 24 hours.

Bazaars have sprung up along the East-West Highway at truck stops and crossroads, spreading untidy rows of thatched tea shops and fruit stalls. Shiny apples, heaps of oranges and bananas displayed against the jungle backdrop of statuesque sal trees and scrubby undergrowth are one of the enduring images of a Terai journey.

Devghat ❹ is located at a sacred confluence *(tribeni)* and has great religious importance. Many believe Sita died here and, as a result, many devout followers also come here to die. In January thousands gather in Devghat for the great purificatory festival of Maha Sankranti *(see page 85)*. Dugout canoes wait to ferry visitors to the shrine, tended by a *baba*, a famous holy man whose counsel is much sought by visiting pilgrims. This is also the take-out point for many Chitwan-bound rafting trips *(see page 303)*.

Narayanghat ❺, 10 km (6 miles) south of Devghat, and the adjoining town

BELOW: the only railway in Nepal runs from the Indian border to Janakpur.

of **Bharatpur** are located five hours by car southwest of Kathmandu. The two towns mark the hub of the Terai road network and are gateways to Royal Chitwan National Park. All vehicles, whatever their final destination, must pass through the mushrooming town of Bharatpur, situated on the banks of the Narayani River. There are also four flights daily from Bharatpur to Kathmandu.

Narayanghat is the prototype of a Terai town, with its straight grid roads, pastel-coloured concrete buildings and North Indian-style hotels and restaurants. Shops and stalls sell imported electronic products, fashions, fruit, biscuits and chocolate. Nepalese beer, Fanta and Coke are cooled in huge refrigerators or red portable freezer boxes. Windowless restaurants cooled with ceiling fans provide welcome shelter from hot and dusty streets which throng with gaily painted rickshaws and hooting trucks.

Royal Chitwan National Park

Renowned for centuries as one of the best areas for wildlife viewing in Asia, the diverse flora and fauna of the Terai national parks attract visitors from all over the world *(see page 106)*. Not to be compared with the wide open spaces of Africa, the intimacy of the search and discovery of Asian wildlife thriving in its dense natural habitat is considered by many travellers to be as rewarding as any larger safari.

Whereas yesterday's kings hunted tigers as guests of Maharajahs, today visitors can explore these uniquely beautiful areas in similar style and considerable comfort. For those with more modest ambitions, numerous budget possibilities abound.

Generally the best time for wildlife viewing in the Terai parks and reserves is

Map on page 294–5

Tharu graphic art in the Terai district.

BELOW:
sadhu at Devghat.

The Royal Bengal tiger still survives at Chitwan.

from February to April when the thick ground cover has retreated. By March some of the summer bird migrants have arrived while many of the winter visitors have not yet left. But some enthusiasts enjoy aspects of other seasons, and most safari outfitters remain open from October to June.

Most easy to reach of all the Terai's national parks, **Royal Chitwan National Park ❻** is also considered one of the richest wildlife areas in Asia and boasts the last and largest remaining areas of tall grassland habitat.

The park was formerly a hunting reserve of the ruling Ranas, always keen sportsmen, where every several years a great hunt would be staged during the winter months when the threat of fever was minimal. The Ranas and their guests, who included European royalty and Viceroys of India, bagged huge numbers of tigers and rhinos.

The national park occupies a lowland valley lying between the Siwalik (Churia) and Mahabharat ranges. It is drained by two major rivers, the Narayani and the Rapti. Prior to the 1950s Chitwan was only sparsely inhabited, mainly by Tharu peoples who it is thought developed a resistance to the endemic malaria. After the eradication of malaria, Chitwan was cleared and cultivated and its population tripled in less than a decade.

Poaching then became a problem; the rhinoceros in particular was killed for its valuable horn. In 1964 a sanctuary was declared and a large number of people were moved out and resettled. The *Gaida Gusti* or "Rhino Guards" attempted to patrol the park, but poaching continued. The rhino, thought to have numbered 1,000 in 1950, reached an all-time low of less than 100 individuals in the 1960s.

Only when the national park was established in 1973, with the full protection

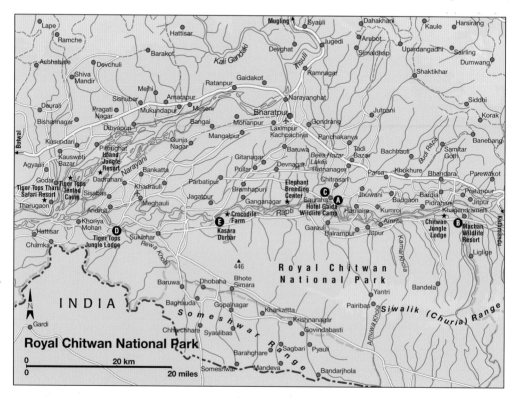

Royal Chitwan National Park

of the Royal Nepalese Army, was poaching and encroachment finally brought under control. In 1976 Royal Chitwan National Park was extended to its present size of 1,040 sq. km (402 sq. miles) *(see page 106)*. Concessions were given to private jungle safari operators to build lodges within the park and tourism developed at a rapid pace.

Visiting Chitwan

The large animals concentrate in the dense forest and tall grasslands of the floodplain. The best way to approach them is on the back of a well-trained elephant. Not only does the elephant offer the best vantage point, but the animal's scent masks that of humans. Rhinos favour marshy ground and indeed some areas of prime habitat are only negotiable by elephant. This is also the safest way to view them, as well as tiger, gaur and sloth bear *(see page 103)*.

Each of the seven lodges and tented camps which operate within the park is permitted to maintain their own stable of elephants. Among the best concessions are **Hotel Gaida Wildlife Camp Ⓐ**, Chitwan Jungle Lodge, **Machan Wildlife Resort Ⓑ**, Island Jungle Resort, Hotel Narayani Safari and Temple Tiger. Outside the park at **Sauraha Ⓒ** are a number of small hotels, the best of which is Royal Park Hotel. It is also possible to hire elephants from the government *hatisar* (elephant camp) at Sauraha. The famous **Tiger Tops Jungle Lodge Ⓓ** and its satellite Tented Camp is the oldest tourist lodge in the area, established in 1965 – predating the existence of the national park. It is renowned as one of the world's finest wildlife establishments and also as the host of the annual World Elephant Polo Championships. The adjacent Tiger Tops Tharu Safari Resort offers such stylish facilities as a swimming pool and riding stables in

Maps:
Area
294–5
Park 302

TIP

Searching out rhinos on foot is exhilarating, but it can be dangerous. Only venture into the park with an experienced guide, and do not encourage him to take you close to the animals. Alternatively, do your rhino-spotting from the safety of an elephant's back.

BELOW: tracking rhinos is the classic Chitwan experience.

addition to wildlife activities. For more information about accommodation in the park refer to the *Travel Tips* section *(see page 339)*.

Travelling in 4WD vehicles is another rewarding way to spot deer, wild boar, rhino, sometimes gaur and occasionally tiger, leopard and sloth bear. Movement in the park is not permitted after dark. As the road network in Chitwan is limited, it is best to combine a drive with a visit to the park headquarters, **Kasara Durbar ❺** (open daily). There is a small museum here (open Sun–Fri) which includes examples of reptiles and butterflies found in the park and the drive also takes in the Gharial Breeding Project where batches of harmless gharial crocodile hatchlings have been raised since 1978 for restocking the Narayani River.

East of Kasara is Lame Tal, a long ox-bow lake with spectacular birdlife and basking crocodiles. Other tals, such as Devi Tal, are good focal points for wildlife viewing. *Machans* (watchtowers) have been constructed overlooking tracts of grassland at Sukibhar in the west on the way to Tiger Tops and near Dumariya in the east.

Peaceful boat or canoe trips down the Narayani River encounter migratory waterfowl, dolphin, marsh mugger and gharial crocodile as well as unrivalled views across the entire width of Nepal to the white Himalayan peaks.

One of Chitwan's greatest assets is the scope it offers for nature walks. For those with curiosity, perseverance and a certain amount of courage, walking is the most profitable way of observing birds, studying vegetation and inspecting animal tracks. Treks of two or more days are also available, which have the advantage of getting away from crowds of less ambitious tourists. But the jungle is not without a very real element of danger, so never set off without being

BELOW: elephant polo championship in Chitwan.

escorted by an expert guide – visitors have been mauled by rhinos. Guides are also invaluable as both a source of information and their trained ability to listen out for wildlife and birds. Experienced guides can be hired at most lodges or at the park headquarters.

It is a half-hour flight from Kathmandu to **Meghauli**, the grass airstrip that serves Tiger Tops. Alternatively it is a pleasant five-hour drive to Chitwan from Kathmandu, via Narayanghat (Bharatpur) to Tadi Bazaar and Sauraha.

Maps:
Area
294–5
Park 302

West of Chitwan

The British- and Indian-built western sections of the East-West Highway opened to traffic comparatively recently: the bridge at Narayanghat was completed in the early 1980s. The excellent stretch of road west of Narayanghat follows the Narayani River through the Chitwan Valley, past a paper factory and the Tuborg brewery. A well-marked village road leads south to the Tiger Tops Tharu Safari Resort, then winds out of the Inner Terai Chitwan valley and through the forested Siwalik hills.

The highway runs between stands of leafy sal trees, complementing the red soil and scattered golden- and cream-coloured houses. From the far-reaching flatlands which stretch along the roadside, people seemingly appear from nowhere. Young children tend water buffaloes and goats grazing alongside the deserted roads.

Located 120 km (75 miles) west of Narayanghat at the base of the foothills is the pleasant crossroads town of Butwal. Gurung and Thakali people originally from the uplands make up the majority of its population. From here, a scenic road runs north through the hills to Pokhara via the viewpoint of Tansen (*see*

Sloth bears thrive in Chitwan's forests.

BELOW: in the forest at Chitwan.

The sacred pipal tree at Lumbini.

page 234). Another route heads south for 20 km (13 miles) to the large industrial town of Siddharthanagar, the border crossing at Sonauli.

This area is full of places of historical and cultural interest. Twenty km (12 miles) west of Siddharthanagar on a well-marked road is **Lumbini** ❼, the birthplace of the Lord Buddha and an important pilgrimage place for all Asia *(see page 311).* There are six daily flights linking Siddharthanagar and Kathmandu. Another ancient civilisation site, **Kapilavastu** ❽, lies 27 km (17 miles) further west at Tilaurakot, Prince Siddhartha's childhood home and the former capital of his father's kingdom. The ruins are thought to be those of the former palace, and the place where Lord Buddha began his journey of enlightenment. Near the dam at Tribenighat, a historic temple marks the site of Sita's banishment, as told in the great *Ramayana* epic.

The East-West Highway then climbs up through the Siwalik range into the beautiful Deokhuri Valley, an Inner Terai dun watered by the Rapti River. This is home to the Dangaura Tharu people whose long mud houses surrounded by fertile fields can be seen from the road. The young women wear their striking black and red skirts and a distinctive headdress adorned with tassels and beads upon which they balance their loads. The less visited Dang Valley lies further north, particularly popular with cyclists.

The western Terai

Until around ten years ago, the easiest way to reach far west Nepal was via India, especially during the monsoon when floods swell the rivers. Beyond the Deokhuri Valley, the highway penetrates the most remote part of the Terai. Here there is the true feeling of the "wild west". The four districts of Banke, Bardia,

BELOW: a typical Terai village.

Kailali and Kanchanpur are still known as the *naya muluk*, or new territories, as they were returned to Nepal by British India as late as 1860. Before the Land Reform Act of 1964, these districts were inhabited by only Dangaura, Katharya and Rana Tharu. Migrants subsequently settled from the hills, clearing and claiming these virgin lands.

Nepalganj ❾ is the far west's largest city and is considered to be one of the hottest places in Nepal. It is also Nepal's most Muslim city, thanks to more than a century of immigration from neighbouring India – mosques and Moghul architecture abound in the city, although many of the mosques are garish, modern and closed to non-Muslims.

For centuries, Nepalganj has also been an important market town, attracting not only Indians but also Tharu and highlanders from Jumla and Tibet to its bustling bazaars north of the main square, Tribuhuwan Chowk, set out on wooden benches.

Today the population, both Indian and Nepalese, is less than 50,000; it has yet to benefit from industrialisation, although small-scale handicraft production such as silver jewellery is evident along the main street.

An important regional communications and transport centre, Nepalganj is the far west's link with Kathmandu. Flights from Nepalganj airport (the country's fourth largest) connect to the hill town of Jumla *(see page 316)* and roads service the Tiger Tops Karnali Lodge and Tented Camp in Royal Bardia National Park and Sukla Phanta Wildlife Reserve near the western border *(see page 106)*. A good road also leads north to the pleasant and fertile valley of Surkhet, now renamed Birendranagar, which was once so malarious that travellers feared to stay even one night.

Map on page 294–5

LEFT: Nepalese Muslim at Nepalganj.
BELOW: royal tiger hunts were popular in the early 1900s.

Terracotta ornamental flowerpot.

BELOW:
sunset reflected
in the Karnali
River of Bardia
National Park.

Royal Bardia National Park

Located in the remote and sparsely settled far west Terai is an untouched preserve for the more adventurous traveller keen on indigenous flora and fauna. **Royal Bardia National Park** ❿ was first gazetted in 1976 as Royal Karnali Wildlife Reserve and the eastern extension was added in 1984, bringing the reserve to today's size of 968 sq. km (374 sq. miles). This became Royal Bardia National Park in 1988 *(see page 106)*.

The Geruwa River, the eastern branch of the great Karnali River which diverges into two main channels and many islands, forms the park's western boundary. The park extends east to the Nepalganj-Surkhet road and includes a large portion of the beautiful Babai River Valley, bounded by two parallel ranges of the Siwalik hills.

Tiger Tops operates the only concession in Bardia; the **Karnali Lodge**, set amid the fascinating Tharu villages on the edge of the forest, and the Karnali Tented Camp on the banks of the river downstream from Chisapani. Several simple, inexpensive lodges are clustered around the park headquarters at Thakurdwara. Most visitors fly to Nepalganj, one-and-a-half hours from Kathmandu, then make the three-hour drive to the park. To drive all the way from Kathmandu to Bardia takes 12 hours through memorable and scenic stretches of the Terai. Although still difficult to get to, the inaccessibility has prevented the crowds that now flock to Chitwan, offering a far more natural experience.

The main appeal of Royal Bardia National Park is being one of the best places on the subcontinent to see the Royal Bengal tiger in the wild and the only park where baiting is permitted on a regular basis. Three-quarters of all the tiger viewings in Bardia are from elephant-back and many are seen from vehicles and

boats, and on walks. West Nepal supports the kingdom's second largest population of this magnificent cat after Chitwan. It is thought that around 50 breeding adults are distributed from Banke through Bardia and Kailai into Kanchanpur. A few leopards live on the forest edges.

Trained elephants can be used to see tiger, rhinoceros and swamp deer in the Manu Tappu and Khaura Khola areas and rides can be booked at Thakurdwara. However, the park has an excellent network of roads and driving is the best way to see the herds of deer that congregate on the open grassland. Most 4WD rides cover the west of the park, through the famous phanta grasses *(see page 96)* and the home of many of Bardia's wild elephant herds. The southern area of the park, also best reached by vehicle, is the roaming ground of the beautiful blackbuck antelope.

There are a number of long walks, especially along the river, which are good for birdwatching and spotting deer and monkeys. River trips by boat or dugout canoe are scenically breathtaking and excellent for seeing waterfowl, gharial and marsh mugger crocodiles, smooth-coated otters and gangetic dolphin. This is also a great way to fish in the park's rivers; species include the huge *mahseer*, popular among sport fishers although the fish must now be released back into the river due to a declining population. A fishing permit is required, available from the park headquarters.

Royal Sukla Phanta Wildlife Reserve

Although small and remote, **Royal Sukla Phanta Wildlife Reserve ⓫**, covering 155 sq. km (60 sq. miles) is another gem of a wildlife sanctuary, tucked into the far southwest corner of Nepal. It is well worth a visit, though the

Map on page 294–5

BELOW:
gharial crocodile.

Map
on page
294–5

*The Terai forests
provide a safe haven
for various species of
lizard.*

BELOW: elegant
Tharu women of
west Nepal.

two-and-a-half hour flights to Mahendranagar are sometimes uncertain. The tented camp concession is operated by Silent Safari (tel: 099 21230).

Sukla Phanta encompasses part of the floodplain of the Sarda River, has thick sal forests and a pretty, small lake called Rani Tal. The preserve has extensive open grasslands and the largest surviving population of endangered swamp deer (*barasingha*), numbering about 2,000. There are many deer concentrated in the open meadows and waterfowl on Rani Tal. The park has more than 450 species of birdlife, including cormorants and eagles. Other wildlife, including an estimated population of 30 tigers, can best be observed from the tall *machans* (watchtowers) or from 4WD vehicles. Entrance to the reserve on foot is not permitted unless accompanied by a guide.

Elephants also make their home in the reserve although, strangely, they are rarely seen. One particularly famous inhabitant was Thula Hatti ("Big Elephant"), believed to be the largest Asian elephant in the world, but he was killed by a mine explosion in 1993, most likely planted by a poacher.

Near the Rani Tal is a round brick compound which many believe was the fort of an ancient Tharu king, although lack of archaeological research renders this more myth than fact for the time being.

Towards India

West of Nepalganj the East-West Highway passes through the untouched forests of Royal Bardia National Park to **Chisapani**, a village on the banks of the Karnali River, 350 km (218 miles) west of Narayanghat. A spectacular, if somewhat incongruous, single-tower suspension bridge – reputedly the longest in the world – now links the far west to the rest of Nepal. An ambitious hydroelectric project is also planned for the area, which may well change its way of life again. As yet, however, very few tourists venture west of Bardia National Park, and the area remains more influenced by the Indian capital than its own.

The border town of **Dhangarhi** draws Indian shoppers in their droves with its imported goods. The challenges of a new cultural identity evident in such remote areas is also apparent in booming **Mahendranagar**, which has doubled its population in the last 10 years and has now grown bigger than Nepalganj. Unless you're in search of Indian-style bustle, however, neither town offers much for tourists other than as bases to explore the nearby nature reserves. In contrast, nearby villages offer some of the more authentic sights of the Terai, inhabited by the native Rana Tharu and distinguished by longhouses and women wearing their traditional colourfully embroidered skirts topped with black shawls.

Although it is unlikely to ever take over from the Himalayan regions as Nepal's primary tourist attraction, the Terai offers a certain fascination as a melting point of Indian and Nepalese hill traditions and a centre of burgeoning commercialism speeding whole-heartedly into the 21st century. Combining this with its unequalled opportunities for viewing wildlife, a visit to the south of the country has an indisputable charm all of its own. ❑

Birthplace of Lord Buddha

Lumbini in southern Nepal is the birthplace of Lord Buddha, born in 543 BC as the Sakya Prince, Siddhartha Gautama. It is situated 21 km (13 miles) west of the modern town of Siddharthanagar, formerly known as Bhairahawa, and is set in 13 sq. km (5 sq. miles) of landscaped gardens.

An important place of pilgrimage for Hindus as well as Buddhists, Lumbini was "lost" for centuries. In the 4th century AD the Chinese monk, Fa-Hien, travelled to India in search of Buddhist manuscripts and returned with vivid descriptions of the remains he found at Lumbini. Already it was in ruins and had been overgrown by the jungle; Fa-Hien wrote: "On the road people have to guard against elephants and lions."

Only in 1895 did archaeologists unearth the inscribed pillar, erected to commemorate the visit of the Mauryan Emperor Ashoka in 249 BC *(see page 28)*. Since 1970 the sacred site has been protected by the Lumbini Development Trust. Excavations have been made and pottery, figurines and coins found among the ancient brick foundations of monasteries and stupas. A new Tibetan monastery has been built, trees planted and a museum, library, hotel and garden are under construction.

The massive Ashoka pillar marks the place of Buddha's birth and the Mayadevi Temple contains a panel depicting the miraculous event. The myth tells how Buddha was conceived by entering his mother's womb in the form of a white elephant. When the time came his mother, Mayadevi, leaning on a fig tree, gave birth to Prince Siddhartha from her right side. She placed the newborn child in a lotus flower, but he stood and walked seven steps in each of the four directions, announcing his great destiny. After seven days Mayadevi died.

The original temple was built by Emperor Ashoka and reconstructed in the 5th century AD in the *shikhara* style. The present building dates from the 19th century and is sheltered by an ancient pipal tree. Adjacent is the sacred pond in which Prince Siddhartha was bathed after his birth. Mayadevi is also greatly revered by Hindus.

The story of the Buddha is known to all his followers. He lived a life of luxury, marrying a princess, fathering a child and enjoying his youth. Only as an adult did he venture beyond the walls of the palace where he encountered a poor man, a sick man and a dead man. He was so disturbed by this suffering that he abandoned his comfortable life to become an ascetic.

Tilaurakot, the ancient capital of Kapilavastu, is 27 km (17 miles) west of Lumbini. In a lovely mango grove, excavations have revealed the brick remains of the eastern and western gates of the palace complex in which Prince Siddhartha lived with his father, King Suddhodhana. The museum in the village contains pieces dating between the 4th century BC and the 4th century AD. Near Tilaurakot are the damaged Ashoka pillars of Niglihawa and Kotihaw. ❑

RIGHT: a Licchavi statue of the Lord Buddha, the Compassionate One.

THE REMOTE WEST

Map on page 316

Western Nepal is a largely untamed region, sparsely populated and so remote from the rest of the country that even visiting Nepalese are mistaken for foreigners

Kathmandu

In western Nepal the Himalaya are at their widest, unfolding as broad ridges generally over 3,600 metres (11,800 ft) known as *lekhs*. The great Karnali River system bevels these high pasturelands into oak-pine forested valleys. Jumla, an administrative and commercial centre, shivers at 2,347 metres (7,677 ft) under thick snow throughout winter, while **Dipayal**, at 600 metres (1,970 ft) records some of the country's highest temperatures. A petered-out monsoon squeezes its last drops onto the west's summer-parched farmlands in the far-reaching rainshadow of the Dhaulagiri massif.

The Khasa Malla kings governed west Nepal and Tibet through the 14th century, when Indian Rajput chieftains fleeing Muslim invaders carved out petty principalities here. Occupational castes followed, settling in the valleys and low hills while Tibetans extended their niche into the inner Himalaya, establishing an unassimilated settlement pattern that persists today. The crusade of Prithvi Narayan Shah reached Jumla in 1788 and thereafter the west answered to Kathmandu, or for a period to neighbouring Mustang.

Today, hilltop *chortens*, crude human effigies and folk song traditions recall the west's mixed ethnic heritage. Religious beliefs show altitudinal preferences: Buddhism in the highlands, Hinduism in the lowlands, with a form of kinship deity worship intertwined.

PRECEDING PAGES: Phoksundo Lake. **LEFT:** yaks in Dolpo. **BELOW:** Jumla farmers and child.

Trekking in the west

Trekkers bound for west Nepal enter a world far removed from the tea houses of Solu Khumbu. Only the hardy need apply – those willing to weather the difficulties for the great rewards of more isolated and rugged Nepal. Except for the Terai and silt-fed valleys, the region is agriculturally impoverished. All food and drink must be carried in as there is hardly any opportunity to restock. Customarily ill-prepared to accommodate outsiders – peoples such as the Thakuris consider it polluting to house a stranger – tents and camping equipment are also required. A reliable trekking guide is invaluable in finding elusive paths and dealing with non-English speaking porters.

Travel to the remote west is no easy jaunt for other reasons too. Many areas are off limits due to government policies, political or otherwise. Trekking agents have long awaited the forecasted opening of the high Mugu and Limi valleys in Humla but, should they open, advance research on current politics would still be necessary. Maoist anti-government insurgency forces have established strongholds scattered throughout Nepal but nowhere more than in the middle hills of the mid-west. However, only Dolpo has been designated by foreign diplomatic agencies as meriting extreme caution status for foreigners. To date, no

TIP

Royal Nepal Airlines
(RNAC) is the only
carrier that services
Jumla, Dolpo and
Humla, from
Nepalganj, with four
flights per week.
Winter sees heavy
cancellations due to
fog in the south and
snow in the north. The
only chance for
advance reservations
is from the RNAC office.
Prices range from
approximately
US$60 to 90.

tourists have met with Maoist violence (although some have been forced to make pay-offs) but it is essential to check out all trekking plans with a reputable agency which is up-to-date with the political situation in that area.

Jumla ❶ is where most treks begin. **Rara National Park ❷** is the far west's most popular trekking area, though it receives only a few tourists each year. Set at 2,980 metres (9,777 ft), Rara Daha's (Lake) blue waters reflect a snow-clad Ghurchi Lekh framed in evergreens. During November and April, shoreline reeds are aflutter with migrating wildfowl. The 106-sq. km (41-sq. mile) protected area harbours the Himalayan black bear, *thar*, musk deer, red panda, otter and monkey *(see page 101)*.

Two main trails connect Jumla to Rara, each requiring approximately six days return. The more westerly route heads north from Jumla, up the valley and across grassy slopes, reaching Hada Sinja, the old Khasa Malla capital, in two days. Across the river the old palace is in ruins, but a temple to Bhagvati, goddess of justice, is worth a view. You have the choice of the longer, easier Gorosingha route or the steeper, shorter Okarpata route. Both cross the Ghurchi Mara and traverse a 3,800-metre (12,500-ft) ridge overlooking Rara Lake. Forests of pine, birch and rhododendron lead to a bridge with posts carved into human likenesses, spanning the final approach to Rara Lake. It takes one full day to walk the 20-km (13-mile) trail around the largest lake in Nepal.

The return to Jumla leaves from the lake's southern rim and descends to **Pina** (2,430 metres/7,970 ft). Once over Ghurchi Lagna (3,456 metres/11,340 ft), the trail passes Bumra and the Lah Gad River and climbs to a meadow where it forks. The westerly branch crosses Danphya Lagna (3,658 metres/12,000 ft); the easterly route descends along riverbanks. Both lead back to Jumla.

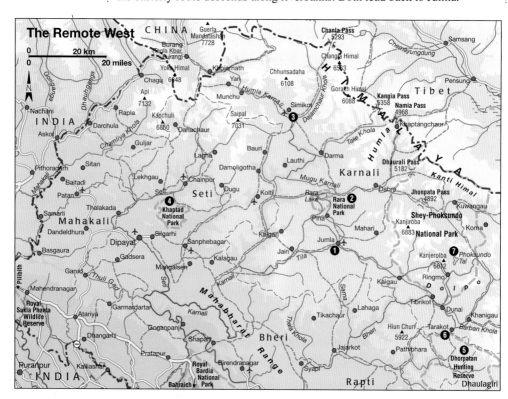

The Remote West

Map on page 316

Humla

The distance from Jumla to **Humla** is far greater than the jingle in their names implies. Located 12 or more hard days' walk northwest of Jumla, Humla has known a handful of Westerners and few of the modern world's accoutrements. Until the mid-1990s the majority following this route were pastoralist Humli farmers taking their sheep and goats along the great "salt for grain" trail to lowland Aacham. Increased supply of government salt and grain had already diminished local investment in pastoralism, but when population land pressure led Aacham to increase their grazing fees, Humlis responded by wholesaling their sheep herds and the historic trade route dropped to a trickle. However, Hindu and Buddhist pilgrims still bisect Humla en route to holy Lake Mansarovar and Mount Kailas, the centre of the world for Buddhists, in Tibet *(see page 55)*.

Rhododendrons are abundant at moderate altitudes in western Nepal.

With the fall of their caravan lifestyle, however, other aspects of local life unravelled. Humla had a unique social niche with their polyandric marriage system – with some men always off on trade or shepherding, the tradition of one wife to many brothers held sway for centuries. With all the men now coming home, the family seams are bursting, the economy is stunned and Humla has taken vigorous steps to re-invent itself. They have the national lead in forestlands owned by the community and are successfully processing non-timber forest products such as herbal oils. With the lead of their first educated woman, Babita Lama, Humla has four health clinics, successful crafts exportation and a sharp increase in girls' enrolment in school.

BELOW: western Nepal offers great trekking for those determined to get off the beaten track.

The trail from Jumla to Humla goes west from Sinja, joining the Khater Khola, the river that drains Rara Lake, following its lush riparian lands before joining the main north-south trade route below Barchya on the Karnali. From dry

Circumambulation around Mount Kailas is an important religious ritual, called parikama *by Hindus and* kora *by Tibetan Buddhists. The latter believe that it wipes away the sins of a lifetime.*

riverbanks, the trail rises to cross 3,800-metre (12,500-ft) Munya La. At trail choice points, check with locals on weather and trail maintenance. Whether you follow the Karnali or fly in from Nepalganj, you will arrive at **Simikot ❸**, district headquarters of Humla.

Mountains, valleys and national parks

The foremost draw for foreign travellers to Humla is its short route to Mount Kailas. To reach Mount Kailas, source of the Humla Karnali and three other great rivers of Central Asia, head north out of town towards **Munchu**, the Nepal departure police checkpost two days short of the border to Tibet. It is essential that you plan ahead so that you are met at the border, otherwise the Chinese authorities will not permit you to cross. You will be driven to Taklakot, a vibrant old trade centre, pulling peoples of exotic cultures throughout the region. From here it is just 100 km (60 miles) to Darchan, the first stop at the base of Mount Kailas, where at least two nights are required to acclimatise before making the four-day circuit.

Khaptad National Park ❹ guards a place of religious importance as well as *lekhs* and high pastures *(see page 106).* Five of the park's 225 sq. km (89 sq. miles) are sacred, sheltering shrines and streams that feed the Ganges river.

Getting to Khaptad is not difficult; the four western airports (Kolti, Sanphebagar, Chainpur and Dipayal) can be reached within two to three days' walk of the park. From Chainpur in the Seti Valley, the trail mounts the 3,050-metre (10,000-ft) Khaptad Lekh to the park's headquarters. An alternative return route heads south to Silgarhi, a Newari hill bazaar with stone-paved streets. Seven to ten days are needed for the trip.

BELOW: yak caravan in the Karnali Valley.

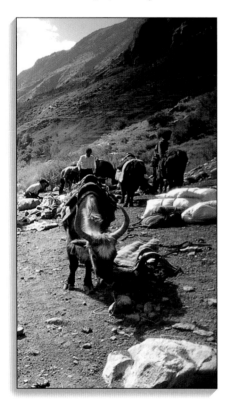

DOLPO'S HARDY SALT TRADERS

Sequestered from the outside world by tortuously high mountain passes and restricted entry, Dolpo has long fascinated and frustrated travellers. For centuries, a trans-Himalayan salt trade was the mainstay economy of Nepal's mountain people. Terai-grown grains brought up during winter were exchanged for the essential salt as well as wool, butter and Tibetan brick tea. Every summer, yak caravans crossed snowbound passes, well over 4,000 metres (13,200 ft), sometimes enduring days without food and nights at temperatures down to −20°C (−4°F). Although the advent of iodised salt has made the value of Tibetan salt plummet, the great herds still thunder in Dolpo.

David Snellgrove first revealed the mysteries of Dolpo in his book *Himalayan Pilgrimage* (1961). More recently Eric Valle's Academy Award-nominated feature film *Caravan* (1999) brought Dolpo to the world's attention again. The film chronicles the salt traders' rugged life, mixed with a depiction of the classic rift between youth's urgent pride and the elders' respect for the mysterious authority of the mountain gods. By the beginning of 2000 *Caravan* had run for six months and counting, to packed audiences crackling with the excitement of Nepalese thrilled with the beauties of their own hidden culture.

Mysterious Dolpo

In 1989, the valleys leading to Dolpo's **Shey-Phoksundo National Park** were de-restricted to organised trekking groups who are self-sufficient in food and fuel. Shey Gompa and the rest of the 1,373-sq. km (531-sq. mile) park above Phoksundo Lake are also accessible for organised groups with special permits. These high mountain regions were featured in Peter Matthiesen's book *The Snow Leopard*.

A three- to four-week trek into **Dolpo** requires the mindset to endure a remote, spartan landscape. There are several approach routes; from Pokhara, Jumla, or following the path up the Bheri River. Drive to Baglung on a good, paved road and start walking, or drive to Maldunga and then a further 10km (6 miles) on a very rough road to Beni.

Tarap lady in the Dolpo region.

Village tea houses are available along this corridor as far as Lumsum, from where the trail climbs steeply through pine and rhododendron forest to Jaljala Pass (3,415 metres/11,200 ft). A *chautara* (tree-shaded rest stop) marks the top, where a fine camp spot looks over the Dhaulagiri and Annapurna Himals. Dhorpatan (2,760 metres, 9,055 ft) is reachable in seven days from Pokhara.

Dhorpatan lies over a 2,930-metre (9,600-ft) pass, five or six days from the trailhead. At the **Dhorpatan Hunting Reserve ❺**, blue sheep and other prized animals can be hunted with a permit. The next leg of the journey, Dhorpatan to **Dunai**, takes a rollercoaster track over three passes through a desolate landscape. The next stopping point is **Tarakot ❻**, known locally as Dzong for its hilltop fortress.

BELOW: Ringmo, at the southern end of Phoksundo Tal. **FOLLOWING PAGE:** women of the hills.

From Dunai, the district headquarters, two trails lead north. If the locals report it in good repair, take the trail up the Suli Gad River. There are lodges in Chepko and Ringmo and forest walks. After the Palam park entrance, where your entrance ticket and goods will be checked, the trail winds through a narrow gorge, passing close to a magnificent waterfall. The highest in Nepal, it tumbles 1,670 metres (5,480 ft) down a series of rock shelves.

Hikers' first glimpse of **Phoksundo Tal ❼** reveals a white glimmer of silver birch edging the lake's turquoise-blue waters, set in a cleft between rocks that rise 2,000 metres (6,500 ft). Kanjiroba, at 6,883 metres (22,582 ft) the highest in the region, can be seen from the tops of these surrounding peaks. Blue sheep, musk deer, goral, snow leopard, *thar* and bear inhabit the park, set aside to protect an ecosystem typical of the high arid Tibetan plateau. At the southern end of the lake sits the *gompa*-rich hamlet of **Ringmo** (3,630 metres/11,900 ft) whose inhabitants subsist on buckwheat and potatoes.

Turning back down the Suli Gad and continuing west to **Tibrikot**, another fort town, the trail diverges, southward along the Bheri to Jajarkot and Surkhet, accessible by road from Nepalganj or west to Jumla. Most trekkers prefer the five- to six-day journey to Jumla, across the 3,840-metre (12,590-ft) Balangra Pass and on through Rimi to Napokuna in the upper Tila Valley. The entire Pokhara or Tansen-Dolpo-Jumla trek can also be done in reverse. In either direction, weather will be a major factor. ❑

INSIGHT GUIDES

TRAVEL TIPS

Insight Guides Website
www.insightguides.com

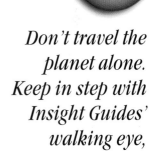

Don't travel the planet alone. Keep in step with Insight Guides' walking eye, just a click away

New Insight Maps

Maps in Insight Guides are tailored to complement the text. But when you're on the road you sometimes need the big picture that only a large-scale map can provide. This new range of durable Insight Fleximaps has been designed to meet just that need.

Detailed, clear cartography
makes the comprehensive route and city maps easy to follow, highlights all the major tourist sites and provides valuable motoring information plus a full index.

Informative and easy to use
with additional text and photographs covering a destination's top 10 essential sites, plus useful addresses, facts about the destination and handy tips on getting around.

Laminated finish
allows you to mark your route on the map using a non-permanent marker pen, and wipe it off. It makes the maps more durable and easier to fold than traditional maps.

The first titles
cover many popular destinations. They include Algarve, Amsterdam, Bangkok, California, Cyprus, Dominican Republic, Florence, Hong Kong, Ireland, London, Mallorca, Paris, Prague, Rome, San Francisco, Sydney, Thailand, Tuscany, USA Southwest, Venice, and Vienna.

✵ INSIGHT GUIDES
The world's largest collection of visual travel guides

CONTENTS

Getting Acquainted

The Place

Area: 147,181 sq. km (56,827 sq. miles).
Capital: Kathmandu.
Highest mountain: Mount Everest (8,850 metres/29,035 ft).
Population: 22 million.
Languages: Officially Nepali, but also a variety of other languages and dialects.
Religion: Hindu (86 percent); Buddhist (8 percent); Muslim (3 percent).
Time Zone: GMT + 5 hours, 45 minutes. When it is midday in Kathmandu, it is 6.15am in London, 1.15am in New York. When daylight saving time operates in Europe and America during the summer, the time difference is reduced by one hour.
Currency: Nepalese rupee (NRS).
Weights and measures: metric.
Electricity: 220 volts.
International dialling code: 977.

Geography

Nepal is surrounded by India and shares a common border to the north with the Tibet Autonomous Region of the People's Republic of China. A rectangle 885 km (553 miles) long and averaging only 160 km (100 miles) from north to south, Nepal bends to follow the curve of the central Himalaya. A country the size of Austria and Switzerland combined, its astonishingly varied topography ranges from the highest mountains on earth to the tropical lowlands of the Terai.

The country is entirely mountainous except for the temperate valleys spread across its middle and the narrow strip of plain along the southern border. The Himalaya was formed by the clash of two large continental plates, the Indian subcontinent and Eurasia, in a process that began 130 million years ago. Studies of rock layers suggest the upheavals displaced the Tethys Sea which previously covered much of the land. The mountains are still in the process of adjustment and the Indian subcontinental plate continues to push into Asia, resulting in land slips, glacial activity and occasional earthquakes. At the same time the Himalaya are wearing down, as all young mountains do, pounded by monsoon rains, constant freezing and thawing which cracks and erodes the rocks.

The People

Nepal's population is about 22 million, with 45 percent of it under the age of 15. Approximately 15 percent live in urban areas. The annual rate of population growth is 2.4 percent. More than 36 recognised ethnic groups, with different cultural identities and as many as 50 distinct languages, make their home in Nepal. The prevailing pattern of Hinduism to the south and Buddhism to the north is interwoven with Tantrism, animist rites and shamanistic practices (see page 62). Both major religions co-exist in many parts of the country but they come together in the homogeneous society of the Kathmandu Valley.

The Indo-Aryan population consists of 52 percent Nepalese, 11 percent Maithili, 8 percent Bhojpuri and 3.6 percent Tharu. The Tibetan-Burmese groups are 3.5 percent Tamang, 3 percent Newari, 1.4 percent Magar, 1.2 percent Gurung, 0.2 percent Limbu, and around 60,000 Tibetans. Around 52 percent of the population speak Nepali, 11 percent Maithili and 8 percent Bhojpuri. The Tibetan-Burmese languages are Tamang, Newari and Tharu.

Official figures state that 86 percent of the population are Hindu, 8 percent Buddhist, 3 percent Muslim and approximately 50,000 are Christians. Yet independent surveys suggest that these official percentages are weighted for political reasons and there are significantly more practising Buddhists.

Government

In 1990, the absolute monarchy of Nepal was turned into a constitutional Hindu monarchy (see page 39). The power of King Birendra, who came to the throne in 1972, was reduced and a multi-party system and a democratic legal system was introduced.

The parliament consists of the Lower House with 205 MPs who are elected every five years and the National Assembly whose 60 members are re-elected every six years. Legislative powers are in the hands of both houses and the king has restricted powers to propose changes in bills presented for his signature and to create ordinances.

Nepal is divided into 14 regions and 75 districts. Its administrative centre is Kathmandu. The highest court is the Supreme Court and there are several Courts of Appeal. Theoretically every district has a district court but not all are functioning or even exist. The highest commander of the Royal Nepal Army is the king, who is bound by the decisions of the National Defence Council.

More than 50 political parties are registered with the Election Commission, most of them splinter groups struggling for a piece of the pie. The two main players on the political scene are the Nepalese Congress Party and the Communist Party of Nepal-United Marxist-Leninist (UML). The National Democrats or Rastriya Prajatantra Party (RPP), led by members of the old panchayat regime (see page 38), form a smaller party with the power to provide crucial swing votes, which tends to shift its allegiance according to the direction of the political wind.

The first Nepalese Congress government, headed by Prime Minister Girija Koirala, lasted from May 1991 to November 1994. It was replaced with a UML government headed by Man Mohan Adhikari, making Nepal, for a brief period, the world's first and only Communist Hindu monarchical democracy. Since 1995 there have been at least half a dozen changes in the premiership; most have headed coalition governments with shifting combinations of members from Congress, UML, RPP and the small Nepal Sabdhavana Party.

Political infighting often leads to upheavals and demonstrations in the capital. On *bandh* days shops and transport are shut down. Public disillusionment with party disputes and corruption is increasing.

Another problem involves the gradual spread to the centre of a terrorist campaign led by a Maoist rebel faction based in impoverished western Nepal.

Economy and Welfare

Statistically, Nepal ranks among the world's poorest countries. With a per-capita GDP averaging around US$222 per year, that is among the 10 lowest national incomes in the world. About half of Nepal's population are considered to be below the poverty line, but in reality most Nepalese live in a largely non-commercial environment in which such figures are irrelevant.

Around 80 percent of the population is dependent on agriculture for its livelihood, most of them subsistence farmers working small plots carved into terraced hillsides. Since only 21 percent of Nepal's total area is arable land, farmers must rely on intensive cropping methods. Irrigated land yields rice, vegetables and wheat, while dry fields grow corn, millet, potatoes, lentils and flowering mustard (used to produce cooking oil). Favourable climatic conditions allow for two or even three crops per year, while the many different micro-climates

created by the country's varied topography allows for the cultivation of valuable cash crops – tea, coffee, fruits, vegetables and spices – opportunities being taken up by enterprising farmers.

Livestock are an important part of the farming economy, relying on the country's 12 percent of permanent pasture land. Water buffalo, goats, sheep and chickens are common, along with yaks and yak-cattle crossbreeds such as *chauri*, *dzopkio* and *dzo* at higher altitudes.

Manufacturing, service and industry constitute a relatively small portion (less than 20 percent) of Nepal's GDP. Hand-knotted Tibetan carpets are the biggest employer and among the largest money-makers, bringing in around US$150 million per year. Handmade garments including pashmina wool products are another large foreign exchange earner (*see page 80*). Tourism contributes to the domestic economy as well, with more than 450,000 international visitors in 1999 and about US$150 million in

Climate and When to Go

From the snow of the higher peaks to the tropical expanses of the lowlands, Nepal enjoys an extreme variety of climates. Altitude and aspect are the most influential factors. The south is tropical with a warm and humid climate ; temperatures range between a pre-monsoon daytime maximum of 37°C (99°F) and a winter nighttime minimum of 8°C (46°F). The central part of the country with its many valleys offers a pleasant climate with temperatures between 28°C (82°F) and 2°C (36°F). The north, however, displays Alpine conditions above 3,500 metres (11,480 ft), with very low temperatures during the winter months. Temperatures in the mountain areas range between 16°C (61°F) and – 6°C (20°F), depending on the altitude and time of year.

With an elevation of about 1,350 metres (4,400 ft), the Kathmandu Valley has warm summers

and cool winters and boasts one of the most congenial climates and most hours of sunshine of any capital city. The cold season from October to March is the best time to visit.

Night-time temperatures may drop to near freezing point, but the sun warms the atmosphere by day, so that the mercury typically climbs to around 23°C (73°F) by midday. The sky is generally clear and bright; the air is dry and warm. In the winter there is frequently an early morning mist – a result of the rapid heating of the cold night air. October and February are particularly pleasant months.

The weather is noticeably warmer in the Pokhara Valley, where temperatures rise to 30°C (86°F) at midday in the lower altitude. In April, May and early June the weather becomes hot and stuffy, with occasional evening thunderstorms. Nature is rampant

at this time, but the brightly coloured landscapes are often shrouded in a heat haze.

By the end of June the monsoon arrives, heralded by pre-monsoon rains which normally start in May. The rainy season lasts three months, during which time the Himalaya usually remain out of sight. The rains create some flooding but it is still possible to visit the Kathmandu Valley and many visitors enjoy this quiet time of year. Most trekking stops with the proliferation of leeches (*jugas*), and the lowlands are sometimes cut off by swollen rivers and occasional landslides. But summer is the best time to trek to the northern areas of Mustang and Dolpo, in the rain-shadow of the mountains.

The monsoon ends around mid-September. Autumn brings clearer skies, cooler nights and the lush greens of the post-monsoon period give way to a brown and gold land.

foreign-exchange earnings. Foreign aid funds as much as 30 percent of Nepal's regular budget, and 40 to 60 percent of the development budget. Major donors include Japan, Denmark, Germany, the Asian Development Bank, the World Bank and various United Nations organisations.

Nepal's geographical location between two powerful states forces the country to export luxury items and to import staple goods. Most products reach Nepal via India, with Calcutta as the only official export harbour. As soon as political difficulties arise India is not shy to use economic blackmail against Nepal. The Nepalese government is keen to support the country's independence by promoting agricultural productivity, industrial smallholdings in specific areas, the production of energy and tourism. At the same time it is trying to negotiate an alternative access route to the sea and to improve trade relations with China and Tibet.

The country's health situation has improved immensely in the past 50 years, but serious problems remain. The national life expectancy for men is around 58 and for women about 57, reflecting a high infant mortality rate. About 75 out of 1,000 babies die by their first birthday and one out of every 100 children dies before the age of five, victims of diarrhoea, disease or respiratory infections compounded by widespread malnutrition. The government has established a network of district hospitals and health posts and is training a cadre of community health volunteers to intervene at village level. Gastrointestinal illnesses such as dysentery and giardia are common, as are hepatitis and typhoid, all spread by unsanitary drinking water.

Education receives a fairly high public priority. National adult literacy rates are still low at 48 percent but have risen from the 24 percent in 1981. Literacy is much higher in the under-15 age group (77 percent for boys and 56 percent for girls).

Calendars

Five different calendars are used simultaneously in Nepal. These include the Gregorian calendar familiar to the West and the Tibetan calendar called *Bhot Byalo* (first introduced in 127 BC).

The official calendar is the *Vikram Sambat*, named after the legendary North Indian king Vikramaditya. Day One of Vikram Sambat was 23 February, 57 BC, and the months are determined by the moon phases. Following the moon year the Nepalese celebrate New Year's Day in mid-April. As the lunar year consists only of 354 days it requires seven additional months every 19 years. *Vikram Sambat* is used in the royal household, newspapers, public services and government bureaucracy.

The fiscal year begins in mid-July. The Nepalese year is 365 days long, as in the West, with 12 months ranging in length from 29 to 32 days. These calendar months starting mid-April are called *Baisakh* (31 days), *Jesth* (31 days), *Asadh* (32 days), *Srawan* (32 days), *Bhadra* (31 days), *Ashwin* (30 days), *Kartik* (30 days), *Marga* (29 days), *Poush* (30 days), *Magha* (29 days), *Falgun* (30 days) and *Chaitra* (30 days).

The seven days of the week have been named according to the planets. They are: *Aityabar* (Sunday – the day of the sun), *Somabar* (Monday – the day of the moon), *Mangalbar* (Tuesday – the day of Mars), *Budhabar* (Wednesday – the day of Mercury), *Bihibar* (Thursday – the day of Jupiter or of the Lord), *Sukrabar* (Friday – the day of *Venus*) and *Shanibar* (Saturday – the day of Saturn).

Another traditional calendar is *Nepal Samat* (introduced in AD 879–89). Buddhist astrologers count the days according to *Shaka Samat* (introduced in approximately AD 77).

Culture and Etiquette

Nepalese cultures are strange and exotic and many visitors are uncertain how to deal with the people directly because they do not speak their language and do not know their customs and values. Misunderstandings and prejudice can make encounters difficult.

The more you know about the history, the economic and political developments and particularly the cultural background the more you will be able to understand what you see and hear. Refer to the appropriate travel literature (*see page 359*) or contact the appropriate organisations (*see page 328*).

The Nepalese are friendly, helpful, polite and tolerant towards visitors and will make you feel at home. The first greeting is not marked by shaking hands but by folding the hand in front of the chest and saying "*Namaste*". It is normal to use first-name terms.

A Nepalese means "no" when he nods and "yes" when he shakes his head sideways. But a "yes" may only signify that he is trying to avoid a negative answer which is deemed to be impolite. Even a direct refusal will often be disguised with a careful and indirect wording. No answer to a question is also considered to be very bad manners; a vague and imprecise reply is infinitely preferable. A dismissive gesture means the opposite: "Come here!" It is not the custom to thank somebody profusely for a present or some help, as the pleasure is normally evident from other gestures.

The Nepalese value self-control and equanimity very highly. Anyone showing lack of self-control or displaying aggressive behaviour in public quickly loses their respect. Cuddles in public are also not accepted. Immodest or revealing clothing should be avoided.

Although the cultures of many Nepalese groups differ greatly from each other they all have a deep-rooted religious feeling which enters all parts of life. Many customs have a religious or even magical background whereas others may just be based on practicality or hygiene.

Always respect religious sites and rites. Honour the mythical and religious Nepalese lifestyle by walking clockwise around a stupa, *chorten* or *mani* wall. Take your shoes off before entering a temple or a shrine. Comply with good grace if you are asked not to enter a certain precinct or not to photograph a shrine. The reasons for enforcing a taboo are as evident for the local people as they are obscure to you.

The Nepalese understand that Western values are different from theirs. Even if they are shocked by your behaviour, they will explain it as primitive barbarianism and will not pursue the matter as long as they do not think the gods are offended. First of all, know and accept the fact that you are a foreigner and therefore ritually "polluted". Thus some seemingly innocent act on your part which could have been tolerated of a Nepalese might have unpleasant repercussions. The apparent familiarity with which the Nepalese behave towards idols should be no invitation for you to imitate them by climbing on statues or similar.

Men and women dressed in white are in mourning and should not be touched under any circumstances. Stepping over the feet or the body of a person rather than walking around him is not done. Never point at a person with your foot as it is believed to be "polluted". This is easily done when crossing your legs on the floor.

Children frequently chant the magic words "*Rupee! Paisa!*" with palms extended. It is mostly a game. Ignore them and they will smile and walk away. Should they insist, grown-ups will shout and scatter them – the Nepalese are very proud. Refrain from giving any money. If you want to support the Nepalese you should contact the appropriate organisations. Giving sweets is also a bad idea since there are very few dentists in the country. Often, rowdy crowds of

children will gather round you. Make sure your bag is closed and your camera equipment secure. Mostly they will simply annoy you by popping up between your camera and the site you want to photograph. Ask a friend to distract them, or else give up until they do likewise.

If you are invited into a Nepalese home, follow these rules: take off your shoes before entering a house or a room; treat the kitchen or the cooking and eating area with the utmost respect; on no account should you go without an explicit invitation – remember the hearth in a home is sacred; never throw rubbish into the fire. Little presents for the children are welcome but will not be opened before your eyes.

The Nepalese use water and the left hand to cleanse oneself after going to the toilet. Therefore nothing should be accepted, and especially not offered, with the left hand only. If you do offer or accept anything then do so with both hands if this is practical or certainly using your right hand. This will please your host very much. Using both hands to give or receive signifies that you honour the offering and the recipient or giver.

Never offer to share your "polluted" food – that is food you have already tasted, bitten into or even touched with your used fork or spoon. Nepalese often eat squatting on the ground. Do not stand in front of a person who is eating because your feet will be directly in front of his plate of food. The sociable part of the evening takes place before the meal so that the visit draws to a close with the end of the meal. Do not forget to praise the food before you leave.

Planning the Trip

Passports and Visas

Except for Indian citizens, all passport holders require a visa for entry into Nepal. A single-entry tourist visa for 60 days can be obtained from any Royal Nepalese Embassy or Consulate upon payment of US$30 (or local currency equivalent). It is also possible to get visas at Kathmandu's Tribhuvan airport, the Kodari border with China, or Indian border entry points into Nepal (*see page 293*). You will need a passport valid for at least six months and a passport-size photo, and it is useful to bring exact change. Visitors who require single, double or multiple re-entry visas within the 60-day period can pay an additional US$25, US$40 and US$60 respectively.

Tourist visas will not be granted for more than five months in any 12-month period. After the first visa issued within any 12-month period, all subsequent visas cost US$50 per entry valid for a 60-day period.

Extensions of visas in Nepal are available from the **Department of Immigration** in Kathmandu at the cost of US$50 for each additional month. These must be applied for before the visa expires. Visa extensions can also be made at the Pokhara Immigration Office (tel: 21167) which is located between the airport and the lakeside (*see page 230*).

Trek permits are no longer necessary for most trekking areas in Nepal. If travel is planned to a remote or restricted area it is mandatory to use a registered trekking agent to make arrangements. They will process the remote area permits as part of the service.

Visas for China, Tibet and India

Travellers wishing to visit Tibet and China must apply for a visa at the appropriate Chinese embassy for which you need travel confirmation from your travel agent. Travellers coming from China may get their visa at the border point in Kodari.

Travellers wishing to visit India can get their visas before they leave home, or from the Indian Embassy at Lainchaur in Kathmandu (tel: 410900), but allow two weeks for the application and clearance process. Travellers coming from India by land or air can get their Nepal visas at the point of entry.

Department of Immigration
New Baneswar, Kathmandu.
Tel: 494273, 494337.
Open Mon–Fri, 9am–5pm, but applications must be submitted before midday.

Customs

Travellers may bring in 200 cigarettes, 50 cigars or 250 grams of tobacco, one bottle of liquor and 15 rolls of film. Also duty-free on condition they are exported when you leave are the following personal effects: one pair of binoculars, one still camera, one video camera, one laptop computer and one portable music system. Please check with the appropriate embassy or consulate if you need to bring in special work equipment.

Passengers arriving at Tribhuvan International Airport without any dutiable articles can proceed through the Green Channel for quick clearance without a baggage check. Those carrying dutiable items are required to pass through the Red Channel for detailed customs clearance. Prohibited items are firearms and ammunition (unless an import licence has been obtained in advance), radio transmitters, walkie-talkies and drugs. Film permits are required for 16mm cameras.

You must also clear customs when you leave Nepal. To avoid hassles be aware of the following:
• Souvenirs can be exported freely but antiques and art objects require a special certificate from the

Department of Archaeology in Kathmandu. It takes at least two days to secure. It is forbidden to export any object more than 100 years old.
• The export of precious and rare commodities is strictly forbidden. These include precious stones, gold, silver, weapons and drugs. Animal hides, fangs or even live wild animals may not be exported without special licences. Live pets such as Tibetan dogs may be taken out.
• Keep receipts for any handicrafts and purchases you have made and remember to have Foreign Exchange Encashment Receipts ready for inspection if necessary.

TIA Customs Office
Tel: 470110/472266.
Department of Archaeology
National Archives Building, Ram Shah Path, Kathmandu.
Tel: 250683/5.

Money Matters

The local currency is the Nepalese rupee or rupiya (NRS). There are 100 paisa to one rupee. Bank notes come in denominations of 1,000, 500, 100, 50, 25, 20, 10, 5, 2 and 1 rupees. Gold-toned coins are issued as NRS 2 and 1, while aluminium coins come in NRS 1, 50, 25, 10 and 5 paisa. Fifty paisa is one mohar; 25 paisa is one sukaa.

Money can be changed at Tribhuvan International Airport and at any number of banks and foreign exchange counters in Kathmandu. It is illegal to exchange foreign-currency with individuals other than authorised dealers. Hotel exchange rates are generally slightly below the bank rates, which fluctuate against a basket of currencies and are published daily on the back page of The Rising Nepal newspaper. Be sure to save Encashment Receipts in case surplus rupees need to be exchanged on departure. The former black market has virtually disappeared with government efforts to make the rupee more fully convertible.

Banks are open 9.15am–3pm Monday through Friday. The counters of licensed money-changers are

Major Banks

Nepal Bank Ltd
New Road, Kathmandu.
Tel: 221185.
Rastriya Banijya Bank
Bishal Bazaar, Kathmandu.
Tel: 228335.
Nepal Grindlays Bank
Thamel, Kathmandu.
Tel: 260440.
Himalayan Bank
Thamel, Kathmandu.
Tel: 227749.
Nepal Arab Bank (NABIL)
Kantipath, Kathmandu.
Tel: 227181.
Nepal Indosuez Bank
Durbar Marg, Kathmandu.
Tel: 228229.

open 12 hours a day. Most hotel, airline and travel agency payments are required to be made in foreign exchange.

Credit Cards and Travellers' Cheques

Credit cards such as American Express, Diner's Club, Mastercard and Visa are widely accepted in the Kathmandu Valley, though many shops will add the card company's 5 percent commission onto bills.

For lost or replacement credit cards contact the local representatives for Visa and Mastercard, the **Alpine Travel Service**, or the **American Express** office.

You may purchase US dollar travellers' cheques with American Express credit cards at the American Express office, or with Visa or Mastercard at Nepal Grindlays Bank. You can receive money quite conveniently through Western Union Money Transfer. Contact the local agent, **Annapurna Tours and Travels**. It's also possible to have money sent to you at local foreign banks to be collected in dollar travellers' cheques, but this procedure is not recommended as it almost always involves more time and trouble than anticipated.

Excess Nepalese rupees can be converted back into hard currency at the end of your stay.

Keep exchange receipts from the bank to facilitate these transactions.

Alpine Travel Service
Durbar Marg, Kathmandu.
Tel: 225020/225362.
Open 9.30am–4.30pm, Sun–Fri.

American Express
Jamal, Kathmandu.
Tel: 226172/227635.
Open 10am–1pm, 2–5pm, Sun–Fri.

Annapurna Tours and Travels
Durbar Marg, Kathmandu.
Tel: 223530/254821.

What to Wear

Your wardrobe will depend upon when you are travelling to Nepal and what you intend to do there. Unless you are planning to meet government or embassy officials, there is no need to bring anything but casual clothing.

From mid-September to March light clothing is fine in the Kathmandu Valley during the daytime but for evenings and early mornings bring a fleece, heavy sweater or a thick jacket. Blue jeans, corduroy trousers or below-the-knee skirts are in order and comfortable shoes are a must, even if you do not intend to go trekking . Do not bother to bring a raincoat; a locally bought umbrella will suffice against the sun as well as the rain.

Special gear for trekking can be hired or bought in Pokhara or Kathmandu in Western sizes.

From April to September only light clothes, preferably cotton, are needed in Kathmandu. Avoid synthetic fibres which irritate the skin.

The Terai, being lower in altitude, is generally warmer than Kathmandu throughout the year. Safari-type clothing is most appropriate for visits to the lowland national parks. But the cold winter nights in December and January make a sweater and jacket essential.

Jungle areas require light cotton clothing in safari colours (soft yellow, green, brown). Remember to take a sunhat and suncream. Also pack your bathing costume but make sure that nobody can see you when you are swimming because naked bodies always cause a stir.

Getting There

By Air

More than 90 percent of non-Indian visitors to Nepal arrive by air at Tribhuvan International Airport, about 6.5 km (4 miles) from Kathmandu.

Several airlines serve Nepal, including the national carrier Royal Nepal Airlines Corporation (RNAC). Others include Aeroflot, Austrian Airlines, Biman Bangladesh Airlines, China Southwest Airlines, Druk Air, Gulf Air, Indian Airlines, Pakistan International Airlines, Qatar Airways, Singapore Airlines, Transavia and Thai International. Kathmandu is connected by direct flights to Abu Dhabi, Amsterdam, Bangkok, Bahrain, Calcutta, Delhi, Dhaka, Doha, Dubai, Frankfurt, Hong Kong, Karachi, Lhasa, London, Moscow, Osaka, Paris, Paro (Bhutan), Shanghai, Singapore and Vienna.

Flying in from the east you can see many of the world's highest mountains, including Mount Everest. The thrice-weekly service to Lhasa flies over the Himalayas and is one of the most spectacular flights in the world. Check with local travel agents (*see page 330*) as such flights are seasonal.

All air fares must be paid in foreign exchange by foreigners in Nepal. Only Nepalese and Indian nationals may pay in rupees for any flight between Nepal and India.

Individual travellers flying during the main season (October–April) should confirm their outward and return flights at the same time. Be sure to reconfirm your international departure tickets again not less than three days before departure or they will be subject to cancellation. The baggage allowance on international flights is 20 kg (44 lbs) in economy class. Overweight charges will be levied in foreign exchange.

By Rail

Within India, trains are a convenient means of transportation, but there is no railway to speak of in Nepal. A 47-km (29-mile) line was built in 1925 between Raxaul, India, and Amlekhganj, south of Kathmandu.

Departure Tax

The following departure taxes are payable upon check-in on all departing international flights. Flights to other SAARC countries (ie Bangladesh, Bhutan, India, Maldives, Pakistan, Sri Lanka): NRS 900.
To all other countries: NRS 1,000. For domestic flights: NRS 100. Children under two and diplomats are free of departure taxes.

Further east, a second line was built in 1940 between the Indian border and Janakpur of some 50 km (31 miles). But that's all.

Combining Indian rail with Indian and Nepalese roads, it takes about three days from Delhi to Kathmandu via Varanasi (Benares) and Patna, crossing the border at Birganj. Coming from the Indian hillstation of Darjeeling, you can take the train to Siliguri. From there it is a one-hour taxi ride to Kakarbhitta, a Nepalese border post from where you can take a bus or taxi to Biratnagar. Travellers going to Darjeeling via Kakarbhitta by road need a special visa. Those wishing to enter the Indian state of Sikkim can get a 15-day tourist visa at Siligiri.

By Road

In addition to Tribhuvan Airport there are several other official entry points. Check local political conditions: crises may cause borders to close temporarily. These points are: **Birganj** (Narayani Zone) near Raxaul, India, the most common entry point for overland travellers; **Kodari** (Bagmati Zone) on the Chinese-Tibetan border, open to tourists with Chinese visas, providing road-access to Lhasa. Vehicles have to be changed at the border because Chinese vehicles are only permitted in China and Nepalese vehicles only in Nepal. A permit to use one's own vehicle is given rarely and after long negotiation; **Mahendranager** (Mahakali Zone) at the eastern corner of Mahendra Raj Marg, the most important east-west connection in Nepal;

Nepalganj (Bheri Zone) with connection to Mahendra Raj Marg; **Sonauli** (Lumbini Zone) near Bhairawa on the road to Pokhara; **Kakarbhitta** (Mechi Zone) with connections to Darjeeling, Sikkim and Siligiri (India).

If you are entering Nepal by private car from India, be prepared to wait for several hours to get through any of the border posts. A *carnet de passage en douanes* is required for cars and motorcycles. This exempts the vehicle owner from customs duty for three months. A driver's licence is also required.

Third-party insurance is not legally required but comprehensive cover is recommended.

Royal Nepalese Missions Overseas

Australia: Level 13, 92 Pitt Street, Sydney, NSW 2000.
Tel: (02) 9233 6161;
fax: (02) 9223 6144;
Suite 712, 127 Creek St,
Brisbane, QLD 4000.
Tel: (07) 3220 2007;
fax: (07) 3211 9885;
16 Robinson St, Suite 2,
Nedlands, WA 6009.
Tel: (09) 386 2102;
fax: (08) 9386 3087.
Canada: 200 Bay St, Toronto.
Tel: (416) 865 0200;
fax: (416) 865 0904.
Denmark: 3A Aldersrogade, DK 2100, Copenhagen.
Tel: 3927 3175;
fax: 3920 1245.
France: 45 rue de Acacias, 75017 Paris.
Tel: (01) 4622 4867;
fax: (01) 331 4227 0865;
email: nepal@ worldnet.fr
Germany: Im Hag 15, 53179 Bonn.
Tel: 0228 343097;
fax 0228 856747;
email: nepal.emb.de@t-online.de
Hong Kong: Unit 1206, Greenfield Tower, Concordia Plaza, 1 Science Museum Road, Tsim Sha Tsui, East Kowloon.
Tel: 852 2369 7813;
fax: 852 2824 2970;
email: rncghk@ datainternet.com

India: Barakhamba Road, New Delhi 110002.
Tel: (011) 332 9969;
fax: (011) 332 6857;
email: Ramjanki@ vsnl.net.in;
I National Library Avenue, Alipore, Calcutta 700027. Tel: (033) 479 1117; fax: (033) 479 1410.
Japan: 14-9 Todoroki 7-chome, Setagaya-ku, Tokyo 158-0082.
Tel: (03) 3705 5558;
fax: (03) 3705 8264;
email: nepembjp@ big.or.jp
Pakistan: 301 Mehdi Towers 115A, SMCHS, Shahrah E-Faisal, Karachi. Tel: (021) 453 3611;
fax: (021) 455 0041.
Thailand: 189 Sukhumvit Soi 71, Bangkok 10110. Tel: (02) 391 7240; fax: (02) 381 2406; email: nepembkk@asiaaccess.net.th
UK: 12a Kensington Palace Gardens, London W8 4QU.
Tel: (020) 7229 1594;
fax: (020) 7792 9861;
email: rnel@compuserve.com
USA: 2131 Leroy Place NW, Washington DC 20008.
Tel: (202) 667 4550;
fax: (202) 667 5534;
email: nepali@erols.com
820 Second Ave, Suite 202, New York NY 10017.
Tel: (212) 370 4188;
fax: (212) 953 2038.

Women and Children

As all foreigners are considered the same, there are no special concerns or dangers for women travellers, providing they dress and behave appropriately. Women should wear trousers, long shorts and skirts below the knee as immodest and revealing clothing is asking for trouble. Sticking to these basic rules, even single women can go about in complete confidence without the fear of being bothered.

Travelling with children in Nepal is a wonderful way to break the ice and meet local people as the Nepalese love youngsters. Be sure to stick to basic hygiene rules, however, particularly with very young children.

Practical Tips

Media

Newspapers and Magazines

There are several newspapers published in English in Kathmandu, as well as dozens in Nepali. Nepali dailies and weeklies express various shades of opinion. The government papers are *The Rising Nepal* (*Gorkhapatra* in Nepali). *The Kathmandu Post* covers local and international news and is widely read by expatriates. The English-language weekly, the *Independent*, comes out every Wednesday.

Of the magazines published in Nepal, look for the useful *Nepal Traveller* and *Travellers' Nepal* which are both handed out free. The excellent, environmentally orientated *Himal* magazine covers South Asia monthly and is highly recommended for a regional overview. Its sister publication in Nepali, Nepal's only quality news magazine, is widely read.

The Indian dailies, *International Herald Tribune*, *Time*, *Newsweek*, *The Far East Economic Review*, *Asiaweek*, and *India Today* can be found at newsstands and hotels one day late after publication. A wide variety of other daily, weekly and monthly foreign news publications can be found in bookshops and at newsstands.

Radio and Television

Radio Nepal broadcasts a daily programme of Nepali folk songs, news and stories on 567, 648 and 792 Khz, including two news bulletins in English at 8am and 8pm. Private radio stations have music programmes in English as well as Nepali. These include FM Kathmandu on 100 Mhz, Kantipur FM on 96.1 Mhz and Radio

Sagarmatha on 102.4. Bring a shortwave radio if you are addicted to international news.

Most of the main hotels offer a wide variety of international channels including BBC, CNN, sports and movie channels. Nepal Television started in early 1986 and presents Nepali programmes including the news in English every evening at 9.15pm. Only the Kathmandu Valley and Terai cities receive these programmes. The Terai also receives Indian television, which increasing numbers of Kathmandu residents are picking up with satellite dishes and cable TV.

Postal Services

The General Post Office (tel: 227499) in Kathmandu is located on Kantipath, near the Dharahara Tower. It's open 9am–5pm Monday to Friday for all services, except for the counters selling stamps, postcards and aerogrammes which are open from 7am–4pm. The *Poste Restante* section is open 9am–5pm Monday through Friday. If you use *Poste Restante* ask your correspondents either to write only your family name on the envelope or to write it with a big initial. The letters are kept for three months and then returned to the sender.

Airmail of parcels up to 10 kg (22 lbs) and surface mail of up to 20 kg (44 lbs) can be booked at the foreign parcel counter from 9am–2pm Monday through Friday. Express Mail Service (EMS) is available at the General Post Office, as well as at Thamel, Basantapur and airport postal counters.

Ensure that stamps on letters and postcards are franked in front of you. Main hotels, handicraft shops and private communications centres will also handle mail and this is certainly the easiest way.

Telecommunications

International telephone connections are now excellent, and direct overseas dialling is available in most hotels as well as from numerous small communications

shops in Thamel. The latter are open 8am–11pm daily. Faxes and emails can be sent from hotels, business centres or telecommunications centres. The Central Telegraph Office near Tripureshwar is open 24 hours a day and provides long-distance telephone services as well as fax connections.

Mobile Phones

Mobile phones were introduced to Nepal in January 1999 but they are not international roaming. To use your own handphone, you have to obtain a SIM-card from the local telephone company (tel: 533126). The deposit payment for this card is quite high and only refundable if you are departing in the middle of the month when they are issuing the monthly bills!

Guests staying at top hotels can rent mobile phones. Daily rates usually include all local incoming and outgoing calls but international calls are billed separately.

Internet Facilities

Internet access is easily available in most major towns in Nepal and even in some of the more remote areas if there are telephone lines. Simple cybercafés offering Internet access and communication centres offering international fax and phones are located in all the major tourists areas in Kathmandu and Pokhara. Most of the top hotels offer Internet access from their business centres.

For Internet access in Kathmandu, try **K@mandu Cybermatha Tea House** on Kantipath (tel: 256079), among the best-equipped of the local cybercafés. The **Nanglo Café and Pub** has a cyber corner in Durbar Marg (tel: 222636).

Health

While life-threatening infectious diseases are rare in travellers to Nepal, it is essential to get some good pre-travel advice regarding vaccinations. Make an appointment with your GP, ideally three months before you set off to discuss your

Operator Services

Telephone enquiry: 197
International operator: 186
Operator for India: 187
Internal long-distance calls: 180
Fault reports: 198

vaccine requirements and any medicines that you should bring (*see page 128*).

Make sure all the vaccines you receive are recorded in your International Vaccine booklet and bring this with you. As well as ensuring you are covered for tetanus, polio and diphtheria, visitors to Nepal should consider receiving vaccines against typhoid fever, hepatitis A and B, Japanese encephalitis (for visitors to the Terai during June to October) and rabies. Meningitis A/C should also be considered, especially if you are visiting in the winter months.

Malaria is still transmitted in some parts of the Terai, especially during the monsoon months. To avoid being bitten by mosquitoes use repellents and cover up, especially at dawn and dusk. Sleep under a mosquito net, if possible, and get specific advice about anti-malarial medicine from your GP.

Get some good travel insurance and make sure you are covered for helicopter evacuation to Kathmandu and for air-ambulance evacuation to a regional hospital.

Never drink unboiled or untreated water and do not trust ice cubes anywhere. Make sure you avoid eating raw vegetables, and remember to peel fruit before consuming. The same counts for uncooked fish and seafood. Never walk barefoot and wash your hands often. If you follow these basic guidelines you should avoid many of the intestinal infections which lead to diarrhoea. Should you be unfortunate and get ill, you ought to drink a lot and take enough sugar and salt. Little glucose/electrolyte packs, available from your chemist, are essential.

Minor problems can occur soon after arrival, especially after long flights. "Traveller's tummy" should clear up after a couple of days but, if it is severe and persistent, get a stool test and medical assistance.

Use disinfectant and cover even the smallest wounds. Also cover your head in the sun and avoid contact with stray cats and dogs or wild animals. Remember that unprotected sexual intercourse can lead to severe or fatal illnesses such as hepatitis B or HIV/Aids.

For information on altitude sickness, *see page 351.*

Medical Services
The best facilities for emergencies and accidents are listed below. Avoid the chaotic government-run Bir Hospital near the Tundhikhel.
B & B Hospital
Gwarko.
Tel: 533206.
A new private hospital which offers

excellent orthopaedic services.
CIWEC Clinic
Yak & Yeti Road (off Durbar Marg).
Tel: 228531.
Foreign staff, excellent service (world specialists in diarrhoea) but higher prices than other clinics.
Military Hospital
Chauni.
Tel: 271940.
The best facility for trauma victims.
Nepal International Clinic

Travel Agencies and Tour Operators

Kathmandu Travel Agencies
Adventure Travel Nepal
Lazimpat.
Tel: 411225; fax: 414075/419126; email: info@tigermountain.com
Annapurna Travels & Tours
Durbar Marg.
Tel: 223530; fax: 222966; email: navraj@mos.com.np
Everest Express
Durbar Marg. Tel: 220759; fax: 226795; email: info@everest-express.com.np
Himalayan Holidays
Gairidhara. Tel: 428756; fax: 435467; email: namaste@himhols.wlink.com.np
Kathmandu Travels & Tours
Battisputali.
Tel: 471577; fax: 471379; email: dwarika@mos.com.np
Marco Polo
Kamaladi.
Tel: 247215; fax: 244484; email: marco@polo.col.com.np
Natraj Tours & Travels
Ghantaghar.
Tel: 222906; fax: 227372; email: natraj@vishnu.ccsl.com.np
President Travels
Durbar Marg.
Tel: 220245; fax: 221180; email: preintl@mos.com.np
Sita World Travel (Nepal)
Tridevi Marg.
Tel: 418363; fax: 426546; email: sitaktm@sitanep.mos.com.np
Tibet Travels & Tours
Tridevi Marg.
Tel: 249140; fax: 249986; email: kalden@tibet.wlink.com.np

Tours of Enchantment
Lazimpat.
Tel: 415283; fax: 419872; email: shanghol@mos.com.np
Yeti Travels
Durbar Marg.
Tel: 221234; fax:226152/53; email: yeti@vishnu.ccsl.com.np

Pokhara Travel Agencies
Ambassador
Lakeside.
Tel: 21451; fax: 21451.
Samrat
Lakeside.
Tel: 23217; fax: 25050.

Trekking Agencies
Amadablam Adventure Group
Kamal Pokhari, Kathmandu.
Tel: 414644; fax: 416029; email: sales@amadablam.wlink.com.np
Asian Trekking
Tridevi Marg, Kathmandu.
Tel: 415506; fax: 411878; email: asianadv@mos.com.np
Everest Treks
Kamaladi, Kathmandu.
Tel: 226358; fax: 224031.
Himalayan Journeys
Kantipath, Kathmandu.
Tel: 226138; fax: 227068; email: hjtrek@mos.com.np
International Trekkers
Chabhil, Kathmandu.
Tel: 371397; fax: 371561; email: nepal@intrek.wlink.com.np
Malla Treks
Lainchaur, Kathmandu.
Tel: 410089; fax: 423143; email: surendra@malla.trk.mos.com.np
Mountain Travel Nepal
Lazimpat, Kathmandu.

Tel: 411225; fax: 414075/419126; email: info@tigermountain.com
Sherpa Cooperative Trekking
Durbar Marg, Kathmandu.
Tel: 224068; fax: 227983; email: sherpaco@trekk.mos.com.np
Sherpa Trekking Service
Kamaladi, Kathmandu.
Tel: 220243; fax: 227243; email: lamasts@wlink.com.np
Thamserku Trekking & Travel
Basundhara, Kathmandu.
Tel: 354491; fax: 354323; email: serku@vishnu.ccsl.com.np

River Trip Specialists
Equator Expeditions
Thamel, Kathmandu.
Tel: 415782; fax: 425801; email: equator@mos.com.np
Great Himalayan Rivers
Lazimpat, Kathmandu.
Tel: 410937; fax: 226608; email: gha@mos.com.np
Himalayan Encounters
Thamel, Kathmandu.
Tel: 417426; fax: 438354; email: raftnepal@himenco.wlink.com.np
Himalayan River Exploration
Lazimpat, Kathmandu.
Tel: 411225; fax: 414075/419126; email: info@tigermountain.com
White Magic
Jyatha, Kathmandu.
Tel: 253225; fax: 249885; email: wmagic@wlink.com.np
Ultimate Descents International (Wet Dreams)
Thamel, Kathmandu.
Tel: 439526; fax: 414765; email: rivers@ultimate.wlink.com.np

Hitti Durbar (across from the Royal Palace).
Tel: 435357.
Run by a Nepalese doctor who trained in Canada.
Patan Hospital
Lagankhel.
Tel: 522278.
Probably the best all-round choice for hospitals.
Teaching Hospital
Maharajganj.
Tel: 416596.
Good all-round facilities, as well as the Kantipath Children's Hospital.

Alternative Facilities

Kathmandu offers many opportunities to experiment with traditional Ayurvedic and Tibetan healing methods, in which patients are diagnosed by pulse, breath and urine, and treated with an array of herbs.
Dr Mana Bajracharya
Mahabaudha (behind Bir Hospital).
Tel: 223960.
An expert practitioner of traditional Hindu Ayurvedic medicine.
Kunphen Tibetan Medical Centre
Chetrapati.
Tel: 251920. Conveniently located dispensary for Tibetan medicine.

Pharmacies

Most medicines that you will require during your visit are readily and cheaply available in Kathmandu without prescription. Ask for an *aushadhi pasal*, literally "medicine shop". Do not rely on the pharmacists but ask for medical assistance when making a diagnosis. Look out for the well-known brand names manufactured under licence in India but check the label carefully as contents may be different from those you are familiar with back home. Also check the dosage carefully. Be aware that antibiotics are readily available and are sometimes even handed out instead of the required analgesics.

Pharmacies can be found in all the major towns of Nepal. For trekkers or those venturing off the beaten track be sure you have what you need with you before you leave.

Foreign Missions and Consulates in Kathmandu

Australia: Bansbari.
Tel: 371678; fax: 371533.
Austria: Naxal.
Tel: 410891; fax: 434891.
Bangladesh: Naxal.
Tel: 414943.
Burma (Myanmar): Chakrapat..
Tel: 521788; fax: 523402.
Canada: Lazimpat.
Tel: 415193; fax: 410422.
China: Baluwatar.
Tel: 411740; fax: 414045.
Denmark: Baluwatar.
Tel: 413010; fax: 411409.
Egypt: Pulchowk.
Tel: 524812.
Finland: Lazimpat.
Tel: 416636; fax: 416703.
France: Lazimpat.
Tel: 412332; fax: 419968.
Germany: Gyaneswor.
Tel: 416832; fax: 416899.
India: Lainchaur.
Tel: 410900; fax: 413132.

Israel: Lazimpat.
Tel: 411811; fax: 413920.
Japan: Panipokhari.
Tel: 414083; fax: 414108.
Netherlands: Kumaripati, Patan.
Tel: 522915; fax: 523155.
New Zealand: Dilli Bazaar.
Tel: 412436, fax: 414750.
Norway: Jawalakhel.
Tel: 521646.
Pakistan: Maharajganj.
Tel: 374024; fax: 374012.
Spain: Battisputali.
Tel: 472328.
Sri Lanka: Baluwater.
Tel: 417406.
Switzerland: Jawalakhel.
Tel: 523468.
Thailand: Bansbari.
Tel: 371410; fax: 371409.
UK: Lainchaur.
Tel: 414588; fax: 411789.
USA: Panipokhari.
Tel: 411179; fax: 419963.

Security and Crime

Nepal is generally regarded as a very safe place but in Kathmandu, as in any capital city, it pays to be careful, especially after dark. Be alert for pickpockets during crowded festivals. Terrorism associated with the Maoist's "People's War" has been going on for some years, mainly in the west of the country, but is not targeted against tourists.

Business Hours

Government offices are open 9am–5pm Monday to Friday for most of the year. Banks open at 10am and close at 3pm, Monday to Friday. Embassies and international organisations are open 9/9.30am to 5/5.30pm, Monday to Friday.

Until mid-1999 Sunday was a full working day for government offices and banks. Many private businesses and shops still operate on a six-day week. Shops seldom open before 10am but do not usually close until 8pm or 9pm.

Religious Services

The Kathmandu International Christian Community (KICC) (tel: 525176) conducts inter-denominational services at 9.30am every Sunday at Lincoln School in Rabi Bhawan. Catholic services are held 5.30pm on Saturday at Hotel del Annapurna and on Sundays at 9am and 5.30pm at the Church of the Assumption in Dobighat. For details of Jewish services contact the Israeli Embassy (tel: 411811). For Muslims the main mosques are in Durbar Marg.

Photography

Different brands and speeds of photographic film are available in Kathmandu and Pokhara at reasonable prices but check the expiry date. Be sure to pack enough film when visiting remote or trekking locations. Film can be reliably developed in Kathmandu, except for specialist transparencies such as Kodachrome. Das Colour Lab on Kantipath, Nepal Colour Lab in Thamel, and Photo Concern on New

Road and in Thamel are among the many shops offering one-hour prints. Photographic shops can also supply batteries and repair cameras: try **Photo Concern** (tel: 223275).

The keen photographer should bring along telephoto as well as wide-angled lenses as these will prove useful to capture the rich variety of wildlife and the mountain landscapes. Fast film for the dark jungles is recommended, though 100

ASA is suitable for most purposes.

When it comes to taking pictures of the Nepalese and their surroundings, tread carefully. Be sensitive and bear in mind that religion and superstition play an integral part in Nepalese life. Do not simply click away at people, statues, shrines, buildings, trees and boulders; what may appear to be innocuous may have deep spiritual significance for the locals. Seek permission

whenever you are in doubt. It is always better to forgo a shot rather than risk offending your hosts.

Weights and Measures

Nepalese use the metric system, but in some circumstances they also stick to traditional measures. As elsewhere in South Asia, they count in *lakh* (unit of 100,000) and

Useful Addresses in Kathmandu

International Organisations

American Express
Durbar Marg.
Tel: 226172; fax: 226152.
Amnesty International
Bag Bazaar.
Tel: 231587; fax: 225489.
British Council
Kantipath.
Tel: 221305; fax: 224076.
CARE, Nepal
Pulchowk.
Tel: 521202.
DFID
Ekantkuna.
Tel: 542980; fax: 542979.
French Cultural Centre
Thapathali.
Tel: 241163; fax: 226152.
Goethe Institute
Sundhara.
Tel: 250871.
GTZ
Pulchowk.
Tel: 523228; fax: 521982.
International Monetary Fund
Tel: 411977; fax: 411673.
Save The Children (UK)
Patan Dhoka.
Fax: 527256.
Save The Children (USA)
Baluwatar.
Tel: 412447; fax: 410375.
UNHCR
Lazimpat.
Tel: 412521; fax: 412853.
United Nations
Pulchowk.
Tel: 523200; fax: 523991.
US AID
Kalimati.
Tel: 270144; fax: 272357.
US Information Service

Gyaneshwor.
Tel: 410041; fax: 415847.
US Peace Corps
Lazimpat.
Tel: 410707; fax: 411762.
Visa
c/o Nepal Grindlays Bank.
Tel: 254002; fax: 226762.
VSO, Voluntary Service Overseas
Lazimpat.
Tel: 413519; fax: 414585.
World Bank
Yak & Yeti Complex, Durbar Marg.
Tel: 226792; fax: 225712.

International Airlines

Aeroflot
Kamaladi.
Tel: 227399; fax: 226161.
Air Canada
Durbar Marg.
Tel: 222838.
Air France
Durbar Marg.
Tel: 223339.
Air India
Hattisar.
Tel: 415637.
Austrian Airlines
Kamaladi.
Tel: 223317l; fax: 241506.
British Airways
Durbar Marg.
Tel: 222266; fax: 226611.
Biman Bangladesh
Naxal.
Tel: 434740; fax: 434869.
Cathay Pacific
Kantipath.
Tel: 411725.
China Southwest Airways
Kamaladi.
Tel: 419770; fax: 416541.

Druk Air
Durbar Marg.
Tel: 225166; fax: 227229.
Gulf Air
Hattisar.
Tel: 430456; fax: 435301.
Indian Airlines
Kamal Pokhari.
Tel: 414596; fax: 419649.
Japan Airlines
Durbar Marg.
Tel: 222838.
Lufthansa
Durbar Marg.
Tel: 223052; fax: 221900.
Northwest Orient Airlines
Lekhnath Marg.
Tel: 418389.
Pakistan International Airlines (PIA)
Durbar Marg.
Tel: 223102.
Qantas Airways
Durbar Marg.
Tel: 220245.
Qatar Airways
Kantipath.
Tel: 256579; fax: 227132.
Royal Nepal Airlines
New Road.
Tel: 220757; fax: 225348.
Singapore Airlines
Durbar Marg.
Tel: 220759; fax: 226795.
Swissair
Hattisar.
Tel: 434607; fax: 434570.
Thai Airways
Durbar Marg.
Tel: 221316; fax: 221130.
Transavia Airlines
Heritage Plaza, Kamaladi.
Tel: 247215; fax: 244484.

crore (unit of 10 million). Heights are usually measured in metres, but sometimes also in feet. (One foot equals 0.305 metres; one metre equals 3.28 feet.) Distances are counted in kilometres. The term *muthi* means "handful", whether it be of vegetables or firewood.

Weights are measured in kilograms with the following exceptions:
• Rice and other cereals, milk and sugar: one *mana* equals a little less that half a litre; one *paathi*, about 0.75 litres (26 fl oz), contains eight *manas*; 160 *manas* equal 20 *paathis* equal one *muri*, about 75 litres (16.5 gallons).
• Vegetables and fruit: one *pau* equals 200 g (7 oz); one *ser* equals four paus, or one kilogram; one *dharni* equals three *sers*, or 2.4 kg (5 lbs).
• Metals: one *tola* is equal to 11.66 g (half an ounce).
• Precious stones: one carat equals 0.2 g.

Electricity

Major towns in Nepal are electrified with 220-volt alternating current, though some fluctuation is usual. Electric razors, hairdryers etc can be used with adaptors. When using a computer or other sensitive electrical equipment, it is essential to use a voltage stabiliser. Power cuts are common in Kathmandu and Pokhara, depending on the season and the level of water in the hydroelectric reservoirs. Large hotels and shops have their own generators to deal with such contingencies.

While larger trekking towns like Namche Bazar have been electrified, the rural electrification programme has a long way to go before it can phase out candles and firesides. A small flashlight and extra batteries are useful.

Tipping

Tipping has become a habit in hotels and restaurants patronised by foreigners. A surcharge of 10 percent and often an additional personal tip are expected. Small favours should be tipped with NRS 20. Taxi drivers need not always be tipped but when they have been especially helpful, about 10 percent of the fare is in order. Some restaurants display tipping boxes at the exit and the contents, about 40 NRS per customer, will be distributed among all staff. A 10 percent tip is also customary in Westernised restaurants. Travel and trekking guides are usually tipped much more. Elsewhere, tipping is discouraged.

Public Holidays

Festival dates vary from year to year because of the difference between the calendars (*see page 85*) and, as many are determined only after complex astrological calculations, your best bet is to contact the **Nepal Tourism Centre.**

The Nepalese are usually happy to allow you to share in their festivities but remain respectful and keep some distance. Remember they are predominantly religious in character, even though they can often get quite rowdy and crowded.

Nepal Tourism Centre
Bhrikuti Mandap, Kathmandu.
Tel: 256909; fax: 256910; email: info@ntb.wlink.com.np

Getting Around

From the Airport

If you are not being met by your travel agent, taxis and private cars are available for a flat NRS 200 fee to most central areas of Kathmandu such as Thamel and New Road. For areas on the edge of the Valley such as Nagarkot and Dhulikhel the fee is NRS 1,000. Buy a ticket at the booth immediately outside the airport exit.

Crowded city buses shuttle between the airport and the municipal bus park for a few rupees. The pick-up point is on the Ring Road, a few minutes' walk from the airport terminal.

On Departure

It is advisable to reconfirm all international air tickets at least 72 hours prior to departure. Royal Nepal Airlines or Indian Airlines air tickets have to receive a reconfirmation stamp from the relevant office; they cannot be reconfirmed over the telephone. For all India destinations a copy of your Indian visa is required.

Airport departure tax is paid at the bank inside the airport prior to check in (*see page 327*).

By Air

Flying is the best way of moving around fast in Nepal although domestic schedules are subject to last-minute changes. A few years ago Royal Nepal Airlines lost its monopoly so the era of the eternal lack of planes has passed due to competing airlines.

The airline spider's web spreads from Kathmandu to the west

(Bajura, Baitadi, Chaurjahari, Dang, Darchula, Dhanghari, Doti, Jumla, Mahendranagar, Nepalganj, Sanphebagar, Silgari, Surkhet, Tikapur); to the centre (Baglung, Bhairawa, Bharatpur, Jomsom, Manang, Meghauli, Pokhara, Simra); and to the east (Bhadrapur, Bhojpur, Biratnagar, Janakpur, Lukla, Lamidanda, Phaplu, Rajbiraj, Ramechhap, Rumjatar, Taplejung and Tumlingtar). Details can be obtained from the domestic airline offices.

There is a two-tier fare system in operation on all routes; one for foreigners and a lower one for Nepalese and Indian nationals. Airport tax of NRS 100 is charged for all domestic flights. Several airports in Nepal such as Biratnagar, Janakpur, Pokhara and Nepalganj now have hard-top runways so flight cancellations are not so frequent. All of the mountain and remote airports are grass airstrips, so delays and cancelled flights due to bad weather are still common. Trekkers can still experience delays due to weather of up to several days from Lukla and Jomsom.

Domestic Airlines

Asian Airlines Helicopters
Thamel, Kathmandu.
Tel: 410086; fax: 423315.
Buddha Air
Hattisar, Kathmandu.
Tel: 437677; fax: 437025;
email: buddhaair@buddhaair.com
Cosmic Air
Heritage Plaza, Kamaladi, Kathmandu.
Tel: 246882; fax: 427084;
email: coi@wlink.com.np
Dynasty Aviation
Lazimpat, Kathmandu.
Tel: 410090; fax: 414627.
Fishtail Air
Tinkune, Kathmandu.
Tel: 485186, fax: 485187.
Gorkha Airlines
Hattisar, Kathmandu.
Tel: 436576; fax: 435430;
email: gorkha@mos.com.np
Karnali Air Services
Sinamangal, Kathmandu.
Tel: 473141; fax: 488288;

It is essential to book and to reconfirm the flight a few days ahead, especially to distant destinations where only the smaller aircraft operate. There are cancellation fees of 10 percent if you cancel 24 hours in advance, 33 percent if less than 24 hours in advance and 100 percent if you fail to show up without informing the airline. If the flight is cancelled due to weather or other causes, your fare is refunded.

Mountain Flights and Helicopters

Several airlines operate one-hour mountain flights, which leave Kathmandu each morning (in clear weather only) to fly east along the Himalaya for a view of Mount Everest, a spectacular trip (*see page 280*).

Five- and nine-seater helicopters can be chartered via travel agents and are charged per flying hour. Used during medical evacuations, sightseeing flights can also be arranged although there are restrictions as to where helicopters can land, especially in protected areas.

email: karnaair@mos.com.np
Lumbini Airways
Min Bhawan, Kathmandu.
Tel: 482728; fax: 483380;
email: lumbini@resv.wlink.com.np
Mountain Air
Hattisar, Kathmandu.
Tel: 435330.
NECON Air
Kalimati, Kathmandu.
Tel: 473860; fax: 471679; email:
reservation@necon.mos.com.np
Royal Nepal Airlines
Kantipath, Kathmandu.
Tel: 226574.
Shangri-La Air
Kamal Pokhari, Kathmandu.
Tel: 439692.
Skyline Air
Tinkune, Kathmandu.
Tel: 481778; fax: 487422;
email: skyline@wlink.com.np
Yeti Airlines
Lazimpat, Kathmandu.
Tel: 421215; fax: 420766.

By Road

In this mountainous country with deep valleys etched between peaks and ranges, roads are vital for bringing together the various communities. But, until Nepal started opening up to the outside world in the 1950s, the kingdom had nothing except village trails and mountain paths. Cross-country trading was generally a tortuous affair measured in weeks and months. Since the 1950s, there have been major efforts to construct roads, many of them built with foreign aid. None were more active than Nepal's big-brotherly neighbours, India and China, who were both prompted by obvious strategic considerations.

During the rainy season whole portions of existing roads are damaged and must be repaired. Maintenance on some roads is slow and it is best to enquire locally before setting off on a long-distance road trip.

There are six major road links. The **Tribhuvan Raj Path**, linking Kathmandu via Hetauda and Birganj with Raxaul at the Indian border 200 km (124 miles) away, was opened in 1956 and built with Indian assistance. The **Arniko Raj Marg** (Highway) or Chinese Road leads from Kathmandu to Bhaktapur and Dhulikhel and then to the Tibetan border at Kodari (*see page 288*). It was built with Chinese support and opened in 1967. Some 110 km (68 miles) long, it suffers from periodic landslides. Check conditions before taking a trip. Chinese engineers also helped to build the **Prithvi Raj Marg** in 1973 which covers the 200 km (124 miles) between Kathmandu and Pokhara. There are two extensions to the Pokhara road: Dumre to Gorkha and Mugling to Narayanghat. In 1970 Indian engineers completed the 188-km (117-mile) extension from Pokhara via Butwal to Sonauli on the Indian border south of Bhairawa, called the **Siddhartha Raj Marg**. The most ambitious road is the result of the cooperation of the former USSR (or its successors), the United States, Britain and India, the **Mahendra Raj Marg**. Popularly known as the East-West Highway, this 1,000-km (620-mile) lowland thoroughfare through the Terai is part of the fabled Pan-Asian Highway linking the Bosphorus with the Far East. China built the 32-km (20-mile) **Ring Road** around Kathmandu and Chinese technicians have also installed a trolley-bus service between Kathmandu and Bhaktapur. East of Kathmandu the Swiss-built highway from Lamosangu to Jiri stretches 110 km (68 miles) and was completed after 10 years in 1985.

A seventh road link currently under construction will open a new access route from Kathmandu to the Terai. When completed, the Sindhuli Highway will lead from Dhulikhel to Janakpur.

Now that the major road links have been established, locally built roads are creeping deeper into the mountains. Scars can be seen on the hills around Kathmandu Valley and the road north from Trisuli Bazaar now stretches into Langtang National Park (*see page 253*).

Public Transport

Buses

All roads are plied by local bus services, with express coaches on the main routes. A bus ride in Nepal is a bumpy, noisy, smelly and slow affair that nevertheless can be fun. Some of these antediluvian beasts are mere sheet-metal boxes on wheels, but they eventually arrive at their destinations, even if passengers have to occasionally alight on the steepest climbs. No matter what, they are a cheap way of going about inside and outside of the Kathmandu Valley. They allow for a long, close look at the local folk inside the bus, if not always at the dramatic scenery outside.

Special tourist minibuses ply popular routes to Pokhara and Chitwan; they are about twice as expensive and slightly more comfortable, as well as faster. Offices in Thamel handle tickets and departures (*see page 174*).

Kathmandu Transport

Within Kathmandu, three-wheeled public scooters (*tempos*) can carry up to six passengers, always plying the same route and starting from Rani Pokhari. Also available are black and yellow metered *tempos* which can be privately hired. In 1999 the heavily polluting blue Vikram *tempos* were banned from the streets of Kathmandu and have been replaced by fleets of environmentally friendly electric *tempos* running on batteries.

The gaudily painted, slow-moving, honking rickshaws are still part of the Kathmandu city scene. They are large tricycles with two seats in the back covered by a hood; a man pedals up front. Make sure the driver understands where you are going and the price is settled before you start. Remember rickshaws should cost no more than taxis.

Book long-distance buses one day ahead to be safe. The long-distance bus park is at Gongabu, on the northern side of the Ring Road east of Balaju, in Kathmandu. Buses headed to destinations along the Arniko Highway (including Tatopani and Jiri) leave from the municipal bus park east of the Tundhikhel. In Pokhara, the bus terminal is near the airport on the south side of town. Try **Greenline Tours**, who operate an excellent daily service to Chitwan, Pokhara and Dhulikhel from their private terminal on the edge of Thamel.

Greenline Tours
Tridevi Marg, Kathmandu.
Tel: 253885.

Taxis

Taxis are available to go to most places within the Kathmandu Valley. They have black registration plates with white numbers (private cars have white numbers on red plates). Make sure their meters are working. To hire a taxi for a day-trip within the Kathmandu Valley, negotiate a price before starting your journey.

Private Transport

Car Hire

More reliable than public transport, private cars can be hired from any hotel or travel agency but you are not allowed to drive yourself. The vehicles are less likely to break down than any other mode of transport. Price and interior equipment comparisons are a must. The price usually includes a driver who normally speaks at least a little English. A tip at the trip's conclusion will be welcome, but it is not mandatory, and should not be more than NRS 150. A car can hold three or four people, just like a taxi.

Avis and Hertz are officially represented by American Express on Durbar Marg (*see page 332*). However cars are not rented without drivers and it is not advisable to attempt to drive yourself in Nepal due to the state of the roads and local driving practices.

Rules of the Road

If you do find yourself behind the wheel when in Nepal, follow these rules of the road. Drive on the left and be aware of people and animals on small narrow roads. On mountain roads you should make sure that you are not pushed towards the slope. All accidents lead to severe trouble, particularly when cows – which have holy status for Hindus – are involved. The accidental death of such an animal can lead to a long jail sentence.

Petrol and diesel are available, but do not expect them to correspond to Western-quality standards.

Always carry your passport (or a photocopy showing your visa) when travelling, as there are occasional police checkpoints on all roads.

Mountain Bikes

Many shops in the old part of Kathmandu and in Thamel have mountain bikes for hire along with the old-fashioned Indian and Chinese bicycles. There is no deposit necessary; your hotel or passport number is enough. Make sure the bell works. Along with the brakes, this is the most important part of your bicycle as you will need it to weave through the throng.

Mountain bikes are particularly suited to the back roads of the Kathmandu Valley and further afield (*see page 145*). These can be rented in Kathmandu. **Himalayan Mountain Bikes** organise excellent escorted tours through the valley. Further information is available from Thamel at the Kathmandu Guest House (*see page 337*).

Himalayan Mountain Bikes
PO Box 12673, Kathmandu.
Tel: 437437; fax: 414596.

Motorbikes
It is possible to hire Japanese motorbikes. All that is required is an international driving licence and a deposit.

On Foot
Be prepared to do a lot of walking. Taxis and cars can only take you limited distances. Apart from a few well-trodden spots, most of the interesting sites have to be reached on foot. Nepalese do not count distance by kilometres or miles, but by the number of walking hours involved in a journey.

There is no need to compete with their often brisk pace. A leisurely stroll amid the rice and mustard fields, through villages and across ridges and valleys is certainly the best way to take in the people, their culture and way of life. Do not hesitate to venture off the tourist track; you can expect to be safe wherever you wander and moreover, you will find the people to be more friendly than you had ever imagined. Then you will have the pleasure of discovering this beautiful land and its people for yourself.

Hitchhiking

Hitchhiking is unheard of in Nepal. Even the poorest of the poor pay for a bus or lorry ride. Anybody picking you up will expect some reward unless some friendly foreigner stops for you.

Where to Stay

Choosing a Hotel

Four- and five-star hotels offer a first-class service for foreign visitors. Some two- and three-star hotels can also be recommended. Hotels of international standard require foreign currency. During the spring and autumn seasons, the better hotels operate at near-full capacity so book well in advance.

Most hotels in Kathmandu offer a choice of packages: bed and breakfast (CP); bed, breakfast and one other meal (MAP) and full board (AP). Add 2 percent to these quotes for the new Government Tourism Tax and 10 percent for VAT, a total of 12 percent.

There are plenty of less glamorous but quite adequate hotels and lodges in Kathmandu to suit everyone's taste and budget. Toilet facilities and showers may or may not be communal and heating is often extra. These are mostly located in the Thamel district (*see page 174*). Private accommodation and homestays are another inexpensive alternative.

On the popular trekking trails, most villages offer small lodges or tea houses, usually with minimal facilities, dormitory accommodation (only a few offer single and double rooms) and simple food.

Hotel Listings

KATHMANDU

Luxury
Hotel de l'Annapurna
Durbar Marg
Tel: 221711/223602
Fax: 225236
Email: apurna@taj.mos.com.np
A Taj Leisure hotel with 160 rooms.

Central location. Swimming pool and tennis court. Asian restaurants with live music, Indian and European snacks.

Dwarikas's Kathmandu Village Hotel
Batisputali
Tel: 470770/472328
Fax: 471379
Email: dwarika@mos.com.np
Ten minutes from the airport. Beautifully constructed rooms and suites in traditional Newar style using antique materials. The restaurants are both local and European. 70 rooms.

Everest Hotel
Naya Baneswar
Tel: 488100/099
Fax: 490288
Email: admin@everesthotel.com.np
Ten minutes from the airport. Pool, tennis, health facilities, business centre, restaurants (local and Asian cuisine) with live music, café (European and Oriental food), casino and discotheque. Beautiful view of the Himalaya. 162 rooms.

Hyatt Regency Kathmandu
Boudhanath
Tel: 491234
Fax: 490033
Very new hotel with 290 rooms. Swimming pool, health club, restaurants, bars.

Le Meridien Kathmandu
Boudhanath
Tel: 244154
Fax: 226414
Email: meridien@col.com.np
Scheduled to open early 2001 with 102 rooms. Beautiful world-class 18-hole, par-72 Gleneagles-designed golf course opened 1999.

Radisson Hotel Kathmandu
Lazimpat
Tel: 419358
Fax: 411720
Email: radkat@mos.com.np
Central. 172 rooms. Swimming pool, health and spa centre, bar, restaurants with live music (local, Indian and European cuisine).

Soaltee Crowne Plaza
Tahachal
Tel: 272550
Fax: 272205
Email: crowneplaza@shicp.com.np
Formerly named Holiday Inn and

Oberoi. Ten suites, seven regal suites and 300 rooms. Thirty minutes from city centre, casino, pool, tennis, health club, beauty parlour, bar, café and restaurants with live music (local, Indian, European and international cuisine).

Hotel Yak & Yeti
Durbar Marg
Tel: 248999/240520
Fax: 227782
Email: reservation@yakandyeti.com
Excellent location in a converted Rana palace with 270 rooms and an elegant executive floor. Pool, tennis, fitness centre, business centre, restaurants (local, Indian, vegetarian, Russian) and café.

Expensive
Bluestar Hotel
Tripureshwor
Tel: 228833
Fax: 226820
Email: hotel@bluestar.mos.com.np
Bar, café, business centre, restaurants (Indian, Chinese and European). 100 rooms.

Grand Hotel
Tahachal
Tel: 282481
Fax: 424667
Located 20 minutes from the city centre, 84 rooms, restaurants (European and Indian).

Hotel Himalaya
Patan
Tel: 523900
Fax: 523909
Email: himalaya@-
lalitpur.mos.com.np
Pool, café, bar, restaurants (local, Indian, Japanese, European). Friendly service.

Malla Hotel
Lekhnath Marg
Tel: 410620/968
Fax: 418382
Email: malla@htlgrp.mos.com.np
Lovely garden. Café, bar, restaurants (Indian, Chinese and European). 75 rooms.

Royal Singi
Lal Durbar
Tel: 424190
Fax: 424189
Central, close to business and tourist centres with 85 rooms. Excellent Chinese restaurant.

Hotel Shangrila
Lazimpat
Tel: 412999
Fax: 414184
Email: hosang@mos.com.np
Beautiful garden with swimming pool, good beauty parlour, garden, bar and restaurants (Chinese, European). 80 rooms.

Sherpa
Durbar Marg
Tel: 227000
Fax: 222026
Email: sherpa@ccsl.com.np
Central, roof terrace, café, bar, BBQ restaurant (Indian and European). 80 rooms.

Moderate
Garden Hotel
Naya Bazaar, Thamel
Tel: 411951
Fax: 418072
Email: garden@wlink.com.np
Located five minutes' walk from Thamel. Restaurant, bar, 50 rooms.

Hotel Manang
Thamel
Tel: 410993
Fax: 415821
Email: htlmanang@vishnu.ccsl.com.np
Central location, nice roof terrace, 55 rooms.

Hotel Marshyangdi
Thamel
Tel: 414105/412129
Fax: 410008
Email: htlgold@mos.com.np
A video and a reading room, café, bar, restaurants (local, Indian, Chinese and European).

Hotel Mountain
Kantipath
Tel: 246744
Fax: 249736
Email: mountain@vishnu.ccsl.com.np
Central, nice coffee shop, 56 rooms.

Hotel Shanker
Lazimpat
Tel: 410151
Fax: 412691
Email: hotelshanker@mos.com.np
Former Rana palace with old-world charm, large park, restaurants (local, Indian and European), with 200 rooms.

Price Guide

The following price categories are for the cost of a double room, including breakfast, before tax.
Luxury: More than US$150
Expensive: US$100–150
Moderate: US$50–100
Budget: Less than US$50

Summit Hotel
Kupondole Heights
Tel: 524694
Fax: 523737
Email: summit@wlink.com.np
Large garden, good views, pool, restaurant, 75 traditional rooms.

Hotel Tibet
Lazimpat
Tel: 429085
Fax: 410957
Email: hotel@tibet.mos.com.np
A well-managed hotel with excellent service and 55 rooms.

Hotel Vajra
Bijeswari
Tel: 271545/272719
Fax: 271695
Email: vajra@mos.com.np
A cultural experience with Tibetan style rooftop bar, large garden, sauna, library, live entertainment, restaurant (local, Tibetan and European), 51 rooms.

Budget
Kantipur Temple House
Chusyabahal
Tel: 250131
Fax: 250078
Email: kantipur@tmhouse.wlink.com.np
Lovely small hotel with all 32 rooms furnished in traditional décor.

Kathmandu Guest House
Thamel
Tel: 413632/418733
Fax: 417133
Email: ktmguest@ecomail.com.np
Most famous and central of the Thamel lodges. Cable TV, restaurant (local) and 80 rooms.

Mustang Holiday Inn
Jyatha
Tel: 249041
Fax: 249016
Email: ntv@mhiwlink.com.np
An old favourite with a central yet

quiet location, 45 rooms, rooftop terrace and garden.

Tibet Guest House
Chetrapati
Tel: 251763
Fax: 260518
Email: tibet@guesths.mos.com.np
Well located, friendly service, 55 clean rooms, restaurant (European, Tibetan, Indian and Chinese).

DHULIKHEL

Expensive
Dhulikhel Mountain Resort
Dhulikhel
Tel: 011-61466
Reservations: PO Box 3203, Lazimpat, Kathmandu
Tel: 420774/413737
Fax: 420778
Perched high on a bluff past the village. Good food and comfortable accommodation with superb views of the mountains. Only one hour's drive from Kathmandu.

Mirabel Resort
Dhulikhel
Tel: 248054
Fax: 226642
Mountain views in a convenient location on the edge of the village.

Moderate
Dhulikhel Lodge Resort
Dhulikhel
Tel: 011-61114
Reservations: PO Box 6020, Kamaladi, Kathmandu
Tel: 222389
Fax: 222926
Very nice rooms with picture windows overlooking rice terraces and Himalayan panoramas. Restaurant with indoor and outdoor dining and terraced gardens.

Himalayan Horizon Sun-N-Snow Hotel
Dhulikhel
Tel: 011-6129
Reservations: PO Box 1583, Durbar Marg, Kathmandu
Tel: 247183
Fax: 225092
Email: hi.horizon@dhulikhel.wlink.com.np
Nepalese-style building but with modern facilities.

Himalayan Shangrila Resort
Dhulikhel
Tel: 427837
Fax: 423939
Email: himalayan@hsr.wlink.mos.com.np
Quiet location, traditionally styled rooms with great mountain views, bar, restaurant.

Price Guide

The following price categories are for the cost of a double room, including breakfast, before tax.
Luxury: More than US$150
Expensive: US$100–150
Moderate: US$50–100
Budget: Less than US$50

KATHMANDU VALLEY

Expensive
Club Himalaya
Nagarkot
Tel: 413632
Fax: 417133
Great views with indoor swimming pool, health club, bar, restaurants.

Moderate
Everest Panorama Resort
Daman
Tel: 057-40382
Reservations: Kamal Pokhari, Kathmandu
Tel: 428500
Fax: 416029
Located 90 km (55 miles) from Kathmandu on the Tribhuvan Raj Path. Tranquil setting with views of the Himalaya, bar, restaurant (local, European, Indian and Chinese).

Haatiban Himalayan Heights Resort
Pharping
Tel: 371537
Fax: 371561
Email: nepal@intrek.wlink.com.np
Great views of the Himalaya across the Kathmandu Valley. Comfortable rooms, restaurant and bar with central fireplace.

Malla Alpine Resort
Kalitar-Tika Bhairav
Tel: 228668
Reservations: PO Box 6809, Lekhnath Marg, Kathmandu

Tel: 410620
Fax: 418382
Located in a peaceful corner of the valley with 18 ethnic-styled bungalows, bar and restaurant.

Riverside Springs Resort
Kurintar
Tel: 056-29429
Reservations: Hitti Durbar, Kathmandu
Tel: 241408
Fax: 232163
Email: nangint@ccsl.com.np
Located 100 km (60 miles) south-west of Kathmandu along the Prithvi Raj Marg on the banks of the Trisuli River. Pool, bar and restaurant.

MANAKAMANA

Manakamana Village Resort
Kurintar
Tel: 230287
Fax: 252570
Offering day-trips to the Manakamana Temple inclusive of cable car ticket, the resort has 8 double rooms and a Village Restaurant.

POKHARA AND POKHARA VALLEY

Pokhara's lodgings include several luxury hotels on the outskirts of town and an assortment of classes and prices. The location on the edge of Phewa Lake is scenic, with boats easily rented. In season, however, the tourist strip can become a bit overcrowded. Recent developments tend to avoid the lakeside and have found some lovely sites in the foothills.

Luxury
Fulbari Resort
Tel: 061-23451
Fax: 061-28482
Email: resv@fulbari.com.np
Beautiful 165-room resort hotel located 20 minutes from the airport. Heated outdoor swimming pool, fitness centre, tennis courts, disco, casino, nine-hole golf course, six restaurants and bars.

Shangrila Village
Tel: 061-22122
Fax: 061-21995
Email: hosangp@village.mos.
com.np
Exquisitely landscaped resort
located 15 minutes from Lakeside;
shuttle buses provided. Lovely
rooms, good restaurant and a pool.

Tiger Mountain Pokhara Lodge
Reservations:
Tel: Kathmandu 411225
Fax: 414075/419126
Email info@tigermountain.com
Located a half-hour's drive northeast of town, this award-winning
resort is spectacularly sited on a
hilltop ridge facing the Himalaya.
Nineteen rooms are located in 13
individual bungalows built around a
beautiful main lodge featuring local
architecture. A swimming pool
complements the terraced gardens.

Expensive

Bluebird Hotel
Tel: 061-25480
Fax: 061-26260
Email: hotel@bluebird.mos.com.np
Located behind the airport. Health
club, restaurants, bar.

Fishtail Lodge
Lakeside
Tel: 061-20071
Fax: 061-20072
Email: fishtail@lodge.mos.com.np
Great location on the edge of the
lake, this old favourite has recently
been renovated.

Trek Lodge Ker & Downey
Maharajganj
Tel: 061-416751
Fax: 061-410407
Email: nepadv@asia.mos.com.np
This trek circuit links three pleasant
purpose-built lodges with guided
walks between: Sanctuary Lodge at
Birethanti, Himalaya Lodge at
Ghandruk and Basanta Lodge at
Dhampus

Moderate

Base Camp Resort
Lakeside
Tel: 061-21226
Fax: 061-20903
Email: basecamp@bcr.mos.com.np
Central location with comfortable
rooms.

Begnas Lake Resort & Villas
Sundari Danda, Begnas Lake
Tel: 061-29330
Fax: 01-249324
Email: villas@begnas.mos.com.np
Tranquil location 12 km (8 miles)
from Pokhara on the banks of
Begnas Lake, rustic rooms,
restaurant, bar.

Dragon Hotel
Damside
Tel: 061-20391
Tibetan-themed décor,
air-conditioning.

New Hotel Crystal
Tel: 061-20035
Email: ajsthapit@mos.com.np
Near the airport with fine views.

Trek Lodge Laxmi Lodge
Birethanti
Fax: 061-21523
Email: oskar@mos.com.np
Situated in the midst of a pretty
trekking village, this modest lodge
was the brainchild of British poet
Dominic Sasse. Perfect for retreats
and longer stays.

Budget

Hotel Barahi
Lakeside
Tel: 061-23017/23526
Fax: 061-23072
Email: barahi@cnet.wlink.com.np
Landscaped garden and
comfortable rooms, set on a
quiet road.

Fewa
Lakeside
Tel: 061-20151
Email: mike@fewa.mos.com.np
Managed by Mike of Mike's
Breakfast fame (*see page 342*),
this simple lodge has basic
rooms but an excellent
attached restaurant, and a
wonderful location right on the
waterfront.

Monalisa
Tel: 061-20863
A well-managed, clean and simple
place with spectacular views of
the lake and mountains from
terraces.

Mount Annapurna
Tel: 061-20037
Fax: 061-20027
Tibetan-owned hotel near the
airport with a pleasant garden.

**Trek Lodge Sirubari Village
Resort**
Tel: 061-430187
Fax: 061-435027
Email: village@nep.mos.com.np
Located near Pokhara this beautiful
Gurung village is ideal for those
wanting to experience real
Nepalese life. All accommodation
and meals are organised through
homestays with a local family.

THE ANNAPURNAS

Expensive

Jomsom Mountain Resort
Jomsom
Tel: 427150
Fax: 427084
Newly opened, this five-star resort
aims to give luxury service deep in
the Annapurnas, accessible by daily
flights to Jomsom.

THE EVEREST REGION

Many pleasant and inexpensive
lodges can be found in the Everest
area. The best are clustered in
Namche Bazar and have heated
restaurants. Listed here are hotels
that have reservation offices in
Kathmandu.

Luxury

Hotel Everest View
Reservations: PO Box 283, Durbar
Marg, Kathmandu
Tel: 224271
Fax: 227289
Fantastic views from one of the
highest hotels in the world, located
at a 3,800-metre (12,460-ft)
altitude about 30 minutes' walk
from the Syangboche airstrip.
Oxygen and bath in every room.

Moderate

Hotel del Sherpa
Reservations: PO Box 1091,
Kathmandu
Tel: 038 20213
Only 10 minutes' walk from the
Phaplu airstrip, this lovely and
unique hotel features rooms
decorated in Tibetan style, a
spacious garden and a sauna.

ROYAL CHITWAN NATIONAL PARK

Listed here are lodges which have been granted concessions to operate within the park by the government. There is no system of star rating and most offer a package fully inclusive of meals and jungle excursions. All have reservation offices in Kathmandu which will also arrange transport, either by air, or a 4–5-hour drive from the capital. Taxes and park entry fees are extra. The official season runs from September to June, but some remain open during the monsoon.

Luxury
Tiger Tops Jungle Lodge and Tented Camp
Reservations: PO Box 242, Kathmandu
Tel: 411225
Fax: 414075
Email: info@tigermountain.com
Located in the heart of the park, this famous pioneer ecotourism lodge operates wildlife safaris from the comfort of 20 elegant tree-top rooms. Fully equipped with elephants, trained naturalists, jeep and boat trips and jungle treks. A Tented Camp about 5 km (3 miles) away features 12 safari tents with twin beds. Accessible by daily half-hour flights to Meghauli airstrip, a five-hour drive or a three-day river trip. Prices are inclusive of all guided activities and meals.

Expensive
Gaida Wildlife Camp
Reservations: Durbar Marg, Kathmandu
Tel: 227425
Fax: 227292
Email: gaida@mos.com.np
Located near Sauraha with timber framed buildings and a separate jungle camp. Established 1977.
Machan Wildlife Resort
Reservations: PO Box 3140, Durbar Marg, Kathmandu
Tel: 225001
Fax: 240681
Email: wildlife@machan.mos.com.np
Set in the eastern end of the park, with chalet-style bungalows

decorated with Maithili paintings, a small pool and a tented camp.
Temple Tiger Wildlife Camp
Reservations: PO Box 3968, Kantipath, Kathmandu
Tel: 221585
Fax: 220178
Located in the park's western end, accommodation is in basic bungalows and large "two-room" tents. Shower rooms with hot water provide some comfort.

Price Guide

The following price categories are for the cost of a double room, including breakfast, before tax.
Luxury: More than US$150
Expensive: US$100–150
Moderate: US$50–100
Budget: Less than US$50

Tharu Safari Lodge
Reservations: Tiger Tops, PO Box 242, Kathmandu
Tel: 411225
Fax: 414075
Email: info@tigermountain.com
Set on the edge of the park near the Narayani River, the resort's 24 rooms are decorated in the style of traditional Tharu longhouses. Swimming pool, pony and bullock cart rides and elephant safaris.

Moderate
Chitwan Jungle Lodge
Reservations: PO Box 1281, Durbar Marg, Kathmandu
Tel: 228918
Fax: 228349
Email: wildlife@resort.wlink.com.np
One of the largest lodges (32 rooms), set in the middle of the park east of Sauraha.
Island Jungle Resort
Reservations: Durbar Marg, Kathmandu
Tel: 220162
Fax: 225615
Email: island@mos.com.np
Located on Bandarjhola Island on the Narayani River.
Narayani Safari
Reservations: Narayani Hotel, Patan
Tel: 525015
Fax: 521712

Email: bachan@nbe.mos.com.np
The main hotel is in the town of Bharatpur offering safari excursions from the park headquarters at Kasara Durbar.

SAURAHA (CHITWAN)

There is a plethora of small lodges that have mushroomed on the edge of Chitwan at Sauraha, some of which have offices in Kathmandu.

Moderate
Green Mansions
Reservations: Jamal, Kathmandu
Tel: 231271
Fax: 521057
Set on the edge of the community forest reserve, with peaceful atmosphere and fishpond.

Budget
Royal Park Hotel
Reservations: Thamel, Kathmandu.
Tel: 412987
Fax: 411085
Email: royal@parkhotel.wlink.com.np
Nicely designed and decorated bungalows scattered amid spacious grounds, with an open-air bar overlooking the Rapti River. Good food, including a bakery.
Tiger Camp
Tel: 224318
Fax: 226058
Email: sundar@boodles.mos. com.np
A more budget place with a range of accommodation, including a few machan-style lookout huts on stilts, and a good location overlooking the Rapti River.

LUMBINI

Luxury
Lumbini Hokke Hotel
Lumbini
Tel: 071-80236
Fax: 071-80126
Established and elegant super-deluxe property located just off the road to Tilaurakot, featuring Japanese-style rooms.

ROYAL BARDIA NATIONAL PARK

Acknowledged as one of the best places in South Asia to see tigers in the wild, Karnali is recommended for those who like to get off the beaten track. Some describe it as Chitwan 40 years ago, but Bardia boasts a greater range of wildlife and habitats. Access is by a two-hour drive from Nepalganj, which is connected by several daily flights to Kathmandu. A four-day rafting trip on the Bheri and Karnali rivers can be arranged for adventurers.

Expensive
Karnali Lodge and Tented Camp
Reservations: Tiger Tops, PO Box 242, Kathmandu
Tel: 411225
Fax: 414075
Email: info@tigermountain.com
The lodge, run by Tiger Tops, is on the edge of the forest at the park's southern border, the tented camp on the banks of the Karnali River. Both feature relatively comfortable accommodation, Tiger Tops' excellent service and food, and a full menu of activities, including elephant rides, jeep drives, boat trips and guided jungle walks.

Moderate
The dozen or so simple lodges scattered around park headquarters at Thakurdwara include:
Dolphin Manor
Reservations: Lazimpat, Kathmandu
Tel: 420308
Fax: 415401
Forest Hideaway Hotel & Cottages
Reservations: Thamel, Kathmandu
Tel: 417685
Rhino Lodge
Reservations: Thamel, Kathmandu
Tel: 416918
Fax: 417146
Email: rhinotvl@wlink.com.np

ROYAL SUKLA PHANTA WILDLIFE RESERVE

The only moderate-priced accommodation in this remote reserve involves custom safari camps arranged by **Silent Safari**, PO Box 1679, Jawalakhel, Kathmandu. Tel: 527708; fax: 099 22220. Book in advance. The reserve is reached by flights to Mahendranagar, 10 km (6 miles) to the north.

Camping

Borderland Adventure Centre
Barabise, Tatopani
Tel: 425836
Fax: 435207
Email: info@borderlands.net
Located 16 km (10 miles) from the Tibetan border off the Arniko Highway on the banks of the Bhote Koshi river. Tented accommodation. Activities include canyoning, rafting and biking.
Brigands Bend
Tel: 536072
Fax: 536074
Email: suraj@hilltrek.mos.com.np
Lovely peaceful riverside camp reachable by boat or "flying fox" across the river with excellent food.
Last Resort Adventures
Ten km (6 miles) from the Tibetan border off the Arniko Highway on the banks of the Bhote Koshi river.
Tel: 439526
Fax: 414765
Email: rivers@ultimate.wlink.com.np
Tented accommodation, restaurant, bar, activities include bungee jumping, rock climbing, canyoning, rafting and biking.

Where to Eat

What to Eat

The Nepalese eat three meals a day: breakfast, consisting of sweetened milk tea with a few biscuits, one warm meal at 10am and another in the early evening.

Regional diets depend very much on the respective climate, the agricultural crops, religious beliefs and the social status. In most parts of Nepal, including the Kathmandu Valley, rice is the staple food. Hill people eat potatoes or *tsampa* – raw grain, usually barley, ground and eaten either dry or with milk, tea or water – as a complement to or substitute for rice. It is served with a spicy sauce. The Tibetan mountain tribes prefer *momos* (pasta filled with meat), dried yak meat, pasta hotpots and delicious *rotis* (round flat loaves). The introduction of a potato crop in Sherpa country by the British revolutionised eating habits and Sherpas now survive on potatoes, eating them boiled or baked and dipped in salt and chillis. Potato pancakes eaten with fresh cheese are delicious. *Chapati* (flat bread) diversify the diet of the Terai and *chiura* (ground rice) is typical for the Newari.

Simple households serve the traditional *dhal bhaat* (rice or grain and lentils) daily. If available, it is accompanied by vegetables, eggs, spices (ginger, garlic and chilli) and, in times of festivity, meat (chicken, lamb, goat, yak or buffalo). Some castes eat pork but beef is forbidden in this Hindu kingdom. Another favourite accompaniment are huge radishes which are sometimes made into *achhar* (chutney).

The Nepalese enjoy eating sweets and spicy snacks such as *jelebis* and *laddus*. These come in a variety of shapes and wrappings, ingredients and tastes.

Buffalo milk is turned into clarified butter (*ghee*) or curd sold in earthenware pots. When eating curd (*dahi*) be sure to scrape off the top layer. Dairy products are rare in Asia but fresh milk, butter and cheese are plentiful in Kathmandu.

Fruit from the lowlands is found in Kathmandu as is a wide variety of vegetables but high transport costs make these goods expensive and they are normally sold per piece.

Fresh bread, doughnuts and croissants are found in the bakeries of Durbar Marg, Lazimpat and Thamel in Kathmandu. Most of the big hotels have bakeries.

Fast food outlets are becoming popular in Kathmandu, although McDonald's has still not made its way to Nepal.

Where to Eat

Kathmandu's catering outlets offer a complete range of Nepalese and international cuisine. Prices are low by Western standards. Large hotels tend to have three or four restaurants each, some of them excellent, as well as cafés with snacks. All the restaurants listed below are located in Kathmandu.

Outside Kathmandu it is often difficult to find appealing food, even for a snack. Travellers on day-trips should carry some fresh fruit and a snack from one of the bakeries in Thamel for a midday picnic before repairing to the more substantial menus of Kathmandu. The restaurants below are open for lunch and dinner unless specified.

Restaurant Listings

EUROPEAN/AMERICAN

Base Camp Coffee Shop
Hotel Himalaya
Tel: 523900
Fax: 523909
Email: himalhot@mos.com.np
Very pleasant coffee shop set in a cool white marble foyer overlooking the swimming pool and the Kathmandu Valley. **$$**

Price Guide

The following prices are based on a meal for one, without drinks:
$$$$: More than US$10
$$$: US$7–10
$$: US$4–7
$: Less than US$4

Chez Caroline
Babar Mahal Revisited
Tel: 263070
Serves delicious French fare and is a great lunch spot. **$$$**

Chimney Restaurant
Hotel Yak & Yeti
Tel: 248999
Fax: 227782
Email: businesscentre@ yak&yeti.com
This former Rana palace (*see page 337*) is now an original restaurant with a fine menu still reminiscent of Russian splendour. Central fireplace in a cosy setting but with cramped tables. Open for dinner only. **$$$$**

Gorkha Grill
Soaltee Crowne Plaza, Tahachal
Tel: 272550
Fax: 272205
Email: crowneplaza@shicp.com.np
Most sophisticated restaurant in town offering smart Western food and dancing to a live band. Only open for dinner. **$$$$**

K.C.'s Restaurant & Bambooze Bar
Thamel
Tel: 414387
Very good inexpensive European cuisine with speciality menu: steak, pizza, cake. **$**

Kilroys of Kathmandu
Thamel
Tel: 250440
Irish chef with international experience and entertaining pretensions. Good Indian food as well. **$$$**

Kokonor Restaurant
Hotel Shangrila
Tel: 412999
An atmosphere of French elegance with good French and Chinese food, pianist and a French pastry chef. For winter lunches, the Shangrila has the most attractive garden in town. **$$$$**

Mike's Breakfast
Nag Pokhari
Tel: 424303
Charming old building and garden offering huge American-style breakfasts, lunches and, in season, dinner. The Mexican selections are especially tasty. Something of a Kathmandu institution. Mike also runs the Northfield Café in Thamel and venues in Pokhara. **$**

Nanglo
Durbar Marg
Tel: 222636
Inexpensive Western food and sandwiches served in the courtyard or on the roof. **$**

Simply Shutters Bistro
Babar Mahal Revisited
Tel: 259015
An elegant French-style bistro with an imaginative menu; just the place for a leisurely dinner. **$$$**

Tom & Jerry Bar
Thamel
Pub-style bar, delicious cocktails and music. Meeting place for the younger generation. Bar snacks only. **$**

ITALIAN

Al Fresco Restaurant
Hotel Soaltee Crown Plaza
Tel: 273999
Fax: 272205
Email: alfresco@shicp.com.np
Delicious Italian specialities served in taverna surroundings by the swimming pool. **$$$$**

Fire & Ice
Sanchayakosh Building, Tridevi Marg
Tel: 250210
Continually packed with diners enjoying the delicious thin-crust pizza and soft ice cream which give this cheerful establishment its name. **$$**

Olive Garden
Radisson Hotel
Lazimpat
Tel: 419358
Wonderful Italian specialities with an inventive menu served in a spirited Italianate setting. Particularly popular with the city's expats. **$$$$**

NEPALESE AND INDIAN

Baithak
Babar Mahal Revisited
Tel: 253337
Traditional Rana-style dining on brass plates in an elegant setting beneath ancestral portraits. Start with a drink at the adjacent K2 bar. Dinner only. **$$$$**

Bhancha Ghar (Nepalese Kitchen)
Kamaladi
Tel: 225172
Fax: 419260
Email: keyman@wlink.com.np
Nepalese food served in renovated old Newari house. Evening displays of handicraft-making and bar on the top floor. **$$$**

Bhojan Griha
Dilli Bazaar
Tel: 411603
Delicious Nepalese meals in an enormous restored old building, with local dance and music performances between courses. **$$$$**

Bukhara
Hotel Soaltee Crowne Plaza, Tahachal.
Tel: 272550
Fax: 272205
Email: crowneplaza@shicp.com.np
Wonderful high-quality tandooris and northwest frontier cuisine cooked in an open kitchen and eaten by hand if you dare. **$$$$**

Far Pavilion
Hotel Everest
Tel: 488100
Fax: 490288
Email: admin@hoteleverest.com.np
An elegant Indian dining experience on the top floor with unrivalled views. Dinner only. **$$$**

Ghar-e-Kabab
Hotel de l'Annapurna, Durbar Marg
Tel: 221711
Fax: 259596
Email: apurna@taj.wlink.com.np
Wonderful tandoori and Indian cuisine accompanied by Indian *ghazal* music. Best to book. **$$$**

Krishnarpan
Dwarika's Kathmandu Village Hotel, Batisputali
Tel: 470770
Elegant and innovative Nepalese dining experience in superb surroundings amid a collection of antique woodcarvings. **$$$$**

JAPANESE

Koto
Durbar Marg
Tel: 226025
Delicious Japanese food in a central setting. **$$$**

Tamura Restaurant
Thapathali Heights
Tel: 526732
Hard to find, but worth hunting down for the exquisite décor and impeccably prepared Japanese food. **$$$$**

TIBETAN

Lhasa Kitchen
Hotel Tibet, Lazimpat
Tel: 429085
Typical Tibetan dishes amid authentic surroundings. **$$**

Thakali Bhanchha
Durbar Marg
Tel: 436910
Delicious Tibetan specialities from northern Nepal in pleasant surroundings. **$$**

THAI

Baan Thai
Durbar Marg
Tel: 483140
Kathmandu's best Thai food, in a very popular central location. **$$$**

Drinking Notes

The national drink, *chiya* (tea brewed together with milk, sugar and sometimes spices) is served in small glasses, scalding hot. Up in the mountains, the tea is mixed with yak butter and salt and then churned Tibetan-style. Tea is particularly delicious if brewed with milk and spiced with cinnamon leaves, ginger and cardamom. Lassi is a refreshing sour milk drink which is either served sweet (with lots of fruit) or savoury.

Another popular homemade mountain drink is *chhang*, a powerful sort of beer made with fermented barley, maize, rye or millet. *Arak* (potato alcohol) and *rakshi* (wheat or rice alcohol) are also consumed in great quantities among the locals.

Coca-Cola and Pepsi are bottled in the Kathmandu Valley, as are Sprite, Fanta and other sodas. Tonic water is imported in cans.

Excellent Nepal-brewed beer is widely available. Choose from Golden Eagle, Iceberg, Leo, Star and several foreign brands. Imported liquor and good-quality wine from France and other countries are available from supermarkets and National Trading on Ram Shah Path (tel: 228791) at reasonable prices.

Good-quality rum (*khukri*), gin and vodka are produced locally. If you are a whisky or brandy drinker, however, be warned against the local varieties and stick to the more familiar imports.

Culture

KATHMANDU VALLEY

Patan Museum
Tel: 521492
Situated in the restored Mani
Narayan Chowk in Patan Durbar
Square this is a "must-see" cultural
experience with displays of
Nepalese art, handicrafts and
religious items *(see page 178)*.
Open Wed–Mon 10.30am–5pm.
National Museum
Chauni, near Swayambhunath
Tel: 271478
The country's oldest and largest
collection of archaeological, folk-
loristic and historic exhibits. Open
Wed–Mon, 9am–4pm.
National Art Gallery
Bhaktapur Durbar Square
Tel: 610004.
Open Wed–Mon 10.30am–3.30pm
(see page 184).
National Woodcarving Museum
Pujari Math, Bhaktapur.
Tel: 610005
Open Wed–Mon 10am–4pm.
**National Brass and Bronze
Museum**
Tel: 610448
Dattatraya Square, Bhaktapur.
Open Wed–Mon 10am–4pm.
Museum of Natural History
Southwest of Swayambhunath
Tel: 271899
Features displays on national flora
and fauna. Open Wed–Mon,
10am–5pm.
**Kathmandu Durbar Square
Complex**
This historic area of Kathmandu
includes the Tribhuvan Memorial
Museum (tel: 258034) and the
Mahendra Memorial Museum,
collections of memorabilia focusing
on the lives of the grandfather and

father of Nepal's present king. Open
Tues–Sat, 9.15am–3.30pm.

POKHARA

Annapurna Regional Museum
Prithvi Narayan Campus
Tel: 061-21102
Also known as the Natural History
Museum. Managed by the Anna-
purna Conservation Area Project
(ACAP) it has an exceptional collec-
tion of butterflies, insects, birds
and geology *(see page 231)*. Open
Wed–Mon 9am–4pm.
Pokhara Museum
Between airport and Mahendra Pul
Tel: 061-20413
Reflecting the lifestyles and history
of ethnic groups from western
Nepal. Open daily Wed–Mon
10am–5pm, closes at 3pm Friday.

AROUND NEPAL

Lumbini Museum
Tel: 071-80175
Located in the Cultural Zone this
museum contains coins,
manuscripts and sculptures.
Opposite is the Lumbini
International Research Institute
which provides research facilities
and has a collection of some
12,000 books. Open Wed–Mon,
10am–5pm.
Kapilavastu Museum
Tilaurakot, 27 km (17 miles) west
of Lumbini
Tel: 071-60128

The **Nepal Association of Fine
Arts (NAFA)**, Bal Mandir, Tangal,
organises various art exhibitions
(some also with exhibits for sale)
with traditional and modern
Nepalese paintings.
  Kathmandu also has a range
of active private art galleries,
including the **Siddhartha Gallery**
in Babar Mahal Revisited *(see
page 164)*, and the Indigo
Gallery above Mike's Breakfast
(see page 342).

Ancient coins, pottery and toys are
on display here, dating from
between the 7th century BC and the
4th century AD. Open Wed–Mon,
10am–5pm.
Elephant Museum
In the *hattisar* (elephant camp) in
Bhimphedi, south of the Kathmandu
Valley, there are 85 *howdahs*
(elephant-riding platforms) from the
Rana days.
Tharu Cultural Museum
Thakurdwara, near the entrance to
Royal Bardia National Park
Exhibits costumes, accessories and
household objects which highlight
the art and lifestyle of the Tharus.

The **National Theatre** (*Rastriya
Nachghar*) in Kathmandu shows
plays and music performances.
  The following associations
present cultural and classical dance
performances every evening:
Himalchuli Culture Centre, Hotel
Shankar, Lazimpat, Kathmandu
(Tel: 410151) and the **Everest
Cultural Society** in the Hotel de
l'Annapurna (tel: 221711). The
Ghar-e-Kabab restaurant of the
Annapurnas offers an exquisite
Indian menu, accompanied by
traditional Nepalese music and
ghazal singing.
  Some of the other hotels listed
(see page 336) also have dance
and cultural shows staged in their
restaurants. The **Soaltee Crowne
Plaza** (tel: 272555) features
Nepalese music and dancing every
evening (except Tuesday) in the
Himalchuli Restaurant as well as
dancing to a live band in the Gorkha
Grill restaurant. The **Shangrila Hotel**
(tel: 410620) features *Kala Kunj*
traditional dancing from Bhaktapur
in the garden every Friday evening,
with a buffet barbecue. The **Hotel
Vajra** (tel: 271545) is the place for
cultural gourmets. The excellent
Tibetan musician Pa Gyaltsen
performs here, as does the Kala-
mandapa ensemble (Newari music,
dances from Thimi and classical
Indian music). An institute for
classical Nepalese music, a
permanent art exhibition and a

library complete the picture.

The best show of all is the dancing amid ancient squares and courtyards lit by oil lamps in Patan or Bhaktapur. This must be arranged in advance and is available for groups only – ask your travel agent for details (*see page 330*).

Cinema

The Nepalese love going to the cinema. Kathmandu has quite a few cinemas featuring mainly Indian tear-jerkers; Western visitors may enjoy the reactions of the audience more than the action on the screen.

For Western films, check the programmes of the European, American and Russian cultural centres. Video is flourishing among more privileged Nepalese and video tapes are widely available for rent.

Gambling

Casino Nepal
Soaltee Crowne Plaza Hotel
Tel: 271011
Here you can fritter away small fortunes on baccarat, blackjack, roulette and other games around the clock. The chip value is counted in Indian rupees or foreign exchange. The casino provides a free bus service to ferry you back to your hotel.
Casino Anna
Hotel de l'Annapurna
Tel: 220567
Casino Royal
Hotel Yak & Yeti
Tel: 413999
Both casinos offer standard games or a drink from the hotel bar.

Nightlife

The **Galaxy Discotheque** in the Hotel Everest is open until 1am for hotel guests and members. If you like modern light shows and the latest top hits, this is the place for you. The **Woodlands Dynasty Plaza** also features a disco which is open to everybody, but opening times vary. Check out the trendy **X-Zone Disco** at Lal Durbar, opposite the Disney Store.

Shopping

What to Buy

Kathmandu is a treasure trove for shoppers. Traders appear wherever tourists stray and merchants wait on temple steps. Wares are spread on every pavement but watch out for the junk, fake antiques and souvenir *khukris*. Peer into shops, take your pick or take your leave; try the next boutique or the next stall. There are good buys among the bewildering and dazzling array.

Clothing

Clothes are good value and can be fun, from the lopsided *topis* (caps) to knitted sweaters, mittens and socks; from Tibetan dresses (*chubas*) that fasten at the side to men's Nepalese cotton shirts buttoned diagonally across the chest. *Topis* come in two types; sombre black ones and multicoloured variations. They are similar to the Western tie in that they are a must for all Nepalese visiting government offices, but their asymmetric shape is said to be a replica of Mount Kailas, the most sacred mountain for Buddhists and Hindus.

Nepalese cloth, in red, black and orange, hand-blocked and chequered with dots or geometric designs, is worn by women as blouses or shawls. It is also made into cotton quilts, covered on both sides with thin muslin, giving pastel overtones to the colours.

Wool shawls in a wide variety of colours are established as a major international fashion item; made of the finest goat's wool called pashmina, they are extremely soft, warm and strong (*see page 81*).

Jackets and shoulder bags are made in bright cotton colours in large patchwork. More subtle are those made from the wool used for Tibetan monks' robes and trimmed with striped cloth.

Hand-blocked cotton fabrics are made into dresses, bedspreads and pillow covers by organisations supporting destitute or handicapped women and sold along with weavings, hand-knitted sweaters, and household and gift items at shops in Patan and Kathmandu.

Folk Art

Among the various Nepalese folk objects available and produced in Kathmandu is the national knife, the curved *khukri*, worn in a wooden or leather sheath at the belt and sometimes highly adorned with silver and gold (*see page 224*). Make sure it comes complete with the two tiny blades for sharpening and cleaning.

The *saranghi* is a small four-stringed viola cut from a single piece of wood and played with a horse-hair bow by the *gaine*, the traditional wandering minstrels. Bamboo flutes, sold by vendors who carry them as a huge "tree", make cheap and enchanting gifts.

There are all kinds of hand-beaten copper and brass pots, jugs and jars, sold by their weight but rather heavy to carry home. Tibetan tea bowls are carved from a special wood and lined with silver and silver offering bowls, newly made, are available in Boudhanath.

Hand-made paper is beautifully block-printed or tie-dyed in a variety of designs by the women of Janakpur and sold as wrapping paper, cards and booklets (*see page 298*).

Intricately painted *thangkas* or religious scrolls mounted in silk are sold at a variety of prices. Look for the detail of the work and the amount of gold leaf used (*see page 76*). *Papier-mâché* dance masks are popular and puppets made and sold by the people of Bhaktapur.

Terracotta plant-holders in the shape of elephants, rhinoceros and temple lions or plaques embossed with deities are hand-made in Thimi.

Statuettes of Hindu and Buddhist deities are produced semi-industrially with the ancient "lost wax" process, a speciality of the people of Patan (*see page 75*).

Produced for export are metal filigree animals or Christmas decorations set with small pieces of coloured stones.

Carpets, the hand-made production of which is flourishing with substantial exports especially made for Europe and the US, are excellent value. The ones in the shops, hand-made in private homes and factories, are in traditional Tibetan designs in either bright colours or more subtle "vegetable dyes", though all are in fact chemical colours. The density of knotting, straightness of lines and overall quality of workmanship influence the price of new carpets (*see page 80*). Antique Tibetan carpets, with intricate motifs and beautiful colours, are available at substantially higher prices.

Replicas of Newari woodcarvings seen on temples and 16th- to 17th-century homes can be purchased in handicraft emporiums or at woodcarvers' studios in Bhaktapur.

Antiques

Unless bought from a reputable antiques gallery or certified by specialists, consider many "antique" pieces to have been made yesterday and pay accordingly. Tibetans and Nepalese will not willingly part with their jewels and adornments and, especially when you encounter people on the trail, it is impolite to pressure them to part with their personal heirlooms.

Remember when buying, antiques are forbidden for export if they are more than 100 years old. Certificates are required to prove their younger age if there is any doubt. These and export papers, if necessary, can be obtained from the **Department of Archaeology** (*see page 326*). Here you can also get expert advice on precious and semi-precious stones.

In addition to the old carpets which come in a number of sizes and types, most of the tempting antiques to buy are from Tibet. They include *thangkas*, carved and painted side-tables, metalwork from

east Tibet and jewellery and trinkets made with turquoise, coral, amber, gold and silver. Painted wood chests and cupboards from Tibet blend well with Western interiors but beware of modern copies. Prices are on a par with the world market.

Bargaining is not only expected but an intrinsic part of the Nepalese trading culture. If buying precious stones, you should rely solely on the expert advice of the reputable jewellers at Durbar Marg, New Road, in the bigger hotels or the Department of Archaeology.

Bookshops

Kathmandu has many bookshops with an excellent selection of books about Nepal and a wide range of Asian subjects, written in several languages.

The best shops include **Educational Enterprises** beneath the temple opposite Bir Hospital; **Himalayan Booksellers** with branches in Durbar Marg and Thamel; **Mandala Book Point** (tel: 245570) in Kantipath; **Pilgrim's Bookhouse** in Thamel; and **Ratna Pustak Bhandar** off Bagh Bazaar.

Shopping Areas

The best selection and the best prices are available in the Kathmandu Valley though you will find things to buy all over Nepal. As you sightsee in the valley you will encounter many good shopping areas and, as a general rule, if you see something you really like and the price is not too exorbitant, it is better to buy it than regret not being able to find anything similar! To get an idea of the variety on offer and of the relative qualities and prices, visit the following areas.

Thamel, the tourist area in old Kathmandu, has a good selection of most things, though the crowds may distract you (*see page 174*).

Jawalakhel, south of Patan, has a good selection of carpets. They can be seen being made in the Tibetan Refugee Camp and are displayed in the many shops in the

area (*see page 181*). Patan itself is famous for the manufacture of jewellery and metalwork, still made by traditional methods. Also check out the Patan Museum Shop for unusual gifts (*see page 178*).

Hastakala (Handicrafts) is opposite the entrance to Hotel Himalaya (*see page 337*). All the crafts on sale in this attractive shop run by UNICEF are made by disadvantaged groups under the auspices of the Nepal Women's Organisation, the Mahaguthi and Bhaktapur Craft Printers. The Mahaguthi shops, one just down the hill in Patan and one in Durbar Marg, have similar arrangements, as do the talented designers who run the private Dhukuti, on the same hill.

The shopping and restaurant complex of **Babar Mahal Revisited**, located just south of Singha Durbar, is a must (*see page 164*). A series of purpose-built Rana-style courtyards, it offers an excellent selection of quality shopping for those pressed for time. Look out for the paper shop with imaginative lamp fittings, the pashmina store and the best CD music shop in town. Pasal, in Babar Mahal Revisited, is good for gifts with imaginative local and regional decorative items.

For antiques there are two reliable galleries on **Durbar Marg** with beautiful showrooms; Tibet Ritual Art Gallery, Durbar Marg, is above the Sun Koshi Restaurant and the Potala Gallery is on the first floor across from the Yak & Yeti gate (*see page 337*).

The main shops in Kathmandu for imported articles are on **New Road**, with supermarkets located in Thapatali and Lazimpat. Jewellers and shops selling handicrafts to tourists are centred around Durbar Marg and the big hotels. But beware of the many Indian Kashmiri shops if you are looking for something Nepalese.

Outdoor Activities

Trekking

Permits

Trek permits in Nepal are no longer required. Visitors to national parks can pay their entry fees on arrival, except in the case of the Annapurna Conservation Area when entry permits must be obtained prior to departure from the **Department of Immigration**. Do not forget to bring your passport plus two passport-size photos.

Those visiting remote and restricted areas such as Dolpo and Mustang must make their arrangements through a registered trekking agent who will secure the necessary permit as part of the service (*see page 319*).

If you are attempting a Trekking Peak (*see page 129*) your trekking agent must get a Trekking Peak Permit. Permits for mountaineering peaks that are permitted for expeditions are processed by the **Ministry of Tourism & Civil Aviation** and require the endorsement of your Alpine Club. The fees per person are between US$300 for a Trekking Peak and as much as US$70,000 for Mount Everest. You should allow at least one year for this kind of permit.
Department of Immigration
New Baneswar, Kathmandu.
Tel: 494273/337.

Preparation and Fitness

Anyone who is reasonably fit can trek, but the fitter you are the more you will enjoy it. Do as much walking and exercise as possible in the weeks prior to your trek, to prepare for the effort that will be required of you in Nepal. A thorough medical check-up is recommended

before you go. Inoculations against typhoid, hepatitis and paratyphoid, tetanus and meningitis should be on your list too and start at least six weeks before your departure (*see page 328*).

Food

Water contamination is a problem. On the trail all water should be well boiled or treated with iodine crystals, tincture or tablets. Tincture is available in Kathmandu pharmacies (four drops per litre; allow 20 minutes before drinking). Do not drink from streams or tap water however pure it may look; even chlorine is not effective against amoebic cysts.

Vegetables should not be eaten raw unless properly soaked in an iodine or potassium solution. Peel all fruits or soak in similar solutions. Local food can become tedious for Western stomachs after a few days and sometimes Nepalese cooking oils can upset an unfamiliar digestive system. Bring your own high-energy goodies like chocolate, dried fruits and nuts, powdered drinks, herbal teas and spirits (whisky and brandy, though the local rum is also excellent) if you enjoy a sip on nippy evenings.

Medication

Minor ailments are to be expected. Being at high altitudes and around exotic bacteria puts a strain on the body so that cuts take longer to heal and colds or coughs drag on. On organised group treks, a collective medical kit is provided and the *sirdar* will occasionally have some knowledge of first aid. Some items might be in high demand, however, and it is best to bring your own first-aid kit. This should include:
Gauze bandages
Sterile compresses
Tape and elastic plasters
Laxatives
Pain-relief tablets with codeine
Strong pain-relief tablets
Vaseline
Mild sleeping pills
Decongestant or other cold remedy
Throat lozenges or cough drops
Ophthalmic ointment or drops

Cream against insect bites
Diarrhoea tablets
Medicine for other gastric problems
A broad-spectrum antibiotic
Blister pads or moleskin
Antiseptic and cotton
A good sunblock
Lip salve (to prevent chapping)

Good trekking agencies prepare for emergency evacuations by depositing US$2,000 with the rescue organisation but bad weather may hamper the rescue helicopter.

Precautions

Make sure you take the following special precautions:
Leave passport and valuables (jewellery, credit cards, extra money or travellers' cheques) in the hotel or trekking agent's safe. Carry a photocopy of your passport or driving licence.
Lock up your pack with a small padlock to prevent pilferage or accidental losses.
Your medical kit and toilet gear should be in separate plastic boxes with lids.
Leave your name at your embassy (*see page 328*) before you go on a trek or leave them a copy of your passport and name and policy number of your travel insurance with medical cover, if possible.
Take US$50–100 worth of 5–100-rupee notes for minor expenses (bottled drinks, souvenirs, staff tips) along the way. It is customary, but strictly optional, for a trekking group to pool tip money for the trekking staff, generally dividing it according to relative pay scale, and even to pass on unneeded clothes, shoes or camping knick-knacks. As "thank you" or *dhanyabadh* is not commonly used in this culture, do not be surprised if the receiver just nods or smiles.

Trekking Trails and When to Go

There is an overwhelming number of trekking trails to choose from. Your final choice depends upon the length of time you have available, the season, and your personal interests.

The following list will give you some guidelines. Consult the trekking section of this book and with your trek and travel agent as regions vary as to the time of year.

January to February

This is the best time of year for low-level walks at elevations up to 3,000 metres (10,000 ft) offering pleasant sunny days with clear skies and good mountain views. It is also an excellent time to trek the old trade route between Kathmandu and Pokhara, visit the lower Lamjung Himal areas or trek in the valleys north of Gorkha.

Three good treks are recommended from Pokhara. The so-called **Royal Trek** follows the footsteps of the Prince of Wales for three or four days in the Gurung and Gurkha country northeast of the Pokhara Valley. Great views of Annapurna,

Machhapuchhre and Dhaulagiri are highlights of the six- to ten-day **Ghandruk to Ghorapani circuit trek**. For those with more time, the 15–18-day **Kali Gandaki trek** to Jomsom and Muktinath is in good condition in the winter, although snow is possible at Ghorapani.

North of Kathmandu, the **Langtang and Helambu treks** are both good, as long as you do not venture too high. You may meet some snow above the Sherpa villages of Tarkeghyang and Melamchigaun, but it should not hamper progress (*see page 251*).

Khumbu is only for the hardy as temperatures are cold, but there is sensational scenery and few trekkers. Some delays on Lukla flights can be expected in the event of bad weather.

In late February, spring arrives in Nepal and flowers and rhododendrons begin to bloom at the lower altitudes. Trek before mid-March if you want to beat the spring rush up to 4,000 metres (13,520 ft).

March

Although spring has arrived in the Kathmandu Valley and at the lower levels, high-altitude conditions can still be harsh. Do not plan on being able to cross high passes (5,000 metres/16,400 ft) before mid-April.

March is a good time to start a long trek into **Solu Khumbu** from Jiri, although it is still a little early for Rolwaling. Further east, start mid-month on an excursion to the rhododendron forests of the Milke Danda ridge or for a botanical trek up the Arun river but not yet into

What to Bring for a Trekking Trip

As you are going to walk four to eight hours a day, shoes are of paramount importance. They must be sturdy and comfortable with good tread on the soles; most trekkers hike in trainers at low altitude, though in snow at higher elevations or on rough and rocky terrain good boots are essential. They must accommodate one or two layers of heavy wool or cotton (not nylon) socks, of which you should have a plentiful supply. Light tennis shoes or trainers will help you relax when the day's walking is over.

Many trekkers assume that it will be cold at all times, whereas when treks start low it can be quite hot for a few days. For women, below-the-knee skirts are more comfortable than trousers; in deference to local sensibilities, neither shorts nor tight or revealing tops should be worn. Men should wear either hiking shorts or loosely fitting long trousers which also help prevent insect bites. Thermal underwear can be useful in particularly cold months and at high altitudes. Remember it is better to carry too many clothes than not enough.

When trekking with an organised group, you will normally be asked

to fit all your gear in one pack, to weigh no more than 15 kg (35 lbs). You will carry only a day pack with daytime essentials, such as camera, water bottle, rain gear, sweater or pile jacket, book or writing pad, binoculars and personal items. Your pack should be tough, compact, easily opened, lockable and packed in an organised fashion. For a week's trek below 4,500 metres (14,500 ft), your equipment should include:

● long trekking trousers or skirts
● light rain trousers (Goretex)
● fleece sweaters
● T-shirts/shirts
● sweatshirt
● ski or thermal underwear
● trekking socks
● tennis shoes or trekking sandals
● woollen hat
● gloves or mittens
● sleeping bag (down or synthetic fibre)
● foam mattress
● anorak or Goretex jacket
● umbrella
● telescope walking stick
● sunglasses and sunhat
● towel
● medical kit

● plastic water bottle
● day pack

For above 4,500 metres (14,700 ft) add one pair of gaiters (rain trousers can suffice) for walking through snow, glacier goggles, and boot protector (such as snow seal) unless boots are made of Goretex.

You will also need a torch and spare batteries, candles, a lighter, a pocket knife with scissors, spare shoelaces, string, safety pins, a supply of toilet paper and small plastic bags to protect food, carry rubbish or wrap wet or dirty clothes in, and several large ones to stuff sleeping bag and pack contents into in case of rain. A notebook and pen doubles as a diary and bring a book or cards for the long evenings. An umbrella is handy for showers and to shade the sun. Trekking maps of most areas can be purchased at Kathmandu bookshops (*see page 174*).

Much of this gear can be bought or rented from the trekking shops of Thamel and Chetrapati, though it is best to arrive self-sufficient. If you are trekking alone, you need to add tents, food and cooking and eating utensils to this list.

Makalu Base Camp. **Jugal** is also rewarding for wilderness treks but expect spring flowers only late in the month.

All Langtang, Helambu and Pokhara-based treks are feasible, though some mountain haze may develop during the second half of the month. The **Dhorpatan** (from Tansen or Beni) and lower **Dhaulagiri** areas are a lovely alternative to the Annapurnas late in the month.

Out west, the valleys below **Khaptad** are pleasantly temperate and the rhododendrons are brilliant.

April

In this high season, temperatures are warm in the lower altitudes but there is a likelihood of afternoon clouds and showers in most areas. But this is the best month for flowers in the mountains and the favoured season for Alpine treks and climbing.

This is a superb month to spend high in the mountains around **Manang** and climbing is possible on Chulu and Pisang. After mid-April the Thorung La pass is usually open, critical to completing the classic **Annapurna Circuit** trek. Beware of avalanche danger in the Annapurna Sanctuary, though the Machhapuchhre Base Camp area is good for wildlife after the middle of the month.

For the adventurous, the high altitudes of the Dhaulagiri glacier region are at their best as is the rugged remote terrain of **Manaslu** and **Dudh Pokhari**.

This is an excellent time for treks to the higher altitudes, such as in east Nepal, to the **Milke Danda** ridge and Alpine treks to the base camps of **Kanchenjunga** and **Makalu**. It is also one of the best times to visit the Khumbu, although the low-level walk in from Jiri can be disappointing due to increasing haze and heat. Now is the time for Alpine and climbing treks to **Rolwaling** and the Hinku, Hongu and climbs of **Island Peak** and **Mera**.

Treks into the **Jugal Himal** are fairly tough but rewarding for the off-the-beaten-track adventurer.

Spring flowers are beautiful. Between Helambu and Langtang, visits to the **Gosainkund Lakes** are attractive. En route to Langtang, Trisuli Bazaar and Dhunche are hot, but are worth enduring to reach the high-altitude forests and wild flowers. A return via the Tirudanda or on to Gorkha enters seldom-trekked highland areas.

Short two- to five-day treks around the **Kathmandu Valley** are popular now as they are higher, therefore cooler, than short treks out of Pokhara.

In the far west of the country, treks to Rara Lake and Dolpo start in **Jumla**. The "Upper Dolpo" region is only open to organised groups with special permits. "Lower Dolpo" is open to individual trekkers but is logistically complex because of difficult access and food deficits in this remote region. Don't start a trek before late April or snow will bar the way.

May to June

In these pre-monsoon months, there is haze and heat at all lower elevations and occasional heavy showers. If you are trekking, aim to get to the higher altitudes quickly. Some of the better areas at this time are **Khumbu**, flying in and out of Lukla, **Rolwaling**, **Hongu**, the Ganja La or Tilman's Col areas of **Langtang** and the **Around Annapurna** trek. **Kathmandu Valley** walks are pleasurable (*see page 203*).

July to Mid-September

Keen botanists and students of leeches will enjoy this monsoon time of year. Although not generally recommended for trekking, the terrain is lovely in the higher regions and rainshadow areas, such as Muktinath, Manang and Langtang to a certain extent, as well as Dolpo and the far west. Although rainfall may not be continuous and sunny days and mountain views do occur, trekkers must realise that rain, leeches, slippery paths and swollen rivers will hamper their progress. Various Alpine wild flowers and plants are at their zenith at this time, spectacular in

upper Khumbu. These months are also ideal for **Dolpo** and the **Mustang** region near the Tibetan border.

Mid-September to Mid-October

The monsoon tails off about this time and the countryside is fresh and green. When the mountains are free of clouds, the views are crystal clear though there are still a lot of showers at lower altitudes. Recommendations for trekking routes are much the same as for April and May, though high passes may be snowed over.

Mid-October to Mid-November

This is the "high season" for trekking and with good reason. It is the classic time for high-altitude Alpine and climbing treks and in general has the most reliable clear weather, although rain is not unheard of. The more popular routes are congested at this time; these include the Khumbu where the sheer weight of numbers create inevitable flight delays at Lukla but previously forbidden private airlines are now lightening the load. Even more crowded is the Pokhara region, especially the Kali Gandaki Valley, though weather-wise the Annapurna Sanctuary is at its best.

This is the time to get off the beaten track and enjoy trips to east or west Nepal, **Jugal Himal**, **Ganesh Himal** and **Tirudanda** or routes between Pokhara and Kathmandu. Throughout this autumn period many colourful religious festivals take place to ensure a good harvest in the fields (*see page 90*).

Mid-November to Mid-December

This period offers stable, winter weather as the rain and snow does not start until mid-December. It also has the added advantage of avoiding the previous month's crowds. With crops harvested, the countryside lacks colour but the clarity of mountain views is superb and there is plenty of variety and walking conditions are pleasant.

Low level and short treks up to about 3,700 metres (12,000 ft) are at their best at this time of year. The **Pokhara** region is ideal as are

Helambu, Langtang and **Gorkha**.
The **Khumbu** is still good though
getting colder and the Lukla flights
more reliable than at the height of
the season. Remember that most
of the high passes cannot be safely
crossed because of snow after the
middle of December.

Trekking Etiquette

Hiking in the hills is generally safe.
Learning a bit of Nepalese language
will open many a door and helps
when asking directions. Remember
that farmers often have little concept of time and may unintentionally
exaggerate by hours, either way.
Trail directions should be repeatedly
sought as each villager has their
own version. Distance is always
measured in hours, not kilometres
which are irrelevant in such an up-
and-down country.

When putting together a group of
fellow trekkers, be sure to discuss
each person's expectations for the
trip in terms of pace, rest days,
special interests (photography,
birds, fishing, cultural interactions,
solitude, etc) and whether it is the
destination or the process of
getting there which is most
important. This should help assure
a smooth, congenial trek.

Whereas no-one is likely to
openly criticise you if you make a
cultural *faux pas*, out of respect for
the Nepalese and to ensure a
better rapport between you, your
staff and the villagers, try to be
sensitive to religious beliefs and
local practices. For example, on
your trek you will come across
stupas and *chortens* of various
sizes and conditions. They are
revered, regardless of their size,
with great devotion and were built
to pacify local demons, deities or
the spirit of some dead person. It is
inappropriate to sit or climb on
chortens and they should be
passed with the right shoulder in a
clockwise direction. Lamas' prayer
wheels whirl prayers out in a
clockwise direction only. All circum-
ambulations of temples, stupas and
chortens must follow clockwise the
revolution of the universe.

In Buddhist areas you will see

mani stones placed around *chortens* or stacked to make a *mani*
wall. These flat stones are carved
with inscriptions, prayers and
supplications which have been
artistically engraved with devotion.
Though the temptation may be
great, because of the beauty and
small size of these stones, do not
take them for souvenirs. The
removal of these stones from their
place of offering is sacrilege.

At some crossroads you may find
bits and pieces of coloured cloth, a
bamboo framework with threads
woven into an intricate design, or
dyed flour dumplings lying on the
ground. Be careful not to touch
these or step on them. These
offerings are made to malignant
demons and deities and should be
passed on the left.

Avoid touching a Nepali dressed
all in white. His white cap, white
clothes and non-leather shoes
signify his state of mourning for a
close family member.

Prayer flags may look old, ragged
and torn but to the Nepalese and
especially the Sherpas their significance in carrying prayers of suppli-
cation and gratitude never fades.

When looking for a toilet spot in
the bush, be sure that you are not
close to running water or to any holy
relics such as prayer flags, *mani*
walls or *gompas*. Burn and bury, or
carry out, all toilet paper. Carry all
litter to a rubbish pit or to camp
where the staff can burn or bury it.

Help to minimise the burning of
firewood in lodges by being
adequately clothed so as not to rely
on the fire's heat for keeping warm,
by limiting hot showers heated with
wood and by combining orders for
similar food items.

There are many more customs,
rituals and good habits that should
be adhered to (*see page 324*).

On the Trails

A typical day, when trekking with an
organised outfit, begins around
6am with a cup of tea or coffee.
After packing, breakfast of porridge,
eggs, toast or pancakes is served.
Walking starts around 7–7.30am
Late into the morning, trekkers halt

for a substantial hot brunch or
lunch, the cook having gone ahead
to select the site and prepare the
meal. As early as 3 or 4pm the
day's walking is over. Camp for the
night is set up (usually with a toilet
tent), dinner is served, and by 9pm
everyone is thinking of sleep.

You are free to walk at whatever
pace you prefer. Fast or slow, there
will always be a staff guide in front
or behind you. You can hike alone or
in a group, make endless stops to
enjoy the scenery or chat with
passing locals, take photographs or
sip tea in a wayside shop.

If trekking independently, do not
trek alone. Team up with other
trekkers or hire a guide, preferably
from a trekking agency rather than
at the trailhead.

A few hints may increase your
enjoyment:

● Do not try too much too soon.
Walk at your own pace, no matter
what others may say. Watch the way
the porters walk, slowly and steadily.
Go uphill in short steps, feet flat on
the ground, weight forward.
● Go downhill with your knees bent,
using your thigh muscles. Rest as
often as you feel like.
● Drink as much liquid as you can
to compensate for the sweaty hours
under the sun; at high altitudes,
this also helps your body to
acclimatise.
● Shielding your head from the sun
with a hat or umbrella, not only
applying sunscreen to your skin,
helps prevent sunstroke, which
along with dehydration is one of the
most common ailments on the trail.
● Ensure that your feet are in good
condition to walk. Do not wait until
blisters develop.
● Be careful in the night as in
certain areas thieves sometimes
slit tents to steal cameras and
other valuables. Keep your belongings close to you, well inside the
tent, and keep your tent closed
when you are not in it.
● Finally, add to your luggage a
strong dose of patience, understanding and congenial curiosity for
the values and ways of a world that
is different from, and at times,
better organised than your own.

Mountain Rescue

The **Himalayan Rescue Association (HRA)** is a non-profit organisation which strives to prevent casualties in the Nepal Himalaya. The HRA runs Trekkers' Aid Posts at Pheriche in the Khumbu and at Manang in the Annapurnas. They are manned by doctors and equipped to treat and advise on AMS and other medical problems.

As this is an entirely voluntary organisation, donations are welcomed directly to the HRA or channelled through your trekking agency. The HRA has no facilities to arrange helicopter evacuations which must be done through your trekking agent or embassy.

The HRA does not routinely recommend any medicine for preventing AMS though there are two medicines which under certain circumstances are considered useful. Diamox (aceta-zolomide) is the safest for helping to cope with symptoms of mild AMS. The standard dose is 250 mg every 12 hours until symptoms are resolved. Dexamethasone is a powerful drug which can be useful in the treatment of cerebral edema. It should only be used under experienced supervision.

Additional information for independent trekkers can be obtained from the **Kathmandu Environmental Education Programme (KEEP)**. This non-profit organisation is designed to minimise impacts of individual travellers and maximise benefits for local

Altitude Sickness

Anyone trekking above 2,500 metres (8,200 ft) may suffer from altitude sickness (*see page 140*). Known as AMS or Acute Mountain Sickness it can ruin treks and should be treated seriously. Nearly half of the people who have trekked to Everest base camp, for instance, suffer mild AMS and in some cases lives are endangered.

Dr David Shlim, Medical Director of Himalayan Rescue Association and an expert on mountaineering medicine, has developed a three-step approach to avoid death from altitude sickness:
● Early recognition of the symptoms is very important.
● Never ascend with any symptoms.
● Descend only if symptoms are getting worse while resting at the same altitude.

The only prevention is to give one's body time to adjust to high altitude. Those who go too high too fast are liable to be victims of AMS. To minimise the pitfalls of AMS during a trek, travellers should:
● Drink adequate fluids. At 4,300 metres (14,000 ft) for example, the body requires 3–4 litres (5–7 pints) of liquid a day – more if losing much sweat. At low altitudes, especially in the heat, try to drink at least 2–3 litres (3–5 pints) a day, including soups and hot drinks.
● Accept the fact you cannot go very high if your time is short.
● Plan for "rest days" at about 3,700 metres (12,000 ft) and 4,300 metres (14,000ft). This means sleeping at the same altitude for two nights. You can be as active as you wish during the day, and go as high as you like, but descend again to sleep.
● Above 3,700 metres (12,000 ft), do not set up camp more than 450 metres (1,500 ft) higher in any one day, even if you feel fit enough.
● Learn the symptoms of AMS and be alert for them. If you begin to suffer, do not go any higher until the symptoms have disappeared. Often they will clear up within one or two days. Should any of the more serious symptoms appear, descend at once to a lower altitude. Even a descent of 300 metres (1,000 ft) can make a difference.
● Do not go to high altitude if you have heart or lung disease. Check with your doctor if you have doubts.
● Do not expect everyone in your party to acclimatise at the same rate. It is possible that you will need to divide the party so that people who acclimatise more slowly will camp lower than others.
● Take extra precautions when flying into high-altitude STOL airstrips. Take two "rest days" before proceeding further.

Symptoms & Treatment

There are three main types of AMS. Early mountain sickness is the first and acts as a warning. If it goes unheeded, it can progress to pulmonary edema (waterlogged lungs) or cerebral edema (waterlogged brain).
● Early mountain sickness manifests itself in headache, nausea, loss of appetite, sleeplessness, fluid retention and swelling of the body. The cure is to climb no higher until the symptoms have gone.
● Pulmonary edema is characterised by breathlessness, even while resting, and by a persistent cough accompanied by congestion in the chest.
● Cerebral edema is a very serious condition. The symptoms are extreme tiredness, vomiting, severe headache, difficulty in walking (as in drunken, uneven steps), disorientation, abnormal speech and behaviour, drowsiness and eventually unconsciousness. Should any of these symptoms appear, victims must be carried to lower altitude immediately, either on a porter's back or on a yak or pony, and their trek abandoned. Do not delay descent for any reason and begin at night if necessary. Do not wait for helicopter evacuation. The patient must be accompanied and may well not be capable of making correct decisions. You may need to insist that they descend. Medicine is no real substitute for descent. If a doctor is available, he may give medication and oxygen but even with treatment the patient must go down.

people. A visit to their information centre is highly recommended.

Himalayan Rescue Association
Near the Kathmandu Guest House
Tel: 262748
Email: hra@aidpost.mos.com.np
Advice for trekkers is given
11am–9pm daily except Saturday.

Kathmandu Environmental Education Programme (KEEP)
Potala Guest House behind the Tilicho Hotel in Tridevi Marg
Tel: 259567
Fax: 411533
Email: tour@keep.wlink.com.np

River Rafting

Although a relatively new activity in Nepal, the better river-running outfits are well equipped and have highly trained staff. **Himalayan River Exploration** are the pioneers of the industry.

River trips last from one to several days and your choice depends on the time available and where you are heading. White water varies with the time of year as the rivers rise and fall dramatically during the season, depending on rainfall and snowmelt. As a general rule they are at their highest (and the white water at its biggest) during and after the June to September monsoon and drop to their lowest in February and March. By April the snowmelt in the mountains raises the water level.

Most popular is the two-day Bhote Koshi east of Kathmandu and the three-day Trisuli or Seti river trips down to Royal Chitwan National Park (*see page 143*). More remote and adventurous are the three-day Kali Gandaki trip, the four-day Bheri and the 10-day Karnali river trip from above Nepalganj to Royal Bardia National Park. Most exciting of all are the huge rapids on the Sun Koshi river in east Nepal, which take 10 days to run.

In autumn (mid-September to mid-November) and spring (March to May) shorts and bathing suits, a sunhat, T-shirts, trainers and a torch are all that is needed for a short trip. For early autumn and late spring bring a long-sleeved shirt,

Jungle Safaris

Most wildlife operations in Chitwan and Bardia supply basics as you would expect of any hotel. Take casual, washable safari-style clothes in jungle colours – beige and green are the most suitable. Wear baggy shorts in the summer months but take long trousers to protect legs from swishing tall grass while riding elephants. Trainers are the most suitable footwear and jungle hats, mosquito repellent and suncream are useful. The winter months are cold and morning mist makes it

light trousers, an umbrella (for shade and in case it rains) and plenty of sunblock to protect you from the glare off the water. During winter (mid-November to February) in addition to the above bring a thick sweater, warm trousers, a down jacket and rain poncho. All the clothes you bring should not mind getting wet. For use in camp ensure you have a complete change of dry clothes and shoes.

A good river company will provide tents, sleeping bag and liner, foam mattress, towel and a waterproof bag to stow your clothing. You will be given a life jacket and your guide will instruct you in its use. Safety must be taken very seriously on the remote big rivers of Nepal and should be a consideration when you choose your operator. A waterproof "ammo can" is also provided to carry cameras, binoculars, sunglasses and personal items. This is clipped to the boat and is accessible during the day.

Himalayan River Exploration
PO Box 242, Kathmandu
Tel: 411225
Fax: 414075
Email: info@tigermountain.com

Mountain Biking

Except for a few mountain-bike shops in Kathmandu, do not count on borrowing any specialised tools for on-the-road repairs. Self-sufficiency is essential within

chilly – sweaters and jackets are essential from December to February. As a guideline, the Terai is about 1,200 metres (4,000 ft) lower in altitude than Kathmandu and so the weather is always several degrees warmer.

For those lodges that have swimming pools, don't forget your swimming gear. Tiger Tops has a retail outlet discreetly selling their specially designed range of tempting jewellery, cotton jungle wear, souvenirs and local handicrafts.

practical limits. Bring all the tools you will need for repairs and routine maintenance, including tyre irons, a tube patch kit, an extra tube, a chain tool, a spoke wrench, allen keys and screwdrivers. Less frequently required components are cone wrenches, a headset wrench, a bottom bracket tool, a spanner, extra spokes, extra brake cables and pads, and an extra rear derailleur. And do not forget the obvious, such as water bottles, a sturdy lock that can stretch around a fixed object, a helmet, gloves, a pump and definitely a bell.

Panniers are the preferred mode for carrying your gear while biking in Nepal. Racks and panniers must be durable as many roads are rough and full of potholes. Bring small padlocks to protect them. Riders taking to the trails may prefer to carry their equipment in a medium-sized, snug-fitting backpack, as panniers often hinder a bike's manoeuvrability on rugged terrain. Also, it is easier to carry a bike on your shoulders this way.

A "portager" is an essential piece of gear for carrying your bike, which you will probably be doing frequently. The "portager" is a strap which mounts beneath the central bar and allows the bike to rest fairly comfortably on your shoulder. But on long, uphill totes, you may want to attach the bike to your backpack with nylon webbing to better distribute the weight.

Before leaving home, test your equipment thoroughly and take an extended ride on bumpy terrain fully loaded to make sure that the panniers and rack sit solidly and that you can balance and ride easily wearing a loaded pack.

Be cautious at all times, on roads or trails, of other travellers: loaded porters and stock animals, women and children regularly ply the way and hardly expect to encounter a fast-coming bicyclist. Ring your bell habitually. Move to the inside when animals are passing to avoid being nudged off the trail. Stay on the roads and trails at all times, as off-road riding only contributes to Nepal's already serious soil erosion problems.

Dress modestly (for men long shorts are acceptable, always with a shirt; for women, loose trousers or skirt to below the knee and an unrevealing top), and try to be tolerant of villagers' curiosity which is seldom with malice. In some parks and reserves, bicycle use is strictly prohibited. Check the rules before leaving Kathmandu.

Other Outdoor Adventures

Aerial Views
An unparalleled view of the Kathmandu Valley and the mountains ringing it can be obtained from the hot-air balloon flights arranged by **Balloon Sunrise Nepal**. Similarly spectacular views above Pokhara come from the motorised glider flights operated by **Avia Club Nepal**.

The famous pilgrimage temple of Manakamana can be reached by Nepal's first cable-car (*see page 223*). This international standard Austrian-built cable-car system covers the 2.8 km (1.7 miles) from the main Prithvi Highway at Kuringhat to the temple in less than 10 minutes. Enjoy spectacular views of Manaslu, Himalchuli and the Annapurna Himal from the car. The tourist fare (around US$10 per person) is payable in foreign currency. Contact **Manakamana Darshan Ltd** for more details on riding the cable car.

Pony trekking
Pony trekking can be arranged out of Pokhara for guests of the Tiger Mountain Pokhara Lodge (*see page 339*). Others can contact **Himalayan Pony Trek** for day and half-day village visits and fun rides for children.

Himalayan Pony Trek
Tel: 061-24114
Fax: 061-22809
Email: jhalak@cnet.wlink.com.np

Adventure Sports
Nepal's first bungee jump opened in October 1999, located 160 metres (525 ft) over the Bhote Koshi gorge, just 5 km (3 miles) from the Tibetan border and operated by **Last Resort Adventures**. Rock climbing, canyoning and mountain biking is available from **The Borderland Adventure Centre**. Located 16 km (10 miles) from the Tibetan border off the Arniko Highway on the banks of the Bhotse Koshi river.

Balloon Sunrise Nepal
Lazimpat, Kathmandu
Tel: 424131
Fax: 424157
Email: balloon@sunrise.mos.com.np

Avia Club Nepal
PO Box 2913, Durbar Marg, Kathmandu
Tel: 412830
Fax: 415266
Pokhara
Tel: 061-25944
Fax: 061-25192
Email: nepal@aviaclub.mos.com.np

Manakamana Darshan Ltd
Naxal
Tel: 434690/648
Fax: 434515
Email: chitwan@cc.wlink.com.np

Last Resort Adventures
Thamel, Kathmandu
Tel: 439526
Fax: 414765
Email: rivers@ultimate.wlink.com.np

The Borderland Adventure Centre
Barhabise, Tatopani, Kathmandu
Tel: 425836
Fax: 435207
Email: info@borderlands.net

Sport

Participant Sports

Sport as a pastime or occupation is an alien concept in Nepal. It has only recently been promoted into schools and the military. Football (soccer) and cricket have become popular while cycling, particularly mountain biking, and jogging are attracting some devotees.

Paradoxically, for such a mountainous country, commercial skiing is out of the question, though a few cross-country enthusiasts and mountaineering expeditions do try. There are no ski-lifts, the steepness of the slopes and the high snow line (bringing with it altitude problems) make skiing impractical.

Some sports can be enjoyed in and around Kathmandu though facilities are limited and mainly belong to hotels and private clubs.

Golf
Gokarna Forest Golf Resort's opening in 1999 introduced championship standard golf facilities to Nepal with a course set amid the king's private forest that is acknowledged as one of the best and most beautiful in South Asia. Associated with Le Meridien Kathmandu, guests are welcome to the 18-hole, 72-par course designed by Gleneagles, Scotland. The **Royal Nepal Golf Club** near Kathmandu's airport has a nine-hole course and welcomes visitors. There are also two nine-hole golf courses in Pokhara, one for Fulbari Resort guests and the entertaining and challenging **Himalayan Golf Course**, run by a former Gurkha golf enthusiast.

Swimming
Hotel guests and members can use the tennis courts and pools at the

Soaltee Crowne Plaza, Yak & Yeti, Radisson, Everest, Annapurna, Himalaya, Shangrila and Narayani hotels and for small entrance fees some allow drop-in day use (*see page 336*).

Prudence is needed when bathing in mountain torrents because of swift, treacherous currents. The larger rivers in the Terai are safe but keep an eye out for the occasional crocodile.

Fishing

Lowland rivers and valley lakes are often good fishing grounds. Besides the small fry, the two main catches are asla, a kind of trout, and the larger mahseer which grow to huge proportions. February, March, October and November are the fishing months. Permits are required in national parks where the fish must be returned. Keen anglers should bring their own tackle. Contact **Tiger Tops** for information on fishing in the Karnali, Babai and Narayani rivers.

Gokarna Forest Golf Resort
Tel: 224399
Fax: 226414
Email: gokarna@mos.com.np
Royal Nepal Golf Club
Tel: 472836
Himalayan Golf Course
Tel: 061 21882
Tiger Tops
Lazimpat, PO Box 242, Kathmandu
Tel: 411225
Fax: 414075

Language

Language and Dialect

There are as many tongues spoken in Nepal as there are races and almost as many dialects as there are village communities. But just as centuries of intermarriage have left the nation without a pure tribe or race, neither is there any one pure language. Throughout history, the main languages have intermingled and influenced one another.

The official language, Nepali, is derived from Pahori, a language of northern India related to Hindi. Nepali and Hindi use the same writing system called Devanagari. Nepali has also borrowed heavily from some local dialects as well as from Sanskrit, an ancient scholarly language that has survived (like Latin) as a religious medium. Nepali, Sanskrit and Newari – the language of the Newar people, predominant in the Kathmandu Valley – each have their own distinctive traditions. Newari, which uses three different alphabets, has the newer and more abundant literature.

In northern Nepal the Tibetan language – another traditional vehicle for religious teaching – remains widespread both in its classical form and as derived dialects (including Sherpa and Thakali). In southern Nepal, the people of the Terai speak Indo-European dialects. Three times more people speak Maithili, an eastern Terai dialect, than Newari, reflecting the uneven population distribution in Nepal.

English is spoken and understood in official and tourism-related circles. Most taxi drivers and merchants in the Kathmandu Valley region have a working knowledge of English, as do most Sherpas.

Elsewhere you may find it difficult to make yourself understood although the younger generation is fast acquiring some English.

We strongly recommend that you learn a few basic words and expressions. You will get big returns on this small investment in terms of hospitality and respect. Books to help you are available in Kathmandu bookshops (*see page 174*).

Useful Vocabulary

Hello	*namaste*
How are you?	*sanchai chha?*
Yes	*ho*
No	*hoina*
Thank you	*dhanyabadh*
Please	*kripaya*
Good morning (formal)	*subha prabhat*
Goodnight (formal)	*subha ratri*
Goodbye (literally: we'll meet again)	*pheri bhataunla*
Sorry/Excuse me	*maph gaurnus*
How much is it?	*kati parchha*
Where is (place)...?	*kahaa parchha*
Where is (object)...?	*kahaa chha*
Where is (person)...?-	*kahaa hunnuhunchha*
How far?	*kati tada chha*
How long (length)?	*kati lamo chha*
Good/OK	*thikchha*
Cheap	*sasto*
Expensive	*mahango*
Hot (temperature)	*tato*
Hot (spicy food)	*piro*
Cold (temperature)	*chiso*
Cold (feeling)	*jaro*
Free	*furshad*
Open	*khula*
Closed	*bhandha*
I don't understand	*bughina*

Places

Tourist Office	*paryatak office*
Bank	*bank*
Museum	*shangra laya*
Chemist	*aushadhi pasal*
Bus stop	*bus bishoni*

Pronunciation

Nepali is an atonal language. Whatever the length of the word, the accent is always placed on the first or second syllable. Words are pronounced as they are spelled.

Consonants are pronounced as in English, with a few peculiarities:

ch = tch as in bench
chh = tch-h as in pitch here
th = t-h as in hot head
kh = k-h as in dark hole
ph = p-h as in top hat
j = dj as in Jesus
dh = d-h as in adhere

The t, d, th and and dh with a dot beneath them are pronounced by rolling the tongue back to the centre of the roof of the mouth, so the sound produced is like "rt" in cart or "rd" in card.

Vowels are pronounced either long or short:
e = e (ay) as in café
u = oo as in moon (never yu as in mute)
y = yi as in yield (never ai as in my)
i = i as in bin (never ai as in bind)
o = oh as in toe

Nepalese do usually not use the different greetings "good morning", "good afternoon" or "good evening". Instead, when greeting someone, it is polite to clasp your hands together in front of you, bow your head slightly and say *Namaste* (pronounced na-ma-stay). This simple phrase will evoke a smile and warm greeting in return.

Post Office	hulak
Hospital	ashpatal
Church	girgha ghar
Hotel	hotel

Numbers

1	ek
2	dui
3	tin
4	chaar
5	paach
6	chha
7	saat
8	aath
9	nau
10	das
11	eghaara
12	baarha
13	terha
14	chaudha
15	pandhra
16	sorha
17	satra
18	athaara
19	unnais
20	bis
21	ekkaais
22	baais
23	teis
24	chaubis
25	pachchis
26	chhabbis
27	sattaais
28	aththaais
29	unantis
30	tis
40	chaalis
50	pachaas
60	saathi
70	sattari
80	asi
90	nabbe
100	sae, saya
1,000	hajaar
100,000	lakh
1 million	das lakh

Days of the Week

Sunday	Aityabar
Monday	Somabar
Tuesday	Mangalbar
Wednesday	Budhabar
Thursday	Bihibar
Friday	Sukrabar
Saturday	Shanibar

Months of the Year

Nepalese months vary from 29 to 32 days in length, and any one month may have a different number of days from year to year. Therefore no exact correspondence with the western calendar is possible (*see page 324*).

April/May	Baisakh
May/June	Jesth
June/July	Asadh
July/August	Srawan
August/September	Bhadra
September/October	Ashwin
October/November	Kartik
November/December	Marga
December/January	Poush
January/February	Magha
February/March	Falgun
March/April	Chaitra

Glossary

There are many words that you will see again and again during any trip to Nepal which have religious, traditional or vernacular meaning. The following list should help in your understanding.

A

agam – An often secret god which protects the family in a sacred building closed to foreigners.
akha – A traditional place where religious dancing is taught.
Ananda – The Buddha's chief disciple.
Ananta – A huge snake whose coils created Vishnu's bed.
Annapurna – The goddess of abundance; one aspect of Devi.
arak – A whisky fermented from potatoes or grain.
Ashta Matrikas – The eight mother goddesses said to attend on Shiva or Skanda.
Ashta Nag – Eight serpent deities who guard the cardinal directions and keep evil spirits away.
asla – A freshwater mountain trout.
Avalokiteshwara – A *bodhisattva* regarded as the god of mercy in Mahayana Buddhist tradition, and as the compassionate Machhendra in Nepal.
avatar – An incarnation of a deity on earth.

B

Babu – Controversial caste, introduced by a Malla prince.
bahal – A two-storey Buddhist monastery enclosing a courtyard.
bahil – A Buddhist monastery, smaller and simpler than a *bahal*.

bajracharya – A Newar caste of Buddhist priests.

Balarama – The brother of Krishna.

Balkumari – A consort of Bhairav.

betel – A stimulating mixture of the areka nut and chalk wrapped in a betel leaf and chewed.

beyul – A hidden valley, sacred in ancient Tibetan texts.

bhaat – Cooked rice; also refers to a meal (of rice).

bhaati – An inn or tea shop, especially those of the Thakali people.

Bhadrakali – A Tantric goddess and consort of Bhairav.

Bhagavad-Gita – The most important Hindu religious scripture, in which the god Krishna spells out the importance of duty. It is contained in the *Mahabharata*.

Bhairav – The god Shiva in his most terrifying form.

bharad – A reverential title.

Bhimsen – A deity worshipped for his strength and courage.

bhot – High, arid valleys in the Tibetan border region.

bodhi (also bo) – The pipal tree under which Gautama Buddha achieved enlightenment, and any tree so worshipped.

bodhisattva – In Mahayana Buddhist tradition, a person who has attained the enlightened level of Buddhahood, but chose to remain on earth to teach until others are enlightened.

Bön – The pre-Buddhist religion of Tibet, incorporating animism and sorcery.

Bönpo – A follower of the Bön faith.

Brahma – In Hindu mythology, the revered god of creation.

brahman – The highest of Hindu castes, originally that of priests.

Brahmanism – Ancient Indian religion, predecessor of modern Hinduism and Buddhism.

Busadan – Anniversary of the erection of the temple.

C

chaitya – A small stupa, sometimes containing a Buddhist relic, but usually holding mantras or scriptures.

chakra – A round weapon, one of the four objects held by Vishnu.

chapa – A small house annexed to a temple, in which feasts are held and rituals performed.

chapati – A type of bread made from wheat flour.

chautara – A tree-shaded stone-wall resting place.

chhang – A potent mountain beer of fermented grain, usually barley but sometimes maize, rye or millet.

chhetri – The Hindu warrior caste, second in status only to brahmans.

chhura – Beaten rice.

chitrakar – Newar caste of artists.

chiya – Nepalese tea, brewed with milk, sugar and spices.

chorten – A small Buddhist shrine on high mountain regions.

chowk – A palace or public courtyard.

chuba – A Tibetan or Sherpa robe, for man or woman.

crore – A unit of counting equal to 10 million.

D–E

dabur – An urban roadside square, used for religious dancing during festivals and as a marketplace at other times.

Dalai Lama – The reincarnate high priest of Tibetan Buddhism and political leader of Tibetans around the world.

damais – A caste of tailors who form makeshift bands to play religious music for weddings and other occasions.

damaru – A small drum.

damiyen – A traditional stringed instrument, similar to a ukulele.

danphe – The colourful impeyan pheasant, national bird of Nepal.

Dattatraya – A syncretistic deity variously worshipped as an incarnation of Vishnu, a teacher of Shiva, or a cousin of the Buddha.

Devi (or Maha Devi) – "The great goddess". Shiva's *shakti* in her many forms.

dhal – A lentil "soup".

dhal bhaat – A lentil/rice dish.

dhami – A soothsayer and sorcerer; also the priest of a temple, especially one claiming occult powers.

Dharma – Buddhist doctrine, literally "the path".

dharmasala – A public resthouse for travellers and pilgrims.

dharni – A weight measure equal to three sers, or about 3 kg (6.6 lbs).

dhoti – A loose loincloth.

dhyana – Meditation.

dighur – A Thakali system whereby a group of people pool money to annually support one of its members in a chosen financial venture.

digi – A place of congregation and prayer.

doko – A basket, often carried on the head by means of a strap.

dorje – A ritual sceptre or thunderbolt, symbol of the Absolute to Tantric Buddhists. (Also *vajra*.)

dun – Valleys of the Inner Terai.

dungidara – A stone water spout.

Durga – Shiva's *shakti* in one of her most awesome forms.

dwarapala – a door guardian.

dwarmul – The main gate of a building.

dyochhen – A house enshrining protective Tantric deities. Used for common worship.

dzopkyo – A hybrid bull, the cross between a yak and a cow.

dzum – a hybrid cow, the cross between a yak and a cow.

dzu-tch – According to Sherpas, a type of yeti that is about 2.5 metres (8 ft) tall and eats cattle.

ek – The number one, a symbol of unity.

G–H

gaine – A wandering, begging minstrel.

gajur – An often ornate, bell-shaped finial crowning a *bahal*.

Ganesh – The elephant-headed son of Shiva and Parvati. He is worshipped as the god of good luck and the remover of obstacles.

Ganga – A Hindu goddess.

Garuda – A mythical eagle, half-human. The vehicle of Vishnu.

Gautama Buddha – The historical Buddha, born in Lumbini in the 6th century BC.

gelugpa – a Tibetan sect.

ghada – A type of club, one of the weapons of Vishnu and a Tantric symbol.

ghanta – A symbolic Tantric bell, the

female counterpart of the *vajra*.
ghat – A riverside platform for bathing and cremation.
ghee – Clarified butter.
gompa – Tibetan Buddhist monastery.
gopala – A cowherd.
gopis – Cowherd girls; specifically those who cavorted with Krishna in a famous Hindu legend.
Gorakhnath – Historically, an 11th-century yogi who founded a Shairite cult; now popularly regarded as an incarnation of Shiva.
grama – A village.
granthakut – A tall, pointed brick and plaster shrine supported by a one-storey stone base.
guthi – A communal Newar brotherhood serving the purpose of mutual support for members and their extended families.
guthibar – The members of a *guthi*; also a group of families with the same ancestry.
gurr – A Sherpa meal made of spicy potato pancakes with cheese.
Hanuman – A deified monkey; hero of the *Ramayana* epic, he is said to bring success to armies.
hapa – A bamboo rice-measuring device made only in Pyangaon.
Harisiddhi – A fierce Tantric goddess.
harmika – The eyes on a stupa, placed to face the four cardinal directions.
himal – Snowy peak or range.
hiti – A water conduit; a bath or tank with water spouts.
hookah – A waterpipe through which tobacco or hashish is smoked.

I–J

impeyan – Nepal's national bird, a species of pheasant.
Indra – God of rain/rainfall; the chief deity of Brahminism.
jadun – A large vessel for drinking water at public places.
Jagannath – Krishna, worshipped as "Lord of the World".
Jamuna – A Hindu goddess who rides a tortoise.
janti – The groom's party at a wedding.
jarun – A raised stone water tank

with carved spouts.
jatra – Festival.
Jaya Varahi – Vishnu's *shakti* in his incarnation as a boar.
jelebi – A sweet Nepalese snack.
jhaad – Traditional rice beer.
jhankri – A shaman or sorcerer.
Jhankrism – Traditional animism, incorporating occult practices.
jhya – Carved window.
jogini – A mystical goddess.
juga – leech.
jyapu – Newar farmer caste.

K

kalashi – A pot.
Kali – Shiva's *shakti* in her most terrifying form.
kapok – The silk cotton tree.
karma – The cause-and-effect chain of actions, good and bad, from one life to the next.
kata – A ceremonial scarf given to high Tibetan Buddhist figures.
khat – An enclosed wooden shrine, similar in appearance to the portable shrines carried during processions.
khola – River or stream.
khukri – A traditional knife, long and curved, best known as the weapon of Gurkha soldiers.
kot – A small hilltop fortress.
Krishna – The eighth incarnation of Vishnu, heavily worshipped for his activities on earth.
kshepu – A snake-eating figure often depicted on temple *toranas*.
kumari – A young virgin regarded as a living goddess in Kathmandu Valley towns.
kunda – A recessed water tank fed by underground springs.

L

laddu – A sweet Nepalese snack.
lakh – A unit of counting equal to 100,000.
lakhe – Masked dancing.
Lakshmi – The goddess of wealth and consort of Vishnu.
laligurans – Rhododendron, Nepal's national flower.
lama – A Tibetan Buddhist priest.
la – Mountain pass.

lingam (pl. *lingas*) – A symbolic male phallus, generally associated with Shiva.
Lokeshwar – "Lord of the World", a form of Avalokiteshwara to Buddhists and of Shiva to Hindus.
lhu – A desert wind from India.

M

Machhendra – The guardian god of the Kathmandu Valley, guarantor of rain and plenty. The deity is also a popular interpretation of Avalokeshwara or Lokeshwar and is enshrined as the Rato (Red) Machhendra in Patan and the Seto (White) Machhendra in Kathmandu.
Mahabharata – A Hindu epic.
Mahabharat Lekh – A range of hills between the Himalaya and Terai.
maharishi – Literally, "great teacher".
mahseer – A large freshwater fish highly prized in Nepal.
Mahayana – The form of Buddhism prevalent in East Asia, Tibet and Nepal.
Maitreya – The future Buddha.
Majushri – The legendary Buddhist patriarch of the Kathmandu Valley, now often regarded as the god of learning.
makara – A mythical crocodile, often depicted on *toranas*.
mali – A Newar caste of gardeners.
mana – A measure for rice and cereals, milk and sugar, containing a little less than half a litre.
mandala – A sacred diagram envisioned by Tibetan Buddhists as an aid to meditation.
mandap – A roofless Tantric shrine made of brick or wood.
mani – A Tibetan Buddhist prayer inscribed in rock in mountain areas.
mantra – Sacred syllables chanted during meditation by Buddhists.
math – A Hindu priest's house.
migyu – Tibetan name for the yeti.
mih-tch – According to Sherpas, a hostile, man-sized, ape-like yeti.
momos – Tibetan stuffed pasta, somewhat like ravioli.
mudra – A symbolic hand posture or gesture often employed during religious prayer and meditation.
mukdal – A sweet snack.

munja – The sacred thread worn by brahman and chhetri males from the time of puberty.

muri – A dry measure equal to about 75 litres (135 pints). It contains 20 *paathis* or 160 *manas*.

muthi – A measure equal to "a handful".

N

naamlo – A woven rope headstrap with which porters carry the *doko*.

naga – Snake, especially a legendary or a deified serpent.

nak – Female yak.

namaste – A very common word of greeting, often translated as: "I salute all divine qualities in you."

Nandi – A bull, Shiva's vehicle and a symbol of fecundity.

nanglo – A cane tray.

nani – A type of *bahal* containing a large courtyard surrounded by residences, also including a Buddhist shrine.

Narayan – Vishnu represented as the creator of life. A lotus from Narayan's navel issued Brahma.

Narsingh – Vishnu's incarnation as a lion.

nath – Literally, "place".

nirvana – Extinction of self, the goal of Buddhist meditation.

Nriteshwar – The god of dance.

P

paathi – A dry measure equal to eight *manas* or 30 litres (55 pints).

padma – The lotus flower.

pahar – The heavily eroded central zone of hills and valleys between the Himalaya and Mahabharat Lekh.

panchayat – A government system of elected councils at local, regional and national levels.

Parvati – Shiva's consort, displaying both serene and fearful aspects.

pashmina – A shawl or blanket made of fine goat's wool.

Pashupati – Shiva in his aspect as "Lord of the Beasts". Symbolised by the *lingam*, he is believed to bring fecundity.

pasni – Hindu rice-feeding ceremony conducted for seven-month-old babies, and repeated for old people of 77 years and seven months.

patasi – A sari-like dress, especially popular in Bhaktapur.

path – A small raised platform which provides shelter for travellers on important routes.

pathi – A liquid measurement, just under 4.5 litres (1 gallon).

patuka – A waistcloth in which to carry small objects or babies.

pau – A measure for vegetables and fruit, equal to 250 g (9 oz).

paubha – Traditional Newari painting, usually religious in motif.

pith – An open shrine dedicated to a Tantric goddess.

pokhari – A large pond or lake.

preta – A spirit of the dead.

puja – Ritual offerings to the gods.

pukhu – A pond.

punya – Merit earned through actions and religious devotion.

puri – Town.

R

rakshi – Wheat or rice liquor.

Rama – The seventh incarnation of Vishnu. A prince, hero of the *Ramayana* epic.

Ramayana – The most widely known Hindu legend, in which Rama, with the aid of Hanuman and Garuda, rescues his wife, Sita, from the demon king Rawana.

Rawana – the anti-hero of the *Ramayana*.

rikhi doro – A golden thread which Shiva devotees tie around their wrists to ward off evil and disease.

rimpoche – The abbot of a Tibetan Buddhist monastery (*gompa*).

Rudrayani – A Kathmandu Valley nature goddess. Also known as Shekali Mai.

S

sadhu – A Hindu mendicant.

sajha – Cooperative, organised in the 1970s to deal with inequalities in land sharing.

sal – A strong timber tree of the lower slopes of Himalayan foothills.

sampradaya – A religious sect or community.

samsara – The eternal reincarnation cycle (in South Asia).

sankha – The conch shell, one of the four symbols held by Vishnu. It is widely used in Hindu temples and shrines during prayer.

sanyasin – A religious ascetic who has renounced his ties to society.

saranghi – A four-stringed viola shaped from one piece of wood and played with a horsehair bow.

Saraswati – Brahma's consort, worshipped in Nepal as the Hindu goddess of learning.

satal – A pilgrim's house.

ser – A unit of weight equal to four *paus*, or about 1 kg (2 lbs).

serow – A wild Himalayan antelope.

shakti – Shiva's consort, literally, the dynamic element in the male-female relationship, and the female aspect of the Tantric Absolute.

shaligram – A black ammonite fossil regarded as sacred by Vishnu devotees.

shandula – A mythical bird, a griffin.

shikhara – A brick or stone temple of geometrical shape with a tall central spire.

Shitala Mai – A former ogress who became a protector of children, worshipped at Swayambhunath.

Shiva – The most awesome of Hindu gods. He destroys all things, good as well as evil, allowing new creation to take shape.

shrestha – A Newar caste.

sirdar – A guide, usually a Sherpa, who leads trekking groups.

sindur – A votive mixture made of red dust combined with mustard oil.

Sita – Rama's wife, heroine of the *Ramayana*. She is worshipped in Janakpur, her legendary birthplace.

Skanda – The Hindu god of war.

stupa – A bell-shaped relic chamber.

sudra – Lowest of the Hindu castes, commonly thought to have descended from Brahma's feet.

sundhara – A fountain with a golden spout.

Surjya – The sun god, often identified with Vishnu.

suttee – Former Indian practice of immolating widows on their husbands' funeral pyres.

T–U

tabla – A traditional hand drum.
tal – A lake.
Taleju Bhawani – The Nepalese goddess, originally a South Indian deity; an aspect of Devi.
Tara – Historically a Nepalese princess, now deified by Buddhists and Hindus.
Thakuri – The high Hindu caste.
thangka – Religious scroll painting.
thar – A wild Himalayan goat.
thelma – According to Sherpas, a small, reddish, ape-like yeti.
thukba – A thick Tibetan soup.
tika – A colourful vermilion powder applied by Hindus to the forehead, between the eyes, as a symbol of the presence of the divine.
tola – A metal measure equal to 11.5 g (0.5 oz).
tole – A street.
topi – The formal, traditional Nepalese cap.
torana – A decorative carved crest suspended over the door of a sanctum, with the figure of the enshrined deity at its centre.
trisul – The trident, chief symbol of the god Shiva.
tsampa – Raw grain, usually ground and mixed with milk, tea or water. A traditional mountain food.
tulku – In Tibetan Buddhism, a religious figure regarded as a rein-carnation of a great past lama.
tulsi – A sacred basil plant.
tunal – Carved strut of a temple.
tympanum – A decorative crest beneath the peak of a roof.
Uma – Shiva's consort in one of her many aspects.
Upanishaden – Early religious Brahman texts.
Upanishads – Early Brahmanistic religious texts; speculations on Vedic thought.

V

vaisya – The "middle class" caste of merchants and farmers.
vajra (also *dorje*) – In Tantric Buddhism, a ritual thunderbolt or curved sceptre symbolising the Absolute. It also represents power and male energy.

varahi – A god incarnated as a boar.
Vedas – The earliest Brahmanistic religious verses, dating from the second millennium BC. They define a polytheistic faith.
veden – Earliest Brahman texts with polytheistic tendencies (2000 BC)
vedica – A sacrificial altar.
vihara – A Buddhist monastery, encompassing a *bahal* and a *bahil*.
Vikrantha (also Vamana) – Vishnu in his fifth incarnation, as a dwarf.
Vishnu – One of the Hindu trinity, a god who preserves life and the world itself. In Nepal, he is most commonly represented as Narayan.

Y–Z

yab-yum – Tantric erotica, a symbol of unity and oneness.
yak – Nepalese cattle perfectly adapted to the climate. It gives food and wool to the people and can carry large weights.
yeh-tch – The Sherpa name for the yeti; literally, "man of the rocky places".
yeti – A mythical anthropoid of Nepal's highest elevations, often referred to in the west as "The Abominable Snowman".
yoni – A hole in a stone, said to symbolise the female sexual aspect. Usually seen together with a *lingam.*
zamindari – A system of absentee landlordism, officially abolished in 1955 but still perpetuated in some regions.

Further Reading

General and History

The Wildest Dreams of Kew: A Profile of Nepal by Jeremy Bernstein (NY: Simon and Schuster, 1970). Personal travelogue.
My Kind of Kathmandu: An Artist's Impression of the Emereld Valley by Desmond Doig (India: Indus, 1994). Charming and nostalgic account of life in Nepal in the 1970s illustrated with the author's superb watercolours.
Building Bridges to the Third World: Memories of Nepal 1950–1992 by Tony Hagen (India: Book Faith, 1994).
Nepal: The Kingdom in the Himalaya by Tony Hagen (Berne: Kummerly and Frey, 1961, updated 1998). Geographical study with many photos and maps. Still one of the best books by one of the first men to travel widely in the country.
Trespassers on the Roof of the World by Peter Hopkirk (Oxford University Press, 1990). Fascinating account the clandestine manoeuvres of the pundit surveyor-spies, and others, in the era of the Great Game.
Tiger for Breakfast by Michel Peissel (London: Hodder, 1966). The story of the legendary Boris Lissanevitch.
Offerings From Nepal by Craig Potton with Lisa Choegyal (Craig Potton Publishing, New Zealand 1995). Refreshing and unusual images of Nepal by one of New Zealand's most accomplished photographers.
Kathmandu City on the Edge of the World by Patricia Roberts and Thomas L. Kelly. A beautiful illustrated book on the Kathmandu Valley, its history and festivals.
The Mountain is Young by Han Suyin (Jonathan Cape, 1958). Novel set in 1950s Nepal featuring many recognisable characters.

People, Art and Culture

Festivals of Nepal by Mary M. Anderson (Allen and Unwin, 1971).

The Last Forbidden Kingdom: Mustang Land of Tibetan Buddhism by Vanessa Schuurbeque Boeye and Clara Marullo (Thames & Hudson London 1995). Best photographic book of Mustang by the award-winning filmmakers.

Trans-Himalayan Traders: Economy, Society and Culture in Northwest Nepal by James F. Fisher (Berkeley: University of California 1986). An anthropological study of the people of Dolpo.

Kathmandu, the Forbidden Valley by Ian Lloyd with Wendy Moore (Time Books International, New Delhi 1990).

East of Lo Monthang: In the Land of Mustang by Peter Matthiessen with Thomas Laird (Shambhala, Boston 1995). Evocative book by one of the great travel writers.

Kathmandu Valley: The Preservation of Physical Environment and Cultural Heritage by Carl Prusha (two volumes; Vienna: Anton Schroll, 1975). Prepared by His Majesty's Government of Nepal in collaboration with UNESCO and the United Nations.

Nepal Mandala: A Cultural Study of the Kathmandu Valley by Mary Shepherd Slusser (Princeton University Press 1982). Superb definitive work and inventory of the art and architecture of the Kathmandu Valley in two volumes.

Buddhist Himalaya by David L. Snellgrove (Oxford: Bruno Cassirer, 1957). Excellent survey.

Caravans of the Himalaya by Eric Valli and Diane Summers (National Geographic Society 1994). Stunning photographs of the ancient salt trade of high west Nepal, immortalised in the film *Caravan*.

Natural History

Birds of Nepal by R.L. Fleming Sr and Jr. and L.S. Bangdel (Kathmandu: Avalok, 1979). Definitive work with good illustrations.

Heart of the Jungle: the Wildlife of Chitwan, Nepal by K.K. Gurung (André Deutsch and Tiger Tops, 1983). In-depth survey of the fauna of Royal Chitwan National Park with lovely drawings by the author.

Vanishing Tracks: Four Years Among the Snow Leopards of Nepal by Darla Hillard (New York: Arbor House, 1989). A study of life in the western Himalaya with zoologist Rodney Jackson.

A Guide to the Birds of Nepal by Carol and Tim Inskipp (Dover. New Hampshire: Tanager Books, 1985).

A Birdwatcher's Guide to Nepal by Carol Inskipp (Bird Watchers' Guides, 1988).

Medicinal Plants of Nepal Himalaya by N.P. Manandhar (Kathmandu: Ratna Pustak Bhandar, 1980).

The Face of the Tiger by Charles McDougal (Rivington Books and André Deutsch, 1977). The classic work on the Bengal tiger, by the director of Tiger Tops.

Himalayan Flowers and Trees by D. Mierow and T.B. Shrestha (Kathmandu: Saha-yogi Prakashan, 1978). Good handbook.

Royal Chitwan National Park: Wildlife Heritage of Nepal by Hemanta R. Mishra and Margaret Jeffries (Seattle, The Mountaineers 1991). Comprehensive guide.

Concise Flowers of the Himalaya by Oleg Polunin and Adam Stainton (New Delhi: Oxford University Press, 1987). A much-needed work.

Butterflies of Nepal (Central Himalaya) by Colin Smith (Bangkok: Teopress, 1989).

Development Ecology of the Arun Basin by T.B. Shrestha (Kathmandu: ICIMOD 1989).

Forests of Nepal by J.D.A. Stainton (London: Murray, 1972). Standard work on the flora of Nepal.

Enjoy Trees: A simple guide to some of the shrubs found in Nepal by Adrian and Jimmy Storrs (Kathmandu: Shahayogi Press, 1987).

Honey Hunters of Nepal by Eric Valli and Diane Summers (USA: Harry N. Abrams, 1988). Beautiful documentation of an ancient and dangerous tradition collecting honey from the cliffs of west Nepal.

Trekking and Mountaineering

Trekking in the Himalaya by Stan Armington (South Yarra. Vic., Australia: Lonely Planet, 1998). Useful trekking guide.

Trekking in Nepal: A Traveller's Guide by Stephen Bezruschka (Seattle: The Mountaineers, 1991). One of the original books on the subject though now a little dated.

The Pocket Doctor: Your Ticket to Good Health While Travelling by Stephen Bezruschka (Seattle: The Mountaineers 1988). Useful pocket book; never travel without it.

Everest the Hard Way by Chris Bonington (London: Hodder and Stoughton, 1979).

High Exposure: An Enduring Passion for Everest and Unforgiving Places by David Breashears (Simon & Schuster USA 1999). Autobiography by the climber and film-maker who made the Everest IMAX movie.

Last Climb: the Legendary Everest Expeditions of George Mallory by David Breashears, Audrey Salkeld and John Mallory (National Geographic Society, 1999). Gripping account of the 1999 expedition to find the bodies of Mallory and Irvine.

Everest: Mountain Without Mercy by Broughton Coburn (National Geographic Society 1997). Stunning photos and narrative from the Everest IMAX team.

Nepali Aama: Portrait of a Nepalese Hill Woman by Broughton Coburn (Santa Barbara, California: Ross Erikson, 1982).

Everest: The Best Writing and Pictures from Seventy Years of Human Endeavour by Peter Gilman (Little Brown & Co, USA 1993). Wonderful compilation by everyone who matters on the subject.

Annapurna: First Conquest of an 8,000-Metre Peak by Maurice Herzog, Maurice (New York: E.P. Dutton, 1953).

High Adventure by Edmund Hillary (New York: E.P. Dutton, 1955).

Sagarmatha by Edmund Hillary (Apa Publications, 1992). Incomparable collection of unusual and historical photos of Everest donated as a

fundraiser for the Himalayan Trust.
Going Higher: The Story of Man and Altitude by Charles S. Houston (Boston: Little Brown 1987).
The Conquest of the Himalaya by John Hunt (New York: Dutton, 1954).
Our Everest Adventure: The Pictorial History from Kathmandu to the Summit by John Hunt (New York: E.P. Dutton, 1954).
Sagarmatha, Mother of the Universe: The Story of Mount Everest National Park by Margaret Jeffries and Margaret Clarbrough (Auckland: Cobb/Horwood, 1986). Useful guide to the Khumbu.
Into Thin Air: A Personal Account of the Mount Everest Disaster by Jon Krakauer (Villard New York 1997). Widely read account of the 1996 accident on Everest.
Everest: Expedition to the Ultimate by Reinhold Messner (London: Kaye and Ward, 1979).
Trekking in the Everest Region by Jamie McGuinness (Trailblazer, UK 1998). Useful detailed trek guides series aimed at individual trekkers.
Trekking in Langtang, Helambu & Gosainkund by Jamie McGuinness (Trailblazer, UK 1997).
The Trekking Peaks of Nepal by Bill O'Connor (Seattle: Cloudcap Press, 1989 and England: Crowood Press). Excellent guide with useful maps.
Stones of Silence by George B. Schaller (London: André Deutsch, 1980). Report of a naturalist's survey in Dolpo.
Himalaya by Yoshikazu Shirakawa (Tokyo: Shogakukan, 1976. Also New York: Harry N. Abrams, 1977).

Beautiful photographic book.
Man of Everest: The Autobiography of Tenzing by Tenzing Norgay and James Ramsey Ullman (London: George G. Harrap, 1955).
Trekking in the Annapurna Region by Bryn Thomas (Trailblazer, UK 1999). Excellent detailed trek guide aimed at individual trekkers.
Nepal Himalaya by W. Tilman (Cambridge University Press, 1952). Mountaineer's reports of attacks on high peaks.
Journey to Mustang by Giuseppe Tucci, translated by Diana Fussel (Kathmandu: Ratna Pustak Bhandar, 1982).
Americans on Everest: The Official Account Led by Norman G. Dyhrenfurth by James Ramsey Ullman (New York: J.B. Lippincott, 1964).
A Medicine for Mountaineering by James Wilkerson (Seattle: The Mountaineers, 1985).

Other Insight Guides

Insight Guides cover the world, with more than 360 titles in three series. Insight Guides profile a destination and its culture in depth. **Insight Compact Guides** are encyclopaedias in miniature, ideal for on-the-spot reference. **Insight Pocket Guides** provide personal recommendations from an expert and include a full-size fold-out map.
Other Insight Guides which highlight destinations in this region include *India's Western Himalaya*, *China*, and *India*. Insight Pocket

Guides cover both *Nepal* and *Tibet*. **Insight Pocket Guide: Nepal** offers a number of fascinating itineraries in Kathmandu, and further afield.

Insight Pocket Guide: Tibet explores this amazing region on the roof of the world.

Feedback

We do our best to ensure the information in our books is as accurate and up-to-date as possible. The books are updated on a regular basis, using local contacts, who painstakingly add, amend and correct as required. However, some mistakes and omissions are inevitable and we are ultimately reliant on our readers to put us in the picture.

We would welcome your feedback on any details related to your experiences using the book "on the road". Maybe we recommended a hotel that you liked (or another that you didn't), as well as interesting new attractions, or facts and figures you have found out about the country itself. The more details you can give us (particularly with regard to addresses, e-mails and telephone numbers), the better.

We will acknowledge all contributions, and we'll offer an Insight Guide to the best letters received.

Please write to us at:
Insight Guides
APA Publications
PO Box 7910
London SE1 1XF
Or send e-mail to:
insight@apaguide.demon.co.uk

ART & PHOTO CREDITS

Heather Angel 101, 104, 302T
Apa 117
Ardea London 24, 100R, 109
theartarchive 35R
Devendra Basnet 169
J. Batten/Trip 124
Christophe Bluntzer/Impact 120/121
I. Corse/Trip 180T
T. Bognar/Trip 196, 202, 211
Skip Brown 143, 200/201, 247
Kevin Brubriski 12/13, 45R, 46, 54, 61, 62, 86, 112, 113, 154/155, 176, 237, 292, 299, 300, 310, 320
Chris Caldicott 4/5, 144, 198, 218/219, 221, 223T, 281, 304
Chris Caldicott/Axiom 145
Demetrio Carrasco 16/17, 49
Piers Cavendish/Impact 82/83
C. Chuchuay/CPA back cover centre, 167T, 168, 168T, 171, 184T, 229, 232T, 296
David Cottridge/BBC 1
Gerald Cubitt front flap bottom, 4BL, 92/93, 94, 100L, 103, 105L/R, 186T, 252T, 308T, 309, 310T, 317T
Steve Davey/La Belle Aurore 208T, 239T
Nick Dawson/Christine Osborne Pictures 59, 106, 122, 152/153
Jerry Dennis back cover top right, spine top, 119, 123, 126, 193, 231, 232, 242
L & M Dickinson 133
Greg Evans 47, 87L
Alain Evrard 25, 43, 180, 187, 189, 207, 235R
Wendy Brewer Fleming 315
Michael Freeman back cover bottom, 189T, 318
Nick Garbutt/BBC 48, 77
C.N. Gay 18, 84
Jill Gocher 5B
Mark Graham 283
Gurlt/Zollner 235L
C. Hamilton/Trip 116
Blaine Harrington 68, 172, 172T, 177, 178T
Hans Höfer 253
Jim Holmes/Axiom 241
Dave G. Houser 199, 213
W. Jacobs/Trip main back cover
Caroline Jones 129, 245T
Frances Klatzel 60, 156
Rainer Krack/CPA back cover centre right, 71, 72, 75, 87R, 89, 165, 165T, 171T, 174T, 182, 183, 185, 204, 205T,

207T, 210T, 212, 215, 220, 226/227, 228, 230, 230T, 290/291, 298, 298T, 306T, 307
Thomas Laird 28, 29, 30, 31, 32, 40/41, 50, 51, 63, 66/67, 88, 98, 111, 164, 167L/R, 175, 186, 206, 224, 225L/R, 265T, 267, 275, 288, 307R, 311
J. Lamb/Trip 217
Roy Lawrance/Ffotograff 188, 197T, 234T, 301T
Michael Leach/NHPA 118
Tom Le Bas 289
Lisa van Gruisen Collection 74
Craig Lovell 45L, 208, 216
Mary Evans Picture Library 34, 134
Gary McCue 6/7, 22, 58, 135, 137, 268, 273, 285
Jock Montgomery 38, 44, 52/53, 91, 99, 125R, 234, 240, 240T, 250, 255, 256, 257, 272, 272T, 297, 308
Tony Montgomery 142
Jonathan Nesvig 14, 108, 263
Bill O'Connor 97, 102, 136, 138, 248, 254, 271, 274
Christine Osborne/COP spine centre, 114, 181, 248T
Caroline Penn/Impact 115, 246T
Paul Quayle/Axiom 125L, 239
Jill Ranford/Ffotograff 128, 269, 286T
John Reinhard 76
Rex Features 39L/R, 139, 277
Jeff Robertson 286
Rolex Watch Co, Geneva 141
Galen Rowell 19, 20, 23, 36R, 55, 78, 85, 107, 110, 132, 166, 209, 210, 236, 244, 297T
Royal Geographical Society 33, 35L
John Sanday 64
Gautam Sayami 56
David Shale/BBC 261
Chandra Shamsher 26/27
David R. Shlim 140
Toby Smedley/Ffotograff 255T
Paul Steel 233, 293
Martin Stolworthy/Axiom 260, 270
Nicholas Sumner/Bigpiepictures front flap top, 73, 266
Topham Picturepoint 2B, 36L, 37, 65, 223, 276
N. C. Turner/Ffotograff 69, 150/151
Alan Ward/Ffotograff back flap top, 90, 127, 263T, 264, 266T, 269T, 317
Bill Wassman back flap bottom, 2, 10/11, 21, 42, 57, 70, 79, 96, 148/149, 160, 161, 170, 173, 174,

179, 192, 197, 198T, 203, 205, 213T, 214, 215T, 242T, 243, 249, 251, 257T, 265, 280, 282, 285T, 287, 294T, 301, 303, 306, 312/313, 314, 319, 319T
Andrew Wheeler 246
Art Wolfe 8/9, 130/131, 258/259, 270T, 275T, 305, 305T
David Woodfall/NHPA 95, 245

Picture Spreads

Pages 80/81
Top row, left to right:
Gerald Cubitt, Barry Broman, Gerald Cubitt, Chris Caldicott. *Centre row:* Jill Gocher, Michael Freeman. *Bottom row:* Jerry Dennis, Alan Ward/Ffotograff, D. Saunders/Trip.

Pages 146/147
Top row, left to right:
Jill Gocher, Bob Allen/Stockfile Jonathan Blair/Corbis, Bill Wassman. *Centre row:* Frances Klatzel, Tim Barnet, Alan Ward/Ffotograff. *Bottom row:* Anup Shah/BBC, Craig Aurness/Corbis, Jill Gocher.

Pages 190/191
Top row, left to right:
Blaine Harrington, Dave G. Houser, Christine Osborne/COP, Gerald Cubitt. *Centre row:* CPA, Bill Wassman. *Bottom row:* CPA, Chris Caldicott, Bill Wassman.

Pages 278/279
Top row, left to right:
Steve Davey/La Belle Aurore, Bill Wassman, Andrew Wheeler, Alan Ward/Ffotograff. *Centre row:* Peter Adams, Alan Ward/Ffotograff. *Bottom row:* Alan Ward/Ffotograff, Roy Lawrance/Ffotograff, Jill Gocher, Michael Freeman.

Map Production Colourmap Scanning Ltd
© 2000 Apa Publications GmbH & Co.
Verlag KG (Singapore branch)

INSIGHT GUIDE
NepaL

Cartographic Editor **Zoë Goodwin**
Production **Linton Donaldson**
Design Consultants
Carlotta Junger, Graham Mitchener
Picture Research **Hilary Genin, Britta Jaschinski**

Index

Numbers in italics refer to photographs